JEWISH IDENTITIES

JEWISH IDENTITIES

Fifty Intellectuals Answer Ben Gurion

BY

ELIEZER BEN-RAFAEL

BRILL

LEIDEN · BOSTON · KÖLN

2002

This book is printed on acid-free paper.

Library of Congress Cataloging-in Publication data

Ben-Rafael, Eliezer.
  Jewish identities : fifty intellectuals answer Ben Gurion / by Eliezer
  Ben-Rafael.
    p.cm.
  Includes bibliographical references and index.
  ISBN 9004125353 (alk. paper)
  1. Jews—Identity. 2. Jews—Israel—Identity. 3. Ben-Gurion, David,
  1886-1973. I. Title.

  DS143.B46513 2002
  305.892'4—dc21   2002073529

Deutsche Bibliothek – CIP-Einheitsaufnahme

Jewish identities : fifty intellectuals answer Ben Gurion / Eliezer
Ben-Rafael. – Leiden ; Boston ; Köln : Brill, 2002
  ISBN 90-04-12535-3

ISBN   90 04 12535 3

PRINTED IN THE NETHERLANDS

CONTENTS

Acknowledgements ix
Foreword, by Joseph Gorny xi
Preface xix

PART ONE

WHAT IS A JEW?

Introduction 3

CHAPTER ONE: ENTERING THE MODERN ERA 9
The Decline of a Caste 9
Orthodoxy as Conservative Change 12
Non-Orthodox Judaism 16
The Enlightenment in Eastern Europe 20
Zionism and the Bund 22
The Space of Identities 26

CHAPTER TWO: BEN-GURION'S
CORRESPONDENTS 31
A Phoenix Generation 31
Three Syndromes 36
   The Caste Syndrome 37
   The Ethno-cultural Syndrome 41
   The National Syndrome 46
Conclusion 52

CHAPTER THREE: ISRAELI-JEWISH IDENTITIES 56
Introduction 56
Revolution, Unity, and Elitism 57
The Role of Religion 61
Ethnic Divides 66
   The Mizrakhim 67
   Immigrants from the former Soviet Union 70
   Israeli Arabs 72

Ideological Controversies 73
Conflictual Multiculturalism 79

CHAPTER FOUR: JEWISH IDENTITIES IN THE
  DIASPORA—THE CASE OF AMERICA 82
Social Achievements and Demographic Risks 82
A Religion of Congregations 86
The Future at Issue 90
Cultural Ethnicity 94

CHAPTER FIVE: DIVERGENCE AND
  CONVERGENCE OF JEWISH IDENTITIES 99
Beyond Traditional Identity 99
After Migration, the Holocaust, and Establishment of
  the State 103
At the Dawn of the 21st Century 106
"Family Resemblance" and Tensions 110

PART TWO

WHO IS A JEW?

Preamble 117

HISTORICAL INTRODUCTION, by Shalom Ratzaby 119
The Starting Point 119
The Ger before the Destruction of the First Temple 121
From Ezra and Nehemiah to the End of the Second
  Temple Period 127
Conversion as Entrance into Abraham's Covenant 139

BEN-GURION'S QUERY 144

THE LETTERS OF THE SAGES
  1. Shmuel Yossef Agnon 151
  2. Alexander Altmann 153
  3. Henry Baruk 158
  4. Shmuel Hugo Bergmann 166
  5. Isaiah Berlin 168
  6. Yehuda Bourla 177

7. Haim Hermann Cohn 180
8. Louis Eliezer Halevi Finkelstein 194
9. Felix Frankfurter 197
10. Solomon B. Freehof 199
11. Shlomo Goren 204
12. Aryeh Leib Grossnass, Meir Lew, Abraham
    Rappoport, Meir Halevy Steinberg and
    Morris Swift 220
13. Zecharya Hacohen 223
14. Shalom Yitzhak Halevi 230
15. Hayim Hazaz 236
16. Yitzhak Isaac Halevi Herzog 238
17. Abraham Joshua Heschel 240
18. Joseph Shlomo Kahaneman 243
19. Yossef Kappah 247
20. Jacob Kaplan 254
21. Mordecai Menahem Kaplan 257
22. Yekhezkel Kaufmann 261
23. Aaron Kotler 268
24. Dante Lattes 272
25. Saul Lieberman 274
26. Yehuda Leib Hakohen Maimon 278
27. Moshe Maisels 280
28. André Neher 285
29. Salomon Rodrigues Pereira 289
30. Chaim Perelman 290
31. Simon H. Rifkind 293
32. Yecheskiel Sarne 294
33. Joseph Schecter 296
34. Menachem Mendel Schneerson 298
35. Sh. (Shalom Joseph Shapira) Shalom 300
36. Moshe Silberg 303
37. Akiva Ernst Simon 308
38. Leon (Arye) Simon 316
39. Joseph Dov Soloveitchik and Chaim Heller 321
40. Alfredo Shabtai Toaff 323
41. Elio Raffaelo Toaff 327
42. Ephraim A. Urbach 329
43. Yekhiel Weinberg 333
44. Tsevi (Harry A.) Wolfson 347

45. Aaron Zeitlin 351
46. Shlomo Y. Zevin 355

Glossary of Hebrew Words 359
References 364
Index 381

ACKNOWLEDGEMENTS

I want to thank with warmth the Ben-Gurion Center at Sde Boker and the Ben-Gurion Archives for their support and cooperation. This work would never been accomplished without the backing of Tuvia Friling who was then the Director of the Center, Shaul Shragay who took on himself the publication of the original Hebrew version and Nilly Landsberger who was much more than an editor—inquiring with enthusiasm into the slightest details.

My deepest gratitude goes to Joed Elich, the Senior Acquisition Officer for Brill Academic Press who, from the very first moment, showed interest and enthusiasm in this work. I also include here Anita Roodnat, the Editor of the Religion Unit.

My profound thankfulness and appreciation go to Ms Sara Kitai who translated in English the Hebrew version of this work and overcame the numerous intricacies which my own text comprised, as well as those which were inherent to the complexity of the task that the Sages confronted, on behalf of Ben-Gurion's request from them.

I also take the opportunity here to convey my utmost respect for the Sages themselves who had accepted the challenge set by Ben-Gurion, the founder of the State of Israel, to confront in the frame of a simple letter the most complicated issue of Judaism ever, namely, "who and what is a Jew".

In addition, I have to express my best feelings and gratitude to Yossef Gorny and Shalom Ratsabi who both accepted to contribute their precious knowledge to this venture, the former by composing a foreword offering the outlook of a renowned historian, and the latter with a chapter at the measure of his incomparable mastery of the Holy Scriptures.

My wife Miriam, as always, has very much added to this work by her constant encouragement, and I would forget an essential part of this endeavor if I did not mention the warm and exciting family atmosphere where my grandchildren Or, Tomer, Ron and Lian play the major role.

Eliezer Ben-Rafael
Ramat-Hasharon, March 2002

FOREWORD

By Joseph Gorny

In August 1959, Gershom Scholem sent the following letter to the editor of Ha-Boker, Israel's major morning paper at this time:

> I bought Ha-Boker this morning, 3 Av 1959, in order to read the responses of the various "Jewish sages" to the question Who is a Jew. [It reminds me of] ... Leopold Bloom, the hero of James Joyce's famous book Ulysses. This character is, in fact, Jewish "only" in the eyes of the author, in the eyes of his Irish surroundings—and in the eyes of all the readers (the undersigned included). In the eyes of the "Jewish sages" ... however, he is not a Jew at all as [he] the son of a Jewish father and non-Jewish mother, was raised entirely as a non-Jew, and lives entirely as a non-Jew. Nevertheless, everyone considers him a Jew.

This quote shows how far the Jewish People is distinct from other nations. We can see this exceptionalism both in the depth of the rifts within and between communities, and in its efforts to bridge these gaps by means of trans-territorial, trans-cultural, and transnational organizations. In brief, the Jews were early forerunners of a world phenomenon that has been gaining increasing legitimacy in recent times, namely "diasporism". The paradox of the Jewish unity existing, both in consciousness and in practice, alongside divisive social and cultural processes is brought to the fore in the comprehensive—and very different—histories of the Jewish people written by modern Jewish historians such as Marcus Just (1793–1860), Heinrich Graetz (1817–1891), Simon Dubnow (1860–1941), Ben-Zion Dinour (1884–1973), Raphael Mahler (1899–1977), Selo Baron (1895–1989) or Shmuel Ettinger (1919–1988).

For Just, the Jews are primarily a group with a certain religious faith who are in the process of becoming integrated into a society shaped by the Enlightenment. Graetz views the Jews as a spiritual-religious people with a moral mission for the world at large. In the opinion of Dubnow, the Jews are a diasporistic people who, despite their distance from their historical territory, maintain a national ideology by means of a community organization that moves from one center to another over the course of history. Dinour considers the

Jews a people driven throughout its history by a messianic urge
directed toward the Land of Israel. Mahler understands Jewish nationalism as the result of the objective socio-economic conditions of the
Jews wherever they live. Ettinger, who developed his view of history
after the Holocaust and the founding of the State of Israel, finds it
difficult to identify any single predominant trend in modern Jewish
history.

In effect, these historians represent three basic approaches to the
overall definition of Jewish identity: Jews are a spiritual people according to Just and Graetz; a nation relating to a national territory,
according to Dinour and Mahler; a solidaristic entity, according to
Ettinger. Although the nature of Jewish identity is considerably
different in each of the three approaches, they all share two propo-
sitions that touch directly on the subject of this book. First and foremost is the assumption that despite the fundamental differences
between various sectors of the nation, there is something called "the
Jewish People." The second assumption is that the form and content of the Jewish identity has changed over the course of history.

Moreover, despite their differences, all these historians associate
the changes in identity with the declining weight of religion. Graetz
still attributes a central role to the moral commitment, in the religious
sense but Dubnow replaces religion with national consciousness—
even though religion is included in this consciousness as an historical major element. Baron, as for him, considers religion to be part
of Jewish society as a unique culture while for Dinour, religion is
one of the forces driving the national messianic trend. Mahler considers religion to be a major element in the Jews' popular culture,
and at the same time, for Ettinger, religion is one of the components of the dialectical system underlying the collective Jewish identity. This brings us to the central questions discussed in this book:
what is Jewish identity today, and who is a Jew after the Jews have
experienced secularization, and, later on, have even been granted a
homeland of their own—just like many other nations.

Jewish identity has been affected by numerous forces: emancipation in Western Europe and most particularly in the United States,
which made the Jews partners in the historical life of the countries
in which they dwell; anti-Semitism, which gave birth to the Holocaust
and wiped a third of the Jewish people, mainly in Eastern Europe,
off the stage of history; and the national Jewish movement, which
restored to the Jewish people the possibility for independent action

in the historical arena. At this point as told us by Gershom Scholem, the Jewish People faced the challenge to "take responsibility for its deeds and shortcomings". This but opened a major debate about the "normalcy" of the Jewish People.

Indeed, the fact that the Jews established their own state in a given territory made them similar in this sense to other nations, such as the Irish, Italians, Greeks, and Armenians, many, or even most, of whose members live outside their national borders. This dramatic change in the Jewish People and the simultaneous fact that the Jews also enjoyed civil and social status in the societies of their dispersion led to the disappearance of one of the typical characteristics of Jewish identity, the sense of "homelessness". As a result, the delegitimization of diasporism in the classic Zionist formula was no longer relevant, and new notions of "normalcy" applying to Jews were now defined (Gorny, 1990:22).

"General normalization" regards the nation as a territorial-civil entity, and thus denies the notion of the existence of the Jewish People in the universal sense. In this approach, only the Jewish religion, like the Christian or the Muslim, is trans-territorial. This view, propounded by intellectual circles in the Diaspora, can also be found in Israel. In essence, it combines post-Canaanite ideas with the principles of Western liberalism. Its "normalist" nature is embodied in the call to repeal the Law of Return, not only because it is anti-democratic and anti-liberal, discriminating between different categories of individuals in Israel itself (Jews against Arabs), but also because it is seen as to symbolize the desire to artificially, even arbitrarily, preserve and promote an abnormal identity of the Jewish People.

"Particular normalization" is based on the peculiarities of Jewish history. While highlighting the positive aspects of Jewish life in the Diaspora, it acknowledges Israel as the historical-religious center of the Jewish People. Thus, whereas it claims that the continued survival of the Jewish People throughout the world is dependent on the existence of the State of Israel, it does not consider Israel the sole Jewish center. In effect, the advocates of this approach perpetuate Dubnow's notion of "Jewish centers". Particular normalization can be recognized by its concern for Israel, the memory of the Holocaust, and the devotion to preserving the rights and status of the Jews throughout the world, such as the fight against manifestations of anti-Semitism and the past efforts on behalf of the Jews of the Soviet Union.

"Jewish normalization" is basically Zionism à la Ahad Ha'am. It regards the Jews as a single nation and itts proponents see the political and cultural center of the Jews in the Land of Israel, in the shape of the State of Israel. While stressing the spiritual and emotional meaning of life in the Diaspora, they accept that Jewish diasporas will continue to exist outside the borders of Israel. However, they consider their survival as a Jewish community, as opposed to the survival of the Jewish individual, to be dependent on their connection to the Jewish political center in Israel.

Of the three approaches prevailing today at the start of the third millennium, general normalization, while undoubtedly reflecting a latent, subterranean trend in Israel and the Diaspora, is expressed publicly only by small circles of intellectuals. Jewish normalization has suffered a decline in status for two conflicting reasons. First, it has been adversely affected by the success of Zionism, raising the more and more frequently voiced question of whether the time has not come to declare its triumphant completion. Secondly, it has been enfeebled by the increasing internal difficulties in Israeli society, which deal a very grave blow to the ideals that Diaspora Jewry would like to see in the country. In contrast to the waning power of the previous two approaches, particular normalization, relying on the general trends toward multi-culturalism, ethnicity, and diasporism, has been bolstered by the improved status of Jews in society in the realms of finance, culture, and even politics.

Interestingly enough, to the three approaches to normalization correspond three attitudes to these major axes of contemporary Jewish identity, namely, the understanding of the Holocaust, on the one hand, and the allegiance to Israel as a Jewish state, on the other. Those who advocate general normalization—and exhibit a centrifugal perspective toward Jewry—endow the Jewish Holocaust mainly with universal meaning. To their mind, the suffering and devastation of the Jews is identical to other cases in history, such as the Armenian tragedy in World War I, the dropping of the atom bombs on Hiroshima and Nagasaki, the slaughter in Biafra, and even the massacre of the Indians by the European settlers in Northern and Southern America. This attitude sees in Jewish suffering a particular case of a general human evil. On the other hand, the two centripetal views contrast with this approach. Jewish normalization sees the Holocaust as a collective experience that unifies the Jews and underlies their perception of being a single nation. A wide range of views are allied with this approach, from the extreme national-religious stance that perceives Jewish existence as a constant state of emergency, to the national-secular viewpoint which considers the memory of the Holocaust to be the deciding factor in the relations between the Jews and other nations. Particular normalization perceives the Holocaust as a historical memory with a national message, but without any political significance in the present, a position held by moderate, or even conservative, liberal circles. On the one hand, they stress the historical mistake of the liberals who adopted a universal approach to the ideologies and movements that led to the Holocaust, and on the other, they caution against the extreme national integrative approach, fearing it might create a barrier between the Jews and the society in which they live. All three attitudes can be found, albeit to differing degrees, in both Israel and the Diaspora. In view of objective circumstances, there obviously is a stronger tendency toward universalism in the Diaspora than in Israel, and nationalism is stronger in Israel than in the Diaspora.

On the whole, the memory of the Holocaust has created a shared sense of solidarity among the Jews throughout the world, and especially between Israel and the Diaspora (Oron, 1993; Gorny, 1998). At the same time, however, the stronger the salience of the Holocaust, the weaker the salience of the allegiance to the State of Israel, so that the former forces the second out of its central position in the perception of collective Jewish identity. This is so not only because of the understandable sincere emotional impact of anything relating to the Holocaust, but also because of the inevitable difficulties entailed in statehood. Political existence over the course of history is a constant process of loss of faith in myths, disillusionment with one ethos or another, and frustration at the impossibility of realizing utopias. Thus we are led unavoidably to the conclusion that in respect to the two myths that play today the principal roles in the identity of the Jews, rebirth and Holocaust, Jews identify more strongly with the collective tragedy than with the collective achievement. More than benefiting the salience of the Holocaust, this detracts from the salience of the state. This means that over time we can expect developments and trends that are liable to undermine Jewish unity. Such unity will be impossible or meaningless unless Israel holds a central place in the perception of Jewish collective identity.

All these mean that the Jews are not a nation of "sufferers and scholars," the bearers of the divine notion of justice and morality, as Graetz believed; they are not a nation that proves the power of the national consciousness of a community seeking to maintain its singularity even though it lacks a territory of its own, as Dubnow suggested; they are not merely a social-religious collective, as Baron claimed, since they do have a sovereign state of their own; and they are not a society driven by a Zionist messianic urge, as Dinour proposes, or concentrated around a territorial center in the Land of Israel, as Mahler would have it.

The Jews today are vulnerable to the winds of change and split along political, cultural, and religious lines. They are divided between those who are citizens of their own sovereign country, and those who are equal citizens of other countries in the world. They are involved in a variety of cultures—Hebrew, English, French, Spanish, Russian, and more—not only as consumers, but also as creators. They are divided into religious and non-religious groups, and by religious denomination—ultra-Orthodox, modern Orthodox, Conservative, Reform, and others. It is not at all clear whether, in the third millennium, these differences are capable of reforming into new unities in a process similar to that which Ettinger describes as having occurred over the past century. Paradoxically, Israel, the most prominent symbol of the "Jewish People," as it is entirely under Jewish control, is feeding the process of fragmentation.

This brings us back to the words of Gershom Scholem. The definition of a Jew can not be provided by halakha, but only by history. What we are seeking is a definition of the "historical Jew" on the basis of collective historical experience and memory. In negative terms, in this definition a Jew cannot be a member of any other religion, because the historical continuity of the conjunction of religion and nationality in Judaism prevents it. In positive terms, the definition must be pluralistic. The "pluralist Jewish People" is composed of individuals who bear a variety of different identities in terms of ideologies, culture, and citizenship. On the one hand, they are part and parcel of the rapid historical process of social change that has been going on for over two hundred years. On the other hand, they are united by a sense of connectivity, which is sometimes affected by historical afflictions and sometimes motivated by the desire to preserve and sustain their peoplehood and singularity. The connection may be influenced by social circumstances, but it is meta-historical in essence.

These remarks are meant to present my perception as an historian, and will hopefully add a further—although not entirely alien—perspective to the comprehensive, systematic and far-reaching socio-historical analysis by Eliezer Ben-Rafael in the first part of this book, which describes how the Jewish People have dealt with their collective identity since the dawn of the modern era. The analysis focuses on the issue of "What is a Jew?", naturally leading to the question of "Who is a Jew?", which is the subject of the second part of the book. Here, the floor is given to the Jewish "sages" themselves.

PREFACE

Who and what is a Jew? Is there any common denominator between an ultra-Orthodox rabbi of North African origin affiliated to the Shas movement and living in a small town in Southern Israel and a non-religious, perhaps even anti-religious, Berkeley academic who is member of the Movement for a Secular and Humanistic Judaism? Do Jews the world over tend to converge and emphasize their unity as a solidaristic "people" possessing one collective identity—notwithstanding the inevitable cultural disparities—or do they tend to formulate contrasting concepts under the common title of "Jewish identity," perhaps virtually splitting into different "Jewish Peoples"? These questions are at the heart of this book which attempts to present a systematic discussion of Jewish identities in this era of (post-) modernity.

The opportunity for this discussion is offered by a set of texts that has long been ignored by researchers, scholars and students, but which represents an invaluable contribution as yet unexplored and unappreciated. We are referring here to the great debate initiated in 1958 by Ben-Gurion, then Prime Minister of Israel, which involved approximately fifty intellectuals from the Jewish world ("Sages of Israel," as Ben-Gurion referred to them). These men, from the Diaspora as well as Israel, were associated with the most prominent and representative of the major streams of Jewish thought at the time. Some were rabbis and others philosophers, writers, scientists, judges and lawyers. Some were ultra-Orthodox and others modern Orthodox, non-Orthodox or free thinkers. Their letters appear in full (or nearly so) in Part II of this book. Part I is offered as a tribute to these intellectuals who stood up for their convictions.

In 1958, when Israel was ten years old, the Israeli leadership was compelled to deal with the fact that the notion of Jewish identity had become the object of legislation with crucial practical implications: who may benefit from the Law of Return, and who is entitled to Israeli citizenship. In addition to these legal issues, another more symbolic, but no less critical, question related to whom the State of Israel was referring to when it defined itself not only as a Jewish State, but also as the "State of the Jews." One of the primary foci of the debate that developed around these issues naturally concerned the constitutional validity of ancient Talmudic law, or halakha. This was the basis of the controversy that raged in the Knesset—the Israeli Parliament—and the Government over the question of acceptance into Judaism of the children of mixed marriages, where the mother was the non-Jewish spouse. It was this query that Ben-Gurion posed to the "sages": Should the State register these children as Jews, if such is the wish of both parents, who declare "in good faith" that their children do not belong to any other religion?

While the question itself refers to a specific and rather marginal category, it obliged the respondents to confront the much broader problems of Judaism's social boundaries—who is included and who is excluded—and contents—how does one become a Jew or cease to be one. In short, the respondents were being asked for their opinion on who and what is a Jew. Needless to say, independently of the political implications of the responses,[1] the letters constitute an extraordinary range of approaches reflecting the diversity of attitudes in the Jewish world at that time. The interest they arouse stems from the fact that they clearly and unambiguously reveal the major internal debates of modern Judaism, and the nature and limits of the competition for hegemony of the different schools of thought.

Moreover, in 1958 Judaism was still reeling from the unprecedented upheaval in the Jewish condition engendered by three events of overwhelming—and contrasting—significance that occurred within that revolutionary era that had already been sparked with modernity and the emancipation of Jews: the building of a strong American Jewish community by immigrants from Eastern Europe; the decimation and indescribable suffering of the Holocaust; and the creation of a Jewish State in the mythical "promised land." These changes raised acute questions regarding the continuity or discontinuity of the contemporary formulations of Jewish identity vis-à-vis both earlier modern versions, and traditional Judaism itself. Nearly half a century later, it is also of interest to us here to consider the degree to which these letters of the "Sages of Israel" presage the many diverse formulations of Jewish identity that are current today.

---

[1] Ben-Gurion and the Government of Israel understood that there was impossible to ignore *halakhic* requirements without facing the risk of a split in world Jewry. Consequently, they eventually adopted new guidelines that required conversion for the children of non-Jewish mothers in order for them to be registered as "Jews."

These letters, and their links to both earlier and later formulations of Jewish identity, therefore offer us the opportunity to reflect on the essentials of the Jewish collective identity. Accordingly, Part I of this book offers a sociological interpretation of the development and diversification of Jewish identities since entrance into the modern world. We contend that this process, which has entailed a constant questioning of traditional truths and the continuous emergence of new and unexpected formulations, confirms the validity of a paradigm encompassing all identifiable formulations of Jewish identity within one space of possibilities and indicating their relative proximity to or distance from each other.

The starting point for our analysis is the definition of Jewish identity that prevailed in traditional society before the age of modernity: the assertion of total commitment to a "Jewish People," a perception of a cultural singularity expressed in the notions of the "God and Torah of Israel," and a definition of the Jewish condition in respect to non-Jews, in terms of exile and the longing for a Return to the "Land of Israel." With the entry of the Jews into the modern age, these principles were transformed into questions which may be formulated as follows: (1) To what degree is the Jewish People an entity still requiring solidarity once Jews become citizens of non-Jewish states and societies? (2) How should the religious culture associated with Judaism be interpreted in an increasingly secular environment? (3) To what extent does the notion of exile still apply to Jews in modern, often liberal and democratic, states where they are equal citizens, and can the longing for "Return" remain a legitimate collective aspiration in this context?

These questions have been answered in numerous and varied ways. By drawing insights from the letters of the "sages" to Ben-Gurion, three principal contrasting syndromes can be identified which are relevant to the analysis of both previous and later formulations. These syndromes are still battling for hegemony in the Jewish world today. They diverge from each other not only in the content of their answers to the fundamental questions, but also, and primarily, in the facet of collective identity on which they lay stress. The ultra-Orthodox caste syndrome aspires to continue the traditional model, emphasizing the Jews' religious calling that turns them toward themselves and their own deeds. The ethnocultural syndrome sees Judaism as a set of cultural values upheld by Jewish communities throughout the world. The national-territorialist syndrome accentuates the building

of a sovereign Jewish nation grounded in its ancestral land, which
it defines as a national territory.

In respect to content, each syndrome views the dilemma of particularism vs. universalism that has always been inherent to Judaism
in a different light. The caste syndrome maintains the particularism
of the Jews' religious mission, even though it speaks of the redemption of humanity as a whole; the national-territorial syndrome stresses
the universality of the aspiration for national sovereignty, while insis-
ting on the particularism of this aspiration when it comes to the Jews;
the ethnocultural syndrome tends to emphasize the universalistic perspectives of Judaism and to downplay its particularistic aspects. Furthermore, the ethnocultural and national syndromes are eager to underline
their thorough acceptance of modernity, while the caste syndrome
seeks to retain control of how and how much it participates in modernity, refusing to see it as an absolute good. Finally, for the ethno-
cultural syndrome, Judaism is a subculture and can coexist with any
other national identity; for the caste syndrome, it is the principal
identity of the individual but does not exclude a different national
identity; and for the national-territorial syndrome, Jewish sovereignty
is the only way to enable what it calls "full Jewish identity."

Each stream is further divided into a variety of more specific
approaches. On their fringes are the extremist splinters: Naturei Karta
is the militant branch of the anti-Zionist stream among the supporters of the caste syndrome; Diasporist Judaism represents the
extremist position among the followers of the ethnocultural syndrome;
and the Canaanists and Post-Zionists propose a definition of the
Jewish population of Israel in terms that separate them from the rest
of world Jewry. These groups demonstrate the degree to which contemporary Judaism is marked not only by diversity, but also by a
tendency for division and fragmentation. The risks are real. Our
analysis reveals, however, that thus far all the major syndromes and
the more specific models they have spawned still belong to the same
space. They all relate more or less to the same people, draw their
symbols from the same "store," and attach equal importance to the
solidarity of the whole which together they comprise.

From this perspective, our analysis contributes to the wider debate
about collective identity taking place in the social sciences. It starts
from a definition of collective identity in which it is seen as the representation that crystallizes when individuals think of themselves as
a group, and which serves as the basis for both the distinctions and

the resemblances they perceive within that group.[2] This collective identity constructs the individual's "real world" and his or her place in it. While the quest for an identity of this kind is universal, we contend that it has acquired special meaning and intensity in the contemporary world. Whereas in traditional societies, people defined themselves primarily in terms of what they were a priori, this essentialist identity has been minorized in modernity, overshadowed by the identity that individuals achieve by themselves, that is, the "constructed identity."[3] This approach conjures up Wittgenstein's[4] contention of the tendency of individuals to "hang together" (Zusammenhangen) and develop collective identities (1) through social interaction and solidarity, (2) while elaborating common moral codes and symbols, (3) which delineate social boundaries and define the relation between "us" and "they". These three universal facets of collective identity underlie our approach to Jewish identity, as defined above.

The notion of collective identity always refers to a subjective perspective,[5] implying that the same identity may be the object of formulations that differ among individuals and milieus. For the advocates of the primordialist approach,[6] this identity is primarily the expression of an allegiance to ascriptive attributes perceived to be of overpowering intrinsic social importance, independent of circumstances of place and time. Like Jacques Derrida, they hold that human beings cannot free themselves from the metaphysics which construct groups' historical continuity, whether real or imagined.[7] On the other hand, situationists or circumstancialists speak of the construction of identities, emphasizing the contextual conditions of social life.[8] Together

---

[2] C. Calhoun, "Social theory and the politics of identity," in C. Calhoun (Ed.), *Social Theory and the Politics of Identity*, Oxford, Blackwell, 1994, pp. 9–36; F. Barth, "How is the Self conceptualized? Variations among cultures," in U. Neisser and D. A. Jopling (Eds.), *The Conceptual Self in Context: Culture, Experience, Self-Understanding*, Cambridge, Cambridge University Press, 1997, pp. 75–91.

[3] A. Touraine, *Critique de la Modernité*, Paris, Fayard, 1992, pp. 139–174.

[4] T.R. Schatzki, *Social Practices: A Wittgensteinian Approach to Human Activity and the Social*, Cambridge, Cambridge University Press, 1996, pp. 168–198.

[5] R. Plant, "Antinomies of modernist political thought: Reasoning, context and community," in J. Good and I. Velody (Eds.), *The Politics of Modernity*, **référence ?**, 1998, pp. 76–106.

[6] C. Geertz, *Old Societies and New States*, New York, The Free Press, 1965, pp. 105–157.

[7] J. Derrida, *L'Ecriture et la Différence*, Paris, Seuil, 1967, p. 427.

[8] A. Lange and C. Westin, *The Generative Mode of Explanation in Social Psychological*

with the constructionnists, they stress the importance of considerations of cost and benefit for the social actors, relating them to the
evincing or downgrading of collective allegiances. A similar position
is propounded by those who speak of traditions and affiliations in
terms of "invention" and "imagination."[9]

Nevertheless, recognizing the power of collective myths does not
necessarily preclude the influence of practical circumstances on the
strength of their impact. As we see it, this sort of comprehensive
approach is represented by the structuralist school,[10] which considers
any identity to be grounded in "deep structures" that are concretized
in the reality of social life in what are labeled "surface structures."
According to Levi-Strauss,[11] deep structures may involve inner oppo-
sitions, tensions, or even conflicts, between alternative emphases
("binary poles"). The precise phrasings of these constitutive or "primordial" elements of identity necessarily vary "in the open" with life
experiences, individual endeavors, personal preferences, power
configurations, or specific events. In fact, the different phrasings might
be very divergent, although the variability of formulations is not
unlimited. While the sine qua non conditions of allegiance to the
collective may be relatively clear and simple, this is not necessarily
the case for their requirements, which may be subject to endless
variations.

It is in this context that the present volume begins with a discussion of the fundamental dilemmas historically associated with the
traditional principles of Jewishness from which modern Jewish identities developed. We then trace the major alternative formulations as
they emerged successively, considering whether they represent ge-

---

Theories of Race and Ethnic Relations, Stockolm, Centre for Research in Inetrnational
Migration and Ethnicity, Report No. 6, 1985; S. Olzak, "Contemporary Ethnic
Mobilization," *Annual Review of Sociology*, 9, 1983, pp. 355–74.
    [9] E. Hobsbawm and T. Ranger, *The Invention of Tradition*, Cambridge, Cambridge
University Press, 1983.
    [10] L. Drummond, "The cultural continuum: A theory of intersystems," *Man*, 15,
2, 1980, pp. 352–374; T.H. Eriksen, "The Cultural context of ethnic differences,"
Man, 26, 1, 1991, pp. 127–144.
    [11] C. Levi-Strauss, *Race et Histoire*, Paris, Gonthier, 1961, pp. 19–26; J.-M. Benoist,
"Facettes de l'identité," in C. Levi-Strauss (Ed.), *L'Identité*, Paris, PUF, 1977, pp.
13–24; K. Liebkind,"Conceptual approaches to ethnic identity," in K. Liebkind
(Ed.), *New Identities in Europe*, Aldershot, U.K., Gower, 1989, pp. 25–40. See also:
D. Sperber, "Le Structuralisme en anthropologie," in O. Ducrot, T. Todorov et
al., *Qu'est-ce que le structuralisme*, Paris, Seuil, 1968, pp. 220–237.

nuine metamorphoses of the collective identity, or mere variations of previous phrasings. More specifically, we address three periods: the entry of Jews into the modern era, from the end of the 18th century to the end of the 19th; the mid-20th century; and the beginning of the 21st century. At each of these stages, we will present and compare the various formulations offered.

This sort of analysis may be timely in view of the fact that at our epoch, often described as "postmodern," identity appears to be, at one and the same time, both less of an obligation and the object of a more intense quest than ever before.[12] At the very time that loyalty to collective identities no longer seems to be an unavoidable constraint, we are witnessing an "explosion" of collective identities. Now more than ever, they not only reflect, but also shape, social experience. They tend to be embodied in the greatest variety of formulations, which themselves are constantly changing, a notion expressed in Danièle Hervieu-Léger's[13] concept of "identity trajectories." In the same vein, we conceive of Jewish identity as a succession of phases and a diversification of formulations in which different aspects are given new form and new emphases. In this sense, we consider Jewish identity to be a particular emblematic example of collective identity, and therefore instructive in demonstrating the problematic of contemporary collective identities in general. Following our general interest in the study of collective identity, our basic question is: can we still define a space in which all formulations of a same identity can be represented in relation to one another? To use Wittgenstein's words,[14] where does their "family resemblance" lie.

It is also in this context that we see the importance of the letters presented in Part II which were sent to Ben-Gurion in the late 1950s by individuals of outstanding intellectual stature, such as Isaiah Berlin, Chaim Perelman, Mordecai Menachem Kaplan, Menachem Mendel Schneersohn, Joseph Dov Soloveitchik, S.Y. Agnon and many others. They were written in the same period, in response to the same query, by individuals who all saw themselves as profoundly Jewish, in spite

---

[12] Z. Bauman, "From Pilgrim to Tourist—or a short History of Identity," in S. Hall and P. Du Gay P. (Eds.), *Questions of Cutural Identity*, London, Sage, 1996, pp. 18–36.

[13] D. Hervieu-Léger, "The Transmission and Formation of Socioreligious Identities in Modernity: An Analytical Essay," *International Sociology*, 1998, 13, 2, pp. 213–228.

[14] L. Wittgenstein, *Tractatus logico-philosophicus*, suivi de *Investigations philosophiques*, Paris, Gallimard (trad. de l'allemand par P. Klossowski), 1961, para. 67, p. 148.

of their speaking different languages and living in different countries and on different continents. Their common concerns, as well as their diverging perspectives, demonstrate both the degree to which Jewishness adopts singular, yet diverse, contents at a given point in time, and the degree to which it simultaneously expresses historical continuity.

PART ONE

WHAT IS A JEW?

INTRODUCTION

The questions "Who is a Jew?" and "What are the Jews?" are much more than merely the academic province of the social sciences. They resound through all aspects of the issue of collective identity, which is so much a part of modern life. For the individual, collective identity represents a fact of life that must come to bear daily, a fact of life that is also an obligation, a mission, and a responsibility, and one that we are conscious of whenever we think about ourselves (Bauman, 1998). The collective identity contains both universal elements that relate to us as members of the human race, and particular elements that describe those features that make us unique. This duality is at the very heart of the contemporary discourse on the nature of modernity, since unlike in the past, the question "Who am I fundamentally?", that is, in the essentialist sense, is now less significant than the question "What do I do?" in the constructionist sense. Today individuals are expected to shape their own identity and gain recognition of it from others (Calhoun, 1994).

In Wittgenstein's systematic perspective (Schatzki, 1996), collective identity belongs to a series of phenomena that starts with "social practice," a correlate of "sociality"—human beings' predisposition to "hang together". Sociality is the foundation of social activity, which, in effect, is the system of interdependency that gives rise to what we call collective identity. Wittgenstein maintains that being a baker, professor, African-American, or Norwegian is associated with a variety of beliefs, expectations, hopes, feelings, and understandings held by the individual who "belongs" to that category. They enable us to participate in social acts—including the act of speech—in response to the actions of those defined as "not us," and to understand the acts of those included in "us." "Us" here refers to individuals (the "community") who consider their life to represent "us-conditions." It is not far to go from this premise to that of a "cultural community" which upholds shared norms and values, or a "community of intent" with its source in education and the desire to fulfill certain aspirations. Clearly, then, as Barth (1997) states, collective identity should be seen as a dynamic social process, a sort of group project, that emerges through participation in shaping a culture and moral

codes through practical experience. This may explain why the concept of collective identity serves as the heading for studies of self-
perception, the way in which people distinguish themselves from each
other and the way they interpret the fact that they see themselves
as distinct social entities.

At the turn of the 21st century, the concept of collective identity
can serve more than ever before as the basis for understanding collective activity.[1] The enhanced importance of identity today is linked
to the development of the (post-)modern society (Lash and Friedman,
1992), which spurred the "search for identity." At the same time,
identity may be perceived as a cultural-historical affinity beyond the
circumstances of time and place (Geertz, 1965). This perspective is
anchored in recognition of uncontrollable drives for identification.
Derrida (1978) claims that modern man, like his predecessors, can
not free himself of metaphysics, the aspect of identity that interprets,
structures, and manifests the historical continuity of collective identity. Values, symbols, legacies, and commitments, brought together
in "canonized libraries" of some sort, turn collective identity into the
foundation of a historical culture. These "cultural texts" (Denzin,
1994) serve as course books in the schools, are quoted from in official
ceremonies, and are referred to in public addresses. Far-reaching,
they are interpreted by intellectuals, scholars, and priests, and do
not necessarily exist as a single entity or in a single formulation.
Other researchers adopt a different position, explaining the importance of identity primarily in terms of life circumstances. They stress
the changes in identity from one condition to another, and the
influence of considerations of profit and loss, both individual and
collective, which stem from the emphasis or lack of emphasis on features of identity. Hobsbawm and Ranger (1983) even speak of "inven-
ting tradition" in certain circumstances, taking the stance that various
cultural phenomena are, in fact, imaginary entities.

In effect, however, the different approaches relate to different
aspects of collective identity, and therefore are not mutually exclusive. Just as the link to a certain myth might not be contingent on

---

[1] Kimmel notes that in the non-industrialized world, religious fundamentalism is
now the strongest glue of collective identity and social movements. This is particularly true of the Islamic movement in Iran, Algeria, Kashmir, Egypt, and Turkey.
In these countries, fundamentalism aroused an enthusiasm and engendered an
activism that left radical Marxism, the leading political and emotional force of the
first decades of the 20th century, far behind (Kimmel, 1996:72).

circumstances, so particular conditions might strengthen or weaken this link. Taken as a whole, theories indicate a distinction between two levels of discussion in relation to collective identity. The first concerns the basic principles at the root of identity, what might be seen as its "deep structures." The second relates to the different forms in which collective identity may manifest itself, or its "surface structures."

Following Levi-Strauss (1961), deep structures are thus seen as the factors that shape the "basic" collective identity. However, the various structures may make distinct, perhaps even contradictory, demands, thereby generating conflict and endemic dilemmas. These assumptions are quite similar to the manner in which Gellner (1983) and Smith (1987) depict the emergence of national or ethnic-national identity. Furthermore, each of the individual principles of identity may spawn a dilemma between polar opposites, thus placing an additional burden on the individual. This being the case, it appears that, in essence, collective identity does not necessarily lend itself to a single, consistent, and immutable definition. Rather, it may refer to a whole range of formulations that display varying degrees of similarity in respect to the way in which they provide answers to those endemic dilemmas arising from possible contradictions between basic principles. It is therefore conceivable that different versions of identity, reflecting different influences, might exist side by side among people who see themselves as one collective.

In the context of the above, it is our contention that, by definition, a collective identity necessarily implies three different phases. These distinct yet related aspects are associated with different basic principles (or deep structures). The first concerns the way in which people describe their link to the collective and their obligations to it, that is, the practical implications of their definition of themselves as members of the collective. The second relates to the way individuals describe the social, cultural, moral, normative, religious, historical, or linguistic singularity of the collective. The third aspect focuses on the way individuals perceive the place of the collective in relation to "others," both near and far (Lash and Friedman, 1992). These three features of collective identity are not necessarily perceived in the same manner by all sectors or individuals. Different formulations, which are themselves subject to change, may emerge as a result of circumstances, influences, or personal biographies and preferences. Analyzing collective identity in terms of these three major

aspects also enables us to ask which of them is emphasized most
strongly in each of the various formulations. Accordingly, one should
be able to demonstrate how different conceptions, some considerably remote from one another, may be encompassed within the space
of formulations referring to the collective identity under study.
Obviously, however, the wider the distribution of formulations, the
harder it is to view them as relating to the same space of identities,
and even to the same collective.

In this sense, the current volume considers the question of Jewish
identity as a particular case of collective identity. Part I deals with
the dominant formulations of Jewish identity, both contrasting and
similar, and the way in which they deal with the demands of the
modern era. We shall examine conflicting pledges to the "Jewish
people," which substantiate the principle of commitment to the collective; the different images of the "God and Torah (Biblical Teachings)
of Israel," i.e., perceptions of the singularity of the collective; and
the various interpretations of the concept "Land of Israel," which
pertain to the perspectives of the place and status of the collective
in respect to "others." This will bring us to the crucial question: is it
still possible to speak of a single identity, or at least what Wittgenstein
(1961) terms "family resemblance." Wittgenstein chose this analogy
to elaborate on the relation of language games to language, and it
is, in our view, no less appropriate to our discussion here, as it is
an apt description of the way in which a variety of traits—height,
facial features, eye color, posture, temperament, etc.—may diversely,
unevenly, and often quite randomly, become mixed among people
who make up the same extended family.

In the broadest sense, what we are seeking to discover is whether
or not we can still speak, if not of a single Jewish identity, at least
of a family of identities and a shared space of identities. This approach
is similar to that adopted by Hervieu-Léger (1998) in her investigation of Catholic identity in France. She found that different individuals associate that identity with different elements—faith, community,
ethics, culture, or emotional significance—and give them different
weights that change at different stages in their lives. While our own
approach is similar, it focuses on the content of identity itself, considering the various formulations of the collective identity of Jews
both diachronically and synchronically. What we are seeking to identify is the endemic dialectic of the continuity or discontinuity of

Jewish identity from one period to another and between one school of thought and another.

For this analysis, the opinions of Ben-Gurion's correspondents serve as the central link connecting the lack of uniformity that emerged upon entrance into the modern era with the various forms of Jewishness that developed up to the start of the 21st century. As we shall see, these letters represent a treasure house of documentary evidence that not only gives eloquent voice to the phrasings of Jewish identity in the mid-20th century, but also offers a fitting conceptual framework for analysis of the changes that had taken place before and that will take place later on. Ben-Gurion received these letters from Jewish intellectuals in response to a request issued in late 1958. As they were asked to do, the letters consider the question of the boundaries of the collective in respect to the specific problem of how to register the national allegiance of children of mixed marriages. Although this may represent an essentially marginal issue, it relates directly to the problem of defining the nature of the social limits of Judaism and the distinction between those who "belong" and those who do not. This inevitably also entails the question of how a non-Jew can become a Jew, that is, the criteria for inclusion in, and exclusion from, the Jewish collective.

These limits of the collective cannot, of course, be defined independently of the features its members see in it: "Who is a Jew?" derives logically from "What is a Jew?" Nevertheless, the connection between these two questions is not unmediated, unidirectional, or unequivocal. As we shall learn, in practice, inclusion and exclusion are associated not only with ideology and culture, but also with historical circumstances, political challenges, and other interests. All these play a part in determining who to let in and who to leave out, how to get in and how to get out. The letters of the Jewish thinkers illustrate the various models at the heart of the major controversies in the Jewish world since the Emancipation and to this very day.

CHAPTER ONE

ENTERING THE MODERN ERA

The Decline of a Caste

Historical Judaism has always been characterized by a definition of collective identity that stresses religious faith above all else. However, along the continuum of time and place, this identity was not homogenous. Schmueli (1980) lists five phases in Jewish identity, each with a different emphasis: the Bible, the Talmud, political philosophy in Alexandria, Hassidism, and rabbinical culture. The distinctions between them are reflected in very different approaches to issues such as the nature of man, the concept of sin and death, and can be understood in terms of the physical and spiritual conditions under which Jews lived in different periods and places. Sharot (1982) adds that such variety could also have stemmed from the fact that Judaism does not recognize a central religious authority. Even when Maimonides declared that the next world was open only to those who upheld his thirteen articles of faith, other contemporary rabbis begged to differ. It must be remembered that religious studies, the norm among the intellectual elite in Jewish communities, trained scholars in a rational and metaphoric system of disputation that encouraged dissent. The Kabbalah introduced even more approaches and perspectives. This feature of Judaism was further enhanced by the growth of Hassidism, structured as it was around charismatic rabbis who reigned over a court of disciples. The Hassidim (plural of Hassid) split into dozens of varieties and sub-varieties that disputed each other over issues ranging from the role of the rabbi to the presence of God at the Creation. And we have yet to add to this the enmity between the Hassidim and the Mitnaggedim, who wished to preserve the traditional scholarly form of Judaism.

Nonetheless, no matter how profound and heated these controversies, they did not eradicate the shared foundations of the traditional Jewish collective identity with its solid connection to the God and Torah of Israel, the Jewish People, and the Land of Israel. Ever since the exile of the People after the Biblical period—save perhaps

for the phase Schmueli calls "political philosophy"—the principle of
the "God and Torah of Israel" was the dominant aspect of Judaism
which gave meaning and legitimacy to the existence of the Jewish
people and its tie to the Land of Israel. It was this aspect which
justified the preservation of the Jewish people as the object of the
word of God, and which gave significance to the notion of the Land
of Israel as the Promised Land, the site of the worship of God and
acceptance of his commandments. Yet while this identity stresses the
singularity of the collective, it also represents a clearly universal perception: that by its own redemption, the nation would redeem the
world. This is the meaning of the portrayal of the Jewish nation as
"The Chosen People," the most fundamental element of Jewish
monotheism. Although God is one and universal, his words obligate
a specific group charged with the crucial function of redeeming the
world by observing the commandments "within itself" and "among
itself" in its daily life.

The most appropriate sociological label for this type of collective
identity is "caste." Like all collective terms, "caste" refers to the
many social practices that merge discourse (language, ideas, symbols,
etc.) with action (specific activities, unique behavioral patterns, envi-
ronmental and institutional features, etc.) (Smith, 1987). In the case
of a caste, these practices are given clear religious legitimacy that is
anchored in the perception of "purity." Maintaining purity requires
a lack of contact—in some cases absolute—with "others," keeping
the group separate from everyone else. On the other hand, the term
"caste" also relates to the existence of a distinct collective within a
total system. Such a group plays, in its own eyes, a most crucial role
in achieving an overall "supreme" purpose for the benefit of all—
in-groups as well as out-groups—so that the latter is, whether know-
ingly or unknowingly, dependent on the former in this respect. This
is, in fact, the essence of Dumont's (1977) definition, which states
that a caste is a group with an all-encompassing perception of itself
and the organization of its life, but at the same time sees itself as
part of a larger system in which its aspirations are given "transcen-
dental" meaning.

In these terms, the self-definition of the Jews stands in sharp contrast to their portrayal by their Christian and Moslem neighbors in
different eras and places throughout the centuries. The Jews saw
themselves as a superior caste, while the "others" regarded them as
"impure" and "untouchables," a caste of pariahs. Hence, paradoxi-

cally, the Jews and non-Jews remained separate from each other for utterly opposite reasons. By upholding their internal codes, the Jews made it clear that they considered their inferior status in society to be at variance with the "proper" social order. The strict laws of purity and kashrut explicitly prohibited close contact with non-Jews— anything beyond business or practical dealings—and concretized this general caste attitude.

With the coming of the modern era, the caste approach found itself in the eye of a storm of revolutionary ideas, and soon lost its influence over the Jews. The Emancipation widened the rift. Many chose now to express their Judaism in new ways, until eventually the subscribers to traditional Judaism came to represent a small minority. In fact, even prior to the Emancipation, many Jews, sensing the imminent cultural revolution in Europe, championed the notions of equality and personal freedoms (Russell, 1996). They were also convinced that economic and technological developments would bring down the barriers between the groups and sectors in society, leading to a modification not only of their status, but of the Jewish society and religion as well. Indeed, the processes that took place in the course of the 19th century triggered a radical change in relations between Jews and non-Jews, bringing them closer together on the one hand, and spawning modern anti-Semitism on the other. At the same time as the Jews were allowed to return to England and make their home there, for example, it became the fashion in elite circles to try to persuade them to convert to Christianity (Ragussis, 1995). Similarly, while Jews were admitted into the French army, the Dreyfus affair sparked a wave of anti-Semitism.[1]

Above all else, the transformation of the Jews was spurred by their internal dilemmas, which were cast in a new light by the national and the technological-industrial revolutions in Europe. In view of the new social realities, many came to consider the caste model archaic. The search for new formulations of Jewish identity now contended in a "different" way with the basic dilemmas inherent in the traditional definition. The post-traditional outlooks regarded the basic issues—the "deep structures" of Jewish identity—as questions that

---

[1] In the early 1890s, it was discovered that someone in the French army was spying for the Germans. The generals chose to place the blame on Alfred Dreyfus, a Jewish officer. Tried and found guilty, Dreyfus was exiled to Devil's Island. As a result of tireless efforts on the part of his family and well-known writers and public figures, Dreyfus won a retrial in which his name was cleared.

could be given new answers which would ultimately construct the space of "modern" Jewish identities.

The first question related to the concept of the "Jewish People," and asked whether it could still indicate a collective whose definition was primarily religious, or whether it should now be seen as a community in the social, cultural, and even ethical sense. In other words, did the term still refer to an actual collective with the features of a community, sector, or nation, whose existence in the modern world needed no justification beyond the mere fact of its being a collective entity?

The second question related to the concept of the God and Torah of Israel, signifying the singularity of the collective in the traditional identity. How could the singularity of the Jewish nation be indicated in the new secular reality? In reaction to the previous attitude of religious belief, with its emphasis on the unquestioned truth of the past, growing numbers began to wonder whether Judaism might not better be seen as a culture, a collection of symbols, a history, or a shared fate.

The third question concerned the concept of the "Land of Israel," the fundamental response of traditional Judaism to the place of the collective. Accordingly, any place other than the Land of Israel is defined as Galut, that is, exile. In the traditional view, the Land of Israel is not merely a historical religious symbol, but an actual geographical location, a specific place to which the Jews will return "at the time of redemption." It was now asked whether this was in fact the homeland of the Jews, or whether it could be treated as a metaphor with moral, cultural, or ideological meaning.

Answers to these three questions can be found in each of the major streams of the new Judaisms. In effect, they systematically distinguish themselves from one another by their responses to them.

Orthodoxy as Conservative Change

The most dramatic change undergone by the proponents of traditional Judaism in the modern era was their conversion into one of many camps in Jewish society, and ultimately one of the smallest. In their own mind, this situation entailed not only a decline and loss of influence, but also, and primarily, a grave theological problem.

For traditional Judaism, the very existence of the Jewish People is grounded solely on its connection with the God and world of the

Table 1.1: Principles Shared by All Members of Halakhic Judaism*

1. Belief in one God and rejection of idol worship, implying Divine presence in this world.

2. Grounding of relations between the Jewish people and God on their actions.

3. Centrality of the Torah and observance of its commandments by all Jews.

4. Rejection of all alien rituals without denying the possibility of acknowledging legitimate miracles.

5. Recognition of the existence of "mysteries," the power of the letter (the name of God), and the existence of angels.

6. The principle of God as the Creator.

7. Man as the sole purpose of the Creation, subject to Divine Providence.

8. The concept of "Torah" as including both the written and the oral law.

9. Prophecy as a warning that the nation is not righteous.

10. The principle of the Jews as the Chosen People, signifying that they await redemption and return to the Holy Land.

* Following Urbach (1971) .

Bible. Without religion and Talmudic law—halakha—Israel is no different from any other nation, and thus denies its own unique right to exist. Although the particular diagnosis and prognosis for Jewish reality may be subject to different interpretations by the various schools of Hassidim and Mitnaggedim, they all subscribe to the same religious law, that is, to the idea that Judaism and religion are one and the same thing (Urbach, 1971). This approach is demonstrated by the ten principles shared by all observant Jews, according to Urbach (Table 1.1). Six of them stress faith (1, 4, 5, 6, 7, 8), three highlight unquestioned commitment to the collective (2, 3, 9), and one refers to the link with the territorial symbols and gives meaning to the concept of redemption (10).

The response of traditional Judaism to modernism took the form of intense intellectual debate. The different schools came together in what is known as Orthodox Judaism,[2] which devoted its efforts to finding a way to preserve a community faithful to traditional patterns

---

[2] Jonathan Sacks shows that the term "Orthodox Jew" was coined in the debates of Napoleon's "Sandhedrin" in 1807, when Abraham Furtado used it in reference to the traditional rabbis (Sacks, 1993).

of life and to the principles of halakha at the cost of minimal adaptation (Neusner, 1995). This form of Orthodoxy, which emerged in Germany in the first half of the 19th century, maintained its belief in the divine source of the commandments and the absolute ban on altering them in any way. Its leading thinker was Samson Raphael Hirsch (1808–1888), who believed that the Torah represented the truth even in modern times, and that the Jews continued to be a nation with a unique mission. Modernism itself, he claimed, came from God. In *Nineteen Letters on Judaism* (1836), he held that Jews should be encouraged to undertake secular learning and not devote themselves solely to religious studies, as there was no conflict between dedication to the commandments and acquiring a general education. That being said, anyone who did not follow the Orthodox ways was like a "captive infant" unable to discern "Jewish truth," swayed by "alien" influences, lacking in "true Jewish consciousness," and in need of "correction" (Hirsch, 1984).

Other members of Orthodox circles sought more proactive ways to bring secular Jews closer to traditional Judaism, advocating greater flexibility for the sake of "unity." These more moderate camps were opposed to the efforts to persuade "heretics" to renounce their Judaism. Haim Hirschensohn (1857–1935) propounded the theory that a Jewish state could serve as an excellent means of reinstating the former status of religious law while adapting it to modern life. For him, the connection between the Torah and the Jewish people was axiomatic, and he believed halakha could serve as the constitution of the Jewish state, so long as it displayed flexibility toward modern values, such as democracy and the participation of women in elections and government.

In 1912, Agudat Israel was founded in Katowice, Poland. Rather than being a typical political party, it represented the aspiration to reinvent the concept of the "Jewish People" to suit a modern reality that championed individualism (Mittleman, 1996). The founders of Agudat Israel included "modern-traditional" German Jews as well as Jews from Eastern Europe who were more traditional and less modern, among them Mitnaggedim from Lithuania and members of the Gur and Habad Hassidic movements. In essence, the new political framework was a reflection of the blow to traditional Judaism in the modern era, and sought to respond both to the secularization of social life that was increasingly pushing religious observance to the sidelines, and to the new ethos that gave fresh meaning to work, social achievements, and education. These developments placed enormous difficulties in the path of those who remained unwaveringly faithful to halakha and its underlying principles, and who wished to unite Orthodox Judaism under a single political roof, despite the serious rifts within it.

Interestingly enough, the way in which this form of Judaism chose to organize itself, employing the model of a political party with a comprehensive platform, was itself an indication of the influence of modernism. Agudat Israel wished to bring together all observant Jews. While denying any distinction between religion and politics, in the spirit of the Bible, it put this principle into practice by means of what was essentially a political organization, as was typical of secular public life at the time. The question of how much to "modernize" was, however, soon to cause bitter dissension between the Germans and the Eastern Europeans in the new party. The former tended to display a certain willingness to make concessions to modernism, while the latter regarded the party primarily as a tool for fending off the new influences. Seeking to contend with the demand of German society for "educated German Jews," Hirsch, Rosenheim, and others held that Judaism was, above all, a humane religion, and that Agudat Israel propounded the message of universal redemption. The Council of Great Torah Scholars (Mo'etzet Gedolei HaTorah), the party's supreme body, should therefore see itself as a spiritual-political leadership which would some day constitute the Sanhedrin of the Jewish people throughout the world. In contrast, most of the Eastern European members, who were more numerous from the very start, demanded that the party devote less time to intellectual ideological debate with modernism and more to the conflict with secular Jewry in order to contain its influence in the Jewish world. In time, it was this attitude that would prevail. (Bacon, 1996). The German "modernists" believed that Jews should become integrated into general society as observant Jews, whereas the more radical Orthodox—those who would within a few short years become known as the ultra-Orthodox and would come to dominate the party—considered themselves committed to the higher aims of Judaism: a life of religious study, loyalty to traditional symbols, and intense involvement in all aspects of the Jewish communities.

Despite these differences, what united the different Orthodox circles under a single roof was the spread of the "non-Orthodox" streams. These were now gaining the upper hand in many communities.

Non-Orthodox Judaism

Reform Judaism was the first to launch an increasingly fierce systematic attack on traditional Judaism (Neusner, 1995). It began with
a circle of intellectuals who aspired to Enlightenment (Haskala, in
Hebrew) for Jews, and was led by Moses Mendelssohn (1729–1786),
who in 1778 published a German translation of the Pentateuch with
his own rationalistic commentary (*Bi'ur*). According to Mendelssohn,
the Bible represented the law of the early Israelites, who lived under
specific circumstances. The publication of this thesis aroused a furor
in the Jewish traditionalistic public, but despite the heated opposition, the influence of the new attitude was soon to spread to larger
milieus.

Unlike Mendelssohn himself and some of his followers, another
group within the movement—including Naphtali Herz Wessely,
Naphtali Herz Homberg and David Friedlander—was to abandon
the traditional way of life. For them, Mendelssohn's commentary
opened the way to the German language and culture, as well as to
a rationalistic interpretation of the Scriptures (Neusner, 1995:69).
The four epistles of Naphtali Herz Wessely, *Words of Peace and Truth*
(1782), defined as their goal the recruiting of Jewish support for the
reforms of Kaiser Joseph II, who was carrying out a vast project of
cultural and educational modernization and secularization in the
Austrian-Hungarian empire. Wessely distinguished between two separate fields of knowledge. The first was the "teachings of man,"
which included general studies, such as the national language, history, geography and mathematics, along with conduct and ethics.
The second was the "teachings of God," concerned with the sub-
lime religious commandments that were beyond the understanding
of human beings. However important religious studies might be, only
a person knowledgeable in the "teachings of man" was worthy of
the title "human being," so that ultimately this field was preferable.
Now that circumstances had changed and the Jews were no longer
restricted to commerce, Wessely devised a program of studies designed
to prepare students for the conditions of modern life as befit their
talents. This educational approach was well suited to express the
desire to make Jewish society "productive," a call that would be
taken up again by Socialist Zionism over one hundred years later.

Generally speaking, the leaders of the Enlightenment movement
attached huge importance to education and culture. Hence, as early

as 1778, they founded the Hinukh Ne-urim (Education of Youth) School, where students were taught arithmetic, history, geography, French, German, some Bible studies and Hebrew, but no Talmud. Their intention was to present Judaism as a culture with a unique history and values, on a par with other world cultures. It is with this aim in mind that Mendelssohn and his disciples sought to add a literary dimension to Hebrew. In further steps in the same direction, in 1783 in Berlin, they established the Society to Promote the Hebrew Language, and in 1784 the Hebrew journal *Ma'assef* (Collector) (Feiner, 1995), thus taking a revolutionary stride toward the rebirth of the language as a medium for literary secular interests. The same attitude pervaded the movement's network of schools. Teaching in the spirit of Hinukh Ne'urim, this network grew and spread as far as Galicia by the end of the 18th century.

At the same time, there was also an acute desire to introduce changes into religious life. In the house of worship, now known as a "temple", which opened its doors in Hamburg in 1818, all references to the return to Zion were removed from the prayers (Sacks, 1993). The choice of the term "temple" reflected the attitude that the congregation no longer yearned to rebuild the Temple in Jerusalem; Hamburg would do just as well. By the same token, the word "Galut" was understood metaphorically, taking on a positive meaning indicating the moral mission of the Jews wherever they made their home. Within a short time, the movement revoked the laws of kashrut and the Sabbath, and instituted new principles in respect to matters of personal status. Their basic tenet was that the Jews were not a People; Judaism was only a religion of communities. They argued that only their "modernized" formulations could prevent the youth, alienated by traditional Judaism, from renouncing it altogether. Abraham Geiger (1810-1874), one of the foremost spokesman of the Reform Movement, stated that Judaism should display an unfailing willingness to adapt its rules of both ritual and basic concepts to modern realities (Neusner, 1995).

These ideas served as the foundations for the structuring of Reform Judaism in the U.S., where it was given a systematic and established definition at the first conference of rabbis of its kind, held in Pittsburgh in 1885. The participants declared themselves the Central Conference of American Rabbis, and subscribed to a program that recognized the Torah solely as a means of education, reflecting the aspirations of the People of Israel in the Land of Israel in the Biblical period.

This was to be known as the Pittsburgh Platform which, inter alia, claimed that the Torah had primarily been the source of ethical precepts, while in the modern age it should be seen as the cradle of universal culture. Thus the Jews of today were not a nation, but a cultural-religious community with a universal message.

New schools of Reform Judaism continued to hammer out the principles of the movement in the U.S. and elsewhere. Jacob Rader Marcus suggested a cyclical formula whereby each new variety of Judaism was destined to become a tradition that would in turn by questioned by succeeding generations (Neusner, 1995). Indeed, Abraham Cronbach (1995) demonstrates that Reform Judaism in the 20th century is typified by activism in American society and the positions it adopts on social, secular, and political issues, which it believes derive directly from Jewish values.

Over the years, the Reform Movement has shown signs of going in two opposite directions at once. On the one hand, it has no qualms about instituting changes even when they clearly conflict with halakha, and on the other hand it evidences a trend to return to tradition and renew the practice of certain aspects of religious ritual. This duality reflects the attempt to gain legitimacy for its "daring" in return for evidence of fundamental loyalty. It was, in fact, this dilemma that led to the establishment of the Conservative Movement, a new stream of Judaism that occupied the space between traditional-Orthodox Judaism and the Reform Movement.

As a distant echo of Zecharya Frankel in the mid-19th century, Conservatism is a haven for those who are put off by the extremism of the Reform Movement, who wish to maintain a certain degree of uniformity and unity among the Jews, and who look favorably, in principle, on halakha, yet are unwilling to forego the right to change it when it appears "irrelevant." The Conservative Movement was established in New York in 1886 by graduates of the Jewish Theological Seminary who were profoundly influenced by Franz Rosenzweig (1886–1929), and especially his notions of the obligations incumbent on all Jews at this point in time. Adopting a stance between the Orthodox and Reform streams, Rosenzweig advocated an approach that bridged the gap between modernism and loyalty to tradition. As he saw it, even in the modern era, there could be no Judaism without the commandments. Modern life was a new challenge the Jews had to contend with, while observing the commandments to the extent that they were still relevant (Rosenzweig,

1921). Although this approach honors religious law, it is basically subjective, focusing on the "self" and regarding the commandments not as formal-collective dictates, but as a matter of life experience and demands from oneself.

Another theologian with a profound influence on the Conservative Movement was Emil Fackenheim (b. 1916), who in grappling with the question of commitment to Judaism in the modern era maintained that it was of utmost importance to preserve halakha as a collective fact. Thus adopting an "objectivist" approach, in contrast to Rosenzweig, he also stressed the principle of peoplehood as a condition for ensuring that Jewish identity would endure. The combination of observance of the commandments and a collective consciousness, he held, could secure continued Jewish existence in a world in which Jews no longer had absolute faith. Fackenheim's link between religion and nationalism stemmed from his view that only the "practice" of religion could make a Jew part of the Jewish People. Nonetheless, he agreed with Rosenzweig that not all the Biblical requirements were still relevant to all Jews. Aware of the fact that different people observed Jewish law in different ways at different times in their life, he claimed there was no single "true" pattern of Jewish life (Fackenheim, 1987). Spurred by these ideas, the rabbis of the Jewish Theological Seminary formulated an approach that encouraged critical examination of the Scriptures in order to clarify what was "truly" essential to the Jewish faith (Neusner, 1995). While they did not categorically question the majority of commandments, they were closer in spirit to the Reform Movement than to Orthodox Judaism. Louis Ginzburg, a typical spokesman of the Movement, attributed overriding importance to the continuity of the Jewish lifestyle, yet expounded freedom of choice and considerable selectivity in respect to the Oral Law.

Mordecai Kaplan, another member of the Jewish Theological Seminary, took this even farther, arriving at conclusions that served as the basis for the establishment of yet another stream of American Judaism, the Reconstructivists. This movement, influenced by the sociology of Durkheim and the cultural Zionism of Ahad Ha'am, considers Judaism a civilization, rather than a religion in the accepted sense of the term (Kaplan, 1981). According to Kaplan, belief in the supernatural is foreign to Judaism, which is in essence a culture and value system.

The Enlightenment in Eastern Europe

Between the beginnings of the Reform Movement in Central Europe and its later manifestations, alongside similar streams, in the U.S., other important schools were developing in Europe. The first of these was the extension of the Enlightenment (Haskala) Movement in 19th century Eastern Europe. Unlike the Jews in Central Europe, on the whole those in the Eastern part of the continent had never questioned the articles of religious faith and traditional beliefs. Like their Central European coreligionists, however, they too subscribed to philosophical rationalism. Mordecai Aaron Guenzburg (1795–1846), one of the founders of the Enlightenment, refrained from voicing opposition to halakha, coming out only against the "practices," which he claimed were an "unbinding" addition to it. While Guenzburg and his colleagues did not dispute the value of the Talmud and traditional religious studies, they wished to combine them with general education. Nor did later followers of the Enlightenment, such as Moses Leib Lilienblum (*Orkhot Ha-Talmud*, 1868) and Joachim Tarnopol (*An Attempt at a Cautious Contemporary Reform in Judaism*, 1868), instigate a movement for reform. Nonetheless, voicing the opinions of all members of the Enlightenment, Rabbi Yitzhak Baer Levinsohn introduced innovative ideas, such as the obligation to learn the national language, the need for efforts to increase the productivity of Jewish people, and the institution of changes in Jewish education. Consequently, similar to developments in Central Europe, the Enlightenment founded "new" schools and "reformed" elementary schools that taught in Russian, and designed programs for agricultural settlement. In 1841, two schools of "educational reform" were established in Vilna, and in 1845 a school with classes for girls opened its doors in Lvov.

In the wake of the projects initiated by Mendelssohn and his followers in the second half of the 18th century, the members of the Enlightenment—in Eastern as well as Central Europe—also sought to reinstate Hebrew as a language of literature and culture (Feiner, 1995). They raised this innovative approach to Hebrew to the status of an ideology. Jacob Emden, for example, defined it as the natural language of the Jews, and Jonathan Eybeschütz waged a battle against anyone who did not sustain "the Hebrews' language," that is, who did not speak or write it correctly. Writers like Joseph Perl, Yitzhak Arter, Yitzhak Baer Levinsohn (Rival), M.A. Guenzburg,

Abraham Mapu, Abraham Levinsohn (Adam Hacohen), M.L. Lilien-blum, and Judah Leib Gordon (Yalag) wrote at least some of their work in Hebrew. Joshua Heshel Shor and Yitzhak Arter founded the Hebrew paper *Hehalutz*, whose goals included fighting prejudice and waging war on stagnant tradition. The attitude of many fol-lowers of the Enlightenment movement to Hebrew was reinforced by a renewed appreciation of the Bible at the expense of the Talmud. Biblical Hebrew seemed to them the appropriate language for a "healthy" way of life (Arieli, 1997). No longer was Judaism viewed as a religion alone, but as a man-made creation, a cultural phe-nomenon and linguistic legacy no different in essence from the cre-ations of other nations (Graetz, 1986).

This school of thought was encouraged by the research efforts of the Science of Judaism. This new discipline began with the foun-ding of the Society for Culture and Science of the Jews by a group of young members of the Enlightenment who wished to institute "internal reforms" in order to promote the Jews' adjustment to life in the countries in which they lived. The group thus sought to pro-vide cultural foundations that would combine "historical Judaism" with modern science. Although the society was short-lived—it dis-banded when several of its members converted to Christianity—it paved the way for other movements. Within just a few years, the historian Graetz denounced all those schools of thought that viewed Judaism as solely a religion, and stated that the object of study for a Jewish historian was the Jewish People. Nevertheless, none of these trends ever developed into a movement calling for religious changes. Some reformulated the idea of the Chosen People on the basis of an observation of Jewish history, while others held that preserving Jewish tradition would guarantee the continued existence of Judaism. The latter view gained impetus in the 1860s and '70s, when many were disappointed by the Emancipation that had finally reached Eastern Europe. Fundamentally, then, the Enlightenment accepted the principle of commitment to the Jewish People out of recogni-tion of its cultural secular singularity (including the Hebrew lan-guage), but had difficulty defining that singularity without reference to traditional Judaism. In terms of the place of the Jews in relation to "others," they believed they could be a part of the nations among which they lived while maintaining their distinctiveness.

Toward the end of the 19th century, many began to argue that the slogan "Be a human being outside your home and a Jew inside it" was not ushering in any new Jewish reality. Instead, Jews were increasingly converting to Christianity. A new force emerged and soon gained considerable support, particularly from a long line of writers; this group chose the avenue of Jewish nationalism. One of its most outstanding spokesmen was David Gordon (1831–1886), who founded and edited the journal *Hamaggid*. Gordon lashed out at the "naïve" attitude of many Jews to the Emancipation, attacking both the Orthodox groups who opposed anything modern, and the Reform Movement which denied Jewish peoplehood in the name of the Emancipation. In a series of articles, Gordon stated his belief in the national rebirth efforts, considering the Jewish People a nation and Judaism a national culture centered around messianic anticipation of "return" to the Land of Israel. The national aspirations of the Jews, he claimed, did not conflict with the spirit of the time. On the contrary, messianic hope belonged to "the realm of nationalism," and was thus well in line with the nationalism overtaking all of Europe.

During this same period, Peretz Smolenskin (1842–1885) was waging a battle in *Hashakhar*, the journal he founded in Vienna in 1868, against conservative circles on the one hand, and radical members of the Enlightenment on the other. Smolenskin advocated the position that the Jews were first and foremost a nation whose hallmarks were the Hebrew language, messianic hopes, and the spiritual values it had produced over generations. Anyone who denied the national essence of Judaism and the definition of the Jews as a nation was therefore denying Judaism itself. This school of thought was a haven for those members of the Enlightenment who could no longer identify with religious Judaism, but were loath to forego their ethnic-national affiliation with it.

These attitudes, all of which shift the weight of the definition of Judaism from religion to peoplehood, were given voice in the national philosophy of Ahad Ha'am (the pen name of Asher Ginsberg). His writings stressed the cultural rebirth of the Jewish nation and the need to establish a "cultural center" for Judaism in the Land of Israel.

Zionism and the Bund

Two movements founded in the late 19th century, Zionism and the Bund, went even further in distancing themselves from traditional

Judaism. Both were shaped by people familiar with the crisis in Judaism in Eastern Europe at the dawn of the 20th century, but they opted for very different solutions. The national solution of Zionism gained support by suggesting a secular program drawn from the very core of traditional Judaism itself. It defined Jewish life outside the Land of Israel, that is "exile", as "abnormal." Unlike traditional Judaism, which placed its hopes for redemption on observance of the commandments, secular Zionism feared for the future of the Jews in modern Europe, where belligerent national and nationalistic movements were gaining sway. In point of fact, Zionism itself was influenced by the nationalist ideology that based nationhood and statehood on the principle of territory. It thus called for a "territorialization" of Judaism, whereby the ethno-religious identity would be converted into a national identity by mass immigration to the same piece of land that was to be the site of redemption according to traditional Judaism—"the land from which we came" in the collective memory (Katz, 1960; Avineri, 1981). Buber (1973) notes that the word "Zion" is an indication that Jewish nationalism holds the geographical element to be more significant than the collective, a sign of its prime emphasis on highlighting the connection with a specific place that serves as a central symbol throughout Judaism. This explains the eagerness with which it was embraced, as it suggested a revolution that would transform the religious tradition without repudiating it, and would give new meaning to universally familiar symbols.

The rebirth, among the early Zionist immigrants to Palestine, of Hebrew as the language of everyday life is the best example of this approach. Plucking it from the sacred texts and "tossing it out onto the street" to be used for the most prosaic of activities might be considered iconoclastic. It is particularly surprising in view of the fact that those who reinvented Hebrew as a spoken language already had a common tongue—Yiddish. This is the only case in history in which a new language, not native to any of its speakers, successfully became the language of a group which already shared a common tongue. The only possible explanation is that Hebrew was engraved on the collective memory as a symbol of Judaism, even among those with no knowledge of it, so that adopting it as a general-purpose language fulfilled two basic principles of Zionism: the continuity it wished to display in respect to the legacy of the forefathers; and the secular/nationalist transformation it sought to implement in order to

distinguish it from any other form of Jewishness. The power to set
this transformation in motion, moreover, derived from the fact that
the first waves of Zionist immigrants to Palestine constituted a militant cadre imbued with the nationalist cause.

The example of Hebrew shows how far Zionism aspired to be
perceived as a movement that was breathing new life into Jewish
symbols and endowing them with contemporary significance. This
was one of the prime sources of Zionism's power: it broke the mono-
poly of Orthodox Judaism over the symbols of Jewish tradition. The
devotion to these symbols would also be the foundation on which
universal Jewish solidarity with the State of Israel would later be
built.

From another perspective, however, Zionism was at a disadvantage in respect to traditional Judaism. The caste model linked the
redemption of the Jews to that of the whole world, while Zionism
aspired to Jewish redemption alone. Although it came in many varieties, they were all guided by a common ideology: the "normalization of the Jewish people." Thus the Zionists could only hope to
give universal meaning to their philosophy by stressing its connection to some universally valid concept, as in "Socialist Zionism" or
"Liberal Zionism." In other words, they tended to present Zionism
as part of one of the movements offering a social utopia for the
world at large. By doing so, they denied the principle of caste, foregoing any aspirations that conflicted with the demands of secular society, with which Zionism also associated itself. The price they paid,
of course, was to expose Zionism to the criticism of the proponents
of the caste model, who saw it as a form of "collective assimilation"
to the non-Jewish world. The Zionist leaders, David Ben-Gurion,
Moshe Sharett, Berl Katznelson, Zalman Shazar and others, responded
to the critics by claiming that Zionism endeavored to build an
"enlightened society" in the Land of Israel, where the "Chosen
People" would be "a light unto the nations." In their opinion, that
was what the "normalization of the Jewish people" meant (Gorny,
1990). By taking up this challenge to combine a modern secular ideology with a uniquely Jewish inspiration and orientation, the Zionists
hoped to present an ideological alternative to the view of the Jewish
nation as the object of the promise of messianic redemption.

These complex and powerful aspects of Zionism did not make life
easy for the Bund, its major rival for the support of Eastern European
Jewry. Interestingly enough, the constitutional congresses of both

these movements were convened in the same year, 1897. Unlike
Zionism, the Bund aimed at a redefinition of Judaism that rejected
both the religious and the territorial principles. Instead, it suggested
a philosophy of Jewish Socialism that would ally itself with world
Socialism (Neusner, 1995, Peled, 1997).

With its power base mainly in Poland and Russia, the Bund offered
the ideology of a class struggle within the Jewish community, striving to unify the Jewish "proletariat" that would join the revolutionary socialist camp springing up throughout Europe and the rest
of the world. Nevertheless, alongside its Marxism, the Bund recognized the singularity of the Jews, an attitude reflected in its desire
to foster Jewish culture. Whereas Zionism linked the rebirth of the
Jewish nation with the renewal of the Hebrew language, the Bund
wished to preserve and promote the Yiddish culture of the millions
of Jews in Eastern Europe. To do so, it demanded that wherever
they resided, the Jews be granted cultural autonomy in the future
Socialist society. To further this aim, the Bund not only opposed
Zionism, but also vied with its "sister" movements, the Communists
and Socialists, who were unwilling to acknowledge the special nature
of the "Jewish question." This was a particularly difficult struggle,
as the revolutionary movements appealed to the heart and soul of
many young educated Jews who hoped to solve the "Jewish problem" by joining forces with those who proposed a new social order
in which primordial identities would be meaningless.[3] The battle the
Bund fought on two fronts demonstrates its desire to promote, at
one and the same time, a universal utopian society and a Jewish
culture with its own moral precepts (Neusner, 1995).

The conflicting forces that shaped the Bund and its philosophy
are aptly demonstrated by the figure of one of its most prominent
thinkers, Vladimir Medem (1879–1923), a man who was raised in
the Russian Orthodox church but returned to Judaism as a Jewish
Socialist. Speaking for the Bund at the Russian Social Democratic
Party convention in 1903, he introduced the idea of Jewish autonomy

---

[3] The number of Jews who joined the Socialist and Communist movements was
out of all proportion to their share in the population throughout Central and Eastern
Europe. This is reflected in the key posts they held in both branches of the Social
Democratic Party in Russia (more so in the Menshevik faction than the Bolshevik),
the Communist parties in Hungary, Romania and Czechoslovakia, and the Socialist
parties in Germany and Austria.

in Eastern Europe, thereby clashing head-on with the Leninists who labeled this notion a "bourgeois nationalist aberration." Medem insisted on the right of the Jewish proletariat to constitute an independent revolutionary force unwilling to renounce its culture, an attitude that was subsequently given new emphases. Chaim Zhitlowsky (1865–1943), who championed Medem's approach, had no qualms about speaking explicitly of a national Jewish identity. At a certain stage, he actually suggested that the Jewish Socialism of the Bund was a continuation of Jewish tradition and Biblical prophecy.

These attitudes had an impact even beyond the framework of the Bund. The historian Simon Dubnow, for example, drew his inspiration for a program of cultural autonomy from the ideas propounded by the Bund. Yet despite its strength at the turn of the 20th century, the Bund and its activists fell victim to the Russian revolution. The virtual disappearance of the movement from the face of Jewish life was further hastened by the mass Jewish immigration to the West, the tragedy of the Holocaust, and the establishment of the State of Israel.

The Space of Identities

To sum up, in the wake of the dramatic changes in traditional Jewish society from the late 18th century to the last decades of the 19th, attempts to define Jewish identity became a series of questions to which a wide variety of answers were offered. In fact, it could be said that in some ways, Jewish identity was now defined by the very debate over what the term entailed. The different perceptions of the collective identity might be distinguished by the way in which they formulated its deep structures: commitment to the collective—"the Jewish People"; the singularity of the collective—"the God and Torah of Israel"; and the image of the place of the collective in relation to others—"the Land of Israel."

Orthodox Jewry, the most loyal adherent to traditional Judaism, adopted modern models of political and social activity in order to ensure its survival and enhance its influence over Jewish life in the modern era. Now challenged by powerful rivals, it could no longer rely on control of community institutions. Moreover, where in the past it had accepted the marginal status of the Jews in society as a given, it was now forced to operate among Jews who were integrating into society as individuals and citizens, sometimes with considerable success. Orthodox Jewry's activities were designed to demonstrate the relevance of continuity with the past for the present and future. To do so, it relied on sacred principles: (1) "the Jewish People" demands solidarity as a requisite of the Jews' shared fate, and its value lies in accepting the destiny dictated by faith; (2) "the God and Torah of Israel," that is, unequivocal acceptance of the covenant of Abraham and the commandments, defines the singularity of the Jews; (3) "the Land of Israel" is the opposite of the Galut, denoting anyplace other than the Holy Land.

The Reform Movement was the first attempt to face off against halakha and suggested new solutions for the dilemmas of Jewish identity in the modern era, namely: (1) "the Jewish People" is a "congregation of believers" or community, with the distinctions between these two terms apt to be blurred; (2) "the God and Torah of Israel" has selective validity in respect to halakha; Judaism is generally depicted here as a body of universal cultural values; (3) "the Land of Israel" is a metaphor that does not imply anticipating a "return" to any actual place.

Conservative Judaism was the intermediate model between the two extremes, entertaining a more positive view of halakhic tradition than the Reform Movement and a less dogmatic approach to the laws themselves than the Orthodox, i.e.: (1) "the Jewish People" is a cultural community; (2) "the God and Torah of Israel" is seen through the prism of a selective attitude to halakha: unlike the Reformists, there is a desire to observe the commandments in principle, but similarly to them, a religious life is perceived in terms of cultural singularity rather than dogmatic demands; (3) "the Land of Israel," a concept to which they are highly conscious of being committed, wavers between a religious and a moral significance.

The Eastern-European Enlightenment movement spawned a variety of philosophies advocating a search for new approaches to Judaism. Despite their differences, they all shared several common features: (1) "the Jewish People" is a collective of real people with a cultural singularity; (2) "the God and Torah of Israel," while given pride of place, is treated primarily as a set of cultural values and language, although halakha is not actually repudiated; (3) "the Land of Israel" refers to a link to Jewish history and a desire to establish a center to represent Judaism to the world.

Zionism similarly offered its own interpretation of the three deep structures of Jewish identity: (1) "the Jewish People" is a worldwide collective that represents a potential national entity; (2) "the God and Torah of Israel" is the culture from which Zionism draws its symbols, giving them secular contents; (3) "the Land of Israel" is a concept on which Zionism seeks to build a "new" Jewish nation, that is, an actual territory.

Like the Enlightenment, the Bund stressed the nature of Judaism as culture, but was addressing a very specific sector of society – the working class. At the same time, it sought to link itself with national and international revolutionary movements by means of formulations of its own: (1) "the Jewish People" refers, first and foremost, to the Jewish proletariat fighting Jewish capitalists; (2) "the God and Torah of Israel" is perceived in terms of both the popular Yiddish culture of Eastern Europe and the social values anchored in the religious-historical legacy; (3) "the Land of Israel" denotes the aspiration for autonomous cultural camps within the countries of the Diaspora.

These different formulations fashion a very wide space of Jewish identity.

(1) "the Jewish People" is viewed by the Orthodox as solely a religious community; by the Reform and Conservative Movements as an ethnocultural, moral, and religious community; by the Enlightenment as a cultural group; by the Bund as an ethnic group; and by Zionism as a national collective.

(2) "the God and Torah of Israel" is interpreted literally by the Orthodox; is seen as a culture as well as a religion by the Conservatives, who pick and choose those laws which apply to its members; is given secular-cultural meaning by the Enlightenment; national meaning by Zionism; and ethnocultural meaning by the Bund; and is viewed as a set of symbols with primarily universal significance by the Reform Movement.

(3) "the Land of Israel" is perceived by Zionism as a challenge to immigrate to and settle the "historical homeland"; is associated by the Enlightenment with a cultural purpose; is linked by the Orthodox with divine redemption; means cultural autonomy in Eastern Europe in the view of the Bund; and is interpreted as a metaphor for mankind at large by the Reform Movement.

In terms of priorities, for the Orthodox "the God and Torah of Israel" was supreme, followed by "the Jewish People." For the Enlightenment as well, the most important aspect was the singularity of the collective, that is, "the God and Torah of Israel," but it was given cultural-secular meaning; in second place, again, was "the Jewish People." Zionism viewed "the Land of Israel," the national territory of the Jews, as the primary aspect, followed by "the Jewish nation renewing itself," i.e., "the Jewish People" under a new form. The Bund gave pride of place to "the Jewish People" in the sense of the Jewish proletariat, with cultural autonomy coming second. The Reform and Conservative Movements put "the Jewish People" first, but also stressed "the God and Torah of Israel" as they chose to understand this notion.

The distinctions between these formulations are reflected most prominently in their language preferences. The Orthodox, especially the ultra-Orthodox, sought to preserve Hebrew as a sacred tongue to be used only for study, prayer, and ritual (Ben-Rafael, 1994). They thus saw Yiddish, the language of the traditional Ashkenazi community, as most appropriate for everyday use, although wherever they settled they also learned the local language in order to communicate with non-Jewish society. Yiddish was also the language of choice for the Bund, reflecting its popular approach, with its loyalty to the language being expressed in the attempt to promote its evolution into a high-culture language. The Zionists, on the other hand, seeking to create a new culture with links to Jewish history, and influenced by the writers of the Enlightenment, found in modernized Hebrew the code they were looking for. Although the Enlightenment was the first movement to demonstrate the vitality of Jewish culture and Hebrew, this did not prevent many of its members from advocating the use of a non-Jewish language to promote Jewish culture. The Reform and Conservative Movements, who wished to stress that they were part of general society and that Jewish values are universal, chose to employ the languages of the countries of which they were citizens, even for ritual Jewish purposes.

To conclude, then, the common denominator shared by all of these definitions of Jewish identity is the debate over the fundamental questions that occupied the Jews from the moment they abandoned a traditional life (see Table 1.2). While this debate led to a multiplicity of divisions and approaches, three major orientations can be identified: emphasis on the collective, "the Jewish people," represented by the Bund and the non-Orthodox religious movements; emphasis on cultural singularity, "the God and Torah of Israel," represented by the Orthodox and, to a certain extent, the Enlightenment; emphasis on "the Land of Israel," represented by those members of

Table 1.2: Jewish Identities in the 19th Century

Formulations of Judaism	Commitment to the collective		Perceptions of the singularity of the collective		Place of the collective	
	People/ community	Religious imperatives	Religious calling	Cultural "uniqueness"	Geographic terms	Metaphoric terms
Traditional Judaism		x	X		x	
Orthodox Judaism		x	X		x	X
Reform Judaism	X		X	X		X
Enlighten-ment		x	X	X	x	X
Conservative Judaism	X	x	X	X	x	X
Bund	X			X		X
Zionism	X			x	X	

Key: x – positive attitude; X – special emphasis

the Enlightenment who championed a cultural center for the Jewish world, and the Zionists, the most prominent proponents of this aspect of Jewish identity.

One might wonder whether the space of Jewish identity that came into being with the dawn of the modern era was also relevant to the conceptions that prevailed in the Jewish world, in the middle of the 20th Century, after the Jewish condition was again radically transformed, and this time, even more drastically, by the creation of powerful Jewish communities in the New World, the horrors of the eradication of a large part of European Jewry, and the unprecedented establishment of a Jewish State in the Land of Israel. No one could answer this question better than the Jewish intellectuals to whom Ben-Gurion turned in the late '50s with the request to define who and what is a Jew.

CHAPTER TWO

BEN-GURION'S CORRESPONDENTS

A Phoenix Generation

Before the modern condition of Judaism had a chance to take root, the circumstances of Jewish existence again changed dramatically during the first half of the 20th Century: the large-scale immigration of Eastern European Jews turned the U.S. into a thriving and powerful new Jewish center; though, from the end of the 1930s to 1945, the Jewish people suffered the greatest catastrophe in its history in the form of the Holocaust in Europe; yet, the establishment of the State of Israel in 1948 represented a completely new reality which in the context of the foregoing seemed to many as Redemption. Every single Jew born between 1890 and 1910 either personally experienced or was witness to these events. In most cases, they had been born into a traditional Jewish community to become in adulthood citizens of a non-Jewish secular society. They were exposed to universalistic ideologies, and had the time to experience painful disillusionments when these ideologies failed. They witnessed the First World War, the Bolshevik Revolution, and the conflicts between the wars that pitted communists, social-democrats, fascists, and liberals against each other. Some moved to Palestine where they created new patterns of Jewish life, while others resettled in the West where they adopted ways of life that were no less different. Some were themselves victims of the Holocaust, or watched their whole world being destroyed. After the Second World War, came the outbreak of the Cold War, the triumph of Stalinism, and, at the opposite pole, the unprecedented prosperity in the West. Having survived the gravest of dangers and lost everything they held dear, many of the members of this generation and a half somehow found the strength of spirit to reinvent themselves both personally and collectively, many achieving extraordinary social, professional, and economic success. No label more aptly suits these people than the "Phoenix Generation."

The question one may ask here is: How and to what extent did these overwhelming historical events affect the Jewish identity of this generation? Did they create new ideas and perspectives, some sort of new perceptions of Jewishness? Or did they cause a retreat behind earlier "solid" formulations and a refusal to alter them? We can find the answers to these questions in the set of letters sent to Ben-Gurion, on his request, by Jewish thinkers from a variety of walks of life, both in Israel and the Diaspora, who represent major trends in Jewish thought. All of them belong to this exceptional generation. In 1958 they were asked by David Ben-Gurion, the Israeli Prime Minister and founder of the State, to elaborate on the Jewish identity. Their answers offer the best possible means to assess this generation's attitudes toward Jewishness.

In his letter, Ben-Gurion explained that the Government of Israel had appointed a committee comprising the Prime Minister and the Ministers of Justice and the Interior to frame regulations for the recording of the affiliation of the children of mixed marriages whose parents both wished to have them registered as Jewish. The Government, it was stated, had instructed the committee "to consult with Jewish sages in Israel and abroad," and to determine population registry regulations that would accord with the tradition accepted by all Jewish circles, the circumstances of the sovereign Jewish state in which freedom of religion was ensured, and the demands of a society that served as the home for Jews from all over the world. Ben-Gurion also noted that the Government had decided to indicate the national allegiance or religion of adult applicants as "Jewish" if they declared themselves in good faith to be so and were not members of any other religion.

On the face of it, Ben-Gurion was asking for opinions on a specific matter: should the child of a Jewish father and non-Jewish mother be registered as a Jew when the parents so wished, or should some sort of religious ceremony be required? In effect, however, the question actually raised the issue of the relations between Jewish religion and national allegiance after the establishment of a sovereign Jewish state, as well as the contemporary validity of halakha and traditional law for determining "Who is a Jew?". As Israel declared itself a Jewish state, the definition of Jewish identity now became an open legal issue with critical implications. It would determine the way in which a citizen's national allegiance was indicated on the official identity card, who was entitled to Israeli citizenship, who would receive the financial assistance offered new immigrants, and even application for a marriage license. The Law of Return, which grants

Israeli citizenship to any Jew wishing to settle in the country, similarly required a clear operative definition of Jewish identity. Such a definition would also carry considerable weight among Jews abroad, as it would serve to establish their relations with Israel, determining which of them was entitled to settle in Israel as a Jew and who exactly were those people to whom Israel was referring by declaring itself not only a Jewish state, but also the "State of the Jews."

Ben-Gurion wrote to forty-seven noted Jewish figures in Israel and abroad. He received forty-six replies from fifty-one people: one of the forty-seven was unable to respond and asked five colleagues to prepare a single answer in his stead, and two others penned a joint response. The people Ben-Gurion chose were distinguished theologians and men of letters: rabbis, jurists, philosophers, authors, and academics from various fields. They represented major streams in Jewish thinking, although Orthodox figures had a clear advantage. Table 2.1 presents Ben-Gurion's correspondents according to the two criteria he employed: did they come from Israel or the Diaspora, and what was their religious orientation.

These same two criteria will serve for our analysis of the letters. The distinction between Israel and the Diaspora presented no difficulty, and was determined according to place of residence. Those who had moved from Israel to the Diaspora, or vice versa, were categorized according to their residence in 1958. In respect to religious orientation, three categories were chosen: (1) ultra-Orthodox; (2) modern Orthodox and non-Orthodox observant; and (3) attached to symbols and free thinker. The term "ultra-Orthodox" refers to those correspondents who consider the major purpose of their lives to be religious studies and the observance of the commandments and halakha. "Modern Orthodox" relates to Jews who observe the commandments and halakha while leading a normal modern life, and who see themselves as part of modern society. "Non-Orthodox observant" refers to those who define themselves as religious but do not view halakha as binding, that is, the members of denominations other than Orthodox. The term "attached to symbols" is used to indicate secular individuals who feel a link to certain traditional values, and "free thinkers" for those who do not consider themselves religious in any way. Admittedly, these definitions are not entirely free of ambiguities and it is difficult to draw precise borderlines between them. It is conceivable, for instance, that people who devote their lives to religious studies are also involved in modern life, or that those who see themselves as thoroughly non-religious observe certain commandments and would shrink from the label "free thinker." Consequently, the categories should be viewed with caution, and the conclusions that rely upon them should be seen to reflect general trends rather than unequivocal facts.

Tables 2.1 and 2.2 show that the number of ultra-Orthodox correspondents was equal to that of the attached to symbols and free thinker (15 in each category), with a large group of modern Orthodox and non-Orthodox observant (21) between them. These figures indicate that Ben-Gurion wished firstly to learn of the religious approach to the problem, although he also asked for the opinions of individuals outside the Orthodox camp. What is of interest to us here, however, is whether the responses reflect central formulations of Jewish identity, or diverge in different or even opposing directions. As we shall see below, the responses of these Jewish intellectuals can be directly and systematically related to the sociological parameters that Ben-Gurion employed in choosing his correspondents: place of residence and religious orientation.

Table 2.1: Correspondents by Religious Orientation and Place of Residence

ISRAEL		DIASPORA	
(1) Ultra-Orthodox			
Shalom Yihye Yitzhak Halevi	Tel Aviv	A.L. Grossnass, M. Lew, A. Rappoport, A. Steinberg, M. Swift	London
Shlomo J. Zevin	Jerusalem	Chaim Heller, Joseph Dov Soloveitchik	New York-Boston
Joseph Sh. Kahaneman	Bnei Brak	Yekhiel Weinberg	Montreux
Yehuda Leib Hakohen Maimon	Jerusalem	Menachem Mendel Schneerson	New York
Yecheskiel Sarne	Jerusalem	Aaron Kotler	New York
(2) Modern Orthodox & Non-Orthodox Observant			
Ephraim Urbach	Jerusalem	Alexander Altmann	Boston
Shlomo Goren	Tel Aviv	Abraham Yehoshua Heschel	New York
Zekharya Hacohen	Nahalal	Tsevi Wolfson	Boston
Yitskhak (Isaac) Halevi Herzog	Jerusalem	Elio Raffaele Toaff	Rome

Table 2.1 (*cont.*)

ISRAEL		DIASPORA	
Moshe Silberg	Jerusalem	Alfredo Shabtai Toaff	Livorno
Shmuel Yossef Agnon	Jerusalem	Saul Lieberman	New York
Akiva Ernst Simon	Jerusalem	André Neher	Strasbourg
Yossef Kappah	Jerusalem	Salomon Rodrigues Pereira	Amsterdam
		Henry Baruk	Paris
		Louis Eliezer Halevi Finkelstein	New York
		Solomon B. Freehof	Pittsburgh
		Jacob Kaplan	Paris
		Mordecai Menachem Kaplan	New York

(3) Attached to symbols & free thinkers

Samuel Hugo Bergmann	Jerusalem	Isaiah Berlin	Oxford
Yehuda Bourla	Haifa	Dante Lattes	Rome
Hayim Hazaz	Jerusalem	Moshe Maisels	New York
Haim Hermann Cohn	Jerusalem	Leon (Arye) Simon	London
Yekhezkel Kaufmann	Jerusalem	Chaim Perelman	Brussels
Joseph Schechter	Haifa	Felix Frankfurter	Washington
Sh. Shalom	Haifa	Aaron Zeitlin	New York
		Simon H. Rifkind	New York

Table 2.2: Distribution of Correspondents

	Israel	Diaspora	Total
Ultra-Orthodox	5	10	15
Modern Orthodox & non-Orthodox observant	8	13	21
Attached to symbols & free thinkers	7	8	15
Total	20	31	51

In respect to religious orientation, it is abundantly clear from the letters that in the view of the ultra-Orthodox and some of the modern Orthodox, those who wish to be considered Jewish are asked to become part of a "Chosen People." Conversion thus means that a non-Jew must undergo a total personal transformation, which can only be effected through a strict and rigid ritual. A considerable number of the modern Orthodox, however, take a more moderate stance and display greater openness to the special problems encountered by a secular Jewish state when contending with the question "Who is a Jew?" Some of them are very conscious of the fact that original and creative solutions are required, while others are willing to accept new definitions of the relations between state and religion in Israel. Others are even open to the creation of an intermediate category between Jew and non-Jew, such as "Jewish-oriented" or "resident Jew." The non-Orthodox correspondents go further in suggesting innovations. They tend to regard conversion as entrance into a nation and culture more than into a religion *per se*. As they see it, Judaism is not an immutable code of laws, but rather a dynamic pluralistic culture. In this sense, they are similar to the free thinkers, who tend even more strongly to distinguish between two separate phenomena: Judaism as a religion and the Jews as a People. None of them, however, goes so far as to totally ignore the religious element or to suggest that the distinction makes it possible to accept a member of another religion into the Jewish People.

On the other hand, the criterion of place of residence reveals a greater diversity of opinion among the correspondents in the Diaspora than among those in Israel. The Israelis largely take it as given that Israel represents a different sort of Jewish experience than the Diaspora, and that it is the leader of the Jewish world. Interestingly enough, the Israelis also exhibit less flexibility than many of the Diaspora correspondents in respect to the issue at hand, and tend to accept the dictates of halakha, if only for "practical" reasons.

Three Syndromes

When we combine the two criteria—religious orientation and place of residence—we find three groups of attitudes that can be perceived as three syndromes that are distinct from each other in the way they relate to and interpret the basic elements of Jewish identity. We have termed these the caste, ethno-cultural and national syndromes.

The Caste Syndrome

The first syndrome, which represents a rigid and inflexible attitude, emerges primarily from the letters of the ultra-Orthodox both in Israel and the Diaspora, as well as from those of some of the modern Orthodox in the Diaspora. The most conspicuous expression of this syndrome can be found in the letter from the five dayanim (judges) of the Rabbinical Court of London, Aryeh Leib Grossnass, Meir Lew, Abraham Rappoport, Meir Halevy Steinberg, and Morris Swift. They express their disappointment that Ben-Gurion did not choose to rely on the chief rabbis of Israel, who, according to the writers, are the proper authorities for all matters of halakha in the State of Israel and can provide a reasoned, and indeed the only possible, halakhic response. Moreover, they reproach the prime minister for requesting the opinions of people who are in no way associated with halakha and Torah, that is, representatives of non-Orthodox branches of Judaism and free thinkers. The Londonian dayanim go on to express their appreciation for Ben-Gurion's efforts to unite the Jewish people the world over. However, they state unequivocally that it is totally unacceptable for non-Jewish children to become Jews in Israel simply on the basis of their parents' declaration, irrespective of the traditional criteria. In their opinion, disregarding these criteria would inevitably result in disparities and schisms among the Jews, as well as mass assimilation.

Aaron Kotler offers the precise halakhic definition that states that only a child born to a Jewish mother or who has undergone conversion according to religious law can be considered a Jew. In his view, the power of halakha lies in the impossibility of distinguishing between Jewish religion and nation. Any modification of this principle would jeopardize the unity of the nation and its very existence. From this perspective, there is no alternative whatsoever to tradition. Nothing could possibly fill the void left by the Torah if, "heaven forbid," it should disappear from Jewish life. The Jews are unique for the internal justification of their existence, without reference to any external factor. Attempts to alter this quality of the nation would negate its essential nature and threaten its survival.

Menachem Mendel Schneerson, in an extremely formal letter (the first of the two he sent), similarly relates to the issue in terms of tradition, ascribing no value to parental declarations in determining whether or not their children are Jewish. Schneerson unreservedly condemns any desire to invent a new definition of a Jew. In his second, and less formal, letter he addresses Ben-Gurion as a leader whose role requires him to make decisions of the utmost significance for the Jewish people at this moment in time. As such, Schneerson claims, Ben-Gurion must understand that it is unthinkable for the status of the Jewish religion, the core of Jewish life in the Diaspora, to decline at the very time that the Jews are returning to their homeland and establishing a state of their own in which Judaism would acquire its full authority. He stresses that such a circumstance would gravely endanger the continued existence of the nation, as the younger generation might collectively assimilate into the non-Jewish world, turning its back on all Jewish values.

On this point, Joseph Dov Soloveitchik and Chaim Heller, representing the Mitnaggedim, concur with their rival Schneerson, the leader of the Habad Hassids. In their letter they declare that halakha can be the only source for determining "Who is a Jew?", and that there is only one unalterable answer to the question. Consequently, there is no need for interpretation or clarification. Every rabbinical court will always hand down the same ruling regardless of circumstances. Any deviation from it would be disastrous for Judaism. The State of Israel must thus beware of destroying the nation it is claiming to save. In the opinion of Elio Raffaele Toaff as well, there can be no other answer to Ben-Gurion's question than that supplied by halakha. No parental declaration could turn a gentile into a Jew. Alfredo Shabtai Toaff agrees with his son, deploring the very act of posing the question. As it is a religious issue at heart, it can be answered only by halakha. The State of Israel, the center and leader of the Jewish world, could not be allowed to shatter the armor of tradition. Should it do so, it would bring about the assimilation of the Jews throughout the world. As long as Israel aspired to be a Jewish state, it must uphold this principle.

Yekhiel Weinberg is similarly dismayed by the question itself, which, he believes could only have been engendered by misapprehensions. It is perfectly clear to him that the only form of Judaism is that which is faithful to the Torah and commandments, and so there can only be one answer to Ben-Gurion's query. Any type of "liberal Judaism" is no more than a lame distortion. Morality without religion is an illusion, he insists, citing Rabbi Sa'adia Ga'on's assertion that the Jewish nation is only a nation in its faith. Even the most patriotic of Israeli citizens who has lived in the country for years, paid his taxes diligently, and risked his life as a soldier in all its wars, would exclude himself from the Jewish people by converting to another religion. Weinberg notes that Ben-Gurion himself states that the issue of the children of mixed marriages relates only to those who have not been admitted to a different faith, indicating that the prime minister also is aware of the connection between nation and religion in Judaism. Therefore, a non-Jew could only become a Jew through conversion. Not surprisingly, he says, the institution of conversion is as old as Judaism itself—indeed, it began with Abraham—and its meaning has never changed with historical circumstances. For Judaism, conversion does not simply mean becoming a member of another religion, but becoming a party to the covenant between God and the Jewish people. There is no place here for any considerations other than the religious-halakhic. Weinberg concludes that the State of Israel has only two options in respect to the registration of the children of mixed marriages as Jews: it can either require traditional conversion, or it can ignore this requirement and thereby cut itself off from Judaism and split the nation in half.

The opinions of the Israeli ultra-Orthodox are no less rigid. Yitzhak Halevi demands that the prime minister accepts the rabbinical ruling as it follows the dictates of the Torah. The Jewish faith existed prior to the Jewish people; Abraham established the nation after establishing the religion. Thus religion is the primordial principle. It will forever remain the exclusive property of the Jewish people, who survived exile by keeping the faith. After the return from exile in Babylon, Halevi reminds Ben-Gurion, the Prophet Ezra assembled the men and ordered them to send away their non-Jewish wives. These women, who had raised and educated non-Jewish children, were the gravest of dangers to the nation as they could be the cause of its impurity and the loss of its sacred status. Only wives who were willing to convert and become part of the nation, following the example of Ruth who said "Thy people shall be my people and thy God my God," were accepted with open arms.

Joseph Kahaneman reminds Ben-Gurion of the most crucial task with which the Jewish people are charged—redemption—, which obligates the nation to place strict demands on itself. Yehuda Leib Maimon adds that Ben-Gurion is displaying a degree of disrespect by writing to so many different people rather than relying on the ruling of Israel's chief rabbis. Yekhezkel Sarne states bluntly that no consideration in the world can alter one single letter of the Torah and the commandments, and so it shall be until the end of time. Shlomo Zevin

totally rejects the idea that any government whatsoever is entitled
to make decisions in matters of national and religious identity.

A number of the modern Orthodox correspondents outside Israel
adopt the same line as the ultra-Orthodox, arguing in defense of
tradition. In the opinion of Jacob Kaplan, the government should
do everything in its power to prevent mixed marriages in the first
place, and should meticulously comply with halakha when registering its citizens. Salomon Pereira agrees, and is similarly puzzled as
to the need for Ben-Gurion's polling of opinions, particularly as he
has also written to people who have no connection whatsoever with
the study of the Torah. To Saul Lieberman it is obvious that when
a gentile embraces the Jewish people, they should return this love.
But such emotions do not make a person Jewish. If a non-Jewish
mother wishes her child to be Jewish, she should convert and pass
her Judaism onto the child.

Alexander Altmann understands from Ben-Gurion's letter that the
parents involved do not regard themselves as observant Jews, but
rather as members of the Jewish nation. Otherwise, they would
undoubtedly wish their children to convert. Precisely because of this
fact, he feels the need to stress that in Judaism the religious and
national elements are intertwined. The religious aspect is invariably
the foundation of national Jewish identity, and it is the combination
of the two that underlies the concept of the Chosen People. Consequently, there is no choice but to demand conversion from anyone wishing to join the Jewish people. The only thing "that can be
done" is to make conversion as easy as possible and adapt it to the
spirit of the times.

The Conservative rabbi Louis Finkelstein takes the same stance
for reasons of his own. He maintains that any change in traditions
as ancient as this one will inevitably precipitate heated controversy.
Throughout history, these traditions have signified the singularity of
the nation, so that modifying them would detract it from its unique
qualities. He also claims that the most important function of a mother
in bringing up her children is to explain why their Jewish identity
would create particular problems in a marriage where the mother
is not Jewish. Given these circumstances, it is totally unacceptable
for the parents' wishes to be the sole determinant of a child's Judaism.

The correspondents representing this syndrome categorically demand
conversion in the name of tradition. Their views plainly imply that
the survival of the Jewish people as an end in and of itself is of less

significance than the realization of its divine purpose. This formulation of Jewish identity therefore gives precedence to the principle of
"the God and Torah of Israel," with "the Jewish people" in second
place and dependent upon it. The third element of Jewish identity,
"the Land of Israel," is not mentioned per se, but appears only in
reference to the State of Israel as the target of halakhic requirements. Its positive or negative contribution to Judaism is, indeed,
contingent on its acceptance or rejection of these requirements. Hence,
a prominent feature of this perspective is that it isolates itself from
anything that is not part of the internal Jewish world. It demands
that a convert totally renounces his or her former mental and social
identity when taking on the new one. As we have seen, this is very
much in line with the concept of caste, and more precisely, a superior caste. Those of Ben-Gurion's correspondents who expressed this
attitude were thus carrying on the Orthodox Judaism of the previous century which had made it abundantly clear that it wished to
remain faithful to traditional pre-modern Judaism.

The Ethno-cultural Syndrome

Among the Orthodox Diaspora respondents, some adopted a more
flexible stance. To varying degrees, these people were closer in
approach to the syndrome displayed by many of the non-Orthodox
and non-observant, most of whom lived outside Israel. We have
labeled this the "ethno-cultural" syndrome because it highlights "the
Jewish people" dimension of Jewish identity and portrays it as a
group whose culture bears both unique symbols and universal values.

   André Neher, representing a moderate Orthodox approach, emphasizes the danger of widening the gap between Israel and the Diaspora
and between Israel and Judaism. In his opinion, it cannot be denied
that Jewish identity is, above all, a religious issue, and that a person cannot become a Jew except through the conditions defined by
traditional Judaism. At the same time, however, he is aware of the
fact that people who are already Jews can become non-religious without jeopardizing their Jewish status. While he believes that the government of Israel should have no part in determining "Who is a
Jew?", he knows too that it is impossible to separate religious from
national affiliation. Realizing that these principles create complex
problems for a modern country like Israel, he suggests convening a
worldwide conference to discuss the new issues involved in relations

between state and religion so as to preserve the enduring unity of the nation.

In the view of Abraham Heschel, only by maintaining strong links between the Jewish people and its faith can the Jews overcome the dangers of assimilation and ensure their survival as a nation. The risk of impurity is everywhere, including in Israel, despite the sacred character of the state-building effort. Nonetheless, it is also obvious to Heschel that with the establishment of the State of Israel, the relations between state and religion need to be clarified. He is open to new ideas for contending with the new problems and bolstering the cultural foundations shared by all Jews. He also supports the definition of an intermediate status of "Hebrews" for those who identify with the Jewish people yet are unwilling to accept the Jewish faith.

A similar stance is taken by Tsevi Wolfson. On the one hand, it is clear to him that Jewish identity does not exist independently of religious identity: secular Jews remain Jews only by virtue of their observant brethren who are responsible for preserving the raison d'être of Judaism. On the other hand, however, he too suggests instituting a special category such as "Hebrews" for people who do not wish to be Jewish in the religious sense.

The proponents of the ethno-cultural syndrome repeatedly resort to the use of halakhic terms. In this sense, they display a similarity to the advocates of the caste syndrome. At the same time, however, they are open to the possibility of giving Jewish existence a cultural social meaning as a collective entity. As such, they are closer to those who are decidedly outside the Orthodox camp.

Henry Baruk, whose stance lies somewhere between the Orthodox and the traditional, agrees that there is no distinction between religion and nation in Judaism. It is a way of life that gives expression to values and beliefs, which stem from Abraham's covenant with God. As he sees it, the conflict between Jewish culture and modern Western culture makes it harder than ever before to be a Jew. Baruk recognizes that modifications of Judaism are inevitable. In particular, in view of the changes in education and family, he feels it is no longer justified to consider the mother the sole instrument for passing on Jewish identity, and thus recommends that new criteria be formulated. He suggests convening a cross-section of public figures from different sectors, and particularly from religious circles, to consider the possibilities. Furthermore, he also maintains that all those who were persecuted by the Nazis simply because they were Jewish should be recognized as Jews, even if they do not meet halakhic requirements.

Solomon B. Freehof speaks of the fundamental problem involved in converting children too young to understand what it is all about. He considers conversion to be an act of mercy, which can be performed on behalf of someone even if he or she is unaware of it. In the modern era, he notes, there is a growing number of applications for conversion because of the increase in mixed marriages, and under such circumstances, rabbis are naturally cautious. Nevertheless, he believes that Judaism does not prescribe a categorical stance in relation to converts. In fact, *Shulkhan Arukh* contains conflicting approaches, thereby providing rabbis with certain room to maneuver. Freehof advocates the attitudes adopted by the Reform Movement. Stressing the importance of preparing candidates for conversion through the study of ethics and Jewish history, he expresses his distaste for formal halakhic ritual. He realizes, however, that if each community were to perform conversion according to its own practices and rules, those who underwent more liberal procedures would not be recognized as Jews by less liberal circles and would thus have the status of some sort of "semi-converts." Freehof suggests that such people be granted the civil rights accruing to a Jew in Israel, but not be fully accepted into all sectors of Jewish society. They would thus have a status similar to the concept of "resident Jew" that existed in the Second Temple period, which might even encourage them to undergo further, more traditional, conversion at a later stage.

Mordecai Menachem Kaplan is similarly of the opinion that there is no one Jewish tradition. In reference to the special case of Israel, he contends that its relations with the Diaspora are grounded in the Law of Return. At the same time, Israel is a modern country committed to upholding secular principles. Kaplan believes that its secular nature obliges Israel to define the concept "Jew" in such a way that it does not include the principle of faith and enables the children of mixed marriages to be registered as Jews. Aware of the difficulties of his approach, Kaplan advocates compromise. He joins with those proposing an intermediate category such as "resident Jew," although he acknowledges that if and when such children wish to be "ordinary" Jews, they will have to undergo conversion.

The majority of secular correspondents in the Diaspora are of similar mind. Dante Lattes claims that a population registry cannot invoke religious criteria. For the children of mixed marriages to be registered as Jews in a modern Jewish state, it is enough that they are not identified with any other religion. He is convinced that these children will be "good Israelis," as they will attend public schools and receive a Jewish education in Hebrew. National identity cards need only indicate that the information contained therein does not have the sanction of rabbinical law.

Isaiah Berlin distinguishes between two senses of the term "Jew": the formal legalistic halakhic meaning and the broader social meaning as used in everyday life. In the latter sense, a "Jew" is any person who is affiliated and identifies with a Jewish community. If this definition were to be applied in Israel, a secular, liberal, and democratic Jewish state, then people who were considered Jews but did not meet halakhic criteria could be an integral part of the Jewish nation. The fact that they will not be recognized as Jews by the rabbinical establishment does not detract from the need to grant them some sort of "political Jewish" status. Whatever the eventual solution, people already thought of as Jews cannot be required to undergo conversion. Moreover, the government is obliged to recognize the Jewish identity—in the political sense—of children whose Jewish fathers wish them to be brought up as Jews, so long as the mother consents. Like other correspondents, Berlin expresses the opinion that these children will, as a matter of course, become part of Jewish society. Alternatively, he suggests that should his ideas not be acceptable to the Israelis, then labels such as "father a Jew" or "wife of a Jew" might be employed instead. These categories would constitute a sort of legitimate "no-man's land," on condition that they are not translated into permanent status, in which case the children would come to be considered "inferior" or "half" Jews. Berlin is convinced that over time the State of Israel will be forced to make a clearer distinction between the religious and national aspects of Jewish identity in order to further the normalization of the Jewish people.

Chaim Perelman also finds it unthinkable that people who are entitled to automatic Israeli citizenship under the provisions of the Law of Return can not be registered as Jews. While he does not question the exclusive responsibility of the religious authorities for religious affairs, he contends that like every other civilized country, Israel must differentiate between nation and religion, and aspire to reach the stage of full secularization, including in matters of personal status. Admittedly, for historical reasons this position is not yet tenable, and moreover, the State of Israel cannot recognize the members of other religions as Jews. Nevertheless, unlike religious faith, which is under no such obligation, it is incumbent upon a country to enact legislation that suits the circumstances of its citizens' life. Perelman thus proposes establishing some sort of high court composed of parliamentarians, rabbis, and other public figures to devise a new format for relations between state and religion in Israel.

As a rule, Ben-Gurion's Israeli correspondents do not subscribe to this view. Hayim Hazaz is one of the few who does. Although he has deep appreciation for Jewish tradition—indeed, he is convinced that religious observance can be credited with the survival of the Jewish people for so many generations—he wonders what would happen should thousands of mixed couples arrive in Israel. Would the country reject them or force on them a religion that was alien to them? He therefore recommends that such couples be allowed to register their children as Jews if they so wish. Shmuel Hugo Bergmann, in turn, expresses his belief in the sanctity of the Jewish people and the strong link between nation and religion in Israel. That being said, he takes exception to the intransigent perpetuation of outdated practices. We cannot ignore the fact, he claims, that many of those who have settled in Israel have no Jewish roots whatsoever. There is therefore no choice but to institute two partially overlapping categories: self-declared Jews and Jews according to halakha. As a secular state, Israel is obliged to accept the principle of self-declaration regardless of religious criteria.

The most extreme proponent of the ethno-cultural model is Haim Cohn. He asserts that parents have sole responsibility for their children and are thus entitled to determine their identity as they see fit. Accordingly, the registry office is obliged to register children as the parents instruct. If both parents declare their child to be Jewish, the child should, by law, be considered Jewish. Even if the declaration conflicts with halakha, the parents have the legal right to determine that their child should enjoy the same personal status as any other Jew. Given that the mother and father have equal standing, in cases where the parents do not agree, the child's identity should be registered as "unknown." Naturally, registration by the state does not imply that the child is being granted Jewish identity in the religious sense, as the religious establishment has exclusive authority over such matters. This, however, should not be a subject of concern in Israel, as the non-Jewish minority can be expected to become integrated into the Jewish majority.

Hazaz, Bergmann and Cohn thus reject the position that religion alone defines the borders of the collective. Rather, they see Israel as a Jewish state primarily by virtue of its cultural-social character. In this sense, they adopt the same standpoint as their colleagues in the Diaspora who define Judaism in terms of its cultural singularity. The Israelis, however, perceive this singularity through the prism of Israeli experience, that is, as associated with a certain territory, in contrast to those in the Diaspora, where it demonstrates an ethno-cultural principle. Despite this emphasis, all the respondents acknowledge an immutable connection between "the Jewish people" and "the God and Torah of Israel." While they may believe the singularity of the collective to reside in its values, symbols, and practices, rather than in religious faith, none of them proposes an immediate and total separation between state and religion. In this respect, the ethno-cultural syndrome displays a clear continuity with those branches of Judaism, beginning with the Reform movement, that spread throughout the Jewish world in the 19th century with the dawn of the modern era.

On the other hand, these formulations also contain new elements that may be attributed to the transformation of Jewish society in the 20th century, and especially in the 1940s and '50s. The definition of Jews as a group that is ethno-cultural (in the eyes of the non-Israeli correspondents) or national-cultural (in the view of its few Israeli proponents) also evidences the impact of "New World" multi-culturalism. This influence is apparent in the positive attitude to the non-ritualistic practice of Judaism and flexible boundaries for the collective—indeed, so flexible that they allow for intermediate categories between Jew and non-Jew. Moreover, none of these correspondents, save for the Orthodox among them, considers halakha to be particularly relevant at this point in time. Rather, they regard Israel as a form of Jewish practice without indicating the superiority of one type of practice over another. And most significantly, they do not see the traditional society of just a few decades earlier as the focus of Jewish existence in the present.

The National Syndrome

The third syndrome centers around the distinction between Israel and the Diaspora as two different circles of World Jewry and, at the same time, the contention that the "Jewish Israeli nation" in "the Land of Israel" is the center and leader of the Jews as a whole. Their desire to retain this status for Israel within the framework of a Jewish world that remains united around the Jewish State, leads even the free thinkers of this trend to advocate solutions to the problem of "Who is a Jew?" that are acceptable to all, including the most Orthodox. In order to stress the mutual relations between Israel and the Diaspora, these "nationalists" therefore opt for definitions of Jewish identity that represent a common denominator, which leads them to formulations that are very much in line with the demands of halakha. While, indeed, "simplified" Reform conversion in any way, shape, or form is offensive to Orthodox Jews committed to upholding halakha, no Reform Jew would refuse recognizing as Jews people fulfilling stricter requirements. Clearly, then, if Israel were to adopt a definition of Jewish identity that was any less rigid than the halakhic formula, it would irrevocably lose the support of Orthodox Jewry, along with its status as the center of the Jewish world. This is an unacceptable risk for those maintaining that Israel is the center of the Jewish world. The large majority of non-Orthodox Israeli correspondents, along with Zionists from the Diaspora, are particularly sensitive to these considerations.

Among the most enthusiastic Israeli advocates of this syndrome, S.Y. Agnon recognizes the fact that state and religion are often in conflict on specific issues, but maintains that no one ever has the right to "edit" the Torah. Statesmen should focus on matters of state and leave religious questions to the rabbis. By the same token, Agnon is not overly accommodating to converts. As they do not enjoy the "credit of fathers" (zekhut avot) like people who were born Jews, they should be even stricter in observing the commandments. Zekharya Hacohen subscribes to the same view. The First Commandment states that the nation has one God, and its sanctity derives from this precept. Basing his arguments on an extensive historical analysis, he claims that although much non-Jewish blood flows through the veins of the nation, this fact has no religious significance. The only thing that matters is that a man be circumcised and a woman undergo immersion in the mikve (ritual bath). Then and only then can they be Jews.

The Chief Rabbi of Israel, Yitskhak Halevi Herzog, agrees that the commandments are the sole source of Jewish life. It is only by virtue of the Torah that the Jews have survived as a nation for so long, and only by upholding the Torah will they continue to endure until redemption. As the viability of the nation lies in the Torah, any government regulation that violates Jewish law on the issue "Who is a Jew?" will undermine and destroy the foundations on which the state is built. Yossef Kappah similarly insists that Judaism is not a race or tribe, but a religious faith and national identity. Entry into this nation can only be gained through the door of halakhic conversion. Yekhezkel Kaufmann concurs, stating that the inseparability of Jewish religion and nationality is the principle underlying the covenant and the community of people of the covenant. Judaism is not a secular entity, so that there is no such thing as secular law in respect to the registration of the population. The State of Israel may have altered the conditions of Jewish life, but not the definition of Judaism. Its citizens can only be defined as Jewish according to halakha criteria. Declaring that parents can turn a non-Jew into a Jew simply by saying so would be tantamount to establishing a new religious law. The fact that the Jewish religion is fundamentally intertwined with Jewish nationality means that the link between the two cannot be broken.

Ephraim Urbach begins his letter in a similar spirit, expressing regret over the fact that a country vowing not to discriminate on the basis of religion or national identity feels the need to record this information in its identity cards. The only possible justification for such a practice is security considerations. If a population registry is essential, however, citizens cannot be listed as Jews in official documents on the basis of national affiliation as opposed to religious status. This would create insoluble problems if they wished to obtain a marriage license, as long as this function remained the province of Orthodox rabbis. Moreover, Urbach cautions that it has not yet been demonstrated that the children of mixed marriages in Israel tend to become integrated into Jewish society. And clearly, legitimizing such marriages in Israel would also encourage them abroad, where they would lead to the assimilation of Jews into non-Jewish society. Moshe Silberg seconds this view, arguing that no regulations regarding "Who is a Jew?" will ever be accepted by all branches of Judaism. The most they can hope for is some sort of compromise. Furthermore, from the moment Israel, a secular state, granted official authority to halakha in matters of personal status, it must also apply halakhic dictates in registering its citizens so as to ensure the consistency of the judicial system.

Sh. Shalom offers a different perspective. In his opinion, the fact that Jews have suffered throughout history because of their loyalty to their symbols and way of life has turned these into hallowed traditions that future generations are obligated to uphold. Indeed, it was this understanding that led to the establishment of the State of Israel. It is thus perfectly proper to require that anyone wishing to become part of the Jewish people also identify with its symbols and way of life. Shalom believes that the rabbinical authorities act in the best interests of the entire nation, including its secular members, particularly in respect to conversion. After undergoing halakhic conversion, the individual retains the right to decide whether or not to live as an observant Jew.

In his response, Shlomo Goren first addresses the nature of the relations between a mother and her children in Jewish sources, concluding that whether she is a Jew or a gentile, she has a critical influence over her children's religious beliefs. Jewish sources state that the moment the child of a mixed marriage undergoes conversion, he or she attains the same status as a Jew by birth, as if both parents were Jewish. Furthermore, while it is impossible to separate Jewish religion and nationality and that has always been so, no secular government has the authority to determine "Who is a Jew?" Nevertheless, given the country's difficulties in dealing with this problem, there should be no objection to instituting a new category of "professing Judaism" for youngsters who are considering conversion but are not yet ready for it. This would allow for the administrative flexibility needed to provide an answer to the specific problem of how to register the children of mixed marriages. In effect, these positions are close to those expressed by the proponents of the caste syndrome. They differ, however, in that their attitude to Israel is based on the belief that religion is the foundation of Jewish nationalism. This approach can thus be termed "nationalist-religious."

Other non-Orthodox observant and/or liberal Israelis reach the same conclusions but from a different angle. Yehuda Bourla admits that religious ceremonies and rituals of all sorts are alien to him and, in fact, he shies away from anything that hints even slightly at religious coercion. Nevertheless, he considers the rite of circumcision to be the single most important mark of a Jew and must be performed for every male child. Consequently, he supports halakhic conversion. Joseph Schechter begins by confessing that he knows little about Judaism, but understands that religion managed to ensure the survival of the nation to this day despite persecution and impoverishment. He thus objects to the position that Judaism should adapt to the modern world. Modernism, he claims, has brought the human race to the brink of annihilation. Furthermore, although he himself is not Orthodox, he believes that the hand of God is in the Torah, and therefore supports a conservative approach to the issues of circumcision and conversion. Akiva Ernst Simon similarly remarks that even Jews who declare themselves to be "non-observant" or even "non-believers" actually observe a large number of commandments. Among other things, they continue to perform the rite of circumcision, although it might be thoroughly out of tune with the spirit of the times. According to Simon, circumcision has always been the symbol of membership in the Jewish nation, so that eliminating the need for it would be overstepping the bounds of Judaism. All in all, the parents' declaration could not be accepted as the basis of Jewish identity. Anyone wishing to become a member of the nation must undergo a religious ceremony.

As we have seen, this approach is not accepted by many of the correspondents outside Israel, particularly those who are neither ultra-Orthodox nor modern Orthodox. It is displayed, however, by Zionist correspondents who identify with Israel's aspiration to be seen as the leader of the Jewish world. Moshe Maisels notes that halakha has already been afforded official authority in Israel in respect to personal status, so that it is unreasonable for a different approach to be adopted for a related issue like the population registry. It is also unreasonable to suggest that the implementation of different laws in different contexts can make an individual half-Jewish and half-non-Jewish. By the same token, Maisels believes that the link between religion and nationality is at the heart of Judaism and can not be broken. Israel can no longer maintain the anti-traditional attitudes of the Zionist movement, as it now represents a unique form of Jewish life that harkens back to pre-Zionist Judaism and is a continuation of its historical development.

Aaron Zeitlin also distinguishes between the utterly secular notion "Israel" and the term "Jew," with the latter denoting both religious and national content. Only in this nation does the Jewish religion exist, and only this religion exists in this nation, regardless of how many Jews lead a thoroughly religious life. Moreover, since even a non-believing Jew remains a Jew and is a party to Abraham's covenant with God, conversion is the only way in which a non-Jew can become part of the Jewish people. Attempts to devise some sort of category of "administrative Jew" that would meet the requirements of the secular laws governing the population registry but would not be recognized by the religious establishment would never be accepted. The secular government has no authority whatsoever over the question "Who is a Jew?". What is more, any non-religious definition would open an unbridgeable gap between Israel and the Diaspora, where the possibility of defining a Jew without reference to religion does not exist. Leon Arye Simon is similarly loath to a new definition of the term "Jew," fearing that unilateral decisions in Israel would cause a rift with Diaspora Jewry. Furthermore, he is not convinced that the majority of Israelis are interested in doing away with the halakhic definition. Nonetheless, he does not deny that the issue creates problems for Israel as a modern state. As to the matter at hand, he suggests affording the temporary status of "father is a Jew" to children whose mothers are not Jewish, when both parents wish to be part of Jewish society.

All the responses of those supporting the nationalist syndrome give prominence to national considerations, especially unity between Israel and the Diaspora and the centrality of Israel in the Jewish world. As stated above, this position leads to their acceptance of halakhic precepts in regard to conversion, as their validity is universally acknowledged. The religious circles emphasize the halakhic principles underlying the requirements for conversion; those who attribute less importance to religious dictates, including the free-thinking respondents, stress the crucial role of religion in preserving the unity of the Jewish people. The major feature of this syndrome, however, is that it refers to the territorial aspect ("the Land of Israel" in traditional phrasing) in terms of the distinction between the State of Israel and the Jewish Diaspora, and gives it priority over the other two dimensions of identity. Accordingly, it also defines "the Jewish people" in terms of two distinct concepts: "Israeli Jews," that is, the Jews in Israel who constitute the "Israeli nation"; and "Diaspora Jewry," the Jews outside Israel. This is where the element of "the God and Torah of Israel" comes in, as the repertoire of traditional symbols, representing a cultural singularity and shared destiny, is common to both parts of the nation. As the national model therefore requires that the religious symbols be seen as the glue binding Israel and the Diaspora together, in effect it carries on the legacy of the Zionist formulation of Jewish identity. It offers a nationalist

interpretation for the establishment of the State of Israel and proposes a pattern of Jewish-Israeli identity that highlights the central
role of Israel in relation to the Diaspora. However, the syndrome
rejects the original image at the basis of Zionism, which portrayed
the Diaspora "whose time had passed" as the opposite of the Zionist
endeavor, which would now ensure Jewish sovereignty and the Return
to Zion. Instead of this conflictual principle, the nationalist syndrome
stresses the need for unity between Israel and the Diaspora. Israeli
Judaism therefore gives priority to traditional symbols not only as
national symbols, but also as the basis for creating a common ground
for all Jews—under its leadership.

Conclusion

The transformation of Jewish existence in the first half of the 20th
century clearly left its mark on Ben-Gurion's correspondents. The
Holocaust appears to have induced the ultra-Orthodox, following in
the footsteps of Agudat Israel, to dig in their heels to preserve the
halakhic definitions of Jewish identity, making them even less willing to temper the strictness of their requirements. In contrast, liberal society, particularly in the United States where the new Jewish
communities evolved, fostered the openness displayed by the ethno-
cultural syndrome. Finally, the national syndrome, heir to the Zionist
movement, portrayed Jewish experience in light of Israeli realities.

Table 2.3 presents a brief comparative summary of the three syndromes which enables us to identify the points of conflict between
them. While the national syndrome supports halakhic criteria for
becoming a Jew, the caste syndrome places these in the context of
wider halakhic demands and makes the commanding role of Israel
in the Jewish world contingent on its meeting these demands. Both
these syndromes are at odds with the ethno-cultural, which adopts
a pluralistic stance. This approach, typical of non-ultra-Orthodox
Diaspora Jewry, flies in the face of the nationalist syndrome which
elevates Israel as the leader of the Jewish world. Indeed, the uncompromising attitude of the national syndrome in respect to the definition
of Jewish identity clashes head-on with the liberal flexible ethno-
cultural syndrome.

The national syndrome represents a highly distinct perception of
"the Jewish people." From this point of view, it is a collective in

which being Jewish is a "sociological" fact, that is, a fact determined by overriding cultural definitions that are generally accepted without reservation by the individual as a member of society. In this sense, Israeli Jewish identity can be seen to maintain the familiar pattern of traditional society in which the Jewish community was a social, cultural, and political enclave and the Jew was essentially anyone who belonged to that community. It is in the context of this similarity that the Jewish-Israeli identity diverges from the dominant Jewish identities in the modern Diaspora. There, where Jews are also citizens of non-Jewish states, they are directly and individually members of general society before they ally themselves with a Jewish community. Furthermore, similarly to the caste syndrome which distinguishes between those who "follow the right path" and "captive infants," Jewish Israeli identity maintains a dichotomous perception of Jews, differentiating between the Israeli Jewish nation and the Jewish people in general. The former framework is supposedly home to a "complete" Jewish life, whereas in the latter Jewish existence is seen as dependent on non-Jews. In addition, the three syndromes differ not only in their interpretation of the various aspects of Jewish identity, but also in respect to the specific aspect to which they give priority. Although all are anchored in the three deep structures of traditional identity, each stresses a different one—the God and Torah of Israel, the Jewish people, or the Land of Israel.

Furthermore, and as we know from elsewhere (Ben-Rafael, 1994), it can be perceived here that the three syndromes evidenced in the letters also express and concretize their singularity in different linguistic markers. The caste syndrome consecrates the language of Scriptures ("the holy tongue" or Ancient Hebrew), advocates preserving the Yiddish of the former Eastern European community for everyday use, and encourages acquisition of the local tongue—e.g., English in the U.S., Hebrew in Israel—for communicating with the world outside the ultra-Orthodox community. The ethno-cultural syndrome, which places great value on the insertion of Jewish communities into the surrounding culture and society, highlights the use of local languages—English, French, etc. Under the influence of Israeli reality, Hebrew is widely taught to the young as the language of the Jew, but only as a secondary marker and, in most cases, it is acquired up to quite a limited level of mastery. As for the national syndrome, it is primarily marked by the use of Hebrew as the basis of a new national culture, which was for long very reluctant to allow the retention of any other code among Israel's Jewish population.

While these differences confirm the strength of centrifugal tendencies among the three syndromes, there is still evidence of centripetal forces as well. The most telling is the fact that the validity of halakhic criteria is universally accepted. None of the correspondents questions the axiom that a person who is born to a Jewish mother or undergoes halakhic conversion is a Jew. As the overwhelming majority of Jews in the world meet these requirements, regardless of their perception of Judaism, all three syndromes may be said to relate grosso modo to the same people. The differences in the borders of the collective drawn by each syndrome actually leave only a narrow margin outside the overlapping area. Hence, while there may be more than one Jewish identity, there is not more than one Jewish People. What is more, all three syndromes draw their symbols from the same repertoire of traditions, rituals, and narratives. The differences primarily concern their interpretation, understanding, or definition. Similarly, all three syndromes attribute special significance to Israel as the concretization of sovereign Jewish life in "the land of the forefathers," albeit their approach to this and the degree of importance they ascribe to it vary widely from one syndrome to the other. Although the letters contain indications of deep-seated disagreement and mutual estrangement, all the correspondents—both in and outside Israel—acknowledge that anything that affects the status of the Jewish religion in Israel has immediate implications for relations between Israel and the Diaspora.

These similarities notwithstanding, each of the syndromes can be seen to stress a different aspect of Jewish identity. In reference to way of life, the singularity of the Jewish people, the caste syndrome stands out for its unique patterns of dress, ritual, speech, and so on. In respect to the territorial dimension, the national model is at odds with the other two approaches by establishing a dichotomy between the Jews in Israel and those in the rest of the world. As for the perception of commitment to the collective and the nature of its boundaries, the ethno-cultural syndrome, open to innovation and far-reaching change, clashes with the others. Thus, taken together, the three syndromes represent a mix of attitudes that diverge in differing degrees from each other while drawing on the same sources and experiences.

Table 2.3: Comparison of the Three Models of Jewish Identity

	SYNDROMES		
	Caste	Ethno-cultural	National
Social base	Israeli & Diaspora Ultra-Orthodox; Diaspora Orthodox	Some Orthodox, non-Orthodox observant, & liberals mainly in the Diaspora with a few Israelis	Diaspora Zionists; Israeli Orthodox, non-Orthodox observant, & liberals
Primary aspect of identity	*God and Torah of Israel*: preceded nation and the Land; Judaism as covenant of Abraham	*Jewish People*: universal Jewish solidarity; usually special attitude to Israel	*Land of Israel*: Israel as a Jewish state and leader of the Jewish world
Secondary aspect	*Jewish People*: collective guardian of the Torah and traditional Judaism	*God and Torah of Israel*: represents values & symbols subject to interpretation	*Jewish People*: distinction between the "Israeli nation" & the Diaspora
Third aspect	*Land of Israel*: site of redemption; Israel is a Jewish state only if it upholds halakha	*Land of Israel*: symbol of identification; site of Jewish culture	*God and Torah of Israel*: symbols shared by Israel & the Diaspora
Conversion	Insistence on halakhic conversion; a "new Jew" becomes party to Abraham's covenant	Conversion affords entrance into the people but openness to an intermediate category	Maintaining patterns that ensure unity, including halakha

CHAPTER THREE

ISRAELI-JEWISH IDENTITIES

Introduction

As we enter the 21st century, we must ask ourselves whether the formulations of Jewish identity suggested by Ben-Gurion's correspondents are still relevant. Since their letters in the late 1950s, circumstances have again changed drastically. The Cold War, which followed on the heels of World War II, split the world into two hostile ideological camps, producing escalating local and regional conflicts until the fall of the Soviet empire. By the end of the 20th century, the West had achieved unprecedented economic prosperity and seen the rise of an ever expanding middle class. Technological progress in all areas of life, the growth of the metropolis, worldwide corporations, intense globalization, the surge in higher education, and many other far-reaching developments had transformed the lifestyle, expectations, and aspirations of men and women throughout the Western world and beyond.

During the same years, the Jewish world changed no less dramatically, and in some ways even more so, although compared to the previous period, it was a relatively quiet time. It saw the advancement of Jews in many Western countries, where they became part of the middle-class and were disproportionately represented in social elites. For the Jews of Israel, however, things were different. At this time, Israel was contending with a tumultuous Middle East, where the 1948 War of Independence was followed by the Sinai Campaign (1957), the Six Day War (1967) and the Yom Kippur War (1973). The Palestinian problem now became the focus of heightened international tension and persistent military confrontations. Following the Six Day War, in which Israel scored resounding victories over its neighbors in the Sinai, the Golan Heights, and the West Bank, the Jewish state had come to be seen as a regional superpower occupying and repressing a rebellious population. As Israel became increasingly isolated in the world, many Jews in the Diaspora also began to take exception to its actions. Others responded by redoubling their commitment to Israel. On the other hand, ever since the first waves of modern immigration, a Hebrew culture had started to emerge in Israel, producing its own writers and thinkers, as all newcomers adopted the language, whether enthusiastically or hesitantly. The new society of Jews developed patterns of its own in all areas of life, displaying the greatest vitality in the creation of new symbols. Did these new forms represent new versions of Jewish identity? Did they stand in contrast to the versions that developed in parallel throughout the Diaspora, itself experiencing transformation? This chapter addresses the first of these questions; the following chapter will consider the second.

Revolution, Unity, and Elitism

In 2001, the Jewish population of Israel numbered more than five million (out of a total population of over six million), a mere ten percent less than the world's largest Jewish community (the United States). According to DellaPergola (1995), within a few years, more Jews will be living in Israel than in any other country, and by the second decade of the 21st century, it will be home to a majority of the Jewish population worldwide. Jewish identity in Israel is thus understandably critical to the future of Judaism as a whole. However, it is by no means a homogeneous entity in terms of culture or even language.

Ever since the period of Israel's founding fathers, the major force pushing for cultural unity in the country has been the ideology of "the ingathering of the exiles," aspiring not only to welcome Jews from all over the world, but to create a new national Israeli culture as well. A crucial element in achieving this objective was the resurrection of Hebrew as a spoken language and its adoption as the legitimate national tongue with priority over other native languages, both Jewish and non-Jewish. While the successful transition to Hebrew drew in large part from the work of the Enlightenment in Europe, it was essentially made possible by the fact that Hebrew was preserved in the collective memory of all Jews as "the original Jewish tongue" and the language of Scriptures. The Zionists in Israel could call on this knowledge in their endeavors to turn Hebrew into a national language to be used also for secular, everyday, purposes. Obviously, the initiators of this change, the large majority of whom were from Eastern Europe, were also obliged to adopt Hebrew for use in their personal lives, even though they already shared Yiddish. By doing so, as we already mentioned, they became the first known group to replace their native tongue with another. Moreover, they actually had to invent its lexis and syntax to meet the demands of a new time and place, and thereby, to expose it to a plethora of influences, bringing it closer to European languages, as well as to Yiddish and Arabic (Chomsky, 1957).

Hebrew thus became the central hallmark of the new society, symbolizing the unique Jewish experience in Israel as an alternative to life in the Diaspora, and implying that this experience was superior to any other Jewish reality (Glinert, 1990). Here lays the source of Zionism as a new form of Jewish identity, creating a distinction between the "Jewish people" in general and the "Jewish nation" in Israel. Taken out of the exclusive hands of scholars and rabbis, Hebrew became the sign of a new collective, each of whose members was "breathing life into the language," despite the objections of those who considered it an abomination to use the "holy tongue" for secular purposes. The linguistic revolution also served as the basis for implementing the ideology of national integration when mass immigration began to arrive from numerous countries (Bachi, 1974; Hoffman and Fisherman, 1972). This ideology was formulated by the founding fathers under the influence of the nationalist ideologies familiar to them from Europe. It required that all newcomers merge into one new unified nation. The aspiration for "kibbutz galuyot," the ingathering of the exiles, was thus sustained by the ideal of "mizug galuyot," the fusing of the exiles.

Nevertheless, the desire for linguistic and cultural unification did not always result in unity. In fact, the same models that sought to produce unity promoted new distinctions. The very call for unification implied recognition of the special status of those portrayed as the worthy role models, the first and second generation "pioneers." Furthermore, as in any immigrant society where the newcomers are striving to put down new roots, here too being "native" was a source of social prestige. It is the children of immigrants who fulfill their parents' lofty ambitions and ensure the success of their endeavors. In the case of Israel, the native-born also carried the bulk of the security burden and the armed struggle, reinforcing their image as the "salt of the earth." In addition, the sons and daughters of the pioneers were highly conscious of being the children of people who had adopted a new national Jewish identity, and of themselves representing a "new kind" of Jew who had never known life in the Diaspora. Consequently, they promoted their self-image as a special group. The fact that they were also a minority group for a long time, as more and more immigrants arrived in Israel, added to their luster. As an "elite" which prided itself on this status, they created their own symbols, the most conspicuous of which was a typically nonchalant use of Hebrew that could be acquired only by being born "within the language", that is, in the country.

In point of fact, elitist tendencies had existed in Palestine ever since the arrival of the pioneers (Ochana, 1996). In those days, it was influenced by the Nietzschean myth of the "new man," reconceived as the "new Hebrew." Jabotinsky, the radical Zionist, was particularly fond of quoting Nietzsche. This Nietzschean influence was linked to the Zionists' self-image as the antithesis of Diaspora Jewry. Many held that the Diaspora had destroyed everything that was good in Judaism, and they invariably spoke of it in a derisive patronizing tone. Quite a few of the pioneers displayed a similar attitude to the Diaspora Jews who resettled in Israel. In their eyes, these people continued to bear the "stigma of the Diaspora," unlike the native-born "sabras" (literally, prickly pears), a positive label meant to indicate the essence of "Israeliness" that sprouted from the new form of life in the country. A central element of their elitism was the variety of Hebrew they evolved (Katriel, 1986). A "no-nonsense" language—a laconic style of speech which abhorred euphemisms and high language in general—, it underscored the connection to the Middle East by incorporating numerous Arabic words, and encouraged a blunt, casual, and "natural" way of speaking. By doing so, it expressed repugnance for verbosity, protocol, formality, and sophistry, all traits attributed to Diaspora Jews (Rubinstein, 1977). The sabra activities of hiking the length and breadth of Israel, belonging to a youth movement, spending time on a kibbutz, and serving in the army produced new words that were unfamiliar to those who "didn't belong" (Shamir, 1970). For a long time, entry into this elite was not easy, for those who had arrived in Israel as youngsters but were not born here, those who had left the ultra-Orthodox community but were still close to forms of religiosity, or Yemenites who had been in the country for many years but remained attached to community values. Acceptance, moreover, when it was offered, never dulled the patina of "nativeness," if only on the symbolic level.

That "Israeli" mainstream culture has, however, undergone profound change over the decades. The collectivistic approach that prevailed prior to the establishment of the state and in the first years of statehood has been replaced by a much more individualistic model following demographic, economic and political developments. The etatist ideology that gained in strength in the 1950s and 1960s stressed the need to move from utopia to nation-building. "Pioneer" was redefined to relate to anyone who "contributed" to the state: not only farmers and settlers as in the past, but also professionals, public functionaries, and business people. The country born out of war and still afflicted by security concerns reserved a place of honor for the armed forces, and now placed great stock on a military career. Mass immigration which tripled the population within a few years, brought to the country a broad array of cultural groups that diffused new perspectives and perceptions. Thus a new social order came into being. In this new social reality, numerous myths were shattered, among them the superiority of physical labor, which had been central to the pioneering ethos. Now higher education and professionalism were also considered legitimate pursuits. At the same time, immigration and wars resulted in a constant strengthening of Israel's relations with the Jewish world, now viewed as the country's "natural partners," in contrast to the anti-diaspora mood in vogue among Zionists years before.

These economic, social, and cultural processes also had an impact on the drastic change that overtook the leading forces of society. Along with a constantly growing middle class came the features of Western consumer society while the "1948-generation" (the generation of the War of Independence) had become bureaucrats, financiers, politicians, and businessmen. As this elite came to be defined in terms of achievements, the meritocracy adopted a more formal standard language. The disdain for "foreign" languages disappeared as sources of communication gained in importance. English became virtually a second language at all levels of education, professional life, and business, and fluency in English was now an attribute of status.

Even in this context, some signifiers of native culture persist today and can still be discerned in patterns of speech, dress, and behavior, but their sources are now mainly the army, high school, the university, or pubs. While many of those identified with this culture at the start of the 21st century belong to the middle or upper class, "nativeness" has, however, inevitably lost a considerable chunk of its appeal as it now characterizes a relatively large sector of the population, and not a restricted cohort anymore. Paradoxically, this fact encourages no few individuals to preserve their own features. People who have not internalized the (quite unclear, today) sabra version of Israeli culture, whether born in or outside the country, stand at some distance from it—voluntarily or not. The modern religious, for example, often reject the secular aspect of mainstream "Israeliness," while many of the immigrants from both Western and Eastern countries do not wish to deny their roots.

All in all, however, one may still speak of a version of Jewish identity conveyed by the strongest strata-sabras and non-sabras alike. This dominant version prolongs the national syndrome seen in the letters to Ben-Gurion: a national identity articulating its singularity in secularized symbols and in a new Hebrew culture, and refering to a territory from where Jewishness is viewed as distinguishing Israel from the diaspora. Though, "how Jewish," "Jewish in what way," and "in what sense Jewish" remain, even here, debated questions that, more than elsewhere, are part of the public agenda where a variety of parties oppose the prevailing formulation. Hence, again one is to speak of several Jewish Israeli identities rather than of one. The issues and forces involved can be distinguished in terms of the three aspects of collective identity which serve as our guidelines throughout this discussion: the singularity of the collective which involves the role of religion; commitment to the collective and the role of narrower allegiances; and the place of the collective in respect to worldwide Jewry, as opposed to the relation to the surroundings.

The Role of Religion

The first distinction recognized and established in Israeli society relates to the singularity of the collective; it is the distinction between the ultra-Orthodox and the secular. From the time of the arrival of the first Zionists and the founding of national institutions, the ultra-Orthodox isolated themselves within their own communities. They used Yiddish as their language of everyday communication, and continued to develop their separate educational system. Devoting their greatest efforts to the establishment of "higher yeshivot" (religious colleges for adult men), they ignored the existence of the universities.

Yet despite this "monastic" tendency (Friedmn, 1986), over time they could not entirely keep themselves apart from Israeli Jewish society. Hebrew gradually seeped into the families and communities, until the younger generation was speaking more Hebrew than Yiddish. As the women do not attend yeshiva and often work outside the home in addition to their family responsibilities, Hebrew became their major language of communication. Whether by choice or otherwise, Hebrew has gradually become the first language of the ultra-Orthodox public as a whole, although Yiddish has not died out. This trend is encouraged by the fact that the ultra-Orthodox initiate contact with the secular sector to promote their own specific interests (exemptions from the army for yeshiva students or housing assistance) and are also determined to benefit from all facilities offered by the welfare state. These developments are tangible evidence that with the existence of a Jewish state, the ultra-Orthodox can no longer remain indifferent to government and isolate themselves within their enclaves.

Furthermore, the nature of the connection between the ultra-Orthodox and secular Jewish society also derives from their own definition of Jewish identity. As we have seen, they regard themselves as those who are fulfilling the true destiny of the Jew, that is, the work of God which alone will bring about redemption. This destiny, however, will be realized only when it is recognized by the whole of the Jewish People, therefore virtually compelling the ultra-Orthodox to pay heed to their status in society as the genuine guardians of Judaism. Hence, given the fact that the State of Israel exists and is home to an ever-larger proportion of the Jewish world, by their own convictions the ultra-Orthodox can no longer remain aloof from the rest of society. Moreover, as Israel is a sovereign state, the impact of the ultra-Orthodox on the life of the Jews may be more direct and effective here than anywhere else, a further motivation for them to abandon their isolation. Last but not least, as the religious laws of purity and uncleanness are stricter in the Holy Land, they feel it incumbent upon them to become involved in public affairs.

This orientation, held by the majority of the ultra-Orthodox public, is not necessarily understood by the secular, who may see their conspicuous markers—dress, rituals, esoteric interests—as expressions of their total foreignness to secular culture. This does not, however, prevent the ultra-Orthodox from considering themselves an active and significant—indeed, perhaps the most significant—force in Israeli society. In their own eyes, this is evidenced by the fact that, unlike their counterparts in Antwerp, Golders Green, or Brooklyn, in Israel they use the official language of the country among themselves, have their own political parties that participate in national politics, and are deeply involved in all spheres of public life. In this sense, the ultra-Orthodox community in Israel is decidedly "Israeli," even as it remains, in respect to essential identity issues, an integral part of world ultra-Orthodox Jewry.

The national-religious community exhibits a different type of Israeli-Jewish religious identity. For years, they have taken an active part in political Zionism, representing its "observant wing." On this basis, the national-religious leadership took on themselves the task of providing religious services to the country at large, while at the same time developing frameworks that reproduced, in religious forms, those of secular society: kibbutzim (collective settlements), moshavim (cooperative villages), a university, and so on. On the linguistic front, they have always been, again in contrast to the ultra-Orthodox, among the most zealous defenders of Hebrew, and were responsible for canonizing standard versions of religious texts for ritual use in nation-wide frameworks (such as the Army, national ceremonies or non-ethnic synagogues). This is a reflection of their aspiration to make a unique contribution to Israeli national culture through their familiarity with traditional sources. At the same time, as a religious community in which religious study is a prescribed ritual, they also acknowledge the spiritual authority of the prominent ultra-Orthodox rabbis.

This sector, however, is also confronted by a fundamental dilemma. As a community openly professing to be part of mainstream society, the national-religious declare their commitment to a flexible approach to the secular public. At the same time, their religious orientation defines the Jewish faith as the faith of the Jew, which he or she should recognize as such. This orientation drives them, like the ultra-Orthodox, to aspire to influence Jewish society as a whole. This tension led to the emergence in the 1960s of a group of national-religious activists (known as the "Youngsters") who opposed the established leadership of their movement and its efforts to maintain the status quo in religious-secular relations. The Six Day War and occupation of areas such as Samaria and Judea, which are part of the Biblical concept of the "Land of Israel," pushed the Youngsters onto center stage. Citing sacred texts that spoke of the "divine promise" of the land to the Jews, the new leadership claimed it was a religious duty to hold onto and settle these areas at all costs. This should now, they believed, be a central principle of national policy. This attitude gave birth to the Gush Emunim (Faction of the Faithful) movement, former members of the religious Bnei Akiva youth movement, which worked feverishly to establish settlements. With the rise to power of the right-wing parties in 1977, their endeavors gained momentum, as dozens of new settlements were created across the Green Line (the pre-1967 border between Israel and its Arab neighbors). With the start of Israeli-Palestinian negotiations and the demand for the establishment of a Palestinian state alongside Israel, political contention with the national leadership over withdrawal from the territories intensified. This led to the emergence of radical nationalist groups within Gush Emunim, some of which became involved in underground activity that was sanctioned by their rabbis. The crisis point was reached in November 1995 with the assassination of Prime Minister Yitzhak Rabin.

Unlike the ultra-Orthodox, for whom religious law represents behavioral and moral principles, the political ideology of the national-religious camp under the leadership of the Youngsters considers the singularity of the collective to lie in its overriding duty to fight to maintain control of "holy land." Here the concept of the Land of Israel is not merely the most important of the three aspects of Jewish identity—a hierarchy found in all varieties of Zionism—but takes on mythical uncompromising meaning that redefines the singularity of the collective in both cultural and spiritual terms. The advocates of this approach are unwilling to accept any limitations whatsoever on Jewish settlement in the territories, a stance that inevitably engenders opposition.

Yeshayahu Leibovits (1976), for example, contends that this sort of nationalist-religious orientation represents an imagined world that draws from the "sacred" descriptions of the Kingdom of Israel of Biblical times on the one hand, and from no less mythical descriptions of a messianic future on the other. What is more, such political messianism cannot but engender tensions with those in the national-religious camp—a not inconsiderable number—who continue to represent the original desire of observant Jews to become integrated into national society rather than to lead it.

The complexity of these issues, which involve religious cleavages in the Israeli reality, is primarily rooted in the significance of traditional symbols in the collective identities of Israeli Jews as a whole.

Surveys indicate that the majority of Israeli Jews do not disassociate themselves entirely from the sources of Judaism. For instance, even many of those who declare themselves to be secular celebrate the Jewish holidays, and observe no few rituals. The overwhelming majority of Israeli Jews maintain the custom of a family dinner on Friday night and light Sabbath candles; no less than three-quarters of the Jewish population fasts on Yom Kippur, lights Hanukkah candles, and takes part in a Passover seder. In addition, there is a broad consensus as to the retention of circumcision, bar mitzvah, and a religious wedding ceremony. Such attitudes are expressed by the majority of respondents in all categories, albeit by a smaller majority of the secular population than of the religious.

In brief, a large proportion of Israeli Jews, and not only those who are religious, equate Jewishness with Israeliness (Farago, 1989; Herman, 1988). Levi (1996) and Oron (1993) have found that despite the significant differences in the behavior of the religious and the secular, most Israeli Jews identify strongly with the fact that they are both Jewish and Israeli. Some two-thirds state unequivocally that they feel themselves part of the Jewish people the world over and are proud of it.

On the basis of these findings, some researchers (i.e., Liebman, 1997a; 1997b) claim that the influence of religion is greater than what might be assumed from the fact that a large proportion of the secular public expresses disapproval of the religious parties. Levi (1996), however, cautions against this conclusion, showing that the same religious symbols that characterize the religious population are mainly given secular national meaning by the non-religious. The differences, according to Oron (1993), relate less to behavior than to the fundamental attitude to Judaism where the rift between the religious and secular is real.

In the secular perspective, Judaism is a national culture more than a religion, and surveys reveal that on the cognitive level, Israelis believe the country is split between the religious and the secular, with the two sides having conflicting interests. This feeling does not preclude the fact that respondents tend to fall into intermediary categories in terms of behavior, that is, "partially observant" rather than "strictly observant" at the one end or "absolutely non-observant" at the other (Katz, 1997). This most likely derives from the fact that patterns of behavior with their source in religion are accepted by many respondents regardless of their religious orientation.

Another intriguing finding is the tendency for a conceptual polarization of the definition of "Israeli" among the various religious
camps themselves. The national-religious are the most extreme in
identifying with this term, while the ultra-Orthodox are the most
reserved, with the secular population lying somewhere in the middle.
This phenomenon conflicts with the fact that the two religious groups
both stress, albeit from different perspectives, the primordial aspect
of "Israeliness," that is, Judaism, whereas the secular are less definite
on this question.

These distinctions indirectly reflect the basic conflicts between
nationalism and religion in the Israeli collective identity. They also
play a role in additional and no less crucial aspects of this society,
above all, its ethnic cleavages.

Ethnic Divides

By their very nature, ethnic divides question understanding of the
meaning of membership in the collective, and thus what we have
termed "commitment to the collective." They query how far adherence to the society, when viewed as a whole, involves direct, immediate, and individual allegiance, independent of any other kind of
allegiance, or whether it is in some way mitigated by loyalty to the
ethnic community. In the Israeli reality, certain ethnic divides have
been major actors in the social and political dynamics that have
evolved over the years, and have demonstrated that the members of
the dominant culture are losing their grip on the leadership of the
whole of Israeli society. Starting in the late 1970s, this group, the
core of Israel's middle and upper classes, began to suffer defeat at
the hands of opposing elites that emerged, in the framework of the
democratic regime, from sectors previously considered "marginal."
They include the Mizrakhi (plural: Mizrakhim; from the Middle East
and North Africa) Jews later joined by immigrants from the former
Soviet Union, who started to arrive in the late '80s. Within a short
time, the Israeli Arabs were also to gain strength in the social and
political arenas as a result of both the multiculturalization of Israeli
society and the peace process in the Middle East. While multiculturalization was primarily the outcome of the political strengthening
of Jewish ethnic groups, it also resulted in the widening of the field
of action of Israel's Arab minority; the Oslo Accords of 1992 added

to this change by making this minority a pivotal element between
Israel and the Palestinians.

The Mizrakhim

Underlying the ethnic rifts among Israeli Jews is a particular form
of ethnicity that we may label eda (pl., edot). This Hebrew term
refers to a group whose members see themselves a priori as part of
the broader collective, but who share their own singular understanding and symbols of that collective. Yemenite Jews, for example, who always thought of themselves as part of the Jewish People,
were thoroughly ready, upon arrival in Israel, to consider themselves
part of the Israeli-Jewish collective. In Israel, however, they found
that their Jewishness was different from others' with respect to heritage, rites, language, family models, and more. In effect, their immigration was largely motivated by their religious traditionalism, which
had led them to understand that the establishment of a Jewish state
in Israel heralded the time of redemption. This belief now encouraged the Yemenites to refuse to abandon all the customs and habits
they had always viewed as Judaism itself. As they saw it, it was their
very faithfulness to this Judaism—that is, *their* Judaism—throughout
the generations that had brought them to the Holy Land. According
to this "traditionalist" Zionism, in this respect their religious fervor
in the Diaspora had been as important as the efforts of the pioneers.
At the same time, however, Yemenites also wished to adapt to their
new surroundings and become an indistinguishable part of the Jewish
Israeli nation. They were therefore open to adopting those new ways
of life[1] which they felt were required by their new condition.

Later, by attending post-secondary schools or universities and taking up a career, the children became part of new social frameworks
and were more exposed to the culture prevailing in their environment.
The more willing they were to turn their back on their traditions, the
easier it was for them to "cross over" and join the middle class
which, although predominantly Ashkenazi, wished to sustain an
"Israeli" non-ethnic, culture. Two factors furthered the integration
of men and women of Mizrakhi descent with the capability for social

[1] In fact, the last of the Yemenite Jews to immigrate to Israel, who arrived in
the '90s, could barely see themselves in their "Israeli" cousins, and several asked
to return to Yemen.

mobility. First, the middle class was ideologically open to social
integration, at least for those who were able to rise to the required
status, as obligated by the commitment to "mizug galuyot." Secondly,
as an eda, the Yemenite population accepted the principle of
assimilation as it believed the Jews to be "one nation," even if many
of them were unable to implement this ideology in practical terms
(Ben-Rafael and Sharot, 1991).

Even today, however, some forty percent of the Mizrakhi Jews in
Israel continue to belong to communities that display the features of
low socio-economic groups. These communities perpetuate the poverty
and inequality that began with their initial entrance into Israeli society in the 1950s and '60s. At that time, the establishment, so culturally remote from the new immigrants, typically adopted a
paternalistic attitude to them, settling them in peripheral areas where
social opportunities were scarce. The immigrants themselves were
also lacking in human capital in the sense of predispositions to integrate into a modern economy.[2] As a result of their lack of mobility,
many of these people had little exposure to the dominant culture,
reinforcing the tendency of Mizrakhi communities to preserve their
special character and even promote new symbols.[3]

In time, these communities, which remained influenced by religiosity and tradition, produced a religious elite that became increasingly powerful. In the early stages, it won the support of the Ashkenazi
ultra-Orthodox (mainly the Lithuanians), casting it as an ultra-
Orthodox group, an image it continued to maintain. It did not take
long for Mizrakhi yeshivot to be established under the leadership of
their own rabbis and scholars. Unlike their Ashkenazi counterparts,
who operate within a population that sets itself apart from the secular public, the Mizrakhi rabbis and students are an integral part
of the community at large, particularly in low-status areas, as a result

---

[2] This issue is the subject of harsh controversy between the school of conflict
sociology, represented by S. Smooha, S. Swirski, D. Bernstein and many others,
and the theories regarding the concept of immigrant absorption, represented by
D. Weintraub, M. Shokeid, E. Leshem and others who have investigated the integration of immigrants into society.
[3] As Weingrod (1990) demonstrates, the *hilula*—a festive visit to the tomb of an
individual considered a "saint"—has been gaining in popularity. Another example
of this phenomenon is the Moroccan Mimouna, the holiday of bread that follows
Passover, which gradually became so established that it now has the nature of a
public holiday for "all *edot*." In addition, the religious practices of the different communities are often preserved in the many synagogues constructed for a specific *eda*.

of the conspicuously traditional character of this population. Furthermore, and again in the context of their traditionalist environment, their activities in the community are not limited to religious affairs alone. Rather, they serve as public leaders, as is typical for religious authorities in traditional societies.

However, new patterns were soon to emerge. As Mizrakhi communities became gradually less dependent on the political establishment, they also became more capable of openly expressing their sense of disillusionment at having been relegated to the fringes of society. At this stage, the right-wing nationalist political leanings of this population, symbolically closer to their traditional ethnic cultures, also became apparent. Moreover, until 1977, the right had always been confined to the role of opposition role, so that support for it offered the added advantage of expressing conflictual feelings against an establishment which had "guided" their first steps in the country and was held responsible not only for the successes, but also the failures, of integration.

In 1977, this process led to a political upheaval, creating, for the first time in the history of Israel, the circumstances that made it possible for the right to rise to power. With competition for political hegemony level between the parties on the left and on the right, the power of those sectors that could ally themselves with either side gained unprecedented strength. This new reality led to an impressive rise in the number of Mizrakhi Jews in the various elite groups, at the same time breaking the long-standing public taboo against any attempt to establish a party on the basis of eda, thereby defying the concept of "mizug galuyot."

The first feeble attempt at this was Tami, a party founded by former activists of the national-religious camp. It was followed by Shas, a Mizrakhi ultra-Orthodox faction that carved out a firm place for itself in the political arena. It managed to politicize the new Mizrakhi religious elite under the leadership of religious authorities. By significantly increasing the proportion of religious representatives in the Knesset, Shas also established itself as a leading force in the religious sector in general. It now had the power to play on the religious political field, as well as on the ethnic political. On the one hand, it presented demands typical of a low socio-economic community, and on the other petitioned for cultural and legislative reforms that were religious in nature. What is more, in the circumstances now prevailing, Shas was able to become an actual force within the government.

The motivation behind the efforts of the party's spiritual leader,
Ovadia Yossef, is, in fact, to ultimately make Shas a leading force
in society. One indication of this intent is the systematic use of the
term "Sephardic" rather than "Mizrakhi", although it actually denotes
the descendents of the Jews of Spain in the Golden Age of the 11th
century, a lineage which the majority of communities in the Middle
East and North Africa can not claim. Yossef contends that the
Sephardic culture predominated in the yeshivot in the Land of Israel
for hundreds of years, so that this variety of Judaism is the only one
that can be truly considered to belong to the Holy Land and should
therefore be adopted by all Israeli Jews.

Moreover, the Judaism practiced by the Mizrakhi communities,
he claims, is closer than that of the Ashkenazim's to the Sephardic
legacy, which endows the Mizrakhim with a mission of Israeli-wide
significance, namely, bringing Israel's religious culture back to its
"true" legacy. This may be seen as an elaboration of the ideological foundations for attributing a central role to Mizrakhi communities in Israeli society. On the other hand, it also demands a considerable
sacrifice from these communities: to set aside their individual rituals
and texts for the benefit of their Sephardic brethren. In this spirit,
Shas is working to introduce new forms of prayer and ritual into
those Mizrakhi synagogues and centers that are willing to do its bidding (Leon, 2000).

Immigrants from the Former Soviet Union

The case of the Mizrakhi/Sephardic ethnic groups has had a profound effect on the immigrants from the former Soviet Union (herein:
the "Russians") who learned how ethnicity might become a basis of
political power and how this power could achieve legitimacy by participating in governmental coalitions. This sector has become increasingly powerful in recent years. A large number of immigrants began
to arrive in Israel in 1989, and by 2000 already constituted some
17 percent of the Jewish population of the country. Within a short
time it became clear that they wished to retain the cultural and linguistic values and symbols they had brought with them and which
they considered an integral part of their identity. As these Jews are
no less secular than those who had come from Eastern Europe long
before, they do not speak of a "sacred legacy." They do, however,
view their original culture and language as marks of their being "cul-

tured" and "cosmopolitan."[4] What is more, they have a strong desire to achieve political power and be involved in directing Israeli society. While viewing this ambition as entirely natural, they do not hesitate to familiarize themselves with the culture of their new homeland, and become "Israelis" as they perceive this notion.

In point of fact, after three generations under a hostile Marxist-Leninist regime, these immigrants have a very limited knowledge of Judaism. Many of them learned whatever they know after arriving in Israel, when they were exposed to the Hebrew language and the calendar of Jewish holidays, both of which are signifiers of Jewish identity in the country. From this perspective, the immigrants from the Soviet Union join the Mizrakhi sector as a force for multiculturalism in Israeli society, although the marks of their singularity are non-Jewish rather than Jewish.

On the other hand, many of them have considerable cultural and educational resources, and, according to their own self-image, belong to the middle class. This feature is reflected in their ambition for social mobility and their willingness to invest in promoting the human capital of their children. Indeed, within less than a decade since the arrival of the first immigrants, many are already employed in the various professions. These trends will undoubtedly become even stronger in time. If the immigrants from the former Soviet Union maintain their desire to enhance their status as a distinct cultural group, they may become the first successful example in Israel of the American model of "white ethnics," that is, a middle-class community that sees itself as an integral part of society, while at the same time highlighting the singularity of its culture and identity in various symbolic contexts. There is abundant evidence that the "Russian" immigrants are indeed moving in this direction: the large number of newspapers and journals in Russian they have founded in Israel; the continued creation of Russian literature by immigrant authors; the frequent public events they organize; and more.

This ethnic solidarity also explains the relative ease with which the immigrants were able, within under a decade, to produce a political

---

[4] In the former Soviet Union, many legitimate languages were spoken in the various republics, but Russian was the lingua franca throughout. Wherever they lived, the Jews belonged to the educated classes who knew and used Russian even if they resided in remote republics.

leadership to represent their interests and develop independent political power, rather than joining existing parties. With the massive support of the immigrants, the "Russian" parties that ran in the national elections of 1996 won quite a few seats in the Knesset, and even entered the government coalition.

In brief, while one may expect that quite a few socially mobile Russians will totally assimilate into Israel's middle-class mileus, others may well be willing to retain a form of symbolic ethnicity. In contrast to the Mizrakhi model of eda, which offers its own definitions of Israeli-Jewish identity, Russian "retentionists" would be prone to continue to look for a formulation of identity that enables them to strengthen their Jewishness, develop their Israeliness, and, at the same time, retain aspects of their Russian culture and opportunities for the use of their Russian language. As a group, their primary desire would be for the dominant culture to come to terms with the growing phenomenon of multiculturalism.

Israeli Arabs

In addition to the Russians, there are numerous other ethnic groups in the Jewish population in Israel, such as the Ethiopians, the English-speaking immigrants from South Africa, the US or Britain, the French-speaking immigrants from France, Belgium or Switzerland, and many others. But these groups are relatively small and of little public saliency as collectives. Another group is much more important and stands at a certain distance. Although not part of the Jewish population, it constitutes a major factor in the consolidation of its identity. This is the Arab minority that accounts for 18% of the population, with 90% residing in homogenous towns and villages. Similar to the Mizrakhi community, here too there is a connection between cultural singularity and social disadvantage. Over 80% of Israeli Arabs are employed in the national economy, 60% as blue-collar workers, as compared to 29% of the Jewish population (Lewin-Epstein and Semyonov, 1987). This inequality is undoubtedly a product, among other things, of the Arab-Israeli conflict (Makhou, 1982): all jobs relating to security and sensitive national issues are closed to Arabs. Moreover, in a climate of mistrust, or at best limited trust, Jewish employers in other fields as well often prefer to hire Jews. The social disadvantage of the Arab sector also derives from the fact that in 1948 they were a traditional peasant society, gaining their first experience of modernization only upon entrance into Israeli society (Horowitz and Lissak, 1989).

Unlike the Mizrakhim and Russians, Arabs are recognized as a national minority and consequently afforded the rights that accompany this status: Arabic is the second official language of the country and the language of instruction in the Arab public schools, and the Arab population maintains recognized political institutions, parties, associations, press and literature in its own language. In line with the attitude of the Israeli establishment, the Arabs themselves are determined to preserve a collective Arab-Palestinian identity (Nakhleh, 1975). One consequence of this is that neither the Jews nor the Arab population in general encourage the socially-mobile elements in Arab society—doctors, engineers, businessmen, and the like—to integrate socially into Jewish society. They remain an integral part of the community and often become its leaders. As such, they also bring with them into the community the influence of the dominant culture, to which they are more exposed than others. They thereby reinforce the tendency of Arabs to acquire Hebrew as a necessity of life in Israel and as a tool that affords access to the culture of modernity prevailing in this society, from the areas of employment and consumption, to education and public services. Without altering the contents of their collective identity, they have narrowed, and continue to narrow, the cultural distance that separates them from the Jewish population (Ben-Rafael and Brosh, 1995).

One may assume that in an era of multiculturalism, the position of a minority like the Arab community has been eased, politically and socially, as they are now dealing with a less unified Jewish majority. Nevertheless, the Arab sector continues to represent a challenge for the dominant culture, which is forced to contend with the conflict between the definition of the country as a Jewish state and the image of Israel as a democratic society.

Ideological Controversies

The third aspect of collective identity, the place and status of the collective in respect to "others," is also a source of conflict in Israeli society between two foci of reference that may be seen to be contradictory. On the one hand is the connection to the Jewish world that gave birth to the Zionist concept of the territorialization of

Judaism. On the other hand is the connection to the immediate environment, the Middle East, of which the new entity was fighting (and still fights) to become a part. The problematic nature of this dilemma became apparent in the early stages of the Zionist project with the coining of the term "Hebrew," used to distinguish between the Jews in the Diaspora and those in the Land of Israel, and to underscore the ancient historical link with the region. This distinction reflected a fundamental contradiction in Zionist ideology, which aspired to represent the nationalism of all Jews the world over, yet also afforded higher moral status to those who were ready to renounce the diasporic endeavor and answer the call to "return to Zion."

As early as the 1930s, several intellectuals from the more radical wing of the movement took this contradiction to its extreme conclusion and started advocating that Jews who had immigrated to Israel should cut themselves off entirely from Diaspora Jewry. They went so far as to renounce the label "Jew," declaring themselves "Canaanites," after the ancient Biblical name of the country.[5] The leader of this group, Yonatan Ratosh, insisted that the "Hebrew nation" should divorce itself forever from Jewish tradition in order to enable the "normalization" of the nation "in Zion."[6] Adopting a somewhat more moderate approach, Hillel Kook joined in the demand for a total separation between the Jews in the Diaspora and those in Israel, if only to enable the young state to develop independently. Any Jews wishing to do so could settle in Israel, but they would be required to consider themselves "Hebrews." However, the Holocaust in Europe, establishment of the State of Israel, mass immigration, and Israeli wars were to deliver a death blow to this trend, in all its varieties. These events forced the Canaanites onto the fringes of public life, just as they heightened the solidarity of world Jewry with the State of Israel.

Over time, and paradoxically enough, the Canaanite stance, with its source in anti-Diaspora right-wing Zionism, ultimately joined forces with the anti-Zionist left, which is more concerned with the Palestinian problem, within and outside Israel. Boaz Evron (1988; 1995), for instance, a Canaanite of the first order, claims that at its inception,

---

[5] See Yakov Shavit, 1984.
[6] In 1951, Ratosh founded the Young Hebrews Center whose organ, *Alef*, lobbied for a constitution that would dictate total separation between religion and state and annul the established connection between the Jews and Israel (Gorni, 1990).

Zionism was an ideology of power that sprang from the position of weakness of Diaspora Jewry. Over the years, the tables turned, and Zionism itself came to need the Diaspora in order to contend with its conflict with the Arabs. The key to unraveling this knot, according to Evron, is to alter the basis of the national definition of Israel, establishing it on the principle of territory alone, as in other countries. Only in this way can equality for all the residents of the territory of Israel, without distinction, be achieved. As long as Israel is defined as a Jewish state, the Arab minority will inevitably rebel and the Israel-Palestinian conflict will remain insoluble. Evron is not troubled by the danger for the future of Judaism that is entailed in this attitude. In fact, he anticipates that the Jews everywhere will eventually become assimilated into their surroundings in any case, save for the ultra-Orthodox who will continue to keep themselves apart. He appears insensitive to the fact that by turning his back on Jewish history, he is presenting the Israelis as a nation with no roots, and stripping them of their cultural wellsprings. In addition, he ignores the reality that fifty years after the establishment of the state and one hundred years after the birth of Zionism, Israel is still a society of first and second generation immigrants, making the question "Who is an Israeli?" as difficult to answer as "Who is a Jew?"

Nonetheless, a growing number of voices among Israeli academics and intellectuals have been calling for the "de-Zionization" of Israeli society (Ram, 1995). Yosef Agassi (1990), for example, claims that the evolution of Israeli society is leading it to the ghetto model, the exact opposite of the original intent of the Zionist project. According to Agassi, the only way to halt this regression is to promote the secular character of the country. The Israeli nation should be based on territory, and should be socially and culturally pluralistic. The Jews in Israel belong to the Israeli nation in the same way that those who reside elsewhere belong to other nations. Accordingly, the Law of Return, which allows for any Jew in the world to immigrate to Israel and become a citizen, should be revoked and there should be a distinction between religion and nationality (Agassi, Buber-Agassi, and Brant, 1991). Yonatan Shapira (1996) supports this view, contending that maintaining the connection between state and religion has always been in the interest of the secular political elite, which sought to gain legitimacy for itself through the use of religious and traditional symbols that are more "effective" for political mobilization than secular ideologies. This tactic, which perpetuated the link between

Israel and the Diaspora, irrevocably distorted the liberal nature of
Israeli democracy.

While Agassi and Shapira refrain from directly addressing the
question of the essence of the connection between Jewish identity
and the Jewish religion, their remarks were invoked in the harsh
debates of the '80s and '90s with the emergence of "post-Zionism."
The term refers to the demand not only for the "de-Zionization" of
Israel, but also the "de-Jewishization" of the Jews. In contrast to the
Canaanites, the post-Zionists are not critical of Diaspora Jewry, but
of Israeli Jews themselves, who define the country as a Jewish state
and not "the state of all its citizens." This camp focuses on the
Israeli-Palestinian conflict, placing the blame for the hostility on Israel
and Zionism. It advocates eliminating the reference to Judaism as
the basis of national identity (Furstenberg, 1995), and contends, in
the spirit of naïve materialism (Orr, 1994), that Judaism is essentially a religious belief and as such is destined to disappear—just as
all other religions will presumably disappear in the wake of the
advance of science and secular culture. In other words, they believe
that in any case, Israel will ultimately cease to exist as a Jewish state.
In the name of this conviction, "critical" sociologists and "new" historians attack those of their colleagues—whom they dub "establishment academics"—who refuse to base their scientific and research
efforts on political and ideological theories. Accusations of "conservatism," "collaboration with the political establishment," and "insen-
sitivity to social inequality" (Shalev, 1996) are commonplace in the
work of these academic "Red Guards."

The basic argument of this camp is that Israel was supposedly
created by ousting the Arabs from their lands, and this "original sin"
is enough to morally invalidate everything that has ensued from it
in Israeli society. These historians and sociologists see it as their primary function to debunk the Zionist myths, and as such, they actually act as "revisionists" trying to rewrite the history and socio-political
development of the Jewish experience in Israel. They regard all who
consider otherwise to be partners to oppression in Israeli society: the
oppression of women by men, of non-Ashkenazi Jews by the Ashkenazi,
and of non-Jewish Israelis by the Jews.

In response to this approach, Lissak (1996) accuses the "critics"
of sacrificing legitimate scientific research in favor of the politica-
lization of the scientist. He contends that as a national liberation
movement, Zionism grew out of the reality of the Diaspora, which

it sought to change by resettling the Land of Israel. Only from this perspective can we understand the Zionists' desire to establish an autonomous economy and society, distinct from the Arab population in the country. In a similar vein, Ben-Rafael (1997) shows that only the revolutionary project undertaken by the Zionists can explain phenomena such as the adoption of Hebrew as the official language of communication by people who already had a common tongue. Furthermore, only the combination of circumstances and ideological inspiration could have given birth to a utopian experiment such as the kibbutz.

The "critical" school remains unmoved by these arguments. Shafir (1996) insists that Zionism is simply a chapter in the history of European colonialism. Under this heading, he includes both the conventional sense of colonialism as the domination and direct exploitation of a native population and its resources by an external power, and what is generally called colonization, the creation of a new social order that usurps an existing system. The common denominator between these two concepts is the idea of a certain territory being taken over by an external force. The use of the term "colonialism" to describe both models, however, ignores the glaring historical-sociological fact that no colonialist regime has ever survived decolonization, whereas most of the Western world today, from Australia to the American continents, consists of formerly colonized—but not colonialist—societies. If only because of this radical difference between the two realities, there is no theoretical justification whatsoever in relating to colonialism and colonization as sub-categories of the same phenomenon.

The controversy between academic camps feeds naturally on the contradictions within Zionism and even within Judaism itself. By defining Israel as the state of the Jews, Zionism spawned complex problems: the connection between a national Jewish identity and Jewish identity per se; the connection between religion and state in a secular country; the connection between Israeli Jews and the Arabs who are also Israeli; the relations between the Israelis and the region. Yet, on all these issues, those who reject the Zionist formula have suggested answers that are plagued by contradictions which are no less acute.

In analytic, rather than ideological, terms, the question we could ask is whether it would not be more accurate at this point in time to speak of "beyond Zionism" rather than "post-Zionism." As a rule,

even those who continue to consider themselves Zionists now use
the term in a much less ambitious sense than its originators. With
most of the Jewish communities in the West having achieved established and recognized status, the delegitimization of the Diaspora
and appeal for the immediate resettlement of all Jews in the Jewish
state has long disappeared from the Zionist agenda. It might be said
that Zionism today is based primarily on the simple principle of
Jewish solidarity, a notion that, by definition, relates to Jewish identity wherever Jews are found, irrespective of adherence to the original Zionist ideology.

In Israel, Zionism is generally conceived of as the special commitment of the state to all Jews the world over. This principle, however, might be seen as a corollary of mere Jewish solidarity, in
circumstances in which the Jews constitute the overwhelming majority of the population, unlike in the Diaspora. Jewish solidarity thus
automatically includes the willingness to open the doors of the country to all Jews wishing to enter, especially if they are impelled to do
so by hardship or risk in their country of origin. This is not essentially
different from what Jews may do in New York or London when
they pressure their respective governments to come to the assistance
of Jews in need elsewhere in the world. The only difference is that
here the hands of Jews are not tied by their being a minority, but
enjoy the power of a Jewish majority in a sovereign state. It also
goes without saying that the major institutions devoted to the study
and research of Judaism and Jewish history will be found in the
country in which Jews are the dominant group, thereby affording it
the status of world center of Jewish cultural and spiritual life.

These realities are not dependent on the formality of the Law of
Return or any other declarations of intent. They are simply grounded
in the political fact of the existence of a Jewish majority—whether
or not Israel were to formally declare itself "the state of all its citizens." Moreover, as long as Judaism perpetuates, the territory itself
would continue to be the mythical "Promised Land" and to have a
special aura in the Jewish world. This is in line with the position
held by the more enlightened of the critics of Zionism, such as
Silberstein (1996), who states that the "deconstruction" of the Zionist
discourse might be a positive process whereby the intellectual space
is "freed" for new formulations that are more suitable for the present time. This is the meaning of the term "beyond Zionism."

Conflictual Multiculturalism

As we have seen, Israeli society is divided on all three aspects of collective identity. It is to this reality that David Ochana (1998) is referring when he objects to the full-scale attack being launched on "the last Israelis," the descendents and followers of the founding generation who sustain the dominant culture.

On the whole, we have also seen that most of the different formulations we have considered agree on the importance of the territorial aspect of Israeli identity, and also share a dichotomous distinction between the "Israeli nation" within its territorial borders and the rest of the Jewish world. The Canaanites, national-religious, Mizrakhim, and even Russian immigrants all subscribe to this territorial-national principle which is so central to the dominant culture, even though none of these groups entirely adheres to that culture. Consequently, we might consider these formulations to be part of a cluster of offshoots of the same national model we have already found among certain of Ben-Gurion's correspondents.

This is not to say that each of the groups does not also demand a very real concession on the part of society. The rifts that relate to the singularity of the collective, that is, the divisions between the secular and religious sectors, reveal the vulnerability of the dominant culture as it itself draws its symbols and link to the Land of Israel from the religious tradition. Although it gives them new interpretations, it does not deny their religious source.

In respect to commitment to the collective, Shas calls for the dominant culture to be formulated so as to give legitimacy to, and reflect, Middle Eastern traditions. At the same time, the Russians would like to see less of a demand for cultural unity so that they can take on Israeli Jewish identity while preserving their cultural identity and sense of community. The Israeli Arabs on their part want the dominant culture to define a general Israeli identity that would place them on equal footing with the Jewish population. These claims lay bare another vulnerability. In the name of Zionism itself, mainstream society is obliged to regard each individual Jewish culture as a national asset. Furthermore, Israeli society has always been committed to the principle of equality, a stance that inexorably creates tension when it comes to the minority status of the Arabs in a state defined as Jewish. For the same reason, the dominant culture is vulnerable to ideological attack in respect to its relations with "others." The evolution of Israeli society as multicultural is therefore also multi-conflictual, with the mainstream constituting a three-dimensional arena of tensions.

In view of the many fissures in the reality of Israeli society, we might ask whether it is possible for the different elements to exist without any "glue," or, as Touraine (1997) phrases the question in respect to the emerging multiculturalism of French society, "Can we live together?" The conflicts between the various sectors and the dominant culture inevitably require that they relate to each other. Through these conflicts, they also discover what they have in common. For example, while they are at odds on the issue of their relative status in society, both the ultra-Orthodox and the dominant culture share the same attitude toward the fact that they are Jewish, although the Judaism of the two camps is very different. Similarly, the dominant culture and the Mizrakhi community interpret Jewish nationalism in very different ways, yet for both the Israeli Jewish identity is the source of national identity. And whereas the orientation of the immigrants from the former Soviet Union is much more pluralistic and ethnic than mainstream society may be willing to accept, both sides are agreed that the former are "olim" (immigrants of Jewish descent entitled as such to immigrate), a term with considerably more significance than merely "immigrants." Finally, without disregarding the basic conflict between Arab and Jewish Israelis, both groups are very much part of modern Israeli culture. Ultimately, these similarities bind the warring elements in the arena together.

Linguistic activity illustrates this principle more vividly than any other feature. The Hebrew language is afforded different meanings, and absorbs different influences, in each group. It coexists with Yiddish among the ultra-Orthodox, with Jewish Arabic vernaculars in the Mizrakhi sector, with Russian among the immigrants from the former Soviet Union, and with Arabic among Israeli Arabs. Hebrew is, by necessity, the language of communication for the ultra-Orthodox, and is related to the sacred language whether they like it or not. It is the language of tradition for Mizrakhi Jews, who adopted it enthusiastically when they arrived in Israel. It is the language of the target population for the immigrants from the former Soviet Union, and must be learned in order to integrate into society, although it may not be the language of their media, literature, or family. It is the second language which influences the mother tongue of Israeli Arabs, encouraging their cultural "Israelization" even if it does not effect their basic identity. The national-religious consider it a mark of honor to speak Hebrew with an eloquence that evidences their respect for Jewish sources, and the "native" Israelis carrying on the sabra tradition continue to enjoy playing games of status by displaying a casual form of Hebrew interspersed, nowadays, with numerous borrowings from English. These distinctions in the use of Hebrew, and the different values it has acquired in each sector of the population, reflect the complexity of Israeli society. The most important fact to remember, however, is that Hebrew today is a thriving language that serves as a common base for the entire society, and by virtue of which that society is both a single entity and multicultural at one and the same time.

CHAPTER FOUR

JEWISH IDENTITIES IN THE DIASPORA—THE CASE OF AMERICA

Social Achievements and Demographic Risks

The preceding chapter demonstrates the relation between the numerous contemporary definitions of Jewish identity in Israel and the national model that had already been articulated by some of Ben-Gurion's correspondents. We now turn our attention to the contemporary Diaspora in an attempt to learn whether a similar continuity can be discerned there. We focus specifically on the United States, which has been the foremost Jewish community for several decades. Not only is it home to one-third of the Jews in the world, but it has also produced the strongest Jewish institutions, organizations, and enterprises anywhere outside of Israel.

Representing a relatively significant and vigorous sector of the population, the Jews in America enjoy firmly established social status. They have achieved prominence in significant fields, including the liberal professions, the sciences, the arts, business, and politics. Most belong to the middle or upper-middle class and reside in high-status towns and neighborhoods. In the opinion of Lipset and Raab (1995), this success derives primarily from a cultural convergence between America's dominant culture and the original orientations of its Jewish population. Puritanism, achievement orientation, and universalistic perspectives that typify the culture prevailing in America are not alien to the attitudes that characterized many a Jewish immigrant from Eastern Europe, where frugality and material success were highly valued. One of the many signs of the great popularity of the United States among European Jews was the translation into Yiddish of the writings of Benjamin Franklin, which appeared as far back as around 1800. Another highly significant convergence between the two cultures is the emphasis on education. As early as the start of the 20th century (1908), when the Jews constituted less than 2% of the American population, they already represented 8% of the college students, a trend that has continued to this day.

These features have contributed to the successful integration of the Jews into society. Today they account for 2.5% of the American population, but no less than 50% of the most noted intellectuals, 40% of the American Nobel Prize laureates in the sciences and economics, and 20% of the professors in the leading universities. In the course of time, the Jews have also become the wealthiest ethnic group in the U.S., with the average family income in the late 1980s being twice that of the non-Jewish population.[1] This social mobility has been accompanied by geographical mobility (Goldstein and Goldstein, 1996). In the early part of the 20th century, the large majority of Jews were concentrated in the northeast; by the final decades of the century, they could be found throughout the country. Wherever they settled, they tended to prefer prestigious sections with a high percentage of Jews. The social significance of these facts is made clear by the Jewish demographics in America.

According to the National Jewish Population Survey of 1990, at that time there were around 3.2 million households in the U.S. in which at least one member was a Jew or former Jew. Altogether, these families numbered 8.2 million individuals. Of these, 4.4 million declared themselves Jewish by religion, including 185,000 "Jews by choice" (the term used for converts). Another 1.1 million stated that they were "secular Jews" with no religion, bringing the total to 5.5 million people, representing the core of the Jewish population in America.[2] An additional 210,000 converts to Christianity were identified, as well as 415,000 individuals of Jewish extraction who were members of other religions, 700,000 children of Jewish descent being brought up in other religions, and 1,350,000 non-Jews who lived with Jews (Goldstein, 1992).

These figures are an indication of just how blurred the social

[1] According to Lipset and Raab (1995), in the 1980s, Jews constituted 21% of senior public officials; 40% of the partners in the leading law firms in New York and Washington D.C.; 26% of the journalists and editors of the major media organizations; 59% of the directors, writers, and producers of the most popular television series; 50% of the forty richest families in America (1982) and 23% of the 400 richest; and 7.4% of the directors of the largest companies (1986), 13% of them under the age of 40.

[2] According to Kosmin and Schekner (1995), the population that might be defined as the mainstream of American Jewry numbered 5,900,000 in 1994. The researchers claim the increase can be attributed to Jewish immigrants from the former Soviet Union, who arrive each year in the U.S. in the numbers allowed by the official quota (40,000).

boundaries between Jews and non-Jews are in America. Because Jews tend to live in fashionable sections in which the population is mixed and they are typically in the minority, they are given numerous opportunities for contact with non-Jews. Moreover, the overwhelming majority of Jewish children attend college, where contact with non-Jews is an integral part of routine reality. These facts may explain the high proportion of mixed marriages—about 60% in recent years. This statistic falls to a little over 50% if we subtract the cases in which the non-Jewish spouse converts, and to around 40% if we subtract the marriages in which the wife is Jewish and the husband is not (Lipset and Raab, 1995).

According to research estimates (Wertheimer, 1993), at the end of the 1980s, in one-sixth to one-third of the families throughout the country who were raising their children as Jews, one of the parents was not born Jewish. If that parent had converted, he or she had generally done so in a non-Orthodox framework where conversion is easier. Some chose the Reform movement specifically because it recognizes children as Jewish on the basis of both matrilineal and patrilineal descent (and not only matrilineal as dictated by halakha). Consequently, the largest number of conversions is usually performed by Reform rabbis, a smaller number by Conservative rabbis, and the fewest by Orthodox rabbis (Goldscheider, 1986). In addition, while one of the parents in slightly more than a quarter of all Jewish families (27%) was not Jewish, only a little over 5% of these people undergoes conversion.[3] Furthermore, as a rule interfaith marriages are associated more with divorce, fewer children, and less of an emphasis on the Jewish identity of the Jewish spouse (DellaPergola and Shmeltz, 1989, 1989a).[4]

---

[3] Goldscheider (1986) adds that a third of the Jews who married in the '80s wed non-Jews. A mixed marriage in which the non-Jewish partner did not convert greatly weakened the desire of the children to be Jewish: 65% of the children of a non-Jewish parent who converted wished to be Jewish, whereas the number drops to only 26% when the parent did not convert. In families where the non-Jewish parent had converted, 15% of the children had never been in a synagogue, and 27% had not been bar-mitzvahed. The figures in families where the parent had not undergone conversion are 73% and 81% respectively (Wertheimer, 1993).

[4] Medding (1987) found considerable similarity between homogenous families and heterogeneous families in which the non-Jewish spouse had converted: in both cases, one-sixth displayed "low identification" with Judaism; around one-half "moderate identification," and some one-third "high identification." In contrast, about 70% of the families in which the non-Jewish partner had not converted were characterized by "low identification." This trend is most prominent in the non-Orthodox streams:

However, there is much more to be said about "Jews by choice." McLain (1996) describes their contribution to the Jewish community in the U.S. in very positive terms. She depicts them as devoted members of their temple who are often on its steering committee or Torah readers, and who, on the whole, may well be the "best Jews in the family." Women who have converted, she found, prepare the Sabbath and encourage the other members of their families to study Jewish history. Many tell of "discovering" a Jewish grandmother or grandfather. An important factor in this dynamic is the prominence of Jews in American society, a feature that accounts largely for their appeal. According to McLain, in 1996 there were some two hundred thousand Jews in America who had not been born or had not been brought up as Jews, and by the year 2010, she estimates they will represent from 7% to 10% of all the Jews in the U.S.

Although proselytizing per se is a bone of contention among the various Jewish denominations, conversion in the U.S. is, in fact, a firmly established procedure, with all the denominations generally maintaining special conversion centers.[5] Rabbi Alexander Schindler, a leader of the Reform movement, represents those who support "gaining souls" through conversion and regularly calls for proselytizing among the Christians. The late Conservative Rabbi Robert Gordis also favored returning Judaism to its role as a "light unto

---

"high identification" was displayed by some two-thirds of the Orthodox families, but only 43–48% of the Conservative and 25% of the Reform. In the case of heterogeneous families in which the non-Jewish spouse did not convert, the rate of "moderate identification" drops to 5% for the Conservative and 2% for the Reform. Sixty-two percent of all heterogeneous families showed some degree of identification with both Jewish and Christian symbols, in contrast to 20% of the families in which conversion had occurred.

[5] The centers run by the Reform Movement interpret the principle of taking on the yoke of the commandments mainly in the sense of commitment to the Jewish community. Some Reform rabbis do not even require a candidate for conversion to appear before a rabbinical court or to undergo circumcision. In the past decade, however, the movement appears to be becoming somewhat stricter in order to ensure that its converts are recognized by the rabbis of the other denominations. Conservative institutions, such as the Conservative Center for Conversion to Judaism in Teaneck, New Jersey, tend to demand observance of the commandments and circumcision. Most allow the candidate to choose between individual or class study. They expect the convert to observe the laws of kashrut and the Sabbath, and lay particular stress on learning the tenets of Judaism. Among the Orthodox, preparation for conversion is always one-on-one, with the candidate maintaining an intense connection with an ordained rabbi. The Orthodox rabbi expects converts to observe all the commandments, although he is aware that, like Jews by birth, they will not lose their Jewish identity if they do not do so.

the nations," encouraging the opening of Jewish information offices throughout the U.S. and elsewhere. Some of his followers have launched aggressive publicity campaigns.[6] Others, particularly among the Orthodox, object to this approach on the grounds that it gives legitimacy to mixed marriages and eventually turns people away from Judaism. As they see it, interfaith marriages brought into the world thousands of children whose Judaism is superficial and suspect.

A Religion of Congregations

American Jewry as a whole is thus far from constituting a homogeneous entity. It contains a profusion of streams producing a Jewish pluralism that seems to duplicate the pluralism of American society itself. At one pole of this community is the ultra-Orthodox sector, representing a small minority of the Jewish population in the U.S. To this day, the group sees its principal role in total commitment to faith and a steadfast preservation of Jewish life in order to bring "redemption" closer. The ultra-Orthodox extol devotion to religious studies, and consider their yeshivot to be the jewel in the crown of Jewish aspirations even today. The only thing of importance for the ultra-Orthodox is study and observance of the commandments. The ultra-Orthodox in America, like the original founders of Agudat Israel, are dedicated to upholding traditional Judaism, and invest their greatest efforts in surviving in contemporary times. Accordingly, they make only the smallest possible concessions to the modern world.

Nevertheless, this community is also beset by controversy. For example, while all agree that the Jewish people are connected for all eternity to "the Land of Israel," there are those who would extend this concept to include any place where "we are at peace with God" (Gutenmacher, 1991).

In times of crisis in the Middle East, the ultra-Orthodox usually support Israel within the context of American politics, but they do so without giving up their struggle against secular Zionism. Agudat

---

[6] For example, Rabbi Silver of Southern Florida published advertisements covering several pages of the *New York Times* and *New York Magazine* lauding the "Christians for Moses," an organization that defines itself as Christian but denies that Jesus was the Messiah. In 1994, a course of study was advertised in an even blunter fashion under the heading "The Meaning of Judaism: Are you Curious?" In its first years, the course had thousands of students in twenty cities.

Israel, the roof organization for all ultra-Orthodox groups, denies that the existence of the State of Israel has any theological significance. Many consider living in Israel a virtuous act only in the sense that the country is a part of the Promised Land and is populated by Jews. These people are willing to support Israel morally and financially only in order to promote the adoption of the Torah as the country's constitution. At the same time, however, the Gur community, the largest of the Hassidic sects, expresses firm solidarity with Israel, while the Habad movement takes an active interest in Israeli foreign and security affairs.

The modern Orthodox sharply contrast—and even clash—with the ultra-Orthodox over the question of what sort of compromises to make with modern life and their willingness to find new solutions to the halakhic problems that constantly arise in all areas of life, such as sex life, the status of women, medicine, dress, Sabbath observance, and so on. Following the German Jewish philosophers of the 19th and 20th centuries, they see themselves as an integral part of the modern world in which they wish to maintain their loyalty to religious law. While these communities today account for no more than ten percent of organized Jewry in America, they are widely held in respect: for a goodly proportion of secular Jews, it is, in fact, the modern Orthodox synagogue which they have in mind when they refer to the "synagogue which they do not attend regularly" and which remains, for them, the "natural" house of prayer, and the place where they get circumcised, bar mitzvahed or married.

On the other hand, modern Orthodoxy is also in conflict with Conservative Judaism, let alone Reform Judaism, which do not feel committed to the integral retention of halakhic demands. Indeed, the same issue is also the source of heated debates within these latter movements themselves. One subject of contention among the Conservatives, for instance, has been whether or not women could be counted in a minyan, the quorum of ten individuals required for communal prayer. This controversy eventually developed into the question of whether women could perform ritual duties, up to and including the office of rabbi. It was only in the 1980s that a prayer book and a practical guide written by Isaac Klein were approved and, together with a rabbinical declaration of principles (*Emet ve-Emouna*—Truth and Faith) heralded a new era for the movement. These works contain a reevaluation of halakha from a historical-dynamic perspective, leading to the nullification of numerous religious laws. The new approach welcomes Jewish pluralism and gives legitimacy to the different attitudes of those who are more or less liberal or who accept the authority of halakha to a greater or lesser degree. It denies the principle of the Jews as the Chosen People, and avers an openness of mind to "non-Jewish wisdom." Such flexibility may explain the prominent place of the Conservative movement in Jewish life in America (some 35% of organized Jewry) and the strength of its institutions—synagogues, schools, youth movements or charity organizations (Wertheimer, 1993). The very strength of the Conservative movement was, however, to spawn a new group, the Reconstructionists, who aspire to forms of religious experience unfettered by institutionalization. This new trend accounts for about 2% of organized American Jewry.[7] In its view, involvement in the congregation is a central value of Judaism. Under the heading of havura, or intimate community, it encourages the shared responsibility of all members of the congregation for any matters on the collective agenda, and deems the religious experience to be both individual and collective.

As for the Reform movement, it too has been most successful in strengthening its position in U.S. Jewry, representing today some 30% of organized Jewry and relegating the Orthodox to a lower status. The Reform movement was the first to grant women the right to serve as rabbis and cantors, and in recent years has gone so far as to afford reserved recognition to homosexual congregations. Paradoxically, the movement has also been resurrecting some of the traditional rituals it previously renounced: greater emphasis is being placed on Hebrew, and men are again being required to cover their heads in temple. Some Reform rabbis have even renewed the demand to observe kashrut. In addition, increasing stress is being laid on Israel and solidarity with world Jewry. All of these issues have naturally aroused considerable controversy, ultimately spawning an array of factions, among them Progressive Reform Judaism. According to Furman (1994), the primary role of the Reform temple is the "sacralizing" of Jewish identity, conceived of as innately associated with political liberalism on the one hand, and prophetic Jewish tradition on the other.

---

[7] The Reconstructionists officially split with the Conservative movement in 1963 with the establishment of an independent congregation in New York, followed by its own rabbinical seminary in 1968. Nevertheless, in actuality the group continues to operate in certain instances within the framework of the Conservative movement.

Even beyond the Reform movement, the Jews of America have created a wide range of groups who wish to some degree or another to devise a formulation of Judaism that would divorce it from religion or, at least, religiosity. The most prominent example is Secular Humanistic Judaism, which was founded in 1965 in Detroit and gained somewhat in popularity in the '90s. The congregations allied with this movement number around thirty thousand members, most in the U.S. (Cohn-Sherbok, 1996). As its name implies, the group's ideology assumes a world in which no divine force intervenes, and centers around the belief in the human mind, the power of the individual to determine his or her fate, and the supreme value of human dignity and liberty. According to this approach, the distinction of Judaism lies in its constant battle to ensure its identity and survival. Judaism is defined as a culture with its own languages, ethics, traditions, and historical memories. At the same time, the movement champions democracy, liberalism, and the separation of religion and state, and critically applies the same principle to Israel. In this formulation of Jewish identity, the memory of the Holocaust and Jewish solidarity, as well as the place of the State of Israel, acquire particular significance. The Torah is regarded as a document created in a specific social and cultural context, and Jewish truth as essentially no different from the truth of other religions; rather, it represents a Jewish experience that does not invalidate other experiences. Thus pluralistic in essence, the movement rejects the absolute authority of halakha, and is most profoundly disturbed by the notion of the Jews as the Chosen People. To its mind, the belief in the coming of the Messiah should be interpreted as the aspiration of humankind at large. As the group regards the God and Torah of Israel as solely cultural and ethical concepts, it suggests that Judaism should be seen as a historical-cultural entity with universal values. This variety of Judaism is much in line with American culture and its insistence on universal human values.

What all these different streams seem to have in common, save for the ultra-Orthodox, is their reference to Judaism in terms of a "congregation," mirroring the concept of "peoplehood." Whereas this principle is stated most explicitly by the Reconstructionists, it exists to a certain extent in each of the denominations. Clearly, it reflects the influence of American culture, which, as a liberal culture that advocates open social borders among communities, encourages each ethno-cultural group to promote its own values. It is in this context that the Jewish congregations, and particularly the non-Orthodox branches, are motivated to define flexible boundaries for their communities. The best—and most extreme—example of this influence is the practice common in certain congregations of having a rabbi and a minister officiate at interfaith weddings.

With the exception of the ultra-Orthodox and those of the Orthodox who propound the caste model, what is really at stake for American Jewry is the viability of a unique Jewish culture. The different denominations adopt a variety of definitions that attach universal contents to specifically Jewish symbols, indicating that the Jews in the U.S. regard themselves not only as full citizens, but as citizens who are loyal to the American ethos. At the same time, they see themselves as members of a particular community, part of an entity that goes beyond national borders both in time, to a traditional past, and in place, to the Jewish people worldwide.

The Future at Issue

No less than three-quarters of the Jews in America state that they attend synagogue at least once a year, and around a third declare themselves to be members of some sort of Jewish community organization. When asked to explain what Judaism means to them, over one-half reply that the Jews are first and foremost "a religious community," while about one-fifth describe themselves as "secular." Only one quarter of the respondents maintain no connection with any Jewish institution and perform no religious rituals. Thus the majority respects Jewish ceremonies as part of an ancient honored tradition.[8] On the other hand, the Jews are also conscious of the existence

---

[8] Ritterband and Cohen (1984) show that in New York, for example, no less than nine Jewish households out of ten conduct a Passover seder; some two-thirds also light candles at Hanukkah, attach a mezuzah to their doorpost, and fast on Yom Kippur. One-third of the households light Sabbath candles, separate milk and meat dishes, and eat only kosher meat. While only 12% state that they do not handle money on the Sabbath, three quarters of the Jews in New York identify with a particular Jewish denomination: the majority with the Conservatives, a smaller number with the Reform movement, and the fewest with the Orthodox. Two-thirds of the respondents also declare that they received a Jewish education, and about a half state that they send their children to some type of Jewish school, whether a yeshiva, a Jewish day school, or Sunday school classes. The overwhelming majority (70%) indicate that their three closest friends are Jewish, and around 40% have been to Israel at least once.

of anti-Semitism in their environment: one-half regard it as a very real problem, and another quarter tend to agree with this statement. For many, this awareness is associated with anti-Israeli sentiments.[9]

In an attempt to identify historical trends, Lipset and Raab describe a process in which old-timers tend to assimilate into the non-Jewish population and leave Jewish concerns to new groups: the Jews who immigrated during the colonial period were already assimilated by around 1800, and the same process occurred among the German Jews who arrived eighty years later. This pattern was repeated with the waves of Jewish immigrants who settled in the U.S. in the late 19th and early 20th centuries, and who disappeared from the Jewish scene with the arrival of Eastern European Jews after World War II. The latter would also have assimilated if it were not for the Six Day War in 1967, which awoke unprecedented solidarity with Israel out of the apprehension that the country was being threatened by a repeat of the Holocaust. However, in the 1980s, material prosperity and social achievements again strengthened the tendency of American Jews to loosen their ties to their community. Lipset and Raab note that the National Jewish Population Survey of 1990 revealed a serious erosion of Jewish identity. For instance, only a minority of Jews (20%) continued to object to interfaith marriages for their children.

This state of affairs is reminiscent of Beller's (1989) description of the Jews in Vienna prior to World War II, many of whom had achieved financial and professional success and sought to take advantage of this status to overcome discrimination and assimilate into Christian society. Alderman (1989) paints a similar picture of the Jews in London after the war, who displayed prodigious social mobility and were eager to acquire the respect and approval of the elite, even at the price of indifference to Jewish interests.

Nonetheless, in the eyes of many a commentator, the American Jewish community continues to reveal an outstanding concern for its Judaism. Cooperman (1993) shows that increased Jewish presence in

---

[9] The researchers conclude that the 25% of Jews in America who are not connected to any Jewish institutions or religious organizations are also less concerned about the status of Jews. Their Jewish identity tends to be "nostalgic," without any sense of commitment. At the other extreme, 25% see antisemitism as a real danger, and also maintain a connection with an organized Jewish congregation and perform religious rituals. The remainder of the respondents fall somewhere in between these two poles (Lipset and Raab, 1995).

American universities is making its mark in the form of an impressive spurt in Jewish studies. At the end of the 20th century, there was hardly a university in the country without faculty members specializing in subjects such as Jewish history, the world of the Bible, Jewish philosophy, and other related fields. The large majority of courses, however, were taught on the introductory level, and most of the students were interested in taking no more than one or two of these courses as part of their studies for a different major. Only a very few were actually majoring in Jewish studies. Furthermore, the faculty members teaching these courses were university professors in every sense of the word, representing a critical scientific approach without regard for the moral-educational aspects of their subjects. Very few saw Judaism as a set of values they wished to pass on to the younger generation. Proponents of the Jewish principle of religious studies could only be found in small numbers in yeshivot and rabbinical seminaries. Still, practically every academic publisher issues at least one series of Jewish studies, and a growing number of academic conferences are devoted to Jewish subjects.

With these facts in mind, Glazer (1987), unlike Lipset and Raab, depicts American Jewry in terms of transformation rather than assimilation (see also: Cohen and Fein, 1985; Goldscheider, 1986). Following Sklare, Glazer notes that while Jewish parents are increasingly foregoing their opposition to interfaith marriages, around one half of their sons and daughters, including those born to mixed marriages, are receiving a Jewish education. Although many may be losing a profound sense of Jewish identity, they continue to identify with Judaism on the symbolic level. In effect, the religious and ethnic pluralism typical of American culture enables Jews to feel comfortable as one of many groups in the country. Due to the basic American tolerance for difference, the Jews are encouraged to maintain their particular identity, even if they are not able to provide a precise definition of Judaism.

Researchers have also found that Israel serves as an important element in reinforcing Jewish identity. Here too, however, opinions are divided. The collection of articles edited by Gorni (1990) presents a wide range of views. The Zionist approach, represented by Reform Rabbi Richard Hirsch, claims that the State of Israel was founded by the Jewish people, who must continue to ensure its survival as the basis of Jewish existence even in the Diaspora. Benjamin Halpern, a celebrated American Jewish intellectual, states that Israel is the hub of the Jewish world, and will remain so as long as it maintains its secular character and disassociates itself from denominational rivalries. Arthur Herzberg, a leader of the Conservative movement, contends that despite the success of the Jews in integrating themselves into American society—and indeed, they are very much "at home" in America—Judaism itself is still in the Diaspora. Mordecai Kaplan speaks of American Jewry as a world Jewish center alongside Israel. Stanley Lowell also finds two major Jewish identities in the world today: the national-territorial Israeli identity and the religious identity in the Diaspora. Even more decidedly "diasporistic" attitudes are expressed by other thinkers, such as Eugene Borowitz from the Reform movement's Hebrew Union College in New York, who highlights the universal nature of Judaism and concludes that Israel is a significant, but not necessary, condition of Jewish existence. Emmanuel Scherer, the head of the American Bund, speaks of the international links among Jews, and considers the U.S. to be the main Jewish center. Reform Rabbi Julius Morgenstern claims that the Jews are united primarily by their common history, rather than by any political reality at a given point in time. Others call for an end to the cultural-political hegemony of Israel over the Jewish world, while organizations such as Breira (choice) and the New Jewish Agenda go so far as to espouse the value of Jewish life in the Diaspora.

But intellectual constructs do not necessarily reflect the opinions of the "man in the street." The large majority of American Jews look on Israel as some sort of "homeland," and perhaps even a potential political haven. The fact that most of the Jews in the U.S. do not define themselves as Zionists does not prevent them from seeing Israel as the focus of "tribal" Jewish solidarity (Ellenson, 1993; Gilboa, 1986). Gilboa demonstrates that as early as the mid-'40s, some 80% of American Jews supported the establishment of the State of Israel. Since that time, support and sympathy for the country have virtually become a matter of consensus.[10] Nevertheless, Waxman

---

[10] In 1983, for example, 91% described themselves as "pro-Israeli," and a significant majority regarded the possibility of the destruction of Israel as "a serious personal loss." In 1967, on the eve of the Six Day War, tens of thousands were ready to volunteer to fight for the country, and fundraising for Israel broke all records. The same responses were also found in traditionally anti-Zionist groups, from the Bund to the ultra-Orthodox.

(1991) notes that the Jews in the U.S. are more pro-Israeli than Zionist: they support the existence of the country and the opportunity for any Jews wishing to do so to settle there, but they do not regard immigration to Israel as an ideological obligation.[11]

In fact, for several years there has been growing support in major Jewish circles for the view that a pro-Israeli stance goes hand in hand with their concern for Jewish interests in the U.S. The neoconservatives, for example, were severely hurt by the attacks on the Jews by African-American organizations in the '60s and '70s, after the central Jewish institutions had been firm supporters of the civil rights movement for decades. These attacks led to a great deal of soul-searching, and ultimately resulted in increased determination to promote Jewish interests, with these circles now advocating aggressive political action on behalf of Israel.

However, the Jews, and particularly the liberal groups active in the political arena, must also contend with difficulties on other levels. Their solidarity with Israel frequently leads to misunderstandings on the part of their non-Jewish partners on the left, who generally tend to side with the critics of Israel in the name of the Palestinian cause (Feingold, 1995). The conventional self-definition of the Jews as a religious group also raises the eyebrows of leftist liberals, who, as a rule, do not see a natural link between liberalism and religion. This problem led the writer William Herberg to spell out the rationale for the connection between the Jewish religion and democratic liberal philosophy in *Judaism and Modern Man* (1951). He himself became religious after years of adherence to the radical Marxist camp (Dalin, 1995).

Cultural Ethnicity

All in all, as in the case of Israel, in the U.S. too there is considerable controversy surrounding the question of collective Jewish

---

[11] After the U.N. adopted the 1975 resolution equating Zionist with racism, however, many Jewish leaders started to define themselves as "Zionists" (Waxman, 1991). While only 5–12% of the Jews in America were willing to consider the possibility of actually immigrating, the overwhelming majority expressed solidarity with Israel and supported it in the Middle East conflict. Similar results were found for other issues on the international agenda: over three-quarters believed that the Israeli incursion into Lebanon in 1982 was justified, and in 1984 about one-half stated that Israel should retain control of the whole of the West Bank in any future settlement.

identity, primarily the singularity of the collective and commitment to the collective. There is little difference of opinion in respect to the place and status of the collective, as nearly everyone agrees that Jewish identity here exists side by side with national American identity. For most groups, the connection with Judaism is part of the pattern of being an American. In general terms, the major differences on the various points may be summarized as follows:

- *Commitment to the Jewish people*: membership in the Jewish collective is largely reflected in the U.S. by some sort of association with a community framework that makes it possible to promote a variety of internal and external interests. This connection affords the Jews the status of an organized ethnic-cultural group, one of many such groups in American society, and leaves flexible social boundaries that are open in both directions, contributing to a certain lack of clear definition.
- *The singularity of the collective*: the God and Torah of Israel are open to a large number of contradictory interpretations by the various branches of Judaism and are the basis of what might be called a secondary Jewish pluralism within the broader primary pluralism of American society. With the exception of the ultra-Orthodox and modern Orthodox, denominations share an emphasis on universal Jewish content that endows Judaism with a mission in America and the world over.
- *The place of the collective*: the Jews in the U.S. are keenly aware of being, above all, part of American society. "At home" in the U.S., they do not regard it as a "Gola" and at most use the term in a metaphoric sense. At the same time, a very large proportion of American Jews believe in solidarity with the Jewish people in general, and with the Jews in Israel in particular. Israel is perceived as representing a kind of territorial origin and Jewish national symbols that are significant as such for all Jews.

Save for Orthodox communities, and especially the ultra-Orthodox, the most prominent of the three aspects of Jewish identity among American Jews is the commitment to "the Jewish people." The singularity of the collective, as defined by the formulations of the various denominations, comes second. The territorial aspect, the Land of Israel, is relegated to third place as a result of their self-perception as Americans.

Here, too, the issue of language faithfully reflects the basic features

of the social rifts in American Jewry. Yiddish, the original tongue of
most American Jews, has almost disappeared, preserved only in the
ultra-Orthodox community. Instead, English, the national language,
is the major, and often the only, tongue employed. This is a clear
sign that the Jews perceive themselves as an integral part of American
society and are reluctant to set their community apart by using a
language that would isolate them from their surroundings. By adopting this attitude, they evidence the crucial difference between themselves and their Eastern European forefathers, most of whom lived
in insular enclaves. At the same time, however, Hebrew is still used
in the synagogue, and it is learned in Jewish education as the symbolic language of the Jew. This warrants the acquisition by no few
individuals of a more or less restricted register of Hebrew words and
expressions that may serve as markers of Jewishness, through code-
switching, in relevant speech situations.

All these approaches are allied with the ethno-cultural model we
found in the letters of Ben-Gurion's correspondents in the mid-20th
century. More than ever before, however, the American versions of
these formulations exhibit a highly selective attitude toward the question of which of the traditional symbols of Judaism to conserve and
which to discard. This selectivity has given rise to the claim that
within a few short decades, Judaism will be the province of historians
alone, a "thing of the past" (Lipset and Raab, 1995). One might
contend, on the other hand, that at a time when different models
of Judaism are fighting for dominance, the debates and rivalries
themselves are breathing life into the public Jewish arena. Moreover,
the current state of affairs is an indication of the wide range of forms
that the ethno-cultural syndrome can take.

Alongside the ethno-cultural model, however, we have also seen
that the U.S. today is home to modern Orthodox and ultra-Orthodox
communities as well. The latter in particular continue to represent
a very real alternative to ethno-cultural attitudes. Their communities are centered around religious institutions, and their greatest
resources are channeled to maintaining their patterns of life and
study in a modern society that regards them as an esoteric phenomenon. Above all, they wish to perpetuate their traditional way
of life in terms of dress, ritual, and study. Still communicating among
themselves in Yiddish, they find numerous opportunities to express
their unbreakable link to their Eastern European roots. At the same
time, however, to this day the different ultra-Orthodox communities

remain distinct from one another, each faithful to the views of its individual leader or particular tradition. Nevertheless, they maintain close ties among themselves and with their counterparts throughout the world.

Despite the conspicuous hallmarks which convey a sense of difference and alienation to outsiders, the ultra-Orthodox have also learned the national language and use it. Willingly or otherwise, they have undergone a certain "Americanization" and adapted to their environment, not hesitating even to enter the public arena and attempt to sway local and national politicians. Highly sensitive to their status within the Jewish world as well, the ultra-Orthodox offer educational and cultural institutions aimed at attracting Jews who have "strayed," still struggling to contend with the crisis that stripped them of their hegemony with the coming of the modern era. Thus at the start of the 21st century, the ultra-Orthodox communities (in the U.S., Israel, and elsewhere) continue, albeit in a more flexible manner than in the past, to uphold the old caste syndrome which already characterized Orthodoxy in the 19th century and again appeared in the letters to Ben-Gurion in the middle of the 20th century.

This syndrome, however, is but one of several. For American Jews, be they ultra-Orthodox, Orthodox, Conservative, Reform or secular, as full citizens of an open, democratic, modern, and non-Jewish society, being Jewish demands that each individual define for him or herself the meanings of Judaism. Only through this subjective effort can they clarify for themselves how and how much they wish to embody their Jewish identity. These decisions, which are not necessarily irreversible or unalterable, serve to define for the individual what for him or her is relevant to being Jewish. They make up a complex psychological process that is often lengthy and tortuous, and depict Jewish identity as evolving out of reflection (Cohen, 2000).

In contrast, the Jewish identity of Israeli Jews is primarily anchored in a collective condition. They are Jews first of all because they are members of a collective whose Jewish national identity is taken as a given. Although like all identities, it too is defined by the individuals who are committed to the collective, one of its major aspects lies in the fact that it appears to its adherents as the predominant feature of a society that exists in its own right and is perpetuated by an independent school system, political agenda, and public discourse. As social reality, this type of Jewish identity does not require individual soul-searching; it simply expresses the individual's being part of the

Jewish Israeli nation. Thus, debates over the meaning and demands
of Jewish identity focus on the aims, attitudes, or objectives of the
collective, and pertain to the national public sphere. They actually
divide the polity into rival factions, more or less along ideological
lines, which, to be sure, is not to say that the controversies are not
intense, especially in view of the acute collective challenges repeatedly facing Israel society in the form of wars, mass immigration,
internal rifts, the peace process, etc. All these differentiate the sociological or political meanings of Israeli Jewishness from the psychological or reflective significance of contemporary Diaspora Jewishness.

These distinctions between Israeli and American Jewry illustrate
the differences between the national and ethno-cultural syndromes
of Jewish identity in all their many varieties. Ethnic Jewish identity
is the blend that results from an individual being both Jewish and
a member of a non-Jewish nation. It means standing out as a Jew
within a non-Jewish collective to which one owes primary allegiance.
National Israeli Jewish identity means being a Jew because one is
part of a Jewish nation. While the former is open to "others" and
aspires to coexist with them, the latter relates principally to the sui
generis collective experience. We might speak here of a "psychological" Jewish identity formed by reflection in contrast to a "sociological" identity formed within a collective condition.

The third formula, the caste syndrome, can be found in both
Israel and the U.S. This model seemingly represents a more consistent formulation of identity than the others. Indeed, on both sides
of the Atlantic, the ultra-Orthodox reveal a pattern of commitment
to the Jewish faith from which all other aspects of Jewish identity
derive. We have seen, however, that even within this syndrome, circumstances have created new tendencies. The ultra-Orthodox in the
U.S. may question the future return to Zion in the geographical
sense or propose new metaphoric interpretations, while in Israel they
display a tendency to rub shoulders with their environment and adopt
Hebrew. In other words, although the caste syndrome is still alive
and kicking in the Jewish world, in the U.S. the ultra-Orthodox seem
to be drawing closer to the ethno-cultural syndrome in some respects,
whereas in Israel they exhibit certain features of the national syndrome.

CHAPTER FIVE

DIVERGENCE AND CONVERGENCE OF JEWISH IDENTITIES

Beyond Traditional Identity

A conceptual framework based on the notion of the "space of identity" has been used in the all-above to clarify the distinctions between
and within the different formulations of Jewish identity. Using this
framework, we have considered the different models of identity and
the ways in which they evolve, converge, and diverge. We have seen
that beyond the differences between eras and schools of thought, all
traditional attitudes share three basic principles or deep structures.
The first is the primordial sense of belonging to a single collective
with common patriarchs and matriarchs, embodied in the concept
of "the Jewish people." The second is the perception of the singularity and purpose of the collective, or loyalty to what we have called
"the God and Torah of Israel." The third principle relates to the
place or status of the collective vis-à-vis "others," which in this case
defines everything outside "the Land of Israel" as "exile." While
these three principles give rise to basic dilemmas, interpreted literally, they delineate a sort of "superior caste" with a destiny whose
realization depends solely on the actions of the members of the collective itself.

These principles of traditional Jewish identity have served in our
discussion as criteria for examining the new streams in Judaism that
emerged when traditional society began to crumble. The unequivocal assertions of the caste model became questions that could be
answered in many different ways: What is the nature of the collective commitment of those who now define themselves as members
of "the Jewish people"? How do these Jews interpret the meaning
of "the God and Torah of Israel," or more generally, how do they
view what it is that makes them a "special" entity? What image do
they hold of their connection to "the Land of Israel" and the status of the collective in relation to "others"? The responses have been
framed by moral attitudes, life experience, and historical circumstances,

all of which may be given different weight in different times, places, and circles. Clearly, then, Jewish identity is not a uniform pattern, and each of its formulations is relatively closer to or farther from the others. This is what is meant by "space of identity" to which the different formulations belong as long as they share, to whatever extent, what Wittgenstein (1961) labels "family resemblance." Even if they do not furnish similar answers to the basic questions of identity, they must at least address the same questions. Provided they do so, they cannot be considered totally alien to each other.

When we apply this principle to the formulations of Jewish identity that emerged with the disintegration of traditional society, we find that the "post-traditional" definitions are still grappling with the same dilemmas: affiliation with the Jewish people vs. affiliation with general society; cultural universalism vs. particularism; longing for the Promised Land vs. loyalty to the country of residence. Although certain groups continue to struggle to preserve traditional Judaism, new groups appear alongside, or in opposition, to them, and gain in strength. Table 5.1 summarizes the six varieties of Jewish identity that dominated the Jewish world up to the beginning of the 20th century.

Even Orthodox Judaism, which has always aimed to preserve Jewish tradition and to ensure that its tenets endure, has not been averse to adopting modern political models in order to contend with the situation in which they represent only a minority of the Jews. In Germany, more so than in Eastern Europe, the Orthodox eagerly accepted the challenge of devising a form of Judaism that would go hand in hand with the philosophy of modern man. The Enlightenment movement similarly did not question traditional faith, but rather linked Judaism to rationalism, advocating the incorporation of modern values into Jewish education. It insisted on the need to learn the local language, while viewing Hebrew as the "natural" language for secular Jewish literature. Taking a more drastic approach, the Reform movement questioned the authority of halakha, redefining Judaism as a social/cultural phenomenon. Conservative Judaism took the middle road, while the formulation of Jewish identity offered by the Bund wavered between universalism and particularism and foundered on the debate over how much it was an integral part of the world revolutionary camp and how much a part of the distinct Jewish experience. Zionism proffered a nationalist formula, attributing supreme importance to the Land of Israel as a national territory.

Table 5.1: Modern Formulations of Jewish Identity

	Commitment: "the Jewish people"	Singularity: "the God and Torah of Israel"	Location and status: "the Land of Israel"
Orthodox Judaism	Solidarity with all Jews	Perpetuation of the covenant; aspiration to "bring the nation back in line"	Belief in Messianic return to Zion
Enlightenment	Cultural community based on loyalty to symbols	Respect for both halakha and the values of general society	Understated until the framing of the idea of a cultural/national center
Reform Judaism	Central concept in the sense of "congregation"	Selective approach to traditional symbols; emphasis on universal values	Metaphoric/ symbolic rather than geographical/ territorial
Conservative Judaism	Cultural community, especially for Reconstructionists	Selective approach to halakha (although less flexible than the Reform); religious life as cultural singularity	Moral/theological ideal; support of Zionist project
Bund	Jewish proletariat	Yiddish culture; respect for Jewish values of justice	Cultural autonomy in the future socialist society
Zionism	Ingathering of the exiles & building of the nation	Modern nationalist ideology; symbols drawn from tradition	Central aspect of identity

For the Orthodox, "the Jewish people" was a religious entity; for the Reform a moral community; for the Enlightenment, Conservatives, and Bund an ethno-cultural group; and for the Zionists a national collective. "The God and Torah of Israel" was interpreted literally by the Orthodox; by the Enlightenment as a set of symbols and values to be expanded to include universal perspectives, by the Conservatives as a system of tenets whose validity was subject to constant reevaluation; by the Zionists as symbols that could also be endowed with secular/national meaning; by the Bund as a class culture from which the "bourgeois" was to be eliminated, leaving only the popular/secular; and by the Reform as a system whose universal/humanitarian elements alone should be preserved. In respect to "the Land of Israel," the Enlightenment virtually ignored the issue until some of its members devised the notion of establishing a spiritual/cultural center in Jerusalem; Zionism regarded it as a territorial principle with both symbolic and political significance; Orthodox Judaism associated it with divine redemption; the Bund would gladly have renounced it in exchange for cultural rights anywhere in the world; and the Conservative and Reform movements interpreted it as a moral challenge.

Each of the formulations also gave differential weight to the three aspects of collective identity. For the Orthodox and the Enlightenment, the most important dimension was "the God and Torah of Israel," albeit the latter extended the concept. For the Zionists, the overriding aspect of identity was naturally "the Land of Israel." The Bund stressed membership in "the Jewish people," as did the Reform and Conservative movements, although they did not deny the importance of "the God and Torah of Israel."

These distinctions were reflected in linguistic preferences. The Orthodox, and especially the ultra-Orthodox, insisted on preserving the holy tongue as the language of study, prayer, and ritual. The Ashkenazim among the ultra-Orthodox also remained faithful to Yiddish as the language of everyday life in the community, along with the local language for communication with their surroundings. For the Bund, Yiddish was the only legitimate language of the Jews, particularly the Jewish proletariat. Whereas the Enlightenment emphasized the importance of learning the language of the nations in which the Jews resided, it was also the first to promote Hebrew as the language for creating a secular Jewish culture. It was the Zionists, however, who fought to make Hebrew a national/territorial language, the foundation on which a unified nation in the Land of Israel would be fashioned. The Reform and Conservative movements represented varieties of Judaism that resolutely turned to local non-Jewish languages. Yet, while they saw the Jewish community as an integral part of non-Jewish nations, they also continued to acknowledge Hebrew as the language reflecting Jewish identity and spoken by Israeli Jews.

After Migration, the Holocaust, and Establishment of the State

As we have seen, the upheaval in Jewish reality with entrance into the modern era was merely a precursor to the even more dramatic events that overtook the world in the first half of the 20th century, affecting the Jews considerably more than anything else. The significance of these events for Jewish intellectuals is apparent from the letters of Ben-Gurion's correspondents. We have discerned in them three distinct syndromes of Jewish identity. While they are basically the heirs to previous approaches, they also show the considerable effect of the unique life experience of this generation. The three syndromes and their attitudes to the three dimensions of identity are summarized in Table 5.2.

These syndromes, to be sure, are not the only possible ones, and diverse approaches might combine different aspects of more than one. That being said, it is still possible to speak of three major streams that are distinct from each other in the way in which they perceive the three dimensions of identity. The caste syndrome is represented primarily by the ultra-Orthodox inside and outside Israel, as well as by certain other Orthodox groups. The supporters of this syndrome, like the founders of Agudat Israel before them, see religious faith as the central element of Jewish identity. Their letters evidence a rigidity and sternness that would seem to reveal, among other things, the tragic influence of the Holocaust, which served to reinforce their unfaltering belief in a unique Jewish destiny. At the same time, there is a change in their attitude to the State of Israel, if not to Zionism itself. The very existence of the State of Israel appears to have encouraged them, unlike their predecessors, to come to terms with it despite its being a secular state. This acceptance is accompanied by demands for respect for religious law in the public domain as a measure of Israel's contribution to Judaism.

Table 5.2: Syndromes of Jewish Identity in the Letters to Ben-Gurion

Syndromes	Commitment to the collective	Singularity of the collective	Place of the collective
Caste	Traditional way of life; desire to "bring the nation back in line"	Faith as central element of Judaism	Belief in Messianic return to Zion; halakhic demands on Israel
Ethno-cultural	"peoplehood" as central element of identity	Varied approaches to halakha; belief in need to adapt to modern secular world	Metaphoric interpretation; solidarity with the Jews in Israel
National	Distinction between Israeli nation and Jewish people	System of collective traditional and secular symbols	Central element of identity; extols value of Israeli Judaism

The ethno-cultural syndrome is propounded primarily by scholars in the Diaspora who represent the whole spectrum of attitudes to religion, save for the ultra-Orthodox. As such, it continues the pattern of the various streams that emerged in the previous period: the modern Orthodox, Enlightenment, Reform, Conservative, and the Bund. All of these, whatever their definition of Judaism, saw it as a particular culture indicative of the existence of "the Jewish people." However, the letters of those supporting this model reveal the influence of Jewish experience in the modern Diaspora, their liberal Western attitudes and their belief that the Jewish community can be an integral part of general society.

The national syndrome is advocated mainly by the non-ultra-Orthodox Israeli respondents and the Zionists in the Diaspora. The heir to earlier Zionism, this syndrome was naturally influenced primarily by the establishment of the State of Israel. Its central element is "the Land of Israel" as the necessary territorial foundation of the new Jewish "nation," thereby creating a dichotomous image of world Jewry—Israel on one hand and the Diaspora on the other— with Israel occupying the position of leadership over the Diaspora. This is perceived as one of the major considerations that should determine how the country moulds its Jewish character.

Each of the three syndromes represents a basic challenge to the others. The ethno-cultural syndrome clashes sharply with the other two because of its willingness to accept far-reaching innovations regarding the boundaries of the collective, changes that are anathema to the caste syndrome and uncomfortable for the national. The caste syndrome stands out for the many Jewish signifiers it preserves, which are very different from the civil/secular style of the proponents of the ethno-cultural or national syndromes. The national syndrome, unlike the others, focuses on a specific territorial reality and distinguishes Israeli Jews from those anywhere else in the world.

The letters also reveal the contradictions within the space delineated by the three syndromes taken together. Despite the secular element of the national syndrome, similar in this aspect to the ethnocultural, its advocates tend to acquiesce to Orthodox demands in respect to membership in the collective. Several of the correspondents justify this in instrumental terms, concerned that if Israel were to adopt any other rule, individuals it recognized as Jews would not be accepted as such by the Orthodox. In other words, Israel's claim of being "the state of the Jews" would be rejected by a whole sector of the nation, whereas none of the different streams could deny that a Jew according to halakha was indeed a Jew. The price of adopting Orthodox rules for practical reasons, however, is that the proponents of the national syndrome must agree to participate in religious rituals whether or not they believe in them. This attitude is distasteful to the supporters of the ethno-cultural syndrome, which, although similar in spirit to the national, promotes a universal/moral perspective that opposes religious dictates. The difficulty of this issue for the national syndrome resides in the fact that the ethno-cultural syndrome represents the mainstream of Diaspora Jewry, that is, the very population which Israel aspires to lead, as the center of world Jewry.

Alongside these sources of contention, the three syndromes also converge in major respects. Since the overwhelming majority of Jews in the world do, as a matter of course, meet halakhic conditions of identity, they constitute the relevant collective for all formulations of Jewish identity. Save for a small number of individuals who are not recognized as Jews by the Orthodox, the identity of most Jews is not in question. Hence, at this stage in time it is inappropriate to speak of different "Jewish Peoples" in Israel or elsewhere, but only of different Jewish identities. In addition, all three syndromes draw

their symbols and myths from the same trove of customs and narratives; they are distinct mainly in the way in which they interpret
them. Consequently, the symbols of each syndrome are familiar to
the others, and all three participate to the same discourse. Finally,
nearly all of Ben-Gurion's correspondents relate to "the Land of
Israel," or at least the State of Israel, out of a sense of solidarity.
These common denominators somehow counterbalance the tensions
that exist between the three syndromes.

At the Dawn of the 21st Century

Ben-Gurion's correspondents wrote their responses in the late 50's;
since then, the world at large has again changed, as has the Jewish
world. When considering contemporary Israeli Jewish identities against
this background, it becomes clear that most prevailing formulations
still largely fit the national syndrome as reflected in the letters to
Ben-Gurion. As they did then, they continue to share an emphasis
on the territorial/national principle and the hierarchical dichotomy
between Israeli Jews and "the Jewish People" that it implies. According
to this approach, Israeli Jews are a specific territorial collective and
conduct a "full" Jewish life with its own language, literature, and
lifestyle. Moreover, as a sovereign entity situated on the symbolic
Land of Israel, in the eyes of many the Jewish state now more than
ever constitutes the natural leader of the Jewish world. Nevertheless,
there is still a variety of approaches in many respects. Among the
national religious, for example, some urge an extreme Israeli nationalism, defining the singularity of the collective in terms of religious,
even mystical Messianic, faith. The Mizrakhi religious—represented
by Shas—constitute a sort of "traditional" Zionism, calling for the
incorporation of the symbols of Mizrakhi and Sephardic heritage
into general Israeli culture in place of the secular outlook that has
long dominated. The immigrants from the former Soviet Union want
a definition of Israeli Judaism that would enable them to retain their
ethnic/cultural identity drawn from Russian culture. While the Arabs,
as non-Jewish Israelis, might not appear to have a place in a discussion of Israeli Jewish identity, they are a factor when it comes to
framing a definition of "Israeli" as separate from "Jew." As such,
they lend support to the radical ideologies that challenge the significance
of "the Land of Israel" and question the express definition of Israel

as a Jewish state. The Canaanites stress the territorial aspect of collective identity, taking the dichotomy between Israel and the Diaspora so far as to distinguish between "Hebrew" and "Jew." Rather than aiming their barbs at the Jews in the Diaspora who have chosen not to settle in Israel, the post-Zionists attack Israeli Jews, accusing them of exploiting and oppressing the Arabs. They demand that Israel be a "state of all its citizens," implying "de-Zionization" of the collective identity. Even if we ignore the more extreme positions—such as divorcing Israel from world Jewry as the Canaanites preach, or erasing the country's Jewish character as the post-Zionists would like—the controversies themselves reveal the Achilles heel of Israeli Judaism: the dichotomization between the Israeli Jewish nation and the Jewish People as a whole. This dichotomization necessarily gives rise to debates over the nature of each of these entities, their obligations to each other, and the degree of existing or desirable collaboration between them. The fact that a non-Jewish minority also lives in Israel, and represents the region in which Israel must survive, also plays a role in this debate.

On the other hand, as far as American Jewry (as the leading Diaspora) is concerned, it appears that the various groups continue to relate to Jewish identity in a manner indicative of the ethno-cultural syndrome, with the sole exception of the ultra-Orthodox who still display the features of the caste syndrome. The large majority of American Jews define themselves as one of the many ethnic or cultural groups of which this society is comprised. While cultural ethnicity means that the members of the Jewish community retain their connection to the broader circle of "the Jewish People," this transnational solidarity exists side by side with a flexible approach to the boundaries that distinguish between Jews and non-Jews within American society. Thus even though the different Jewish denominations are well-aware of their commitment to "the Jewish People," they are intimately involved in American life and consciously maintain a Jewish pluralism within American pluralism. The "American" orientation of this community is also reflected in the style of their organization into congregations. The Conservatives, Reconstructionists, Reform, and Humanists all seek to highlight the universal values of Judaism alongside loyalty to its particular traditional symbols. For many, religious faith serves to bolster this attitude. Furthermore, "the Land of Israel" has considerable symbolic significance in the U.S., where Israel is seen as a central element of the Jewish world. This, however, does not entail recognition of Israel as the major, not to say only, Jewish center. In effect, most American Jews do not regard themselves as a Gola. Rather, they perceive of Israel as a "former homeland," an entity deserving of their loyalty and from which they can draw contemporary symbols, but not an actual fatherland. In the same vein, in the collective consciousness of American Jews there is a Jewish tongue which is now Hebrew, rather than Yiddish or any other Jewish Diaspora language. Hence, Hebrew is taught in the Jewish school system as a hallmark of identity. At the same time, only a handful of individuals become fluent Hebrew-speakers, as this language usually plays no role in daily life.

As we have seen, for more than a few commentators, these features are signs of the gradual disappearance of American Jewry as a distinct entity (Lipset and Raab, 1995). This assertion, however, is firmly rejected by those who speak of transformation rather than demise, and these debates are themselves indications of the Achilles heel of the ethno-cultural syndrome. The major challenge it faces is, in fact, the very survival of the Jews among non-Jews in the absense of territorial borders or zealous religious observance. These difficulties are inexorably reflected in the anxious search for compromises regarding issues that arise in general society, and the undaunted attempts to adapt Jewish behavioral patterns to the demands of the times. The desire to make clear that the community is part of society, however, fosters Jewish pluralism and considerably weakens its singularity. At the same time, the ongoing ideological debate undoubtedly contributes to the vigor of American Jewry.

Table 5.3: Jewish Identities in the U.S. and Israel at the Start of the 21st Century

Model	Commitment to the collective	Singularity of the collective	Place of the collective
Caste	Aspiration to "bring the nation back" to faith	Faith as central element of Judaism	Belief in Messianic return to Zion
In America	Idem	Idem	For some "the Land of Israel" may be anywhere

Table 5.3 (*cont.*)

Model	Commitment to the collective	Singularity of the collective	Place of the collective
In Israel	Involvement in public life	Hebrew as first language	Belief in Messianic return to Zion
Ethno-Cultural	"peoplehood" as central element of identity	Belief in need to adapt to modernity	Understood metaphorically
Modern Orthodox	Idem	Acceptance of halakha & modernity	Idem
Conserva-tives	Idem	Selective approach to halakha	Idem
Reconstruc-tionists	The congregation as the center of religious life	Idem	Idem
Reform	Idem	Strongly selective	Idem
Human. Ju.	Idem	Rejection of faith	Idem
Post-Zion.	Jews as ethnics in Israel	Israeli culture	Israel as nation of its citizens
National	Dichotomy Israel/Diaspora	Secularization of symbols	Israel as center
Nat-Relig	Idem	Faith as basis of society	Idem
Mizrakhim	Traditional ethnicity among Jews	Importance of legacy	Idem
Russians	Cultural ethnicity	Retaining original culture	Link to country of origin
Canaanites	Divorcing of Israeliness from Jewishness	Israeli culture	Linked exclusively to territory

On the other hand, the proponents of the caste syndrome are not beset by the dilemmas of national Israeli Judaism or American ethno-cultural Judaism. Religious faith is the overriding element in their notion of collective identity, and it alone justifies the existence of the

Jewish people and the connection to the Land of Israel. For them, the Jews are "the army of the Lord," that is, a mobilized caste. They recognize the State of Israel only in the practical sense and some (more in the Diaspora than in Israel) even contend that "the Land of Israel" refers less to a geographical definition than to a metaphoric concept that indicates any place where the laws of halakha can be upheld. In Israel, however, the ultra-Orthodox communities often tend to display a degree of "Israelization" in a variety of forms, mainly by their increased daily use of Hebrew and involvement in Israeli public life. Volens nolens, the "Israeli" ultra-Orthodox are pressured to recognize Israel as the legitimate Jewish state and to work to influence it from within. In effect, the very demands of halakha are forcing the ultra-Orthodox to renounce their former hostility to Zionism and the Zionist state. As a result, a gap is inevitably opening between the ultra-Orthodox in Israel and in the Diaspora, signaling the weakening of the old view that the significance of the Jewish people and the Land of Israel is contingent solely on faith in the God and Torah of Israel. The transformation undergone by Jewish identity since its traditional formulation thus generated dilemmas that have eventually become its most essential features.

"Family Resemblance" and Tensions

The concept of collective identity is a heading under which we can analyze the self-perceptions of individuals as members of collectives. We have suggested a conceptual framework that recognizes the importance of the factors of time and place, alongside the influence of primordial aspects, in shaping identity. According to this approach, identity brings together principles and basic dilemmas ("deep structures"), which come to bear in the various formulations and emphases ("surface structures") as developed in response to particular circumstances. We focus in this context on three distinct, yet interrelated, dimensions of collective identity: the individual's commitment to the collective of which he or she feels a part; the individual's perception of the singularity of this collective; and the individual's image of the place or status of the collective in relation to "others." With the help of this conceptual framework, we have examined the principles and dilemmas at the foundations of Jewish identity as revealed in the surface structures, that is, in the formulations of Jewish identity in different times and places. In this way, we have been able to learn about the similarity or tendency toward uniformity, as opposed to the distinctions or tendency toward divisiveness, of these formulations which, taken as a whole, represent the range of possibilities of Jewish identity. Our analysis reveals the vigor and diversity of Jewish identity throughout time and until this day. The first major finding is that the three syndromes we deduced from the views of Ben-Gurion's correspondents—ethnicity, nationality, and caste—channel the wide variety of models of Jewish identity that emerged with the disintegration of traditional society. Another finding is that these same syndromes also constitute a framework for a discussion of the many different versions of this identity that evolved in the forty years following the correspondence between these distinguished individuals and Ben-Gurion.

To be sure, it is quite difficult to pinpoint the common denominator that unites the space comprised by the numerous formulations of Jewish identity which we have encountered in our investigation. What we have found, rather, is a relative and uneven proximity and resemblance exhibited by the different formulations vis-à-vis each other. This picture is best described by the Wittgensteinian notion of "family resemblance" (Wittgenstein, 1961). Wittgenstein elaborated on this concept when analyzing the structure of languages. Like his analyses of "word games" that make up distinct codes, we have also found within the space of formulations constituted by Jewish identities those that are very different, at times even contradictory, and yet still display a certain resemblance. The various formulations are manifested in a plethora of attitudes to and aspects of similarity/dissimilarity that are inconsistent and clearly asymmetric, despite the fact that they all derive from the same sources and are dressed in the same symbols drawn from the same founts and featuring in the same narratives. In other words, the different phrasings of Jewish identity are, like word games deleneating a language, similar to each other in the complex sense that a family is made up of closer and more distant relatives who resemble each other to a greater or lesser degree.

More substantively, beyond the fundamental differences in content and definition, all of the formulations we have found center around the basic issues that arose as soon as the validity of the three principles of the traditional Jewish identity were questioned. The moment these principles were transformed from the religious tenets of a cohesive traditional community to objects of interpretation by individuals, circles, and parties, answers of the greatest diversity could be supplied. In addition, we have seen that the various formulations are also distinct from each other in terms of the relative weight they ascribe to each of the three principles we defined (see Figure 5.1).

The distances we have discerned among Jewish identities indicate how the formulations converge into clusters, as well as how distinct they are from each other. All relate to the same social entity and contend with the same basic questions, and it is as such that their differences and similarities can be contained under the heading of "family resemblance." Only in these terms can we find any commonality between Shas in Israel, Secular Humanistic Judaism in the U.S., and the Bund in Europe. In the "family" of Jewish identities, these formulations are indeed "cousins," although very distant ones. Their inclusion within the same space is an indication of its great diversity and the many forms of contention by which it is beset.

Unity that is subject to constant friction, however, can also result in isolationist attitudes, just as certain relatives may cease to consider themselves part of the same family. Thus, for example, the proponents of the caste syndrome might be tempted to exclude those who deny their truths from the community they define as "the Jewish People." Such attitudes have existed within the ultra-Orthodox public since the establishment of Agudat Israel. Against a very different background, the Canaanites have displayed a similar disposition ever since the early days of Zionism.

When these tendencies are reflected in a diagram (Figure 5.1), they yield a configuration in which there is no center, an indication that the various models do not accept the authority of any common central entity. Each presents a different dominant principle, and none is supreme in the eyes of the others. Indeed, the diagram demonstrates the extent to which the range of Jewish identities is typified by rivalry for hegemony between and within each cluster. Like the members of an extended family, these formulations, embodying the pluralism of Jewish identity, are similar or different from each other to differing degrees. They are therefore likely to develop a differential or asymmetric sense of solidarity with or hostility toward their many "relations." The different formulations are not entirely estranged from one another, but neither is it a given that these "relatives" will continue to wish to be part of the same collective. History teaches that it has often been the similarities between groups which, under certain circumstances, have given rise to destructive animosity and unbridgeable gaps.

Given the profusion of demands in the three-dimensional space, it is unlikely that a two-sided polarization will emerge to the extent that it leads the Jewish world, including Israel, to a state of crisis and fission. Because of these same demands, however, it is impossible to predict either which of the formulations, or coalition of formulations, will gain the ascendancy in the space of Jewish identity. What may still be contended is that however closely related the different definitions may be, the very fact that there are so many patterns of "Jewishness" has stripped the concept of the unequivocal clarity that might serve as the common ground for all manners of defining the "single" collective identity.

At each stage of this analysis, we have found the elements of the models we use to examine both the past and the future in the responses to Ben-Gurion written in the late 1950s. The views expressed in these letters have supplied us with a link between the eras, along with the tools for comparing the different schools of thought at each point in time. It is to these letters that we now turn.

Fig. 5.1: The space of Jewish identities by "family resemblance"

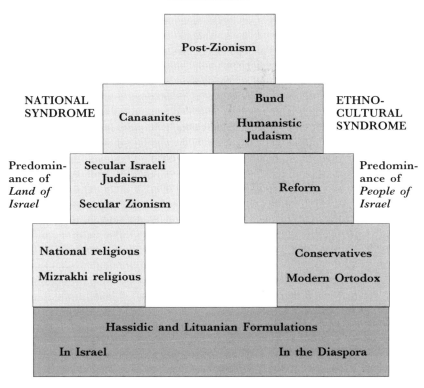

CASTE SYNDROME

Predominance of *God and Torah of Israel*

PART TWO

WHO IS A JEW?

PREAMBLE

This section begins with an introductory chapter by Shalom Ratzaby that investigates the nature of the traditional Jewish identity and thus establishes a frame of reference for the responses to Ben-Gurion's query of the Jewish intellectuals he termed "Jewish Sages." The author describes the changes in the rules of conversion to Judaism in pre-modern times, from the Biblical period to rabbinical literature. This analysis makes it possible for us to assess how far Ben-Gurion's correspondents wished to preserve traditional tenets, or, alternatively, were willing to diverge from them. It thus furthers our attempt at a comprehensive sociological-cultural discussion of Jewish identity.

This chapter is followed by Ben-Gurion's original query, after which we present the 46 responses he received in late 1958 and early 1959 from 51 Jewish intellectuals. The letters are of significance on two levels. The first is what they show about the perception of Jewish identity. In this sense, they are relevant to the discussion in the first part of the book, which drew on the letters to help in our analysis of Jewish thinking before and after this point in time. The second level refers to the debate itself over "Who is a Jew?" Each of the distinguished respondents indicates his definition of the boundaries of the collective and the manner in which an individual may cross over from the non-Jewish to the Jewish side. "Who is a Jew?" is the practical application of the broader question "What is a Jew?" As we shall see, the two issues are not necessarily directly or automatically linked together. As soon as practical matters are involved, circumstantial or instrumental considerations may come into play, along with those that derive from the perception of the collective. As a result, those who propound contradictory formulations of Jewish identity may find themselves supporting similar, or even identical, pragmatic solutions, and the other way around.

Despite the "practical" nature of the question, it would be wrong to imagine that it is easy to define "Who is a Jew." In fact, it is probably simpler to define "Who is not a Jew." However rigid or flexible one's approach, in virtually all formulations of Jewish identity a non-Jew is a person who must undergo conversion in order to become a Jew. In this sense, there would not appear to be much difference between the practices required to enter the collective today and those in effect in the past. However, membership in a traditional Jewish community did not merely mean being party to a very specific way of life, but also, and primarily, being entitled to the collective rights that touched on every major aspect of social life. On the other hand, today citizenship of a country is the essential source of social rights, whereas membership in a Jewish community affords few advantages. In this reality, the cohesiveness of the community cannot be taken for granted and the boundaries of Jewishness have become a matter of debate. In this context, the importance of the letters to Ben-Gurion lies in the fact that they delineate and reflect the most significant controversies over the social boundaries of Judaism.

The responses are presented nearly in full, with the minor exceptions of one which was shortened because of its length and two others from which sections irrelevant to our discussion were removed. Here and there we have omitted citations which overloaded the text.

The current volume was published with the help of the National Archives, through the services of the Ben-Gurion Archives and the Center for the Ben-Gurion Legacy in Sde-Boker (Ben-Gurion University of the Negev). Most of the letters were originally written in Hebrew, save for those by Henry Baruk and Chaim Perelman which were in French, and are presented here in English translation. Those written in English—by Isaiah Berlin, Leon (Arye) Simon, Solomon B. Freehof, Felix Frankfurter, and Simon H. Rifkind—appear here in their original form.

HISTORICAL INTRODUCTION

By Shalom Ratzaby

The Starting Point

The debate over the concept of conversion begins with Biblical sources and continues with the writings of the Sages and rabbinical literature up to and including that being written today. At each stage, the definitions handed down remained valid for centuries despite changing political, cultural, and social circumstances. They indicate and clarify the issues that became bones of contention with the introduction of the changes occasioned by the modern era and the Emancipation. The difficulty of identifying the various levels of Biblical sources is a familiar problem. It becomes even more problematical when the subject is a concept as flexible as "ger" (convert; pl. gerim). The ger of the First Temple Period is not the same as the one in the Second Temple Period, and the ger of the settlement period is most likely not the same as the one in the period of the kingdom.[1] In the Bible, the term serves to indicate the status of a person who settles permanently in a foreign land, generally translated as "stranger."[2] It was only natural, then, that the standing of a ger was more questionable than that of a native, as we can see in the words of the men of Sodom to Lot.[3] Similarly, in reference to the verse "you shall not wrong a stranger,"[4] Rashi explains that anyone who was not born in the country but came to live there from another country is called a "stranger" (*ger*). The term, however, does not only refer to a person in a foreign land, such as Ruth the Moabite, but also to anyone who is not an Israelite, even if he or she was born in the Land of Israel.[5] The "aliens" whom Solomon assigned to be quarriers

---

[1] For the different shades of meaning of this concept, see: Y.A. Seligman, "*ger*", *Encyclopedia Mikrait*, II, p. 546.
[2] Gen. 15:9.
[3] Gen. 19:9.
[4] Ex. 22:20.
[5] See also, *Arukh Ha-shalem*, Kohot, II, p. 344.

and carriers[6] are generally thought to be offspring of the previous inhabitants of the Land of Israel, that is, those who remained after the conquest by the Children of Israel. As Solomon could not banish them, he imposed a labor tax upon them.[7] Since the term ger applies to both those who are not of Israelite stock and those who are not native born, it is not surprising that it also serves in the Bible, along with "resident," to describe the Israelites themselves in respect to God: "But the land must not be sold beyond reclaim, for the land is Mine; you are but strangers resident with Me." (Lev. 25:23).

In time, ger acquired an additional meaning, which eventually became its primary denotation. The attitude which began to dominate after the Babylonian exile defined Judaism, above all, as a religion. Consequently, ger came to refer only to a non-Jew who consciously became a Jew. As the term no longer related to the residence of a foreigner in the Land of Israel, it ceased to be associated with a lengthy process of cultural, and thus also religious, assimilation. In other words, the ger was no longer a person who settled in the Land of Israel for economic, social, or political reasons, but only someone who "became [a] Jew" in the words of the Book of Esther,[8] which dates from after the destruction of the First Temple. In fact, from the Second Temple Period onward, the transition to Judaism took on the nature of a ceremony carefully spelled out by halakha. In this ritual, the ger agrees to accept all of the commandments of the Torah, a commitment which entitles him or her to the same religious rights as a natural-born Jew, including the right to marry within the community. From this point on, in both halakha and actual practice, acknowledging the God of Israel and taking on the yoke of the commandments precede inclusion in the nation and become the essence of converting to Judaism.

The concept of the convert, and thus the nature of the ritual of conversion, would undergo changes reflecting the tensions between the emphasis on Judaism as a religion with a universal message and values, and the view of Judaism as the specific religion of the Jewish people, universal values notwithstanding. Whereas the religious notion of Judaism took shape in territorial frameworks, once the nation was exiled and separated from its homeland, universal religious aspects,

---

[6] I Chron. 22:1–2; II Chron. 2:16–17.
[7] I Ki. 9:20–21; II Chron. 8:7–8.
[8] Esth. 8:17.

such as the principle of monotheism and the Messianic character of world history, began to be seen in a new light. These features, along-side the ethnic and particular traits of Judaism, endowed it with a thoroughly universal nature, as the Messianic vision does not relate only to the Jews. Nevertheless, although ultimately all nations will acknowledge the God of Israel and his commandments, the Jewish people is expected to retain its special status and be the leader of the other nations. These ideas generated internal tensions that came to the fore most prominently in the question of the link between Jewish nationalism and ethnicity, and Judaism as religion. This ten-sion also came to bear in regard to the role and status of the Land of Israel, as the connection between the Jews and the land inevitably has a bearing on the image of Judaism, with implications for the meaning of the act of conversion.

The Ger before the Destruction of the First Temple

As we have seen, "ger" is an extremely ancient concept in Judaism.[9] In the earliest levels of the Bible, it relates even to the Levites, who did not have a share of the land as did the other tribes.[10] Most often, however, it refers to someone who resides in a foreign land, either those who have come to the Land of Israel (such as Ruth the Moabite), or fugitives from neighboring lands.[11] Another large and well-defined group who were also considered gerim (plural of ger) included the Gibeonites and the remnants of the nations that had inhabited the Land of Israel before its conquest and who could not be exiled by the Israelites.[12] Furthermore, the Bible speaks of enslaved gerim, that is, slaves and the children of household servants who were circumcised.[13] As a rule, these gerim took part in Israelite rituals.[14]

---

[9] For the attempt to identify stages in the development of the concept of ger in the Bible, see: Rosenbloom, 1978:19–20.
[10] See, for example, Deut. 18:6; Jud. 17:7–13. Pedersen notes that even after set-tlement, reference to the Israelites as gerim did not entirely disappear.
[11] Is. 16:4; 21:14–15.
[12] I Ki. 9:20–21; I Chron. 22:2. It is worth noting in this context that the com-ments of Israel Ben-Zeev (1982:12) regarding the wave of conversions that over-took the land in the time of David and Solomon is merely an anachronism, attributing to an earlier reality the descriptions and concepts relevant to the Second Temple Period and the generations of the destruction.
[13] See, for example, Gen. 17:12–13.
[14] For example, Ex. 12:44.

Gerim could not become totally assimilated into Israelite society because of its tribal structure. The nation's assets consisted primarily of land, the family and tribal legacy passed down from generation to generation. As the Land of Israel was divided up among the tribes and the individual's membership in the nation as a whole was determined by tribal affiliation, the "strangers" remained gerim, rather than citizens, no matter how long they resided among the Israelites.[15] It is not surprising, therefore, to find that there was a special social status for all gerim, as distinct from landowners, regardless of whether or not they were slaves.[16] We learn from the Biblical text that gerim did not reside on their own land, but rather on the land they worked.[17] Their inferior status also explains the laws providing for their fair treatment,[18] and their inclusion among the recipients of alms.[19] In addition, special reference is made to the gerim who belonged to the nations previously occupying the land, who are known by the general label of "the people that were left" (Kaufman, 1969, 4–5:93). For example, although the Gibeonites[20] lived among the Israelites who settled in their towns,[21] they never became thoroughly assimilated, maintaining their distinct identity throughout the period of the Judges.[22] In the time of Saul, they could be found throughout the Kingdom of Israel,[23] becoming "the king's slaves" together with the members of the other ancient nations, but still known by their national affiliation rather than as individuals.[24]

The religious status of gerim was based on the notion that the Israelites were strangers in Egypt and could therefore empathize with the ger (Rosenbloom, 1978), as well as on the fact that strangers lived among the nation from its earliest days.[25] Indeed, they participated in the performance of the very first commandment—the Passover offering.[26] Similarly, Numbers 9:14 reads: "And when a stranger who

---

[15] Ex. 12:48–49; Lev. 16:29, 17:10–15, 18 and elsewhere.
[16] See, for example, Gen. 23:4.
[17] Lev. 25:23.
[18] Ex. 22:20; Lev. 19:33–34; Deut. 24:14, and elsewhere.
[19] Lev. 19:10, 23:22; Deut. 24:19.
[20] For a discussion of the evolution of the term "ger" to this stage and the implications of this development, see: Meek, 1930:80–172.
[21] Josh. 9:17.
[22] I Sam. 6:21–27.
[23] II Sam. 21:5.
[24] For the Gibeonites after the return to Zion, see: Kaufman, 1969, II: 648.
[25] Ex. 12:48, 12: 38; Lev. 24: 10; Num. 11:4.
[26] Ex. 12:48–49.

resides with you would offer a Passover sacrifice to the Lord, he must offer it in accordance with the rules and rites of the Passover sacrifice. There shall be one law for you, whether stranger or citizen of the country." The same applies to the other offerings commanded by the Torah.[27] What is more, a special warning aimed specifically at gerim appears in respect to the proscriptions considered particularly difficult for them, such as incest, the eating of blood, or taking the name of the Lord in vain, thus indicating that they participated in Jewish ritual and practice. Yet although the Bible goes a long way to ensure the equality and rights of gerim, it does not provide all categories of gerim with the same protection.

The social and economic status of gerim also receives attention in the Bible.[28] They are included in numerous places among those entitled to alms, and are afforded treatment that accords with the Biblical ethic requiring the Israelites to act with compassion and love, which are among the hallmarks of the Lord.[29] On the other hand, gerim are allowed no opportunity to rise from their inferior social status. Ezekiel spoke out against this situation, repeatedly denouncing the cheating of strangers.[30] Not satisfied with broad condemnations alone, he also demanded that they be allotted land among the tribes.[31] Ezekiel's contentions of discrimination notwithstanding, strangers enjoyed the same status as citizens in respect to all the laws of the Torah,[32] and their commitment to the laws of Israel was based on the notion that they had been present at Mount Sinai[33] and at the blessing and cursing on Mount Gerizim and Mount Ebal.[34]

During the period of the kingdom, and particularly in times of prosperity, individuals, families, and entire households came to settle in the Land of Israel. Some achieved very high social standing. Among Saul's officers, for example, we find Doeg the Edomite. Similarly, a battalion of Gittites who had settled with their families in Jerusalem served in David's army.[35] Although they continued to

---

[27] Num. 15:15.
[28] See, for example, Lev. 25:15–16.
[29] See: Ex. 34:6; Ps. 86:103, and elsewhere.
[30] Ez. 22:7.
[31] Ez. 47:22–25.
[32] Ex. 12:19; Lev., 16:29, 17:15, 24:16, 22, and elsewhere.
[33] Deut. 29:10ff.
[34] Jos. 8:33, 35.
[35] II Sam. 15:18–22.

be thought of as strangers,[36] as Kaufman states: "As the 'young men'
consecrated themselves before going to war (I Sam. 21:5–7), we can
assume that the soldiers in those battalions did the same according
to local practice and were included in the rituals of the dominant
religion" (1969, 4–5:192). Nor are gerim missing from the list of
David's bravest warriors, where we find Zelek the Ammonite[37] and
Uriah the Hittite.[38] Another ger, Amasa, the son of Ithra the Ishmaelite,
was even related to David,[39] who went so far as to entrust the Ark
of the Lord to Obed-edom the Gittite.[40]

David also took a wife of Geshur,[41] and his son Solomon had
numerous foreign wives, including Canaanite women from neighboring nations,[42] who could be wedded to Israelites whereas Canaanites
resident in the Land of Israel could not. It is interesting to note here
that the Biblical text[43] seems to indicate that a new attitude toward
intermarriage began to emerge toward the end of Solomon's reign.
We are told that Solomon built altars to the gods of his wives, and
toward the end of his life his heart was even turned away after
"other gods." This might mean that pious circles began to look unfa-
vorably on intermarriage, holding it responsible for Solomon's lack
of wholehearted devotion to the God of Israel. Thus, as many of
Solomon's wives were foreign women whom it was forbidden to
marry, the ancient prohibition against wedding Canaanites was
extended to include all other nations. As Kaufman (1969: 193) points
out, however, the ban existed only in theory for many more years
to come.

The genealogy of the Jewish people also demonstrates that it can
not be seen to have a single ethnic origin. From its very beginnings,
it displays compound roots,[44] its primary elements being Aramaic,
Canaanite (Judah), and Egyptian (Joseph). Over the generations up
to the destruction of the First Temple, the nation was joined by a
large number of foreign households, including the Kenites, such as

---

[36] Ibid. 19.
[37] Ibid. 23:34.
[38] Ibid. 39.
[39] II Sam. 17:25; I Chron. 2:17.
[40] II Sam. 6:10–12.
[41] II Sam. 3:3.
[42] I Ki. 3:1, 11:1, and elsewhere.
[43] I Ki. 11:1–2.
[44] See also: Rosenbloom, 1978:13.

Jael, wife of Heber, who was a heroine and a judge;[45] the Rechabites, one of whom, Jechonadab son of Rechab, played an active role in the destruction of Baal;[46] the Calebs; and others. Moses had a Midian Cushite wife,[47] Ruth the Moabite, the matriarch of the House of David, married Boaz,[48] and Naamah the Ammonite was the mother of the legitimate kings of Judea.[49] As if this were not enough, Biblical law even permits marriage with a prisoner of war.[50]

It is thus extremely difficult to give a precise definition of the Biblical concept of ger. Nevertheless, wherever the term is used, it invariably shares one typical characteristic. It indicates the social and religious status of a group of people of an ethnicity distinct from the majority or dominant nation. Along with the remnants of the previous populations of the Land of Israel, are households that attached themselves to the land and its people for a variety of reasons. After several generations of continuous residence, the descendants of these households, and in some cases even the first generations, came to adopt the beliefs and rituals of the Israelites. One interesting example is the Book of Ruth, which most likely dates from after the return to Zion. It retrospectively rejects the isolationist approach of Ezra,[51] following the earlier concept of ger that prevailed in the First Temple Period, as opposed to the later idea of religious conversion and insularity. The basis of Ruth's conversion lies in her moving to the Land of Israel, and draws on a territorial perception that links the land, God, and the nation. Thus, in response to her mother-in-law Naomi's urging to return, like Orpah, to "her people and her gods" (Ru. 1:15), Ruth replies: "Your people shall be my people, and your God my God" (16). Ruth's declaration shows the willingness for social integration of those who come to live among a foreign nation in a foreign land.[52] Similarly, although from the opposite perspective, David laments the fact that in a foreign land he cannot worship the

---

[45] Jud. 4:11, 17–22, 5:6, 20–24.
[46] II Ki. 10:15.
[47] Ex. 2:21ff.; Nu. 12:1.
[48] Ru. 1:4 ff.
[49] I Ki. 14:21.
[50] Deut. 21:10–14.
[51] For the attitudes in the Book of Ruth and the time of its composition, see: Zakobitz, 1990:20–21, 33–35.
[52] Zakobitz, ibid., 61.

Lord, that is, the God of Israel.[53] Conversion is therefore territorially based rather than universally religious. There is no religious motive for Ruth's conversion; she does not go with Naomi because she has become convinced that the God of Israel is the one great god, but because of her love for her mother-in-law (1:14–17, 2:11). As soon as she arrives in Naomi's land, she is taken under the wings of the God of Israel (1:16, 2:11–12).[54] To summarize, then, in the First Temple Period, the ger was someone who came to live in the Land of Israel and, in the course of time, became culturally and religiously assimilated, adopting the God of Israel and his laws.

The story of Naaman is an exception to this rule. Unlike Ruth, Naaman recognized the distinctiveness of the God of Israel (II Ki. 5:17). Also in contrast to Ruth, whose declaration, as we have seen, is an expression of her willingness to integrate fully into her new nation, after he is healed Naaman exclaims: "Now I know that there is no God in the whole world except in Israel!" (5:15). Naaman thus converts for religious reasons, acknowledging the distinctiveness of the God of Israel, although he continues to reside among his nation of idolaters. What this means is that between the time of the story of Ruth the Moabite and deutero- or even tertio-Isaiah prophecy, a dramatic change had taken place (Kaufman, 1969). Yet even the story of Naaman, the only Biblical instance of anything approaching religious conversion, can be seen as the exception that proves the rule. As to become a Jew means, in the Bible, to live in the Land of Israel and become culturally and religiously assimilated, it is typical that even this one tale of seemingly religious conversion contains no criticism of idolatry. Despite his acknowledgement of the God of Israel, Naaman's words reveal a territorial orientation, "for there is no God in the whole world except in Israel."

Actually, in the First Temple period no non-Israelite believer in the God of Israel who abandoned idolatry for reasons of conscience can be found outside the Land or Nation of Israel. Indeed, none of the rules relating to the eligibility of a ger to participate in Jewish ritual makes any reference to religious belief. For instance, a slave or ger is entitled to partake of the Passover offering after undergoing circumcision, but the ritual of circumcision does not constitute reli-

[53] I Sam. 26:19.
[54] See: Kaufman, 1969:213–214.

gious conversion. Similarly, the conversion of female captives requires only a formal ceremony symbolizing the break from their former nation;[55] there is no mention of any religious ritual whatsoever. As we have seen, even the case of Naaman does not represent true religious conversion. Although he comes to believe in the God of Israel, he takes on himself one commandment alone, to offer a sacrifice to the Lord, and even this is not necessarily conducted according to Jewish law. This concept of the ger can also explain the status of the enslaved gerim in the Philistine towns controlled by Judea in the time of Menasseh (Kaufman, 1969, 6–7). By the same token, the men of Cuth, who were exiled to the Land of Israel, became gerim by virtue of their new home, rather than because of any religious transformation;[56] it was the lions the Lord sent against them that convinced them to study his law. This example is further evidence that conversion was associated with settlement in the Land of Israel.[57] Nevertheless, the very fact that foreigners could worship the God of Israel indicates that even in this ancient period, the definition of Judaism was not entirely particularistic. Only in this sort of broad perception of Judaism could whole units, such as the Gibeonites, the remnants of the Canaanite nations, and families like Kenan, Heber, and others continue to maintain their cultural heritage many generations after they had joined the Israelite nation.

From Ezra and Nehemiah to the End of the Second Temple Period

The period of exile was a watershed in the development of collective Jewish identity, a time of dramatic change in the perception of Judaism and the self-image of the Jews. They now came to define their singularity as distinct from the idolatry surrounding them,[58] and uncovered the universal elements that had been implicit in First Temple Judaism. Maintaining one's faith in God became an absolute value that was not contingent on any territorial, political, or social

---

[55] Deut. 21:10–14.

[56] II Ki. 17:24–41.

[57] See also: Deut. 23:8–9.

[58] The sociologist Max Weber claims that the nation's leaders used religion to ensure its survival in conditions of exile. By means of religious ritual, they created a distinctiveness for the Jews that prevented them from becoming assimilated. See Weber, 1952:336.

factor. The ritual now gave birth to a pattern of religious conversion
based on conscience and acceptance of the Torah. This transformation is apparent from the attitude of the Jews to those who attached
themselves to them in the period of exile and the start of the return
to Zion.[59] Such converts to Judaism for thoroughly religious reasons,
spoken of by deutero-Isaiah,[60] are no longer considered gerim in the
sense of foreigners who came to live among the Israelites, a definition
canceled out by the destruction of the Temple and exile. Called "followers" of Judaism, they did not undergo a religious ritual of conversion, which as such had yet to be devised. Still, they were a new
phenomenon, a fact that resounds in the prophecy of deutero-Isaiah.[61]
Although the act of "professing" Judaism was not encouraged by the
Jews, circumcision was required for anyone wishing to do so. Lacking
in the framework of a Jewish household or tribe, they were looked
on in many ways as outsiders. Deutero-Isaiah declares that they will
not be abandoned. In his prophecy, at the end of days the temple
in Jerusalem will be "a house of prayer for all peoples," including
those nations who are now heathens, some of which are even enemies
of Israel. But they shall remain where they are, sending only dele-
gates to the holy mount. However, this will not be the case in regard
to the "followers" who are faithful to the Lord and his law. In future,
there will be no distinction between them and the Israelites; they
will all ascend the mount together with the dispersed of Israel.[62]
Moreover, deutero-Isaiah, in a vision that encompasses the whole of
world history, states: "Let not the foreigner say, who has attached
himself to the Lord, 'The Lord will keep me apart from His people'"
(56:3).[63]

In view of this attitude, which seems to encourage foreigners to
attach themselves to the Jewish people and speaks out against the
treatment they customarily receive, numerous scholars have attributed the prophecy (from verse 49 on) to tertio-Isaiah, who lived in
the time of Ezra and was among the opponents of his isolationist
views.[64] Whatever the case, as Kaufman claims, "in this vision, set-

[59] Esth. 8:17; Is. 56:3, 6–7.
[60] Or perhaps even tertio-Isaiah, a prophet from the period of the return to Zion.
[61] Is. 56:3, 6–7.
[62] For the valuing of this type of conversion as lower than the concept of universal conversion, see: Kaufman, 1969, I:120–121.
[63] See: Kaufman, ibid.: 135–137.
[64] See: Bamberger, 1939: 15.

tlement in the Land of Israel spells the end of foreignness, it is a destiny and a promise, the reward to the foreigner for attaching himself to the covenant. The religious element is given crucial importance. It is the Jewish religion that turns a foreigner into a member of the nation of Israel and even makes him entitled to the land. Religious thinking in its entirety is contained herein" (1969, 9:137). The vision, however, depicts intent alone. It is most likely that in reality, the status of the "followers" continued to be an embarrassment.

During the period of Ezra and Nehemiah, we find practical attempts to address the issue of the status of those who attached themselves to Israel for religious reasons. The Book of Ezra states that the returned exiles ate of the Passover offering "together with all who joined them in separating themselves from the uncleanness of the nations of the lands to worship the Lord God of Israel" (6:19–21). Similarly, the Book of Nehemiah relates that among those who signed the pledge to God were "all who separated themselves from the peoples of the lands to [follow] the Teachings of God" (10:29). The root of the problem of those who became Jewish lay in the dispute between the returning exiles and the people of the land, particularly the Samaritans.[65] The controversy between the "congregation of returning exiles" and "the people of the land" or "peoples of the land" (Ez. 9:1–2) arose because of social and religious differences between the returning exiles and the Israelite population that had remained in place, consisting of remnants of the kingdoms of Judea and Israel along with foreign elements who had been exiled to the Land of Israel by the Assyrians. Neither these people nor the Samaritans were idolaters. It is reasonable to assume that, like the men of Cuth, the deported foreigners adopted the practices of Israel as an instance of worshipping the local god. Thus, in the story of Zerubbabel's rejection of the Samaritans there is no reference to

---

[65] The following discussion makes no attempt to deal with the complex problem of who the Samaritans were or what their religious culture was, just as no attempt is made to examine the question of who the people of the land were or what kind of religious culture they maintained. The discussion is limited solely to issues relevant to the development of the institution of religious conversion. It is worth noting, however, that in the First Temple Period the term "people of the land" referred to the population with special power to control political and economic life (II Ki. 21:24), and even Haggai still uses the term in a positive sense (2:4). It was only in the time of Ezra that it took on a negative connotation, with the phrase "congregation of returning exiles" now being used to denote the positive.

idolatry as a possible explanation for his decision.[66] In a similar
fashion, among the reasons for the expulsion of the foreign women
by Ezra,[67] there is no hint of idolatry among those who had become
Jews, nor does Nehemiah claim that Sanballat[68] or Obiah[69] were
idolaters.[70] The "congregation of returning exiles" offers no satisfactory explanation for its determined opposition to the participation of
the Samaritans in the Temple building project, but merely states
unequivocally: "It is not for you and us to build a House to our
God, but we alone will build it to the Lord God of Israel" (Ez. 4:3).
However, in light of the isolationist policy of the returning exiles,
led by Ezra and Nehemiah, and the critical importance of the family
tree in determining whether or not a family was of pure Jewish
blood, we may conclude with some certainty that the opposition to
the Samaritans derived from doubts as to the purity of their line
and reservations associated with the new perception of Judaism of
the congregation of the returning exiles. From this time on, conversion was seen primarily as acknowledgement of the God of Israel
and willingness to accept all of his commandments. Until this approach
became institutionalized, full membership in the Jewish people required
a pure line of descent.[71]

The question of the origin of the Samaritans is a matter of con-

[66] Ez. 4:1–4; for a discussion of these verses, see also: Lever, 1958.
[67] Ez. 9:1–10, 44.
[68] However, from documents discovered in the cave of Wadi Dalya it appears
that Sanballat, an opponent of Nehemiah, was a Samaritan pasha whose family
had held this position at least from the mid-5th century B.C. to the occupation of
the land by Alexander the Great. The names of those in this family which are not
Sanballat are Jewish theophoric names, indicating that the family worshipped the
God of Israel. As the Samaritans also worshiped the God of Israel, it would seem
that they and their most distinguished families were considered Jews at this time,
that is, people who had turned their backs on their idolatrous beliefs.
[69] Although the Book of Nehemiah does not state that Tobiah the Ammonite
was a Jew, we learn this from Josephus Flavius' *Antiquities of the Jews* and from the
Xenon papyri. These sources indicate that he was of high status in Transjordan,
and that his family had held a very high position in the Hellenist period. For ancient
sources on the family of Tobiah, see: Mazar, 1980: 270–290; Stern, 1963.
[70] Support for this claim can be found in the fact that Ezra and Nehemiah's
opposition directly defied the stance of the High Priest in Jerusalem, who rejected
their policy out of hand. The High Priest and his circles welcomed the Samaritans
and their families into Temple worship and accepted them as Jews in every way.
Thus, we can assume that the Samaritans, Tobiah the Ammonite, and Sanballat
saw themselves in the same light.
[71] For a comprehensive discussion of the role of religious ritual and halakha in
respect to the ger, see: Finkelstein, 1946, II: 460–462.

troversy. Some claim they were the early inhabitants of the Northern Israelite Kingdom, but as they were not sent into exile, their Judaism took a different form from that shaped by the Israelite tribes in exile in Babylon. Others point to the fact that Samaritan law shows no indications of an early Israelite tradition. They contend, therefore, that they were exiles from Mesopotamian lands who were deported to the Land of Israel by the Assyrian kings, as described in the Book of Kings,[72] and as the Samaritans themselves claim, according to Ezra.[73] Over time, particularly after the return of the exiles and most likely in the wake of the religious reawakening they brought with them, the Samaritans asked to be allowed to take part in the Temple worship of God. However, whereas in the past residence in the Land of Israel and cultural and religious assimilation had been sufficient to make a person a Jew, now, with the perception of Judaism as a religion, this was no longer the case.[74] In addition to these issues, the controversy also hung on political considerations, such as the struggle for hegemony over Jerusalem and the status of the leading circles. It goes without saying, as Kaufman (1969, VIII: 204–207) so clearly explains, that the dispute between the returning exiles and the Samaritans, whatever their origin, would never have arisen had the institution of religious conversion existed at that time.[75] This explanation also suggests that Ezra's single public act before the rise of Nehemiah, the expulsion of the foreign women, may have referred not only to women of other nations, but also to those foreigners who attached themselves to the Jews and came under the wings of the God of Israel.

As we have seen, even here there is no mention of idolatry as a reason for the expulsion. What is more, the act is not sanctioned by Torah law, which does not forbid marriage with foreigners per se. The prohibition against marrying people of other nations relates only to the Canaanites, the former inhabitants of the Land of Israel,[76] the Ammonites and Moabites,[77] and the Edomites and Egyptians.[78] The reason for and validity of the proscription are different in each case.

---

[72] II Ki. 17:24.
[73] Ez. 4:2, 10.
[74] For the problem of the Samaritans, see: Kaufman, 1969, VIII: 201–206.
[75] See also: Rosenbloom, 1978:24–25.
[76] Ex. 34:15–16; Deut. 7:3.
[77] Deut. 23:4–6.
[78] Ibid., 8–9.

The ban on marrying the Canaanites is religious, and is in effect for all times; the Moabites and Ammonites are also forbidden for marriage for eternity, but the reason is historical; the prohibition against marrying Egyptians and Edomites is in effect for three generations alone, also for historical reasons. In contrast, the Book of Ezra contains a total ban on intermarriage, comparing all foreigners to the Canaanites and justifying the injunction in terms of their "abhorrent practices" (Ez. 9:1–2). The prohibition is not only total, but also for all times. In other words, Ezra interpreted the ancient ban on marrying the Canaanite peoples as an injunction against intermarriage in his own time, even when the foreigners were not among those prohibited by Torah law. The justification for this total exclusion is not idolatry or any other religious concern, but rather the apprehension that the reprieve promised by God to his people, "the holy seed," would be revoked if they were to become "intermingled" with other nations.[79] The expulsion of the foreign women, like the rejection of the Samaritans in the time of Zerubbabel or the debate over the construction of the wall under Nehemiah,[80] was thus, above all, a product of the religious and social problems generated by the presence of those who "separated themselves from the peoples of the lands to [follow] the Teachings of God."[81] The High Priest Eliashib and his followers were happy to accept these people as Jews in all respects. Ezra and his circles, however, feared that by not maintaining the integrity of the Jewish people, Judaism, as conceived during the exile in Babylon, would suffer. They advocated the extreme position of religious isolationism, one of whose expressions was the expulsion of the foreign women. As a result, those who attached themselves to the Jews could take part in religious rituals, such as the Passover offering,[82] but were not accepted as thoroughly Jewish, especially as regards marriage. In other words, for Ezra the integrity of the Jews and insistence on their purity as the Chosen People was the foremost consideration, and they therefore viewed the "foreign Jews" as a risk.

As we have seen, at this time Judaism was propounding universal religious values, such as those reflected in the visions of deutero-

---

[79] Ez. 9:6–15.
[80] See: Kaufman, 1969, VIII:312ff.
[81] Neh. 10:29; Kaufman, 1929–1930, I:234–248.
[82] Ez. 6:19–21.

and tertio-Isaiah and in the Psalms. Consequently, it could not accept Ezra's solution, which relied on the line of descent and distinguished between those who attached themselves to Israel on the one hand, and the Jewish people on the other, just as it could not accept the foreigner without proof of his religious faith and separation from his idolatrous past. Thus, up until the Hasmonaean period, we find the isolationist demands of Ezra and Nehemiah alongside polemical literature such as the Books of Ruth and Judith which display the model of the ancient concept of ger.[83]

As a result of the problems involved in the presence of "followers", Second Temple Judaism devised the institution of religious conversion, along with the concept of "ger tzedek," or sincere proselyte, who had nothing in common with the ger of the First Temple period save the name. Judaism was now grounded on a universal religious foundation. Accordingly, the ceremony of religious conversion ignored the specific origin of the foreigner wishing to join with Israel, and afforded him full membership in the nation, which was no longer defined by line of descent. Thus the later books of the Bible, which relate to the period following the destruction of the First Temple and contain various descriptions of the religious conversion of foreigners, eventually established under the concept of "sincere proselyte," who "took refuge under the wings of the Lord."[84] The laws that equate the status of the ger with those of an "ordinary" citizen can probably be attributed to this period as well.[85]

The Hasmonaean period in Judea, saw the emergence of a new form of conversion that might be labeled "political," as it was imposed on the peoples who surrendered to the Hasmonaeans. For example, in the second decade of the 2nd century B.C., the Edomites were converted by John Hyrcanus, an act performed on an entire nation because of expansionist aspirations.[86] Most likely for the same reason, Aristobulus forced Judaism on the Ituraeans in the north in the first decade of the 2nd century B.C., and Alexander Jannaeus (103–76 B.C.) employed a similar tactic in several of the lands he conquered. Some scholars suggest that this situation is reflected in the verses:

---

[83] See: Zakobitz, 1990:20–21, 33–35.

[84] The Vulgate as well distinguishes between the word ger in the earlier levels of the Bible and the term used for those who joined the Jewish people at later stages; see: Rosenbloom, 1978:231–22.

[85] Ex. 12:29; see also: Rosenbloom, ibid.: 22.

[86] For a discussion of this issue, see: Rapaport, 1967:219–230.

"All nations have beset me; by the name of the Lord I will surely cut them down. They beset me, they surround me; by the name of the Lord I will surely cut them down. They beset me like bees; they shall be extinguished like burning thorns; by the name of the Lord I will surely cut them down" (Ps. 118:10–12). Composed at the time of these forced conversions, the psalm employs the rare Hebrew word "amilam" ("cut them down"), a derivative of the word "mila" (circumcision). Thus the meaning here might very well be "I will circumcise them in the name of the Lord."[87] Whatever the interpretation, the fact remains that the policy of forced conversion can explain a large number of laws and customs that appear in the literature of the Sages. According to Rabbi Simon, for instance, the females of Egypt and Edom are eligible for instant conversion. This is a clear indication of the lenient Tannaitic approach to accepting the members of nations forbidden for intermarriage in Biblical law.

The special status of "ger toshav" (resident alien) also appears to have its source in the Hasmonaean period. The Tannaim do not agree, however, as to the meaning of this term. Some hold that a ger toshav is someone who has vowed not to worship idols, others claim it is a person who has committed himself to upholding the laws binding on all mankind, and still others contend it is somebody who has taken on all of the commandments save ritual slaughter. Nonetheless, there is no question in any of their minds that ger toshav refers to a person who has not taken on the yoke of all the commandments, and it is likely that the term refers to those forced to become Jews by the Hasmonaean kings. The political nature of the status also accounts for the restrictions imposed on the resident alien,[88] such as where he can and can not live. The Sages, however, were not concerned with the forced conversions of the Hasmonaeans, and it is doubtful whether the Hasmonaean kings were concerned with halakha. Their actions stemmed solely from political needs. In fact, the official decision regarding the Ammonites was taken by the Sages in Jabneh in the case of a specific individual, "Judah an Ammonite proselyte" (Mishnah, Yadayim 4, 4).

Numerous references to individual gerim also appear in various sources from the first centuries A.D. to the adoption of Christianity

---

[87] See: Bamberger, 1939:16.
[88] See: Orbach, "Ger," *Encyclopedia Ivrit*, XI, column 175.

by the Roman Empire, including the Mishnah, halakhic commentaries, Talmud, Aggadah, and Josephus Flavius. Proselytes came from all walks of life, indicating that religious conversion was a very widespread phenomenon. Had this not been so, the Romans would not have waged such a determined war against it, a position evidenced by the laws from the years following the destruction of the Temple that repeatedly forbid conversion. Indeed, from the last generations of the Second Temple period until the Christianization of Rome, there was a growing wave of converts throughout Asia Minor and in Rome itself, despite the objections of the Roman governors. The movement gained momentum in the generations after the destruction of the Temple, when Judaism, and later Christianity, admitted large masses of converts to their ranks.[89] In this period, Vespasian imposed an annual tax of 2 dinars on every Jew throughout the empire (Josephus 1982), and Suetonius relates that Domitian took pains to collect this levy even from Jews who denied their Judaism, and from women, children and converts (Sifrei, 1994). Domitian was, in fact, noted throughout his life for his hostility not only to the Jews, but also to converts and "believers." More than being a heavy financial burden, the tax represented the enforcement of paganism. Furthermore, it was the first time in Jewish history that the nation suffered legalized discrimination because of its faith. Even in the period stretching from the second half of the 1st century A.D. to the early 3rd century, when the Romans adopted a more tolerant stance toward the Jews in the Land of Israel, they demanded an embargo on proselytizing.[90] Recognition of the religious rights of the Jewish people, therefore, did not obviate the imposition of restrictions upon them. For example, at the orders of Antonius Pius, which revoked what are known as the "devastating decrees" of Hadrian, the Jews were permitted to circumcise their sons,[91] but any attempt to circumcise a proselyte was severely punished. Although by Roman law slaves were the property of their owners, Jews were now forbidden to convert their own slaves.[92] In this sense, nothing changed even in

---

[89] See: Feldman, 1983:188–207; Baron, 1967, I:132–145, II:118–127, III:129–148; Alon, 1977, II:164–166.
[90] See: Alon, ibid.: 107; Avi-Yonah, 1970:56.
[91] For the extension of the injunction against circumcision during the time of Hadrian and the devastating decrees, see: Alon, ibid.: 9–13, 14.
[92] See: Alon, ibid.: 56.

the time of Constantine, who declared Christianity legal and afforded it the same rights previously granted the Jews. When Constantine's son took power, he included the Christians in the prohibition against proselytizing.

Nevertheless, the literature of the Sages contains plentiful evidence of the existence of "those who fear the Lord,"[93] both semi-converts or sincere proselytes, in the first centuries after the destruction of the Temple. Rabbi Eliezer, Rabbi Joshua, and Rabban Gamliel, members of the Jabneh generation, visited Rome where they met with "one of the emperor's senators [who] was a God-fearing man" (Devarim Raba II, 24).[94] It is a well-known fact that the Sages were highly appreciative of those who attached themselves to the Jews, that is, the semi-converts whom they call "righteous" or "good," and assured them a place in the world to come. However, to be considered a true convert, one had to undergo full conversion: circumcision, immersion in the ritual bath, a sacrificial offering, and, of course, whole-hearted commitment to faith in the God of Israel, abandoning idolatry and accepting all the commandments. Just how common conversion was after the destruction of the Temple can also be deduced from the laws framed by Johanan ben Zaccai, which required the convert to donate one-quarter of a silver dinar for the offering when the Temple was rebuilt.[95]

Thus, rabbinical laws regarding religious conversion took shape between the return to Zion and the time of the Mishnah. The halakhic discussion of the issue centered around most of the questions that continue to be of concern to this day, including the definition of the convert, the ritual of conversion, the religious and social status of the convert, and his rights and duties. The religious nature of conversion is most obvious in the Safra homily on the verse "The stranger who resides with you shall be to you as one of your citizens" (Lev. 19:34): "'As one of your citizens'—what is a citizen, he who has taken on himself all the laws of the Torah. From this say a stranger who has taken on himself all the words of the

[93] Some scholars maintain that this phrase in the verse "Let those who fear the Lord declare, His steadfast love is eternal" (Ps. 118:4) actually refers to converts.

[94] There is also evidence of the existence of "those who fear the Lord" in the New Testament, such as in Acts 13:16, 17:4, 17. The phrase also appears on inscriptions in Italy, Greece and Cyrene.

[95] Jerusalem Talmud, Shekalim 88 51b; Babylonian Talmud, K'ritot 9a, Rosh Hashanah 31b; see: Alon 1977, I:1–70; Sifrei, 1994, II:210–211.

Torah except one he is not accepted" (Safra, Kidushim, 8). As halakha began to be consolidated in the Second Temple period, the Temple, as the center of religious ritual, obviously played a major role in the process of religious conversion. For example, a proselyte did not become a Jew until he had been circumcised, immersed in the ritual bath, and brought a beast or dove's nest as an offering. In effect, the act of conversion is comparable to receiving the Torah on Mount Sinai. Thus Rabbi Judah Ha-Nasi explains: "'As you' as your fore-fathers. As your forefathers did not enter the covenant except by circumcision, immersion, and giving of blood [sacrificial offering], so they may not enter the covenant except by circumcision, immersion, and giving of blood."[96] However, despite the analogy with the gran-ting of the Torah on Mount Sinai, the Mishnah distinguishes between the bleeding, the mother giving birth, and the leper, whose offering "is to effect the permission of eating consecrated things," and the ger whose offering "is brought in order to qualify him to enter the congregation [of Israel]" (Babylonian Talmud, K'ritot 8b).

The religious character of conversion from this time on, as well as the irrelevance of the territorial factor, can be seen from the fact that it could be performed outside the Land of Israel, although the proselyte was still required to bring an offering and sacrifice it at the Temple in Jerusalem.[97] In other words, as converts were now undergoing a religious procedure, they had to complete the ritual of conversion at the Temple, the center of religious ritual, but did not need to reside in the Land of Israel. There is indeed evidence that in the Second Temple period, proselytes went to Jerusalem to sacrifice their offerings of conversion, and foreigners went there to undergo the ritual of conversion.[98] Despite the religious character of these acts, however, converting to Judaism and attaching oneself to the Jewish people also took many different forms. We know that some people did not take on Judaism in its entirety. There were those who accepted only the principles of Jewish faith, such as belief in one God, while others adopted certain additional precepts, refraining

---

[96] Num. 15:15; Sifrei Bamidbar, 88; Tractate Gerim, Seven Short Tractates, 84, 4, New York,

[97] Sifrei Bamidbar, 88.

[98] Jerusalem Talmud, Pesachim. See: Sifrei, 1994, I:83. Interestingly, Sifrei inter-prets the journey to Jerusalem as a nationalist act of some sort. However, it seems obvious that going to Jerusalem in order to sacrifice an offering is associated with a religious ritual without any national or territorial significance.

from eating pork and observing the Sabbath, for example.[99] Numerous Greeks accepted the Laws of Israel, and it was hard to find a town without some Greeks who observed the Sabbath and abstained from forbidden food. Nevertheless, "those who fear the Lord" but did not observe all the commandments were not considered gerim. As the Tannaitic tradition states: "If a heathen is prepared to accept the Torah except one religious law, we must not receive him [as an Israelite]. R. Jose son of R. Judah says: Even [if the exception be] one point of the special minutiae of the Scribes' enactments." (Babylonian Talmud, Bekhorot 30b; Mekhiltah of Rabbi Shimon ben Yohai, Hoffman Edition, 30). Still, they were considered candidates for full membership in the Jewish people, as stated in Mekhiltah: "And in the name of Israel they shall be called—those who fear the Lord" (Mekhiltah, Mishpatim). It is not surprising, therefore, that only the act of becoming a Jew for its own sake, undertaken for reasons of conscience and in a willingness to accept all the commandments, with no ulterior motives, extrinsic benefits, or compulsion, was regarded as true conversion. For this reason, the Tanna R. Nehemiah rejects any conversion with even a hint of personal benefit or coercion, such as the "lion-proselytes" (Babylonian Talmud, Yebamot 24b), a reference to the Cuthites who professed their belief in the God of Israel out of fear for their lives after being attacked by lions.

Thus we are now dealing with the institution of conversion as we know it today. Accordingly, in the Tannaitic literature that spells out the precise procedure for conversion, we find that the rabbinical court is to inform the proselyte of "some of the minor commandments and . . . some of the major ones," as well as of the rewards and punishments of the commandments. Only if he accepts both the minor and the major commandments, "he is circumcised forthwith. As soon as he is healed arrangements are made for his immediate ablution, when two learned men must stand by his side and acquaint him with some of the minor commandments and with some of the major ones. When he comes up after his ablution he is deemed to be an Israelite in all respects." (Babylonian Talmud, Yebamot 47b–48a). Thus only when an individual agrees before a religious court to accept the commandments, from the slightest to the greatest, is he

---

[99] See: Lieberman, 1991:52–68.

considered a proper candidate for conversion. This is the start of the conversion process, which includes circumcision, immersion, and a second recitation of the commandments.

In the period of the Hasmonaeans and the new Jewish "statehood," the territorial factor again came to the fore, although it was its political significance that was stressed. Over time, Judaism spread throughout the Roman Empire, with the religious aspect receiving greater attention, particularly in the contention over the issue of conversion. Even in this period, however, conversion could only be completed by sacrificing an offering at the Temple in Jerusalem. Thus we can discern a certain distinction between Jewish identity in the Land of Israel, with an "statist" character so long as the nation enjoys sovereignty, which emphasizes the territorial aspect, and a more "congregational" religious Jewish identity for the Jews elsewhere in the Roman Empire.

At this point in time, dissension arose between the Pharisees and the Sadducees over the role of faith in the "Law of Israel" as opposed to the "Kingdom of Israel." The attitudes of both sides regarding the singularity of the collective were thoroughly particularistic, although the Pharisees were concerned with molding Jewish monotheism while the Sadducees placed less value on the articles of faith. Outside the borders of the Land of Israel, Judaism was enjoying a period of expansion on an exclusively religious basis that stressed its universal values. In light of these distinctions, there can be no question that the religious conversion of the Pharisees in or outside the Land of Israel was a totally different phenomenon from that imposed by the Hasmonaeans on subject nations. For both camps in the Land of Israel, the territorial factor remained a major focus of identity, whereas elsewhere it acquired an essentially symbolic significance.

Conversion as Entrance into Abraham's Covenant

The form of conversion that would achieve hegemony from the time of the Mishnah to the start of the modern era was that defined by the Sages as "entrance into the covenant" or "coming under the wings of the Divine Presence," considered equivalent to being present at the giving of the Torah on Mount Sinai. Several Talmudic discussions indicate, however, that immersion and circumcision were seen as the primary aspects of the ritual, whereas the Sages did not regard the sacrificial offering as an act without which conversion was incomplete.[100] In their view, the offering was designed solely to prepare a proselyte for the ritualistic activities that only a proper Jew was entitled to perform, such as partaking of the offering.[101] The offering as completion of the act of conversion can also be deduced from the remarks of Maimonides: "A proselyte who was circumcised and immersed and did not bring an offering . . . can not partake of the offering . . . .If he brings an offering and becomes a proper Jew he may partake of the holy offering" (Mishneh Torah, Hilkhot Mekhusarei Kapara, 1, 2).[102] A proselyte who does not bring an offering is a convert, but not a ger gamoor, a thorough one. Maimonides explains that a "ger gamoor" is one who is as proper as "any proper Jew."

As we have seen, the Gemara states that the proselyte's offering is meant "to qualify him to enter the congregation [of Israel]" (Babylonian Talmud, K'ritot 8b). In other words, as spelled out by Rabbi Naphtali Zvi Judah Berlin of Volozhin in his interpretation in Safra, the purpose of the offering is not "for the proselyte," as he was already converted by circumcision and immersion, but to make him as pure as any other pure Jew to partake of consecrated food (Emek Hanatziv, Sifrei Parashat 308). In this context, it is interesting to note the response of the Gemara to the question "Without an offering shall we not accept proselytes?" Rabbi Aha bar Jacob replies: "'And when a stranger who has taken up residence with you [Nu. 15:14] etc.'" (K'ritot 9a). This is a reference to the part of the verse that is missing from the Talmudic text, the words "throughout the ages." As Rashi explains: "'Throughout the ages etc.' even after destruction of the Temple (ibid., And when a stranger). In respect to the following verse: "The rest of the congregation. There shall be one law for you and for the resident stranger; it shall be a law for all time throughout the ages. You and the stranger shall be

---

[100] Yebamot 46a–b, as well as other places in the Talmud, contains a discussion of the status of the convert who was circumcised but did not immerse himself or who immersed but was not circumcised. Nowhere is there reference to the status of the proselyte who did not sacrifice an offering.

[101] See: Mishnah, K'ritot 2, 1; Babylonian Talmud, K'ritot 8b.

[102] In his commentary on Mishnah K'ritot 2, 1, Maimonides offers a different view of the role of the offering. In reference to the words of the Tanna Kama, he states: "Tanna Kama says he who was circumcised and immersed may eat of the offering and the sacrifice as a general rule."

alike before the Lord" (Nu. 15:15), the Sifrei states "that will be valid throughout the ages" (P. 89). Similarly, in Nimukei Yosef we find that the sacrificial offering "at this time does not prevent, for it is written throughout the ages and the Lord knows we do not have the giving of blood throughout the ages."[103] That is to say, the possibility of conversion exists for all time, and therefore can not be obviated by circumstances that have been altered by time, such as the discontinuation of the sacrificial offering. However, although the proselyte's offering is no longer required, halakha states that "one who becomes a proselyte at the present time must set aside a quarter for a nest of pigeons" (Babylonian Talmud, Rosh Hashanah, 31b.)[104] Rashi explains that the proselyte must set aside a quarter shekel with which to pay for an offering when the Temple is rebuilt.

This law was not universally accepted. The baraitha that presents the comments of Rabbi Simon ben Eliezer on the subject states: "Rabban Johanan took a vote on it and annulled this rule, because it may lead to wrongdoing" (*Babylonian Talmud, Rosh Hashanah*, 31b).[105] The Gemara lists this as one of the nine laws that Rabban Johanan ben Zaccai amended. Both versions of the Talmud reveal a desire to regulate the practices of the nation so that they are not dependent on the existence of the Temple. In line with this approach, the act of conversion is seen to require two major elements, immersion and circumcision,[106] with the sacrificial offering bearing less weight. In fact, the baraitha that spells out the process of conversion makes no mention whatsoever of the offering, requiring only three elements: a declaration of the proselyte's will and readiness to take on himself Judaism and its commandments without reservation; circumcision; and immersion.

The essence of conversion is clarified by Maimonides in his letter to the convert Obadiah, where he explains that a convert is someone who "left his father and homeland and kingdom of his nation and their power and comprehended in his heart and attached himself to this nation . . . and came under the wings of the Divine Presence and was covered in the dust of the feet of Moses, the teacher of all the prophets, may he rest in peace, and wished for

---

[103] See: Nimukei Yosef, Tannu rabanan, Yebamot 47a.
[104] And in parallel texts: K'ritot 9a; Jerusalem Talmud, Shekalim 8,4.
[105] Ibid.
[106] For a comprehensive discussion of this issue, see: Zohar and Sagi, 1995:85–95.

his commandments" (Responsa of Maimonides, 2). In Hilkhot Malakhim (8, 10), Maimonides also stresses this conscious factor, from which it derives that conversion must not be forced, but that the convert must accept the commandments of his own free will. Here he states that the Torah and commandments were not meant only for the Jewish people, but also "for all those from other nations who wish to become Jews."

While the sacrificial offering may not be necessary, there can be no conversion without acceptance of the commandments. The ritual is merely the final step in a lengthy process whose primary element is the willing commitment of the proselyte to observe the commandments.[107] He must turn his back on his former religious culture and accustom himself to a new way of life, and is therefore said to become "like an infant born to Israel."[108] On the basis of this perception of the Jews as a people only in their religion, many of the foremost rabbis throughout the generations have reiterated that acceptance of the commandments is the determining act in conversion. As it is adoption of the Jewish religion that turns the proselyte into a member of the Jewish people, this entails acceptance of the commandments. Indeed, in all sources, "taking on the yoke of the commandments" is the one unchanging element in determining Jewish identity.[109]

This may help us to understand the meaning of the laws relating to conversion as specified in the baraitha. The commandments and their reward and punishment are enumerated for the proselyte by a religious court, making the declaration of willingness to accept them a binding legal commitment. On the one hand, acquainting proselytes with the commandments creates the foundation for their conscious acceptance; on the other, it minimizes the number of candidates for conversion. The Gemara explains that the candidate is informed of "the sin [of the neglect of the commandment of] Gleanings, the Forgotten Sheaf, the Corner and the Poor Man's Tithe" because "a Noahide would rather be killed than spend so much as a perutah which is not returnable" (Yebamot 47b). As Rashi elucidates: "Since

---

[107] For the meaning of accepting the commandments in different periods, see Zohar and Sagi, 1995.
[108] See also: Lichtenstein, 1971:82–84.
[109] For a discussion of this issue, see: Zohar and Sagi, 1995:213ff.

they are so tightfisted with their money, as it says would rather be killed than spend so much as a perutah, he is informed of the sin of gleanings, etc. lest he withdraw his request to convert" (ibid. 5). Similarly, Hameiri clarifies that idolaters "do not have in the ways of their religions and their idol worship many commandments, and when they hear our many commandments including the most minor will say to themselves how childish they are in such unnecessary pedantry and will recant" (Hameiri on Yebamot 47b). The first enumeration of the commandments is thus the start of the conversion process. Only after the candidate agrees to accept them, can he take the next step, or, in the words of the baraitha: "If he accepted, he is circumcised forthwith." The second enumeration of the commandments by the court takes place during the immersion, after the proselyte has healed from the circumcision. This immersion is the final commitment of the convert to take on the yoke of the commandments. As he rises from the water, the ritual act of conversion is complete and he becomes a member of the Jewish people. As Rashi explains the second immersion: "By means of the immersion he becomes a convert, and thus during the required immersion he must take on the yoke of the commandments" (ibid.) Accepting the enumerated commandments before the court is not a mere declaration, but rather a legal commitment. It is only natural, therefore, that absolute sincerity is a necessary precondition of conversion, just as it is a precondition of a purchase or marriage.

This makes it clear why the convert's act of accepting the commandments is like receiving the Torah on Mount Sinai. Although the need to accept all the commandments does not appear in Shulkhan Arukh, it is demanded by the great majority of rabbinic authorities. In effect, it means acknowledging the Kingdom of Heaven, whereas acceptance of only some of the commandments stems not from the willingness to subject oneself to the Kingdom of Heaven, but from a rational analysis of their particular virtues.[110]

---

[110] See: Shaki, 1984:86–91.

BEN-GURION'S QUERY

Jerusalem
27 October 1958

Dear . . .

I am writing in the wake of a decision taken by the Government of Israel on 15 July 1958 which provides for the establishment of a committee consisting of the Prime Minister, Minister of Justice, and Minister of the Interior, to examine the regulations regarding the registration of children of mixed marriages both of whose parents wish to have them registered as Jews. In its decision, the Government directed the committee to "consult with Jewish sages in Israel and abroad," and formulate registration guidelines "that accord with the tradition accepted by all circles of Judaism, the Orthodox and liberals of all trends, and with the special circumstances of Israel as a sovereign Jewish nation ensuring freedom of conscience and religion and as the center for the ingathering of the exiles."

A population registry has existed in Israel since 1950, with "religion" and "nationhood" among the particulars which the law requires be specified in it. The Ministry of the Interior is responsible for implementing the Population Registry Act, and its officials are authorized by law to demand documents and information from the individuals subject to registration in order to confirm the particulars before they are entered. In accordance with the information in the population registry, each resident is issued an identity card which serves for a variety of purposes. In times of national emergency, each male resident is required to carry his identity card with him at all times.

It has periodically been suggested that the population registry be abolished or that the indication of "religion" or "nationhood" be eliminated, but security and other considerations have thus far prevented acceptance of these proposals and will continue to do so in the foreseeable future. In view of our special circumstances, where it is a practical impossibility to maintain constant and effective protection of all the country's borders from those infiltrating from hostile neighboring nations, who are a source of continuous grave danger to the safety of the country and its citizens, it is imperative that legal residents of Israel be able to identify themselves at all times by means of a document issued them by an authorized body.

The laws of Israel forbid any form of discrimination between individuals on the basis of differences of race, color, nationality, religion, or sex. However, Jews alone enjoy a special extra privilege afforded by the Law of Return. A non-Jew wishing to immigrate to the country must receive permission, and the country is entitled to withhold this permission. Such a person does not become a citizen of Israel by settling in the country, but only in response to a formal request for citizenship that can be submitted after residence in the country for two years. Jews, on the other hand, may immigrate under the Law of Return by virtue of being Jewish (so long as they are not potential criminals who may endanger public safety or suffer from a disease that might endanger public health). Immediately upon arrival in Israel, and after expressing a desire to settle here, they automatically and instantly become Israeli citizens.

For this reason, determining the religion of Israeli citizens is also essential: existing law places matters of marriage and divorce within the jurisdiction of the religious courts—the shari'a court for Muslims, the religious courts of the various denominations for Christians, and the rabbinical courts for Jews. By law, marriage and divorce in Israel are conducted solely according to religious norms and in religious ceremonies; Jewish weddings and divorces are conducted in Israel only according to religious law.

The question has arisen of how to register the "religion" and "nationhood" of the children of mixed marriages when the father is Jewish and the mother is not Jewish and has not converted, but both agree to have the child registered as a Jew. Some contend that as it is a civil registry that does not serve for religious purposes (religious authorities are not required, and as a rule are reluctant, to accept it or rely on it alone), there is no cause to adopt religious criteria for the registry. Others maintain that since "religion" and "nationhood" can not be separated, and since religious affiliation is by its very nature a religious issue, religious criteria should indeed by used for registering both nationhood and religion.

The Government has determined that the religion or nationality of adults will be listed as "Jewish" if they declare themselves in good faith to be Jewish and not a member of another religion. According to the Equal Rights for Women Act in effect in Israel, both parents are legal guardians of their children; if one dies, the other is the legal guardian. Therefore, the declaration of both parents will generally suffice whenever a declaration is required from a minor child. However, the registration of the children of mixed marriages in the population registry has given rise to a question in the case of a mother who is not Jewish and has not converted, but both she and the father agree to register the child as a Jew. Should the child be registered as a Jew on the basis of the parents' wishes and their good-faith declaration that he or she is not a member of another religion, or in addition to the wishes and declaration of the parents, should a ceremony be required for the child to be registered as a Jew? It is on this question that the three-member committee has been charged with making recommendations to the Government after consulting with Jewish sages, as explained above.

In order to ensure a thorough understanding of the problem, four considerations must be noted:

1. In the State of Israel, the principle of freedom of conscience and religion is ensured both in the Declaration of Independence and in the guidelines of all of its governments, which have included representatives of both "religious" and "liberal" parties. All forms of religious or anti-religious coercion are banned, and a Jew may live either an observant or secular life.

2. Israel serves today as the center of the ingathering of the exiles. Immigrants are arriving from East and West, from developed and developing countries, and the merging of the different diasporas and the creation of a single national model is one of the most vital and difficult tasks in the country. Efforts must be made to increase shared and unifying properties and eliminate as far as possible those that separate and divide.

3. The Jewish community in Israel is unlike the Jewish community in the Diaspora. Here we are not a minority subject to the pressure of a foreign culture, and there is no fear that the Jews will become assimilated among the non-Jews as there is in several prosperous free states. On the contrary, here there exists the possibility and trend for a certain assimilation of non-Jews into the Jewish people, particularly in families in which the children of mixed marriages have immigrated to Israel. Whereas mixed marriages abroad are one of the crucial factors

in total assimilation and abandonment of Judaism, the mixed couples who come here, especially from the countries of Eastern Europe, lead to total integration into the Jewish people.

4. On the other hand, the Israeli nation does not see itself as separate from Diaspora Jewry; on the contrary, no Jewish community in the world exhibits such a profound feeling of unity and identity with Jews the world over as the Jewish community in Israel. It is not by chance that the Government guidelines state that the Government will work "to deepen Jewish consciousness among Israeli youth, rooting it in the past and historical legacy of the Jewish people, and to enhance its moral commitment to world Jewry in the awareness of the shared destiny and historical continuity that unite the Jews of every generation throughout the world wherever they may live."

In view of the above, I would be most grateful for your opinion as to how we should act in the matter of registering the children of mixed marriages both of whose parents, the Jewish father and the non-Jewish mother, wish them to be registered as Jews.

Sincerely,

D. Ben-Gurion

THE LETTERS OF THE SAGES

1. SHMUEL YOSSEF AGNON

One of the leading Hebrew writers of modern times, S.Y. Agnon (1888–1970) was awarded the Nobel Prize for Literature in 1966 (with Nelly Sachs). Born in Galicia to a family of merchants allied with the Hassidic Habad movement, he received an informal education. Agnon begun writing in Hebrew and Yiddish as early as age eight, with some of his works published in Ha-Mitzpeh. After arriving in Palestine in 1907, he ceased to write in Yiddish. His first book, Ve-haya Ha-akov Le-mishor (The Crooked Shall be Made Straight; 1912), established his reputation as an author. From 1913–1924, he resided in Germany, supporting himself with odd jobs. He returned to Israel in 1924 and settled in Jerusalem. He now took the name Agnon, from the title of his story "Agunot" (Deserted Wives). Agnon was twice awarded the Israel Prize, in 1954 and 1958. His numerous works of literature include Sippur Pashut (A Simple Story), Tmol Shilshom (Only Yesterday), Atem Raitem (You Have Seen), Sefer Ha-ma'asim (Book of Deeds), and Shira.

6th day of Hanukkah, 5719

Your Excellency, the Prime Minister of Israel, Greetings and strength!

In your modesty you have sought to ask me what should be done about the children of mixed marriages whose parents, both the father and the mother, wish to register them as Jews. I count myself among the faithful of Israel, who are utterly loyal to the Torah, as interpreted by the Sages whose words were set down in Shulkhan Arukh. I therefore have nothing to add or to subtract from their words. May the Lord grant you continued good health and increase your strength and enhance your honor by virtue of your worthy deeds which will never be forgotten by our people.

With deep respect,

S.Y. Agnon

So as not to leave the page blank, forty-nine years ago I spent Passover in Sejera, where I heard a remark attributed to an elderly proselyte who said something like, you who enjoy ancestral rights, when you transgress the laws of the Torah, God does not deal with you so strictly. But we who do not enjoy the ancestral rights of Abraham, Isaac, and Jacob, whose only credit comes from observing the commandments and the religious laws, God judges us for every transgression, however minor. (I convey here the meaning, not the precise wording.)

Allow me to add something about which I was not asked. At the moment, state and religion are like two neighbors who do not regard each other amicably. As a person on whom the safety and welfare of the state rest, you would do well to refrain from concerning yourself with matters of religion, whether for good or ill, in order to leave yourself free for matters of state. I hope you will not take my words as a rebuke of any kind. It is only because I admire and respect you and desire your well being that I have allowed myself to write what I have written.

With best wishes for you and your family,

S.Y. Agnon

2. ALEXANDER ALTMANN

A rabbi and scholar, from 1931 to 1938, Altmann (1906–1987) served as rabbi and professor of philosophy at the rabbinical school in Berlin. In 1938 he went to Manchester, England, where he served as rabbi and founded the Institute for Jewish Studies, which later moved to London. In 1959 he was appointed professor of Jewish Philosophy at Brandeis University and Director of the Institute of Advanced Jewish Studies. Altmann's numerous studies in Jewish philosophy include major works on Sa'adia Gaon and Moses Mendelssohn. He also served as editor of the *Journal of Jewish Studies Scripta Judaica*. His father, Adolph (1879–1944), a rabbi in Trier, Hungary, emigrated to Holland in 1938 and died in Auschwitz.

15 December 1958

Dear Prime Minister,

I received your letter of 27 October in the United States, and am hastening to reply to your request for my opinion concerning the important question occupying the minds of the members of the committee appointed in the wake of the decision of the Government of Israel of 15 July 1958.

As I understand it, in practical terms the question is how to formulate the regulations for the registration of children of mixed marriages where the mother is not Jewish and has not converted to Judaism, but both she and the Jewish father agree that the child should be Jewish—whether to register him as a Jew on the basis of the parents' wishes and their declaration in good faith that he is not a member of another religion, or whether in addition to the parents' agreement and declaration a ceremony of some sort should still be required in order for the child to be registered as a Jew. In other words, the problem is whether the parents' declaration is sufficient to endow their child with the legal status of "Jew," or whether the child must undergo a specific religious act in accordance with the traditional laws of halakha in order to become a member of the Jewish people. Presumably, in these cases the parents do not wish their children to undergo a rite of conversion, as otherwise the problem would not arise and they would naturally apply to an Israeli rabbinical court to have the child converted. It may be assumed that in these instances the parents themselves are not observant and see no need for their child to be accepted as a convert, as they are satisfied with his being Jewish solely in the national sense of the term.

It would appear that this attitude is grounded in the view that the title "Jew" applies even if the religious aspect is totally discarded, and that a person who is not born a Jew can become a member of the Jewish people on the basis of his own personal wishes—or in the case of a child, on the basis of the parents' declaration.

In effect, the question is: Does such a possibility exist, and is there a category of Jews whose Judaism is limited to national affiliation alone?

Clearly, the problem that arises is, in actuality, whether it is permissible for the laws of the State of Israel to distinguish between religion and nationality, or whether such a distinction would be invalid in the State of Israel, and the traditional concept must be retained whereby religion and nationality constitute a single unalterable entity.

Before I attempt to reply to this question, I would like to remark that perhaps a way can be found to implement the Population Registry Act so that the issue of religion and nationality does not arise at all. I would suggest that instead of asking to which religion and nationality an individual belongs, it would be preferable to indicate the ethnic origin of the mother and father alone. The answer to this question would innately indicate the nature of the individual in terms of the security considerations that require a population registry, achieving this purpose in full. As a matter of course, the child of a mixed marriage, whose father is Jewish and mother Polish for example, would be registered in this manner, objectively and according to the clear facts, without attempting to determine the nationality of the child himself. I must state that there is no place for the question of religion and nationality on the identity card of a modern democratic state. On the other hand, the special circumstances prevailing in the State of Israel demand that unusual attention is paid to an individual's extraction. I am told that in the United States as well it is customary to inquire as to the ethnic origin of anyone applying to the consulate for an immigration visa.

Should this suggestion prove unfeasible, the question indicated above will recur and require an answer in principle.

In my opinion, the indivisible identity between nationality and religion is one of the essential aspects of Judaism. In light of Jewish tradition, religion is not a supplement to nationality, but its very essence and root. The ancient Israelite tribes merged into a nation solely under the influence of religious experiences, and the history of the nation and the religion are identical. Ruth the Moabite expressed her desire to devote herself to the Israelite nation by saying: "Your people shall be my people and your God my God." "People" and "God" are linked together, and this bond cannot be broken. Naturally, although a similar unity existed among other nations in the ancient Middle East, for the Jews the religious notion of "the Chosen People" was added, whereby the nation was consecrated from birth to a universal religious function that is its great and glorious destiny. This idea is the single motif running throughout the history of Jewish thought, whatever its schools or manifestations, from Biblical times to the period of the Sages and the philosophy of the Middle Ages and the kabbalists, and it has not lost its vibrancy to this day. We must not ignore the fact that the modern secularization of Christian nations has led to a separation of religion and nationality. Nevertheless, neither the religion nor the nationality of the Christian nations has suffered from this development, as the identity between the two was no more than an historical event incurred at some time by the conquest of a nation and its subjugation to the church; it is not a natural organic connection such as that within the Jewish nation. Franz Rosenzweig was right in saying that the gash between the national myth and the conquering religion has never healed in the soul of the Christian nations, and that one of the reasons for anti-Semitism might be the rebellion of an pagan nation against a religion whose source is in Judaism. In the soul of the Jewish nation, religion and nationality have never clashed; on the contrary, the more a Jew strives to understand his Torah and God, the more he understands his nationality. The whole of the national effort of the Jewish people stems from unity between religious faith and the desire to ensure the survival of the nation. Anyone who jeopardizes this unity is presumably jeopardizing the very heart of the nation. It is clear, therefore, that there can be no recognition of Jewish nationality as separate from religion, and the answer to the question presented above is, absolutely, that the mere statements of the parents, no matter how sincerely they are made, do not have the power to make a child Jewish. In addition to their declaration and the expression of their wishes, the child must undergo conversion according to tradition and halakha.

Thus far I have addressed the theological side of the issue. It is of particular significance precisely at this point in time when we have achieved national rebirth and a sovereign Jewish state has been established in its holy land, since in the wake of the establishment of the state a major change has already taken place in respect to the meaning of the name "Israel." This name has become the term for the citizenship of both Jews and Arabs, as well as those of other nations who join us or are granted Israeli citizenship. As a result of this historical process, the name "Israel" has thus been somewhat stripped of its religious meaning and become a political term. We must therefore take care not to erase the religious meaning of the name "Jew" as well, reducing it to a lower level out of some political secular intent. Such a change is implied in the suggestion to employ the name "Jew" for people who are not worthy of bearing it according to tradition and religion. I believe the name should be reserved only for people who are Jewish by birth or conversion. Naturally, a Jew by birth or conversion remains a Jew forever, even if he does not lead a religious life, as halakha had adopted the rule: "Though he has sinned—he is a Jew."

Introducing a third name such as "Hebrew" for the category of national Jews alone is, in my opinion, not recommended. Who will be satisfied with this title, which is inherently inferior to the title "Jew"? Furthermore, why use additional names and thereby add to the confusion?

The opinion presented here does not conflict with the principle of freedom of religion ensured every inhabitant of the State of Israel. The principle of freedom of conscience and religion denotes only a ban on religious coercion of any sort, and gives every individual the right to adopt whatever religion he desires. The State does not require anyone to observe or not observe any religion whatsoever in his private life. However, clearly if he wishes to enter a religion, he must convert. Mere desire is not enough to make him a member of a community to which he wishes to belong. Just as the individual is free to choose whichever religion he pleases, so the religious authorities must be free to accept or reject him.

I agree wholeheartedly with the considerations enumerated in your letter which stress that the need for "the merging of the different diasporas and the creation of a single national model is one of the most vital tasks in the country." However, precisely for this reason it is important to demand that the children of mixed marriages be accepted as full converts and not semi-converts. Otherwise, the process of integration will not succeed, and these children will forever regard themselves as different and not full Jews. In the desire to help them achieve total integration into the body of the nation, we must take care not to afford them the nature of Jewish nationality alone. There is a danger that unless they are accepted as "sincere proselytes" the possibility of their "entering the congregation of the Lord" by marriage into Jewish families, including religious families, will not be realized. Thus for their own sake, proper conversion should be required, rather than the mere expression of the parents' opinion.

Finally, I would like to stress one more matter. The rabbinate in Israel must, of course, be free to deal as it sees fit with anyone wishing to convert to Judaism. The rabbis have the authority and are responsible to the Lord and to the nation. It is to be hoped, however, that at the crossroads at which we find ourselves at this time, when the different diasporas are coming together in Israel and the country anticipates the arrival of hundreds of thousands of Jews from Eastern Europe, the rabbis will approach the issue of converts charitably and will ease the acceptance into Judaism of those children whose parents have arrived in Israel as a place of refuge and freedom. A serious task is placed on the shoulders of the rabbis to bring those children under the wings of the Divine Presence in order to instill in them affection for the Jewish people and its sacred tradition. I pray that the rabbis in the State of Israel will do everything in their power to further the full integration of these children.

Respectfully,

Alexander Altmann

3. HENRY BARUK

A psychiatrist, Baruk (1897–1999) served as the chief doctor of the Charenton psychiatric hospital from 1931, as a professor at the Sorbonne from 1946, and as the chairman of the French Neurological Society from 1957. He was particularly interested in anthropology and Biblical medicine, publishing works on the connection between religious faith and medical ethics, including *Hebraic Civilization and the Science of Man* (1962) and *Psychiatrie morale, expérimentale, individuelle et sociale* (1965). Baruk was active in Jewish affairs in France and in the Association of Friends of the Hebrew University.

[excerpts]

The enquiry the Government of Israel is conducting in order to define who is a Jew is of great interest. Indeed, the Jewish people is a riddle for other nations and often for itself as well. [. . .]

This difficulty stems from the fact that human beings have rational capacities the use of which generally tend to reduce reality to simple ideas and clear comprehensible concepts. Nevertheless, it is impossible to grasp nature by means of a single idea, as it is considerably more complex. For example, it is customary to distinguish between people, nation, and religion. "People" refers to the families and original group, "nation" to a political territorial group, and "religion" to internal beliefs.

For the Jewish people, however, the situation is different. The Jewish people cannot be characterized by anyone of these three simplistic notions; more precisely, it is a union of all three. It is a people, a nation, and a religion at one and the same time, and so cannot be defined as anyone alone. Although some believe that the Jewish people can be defined as a special race, in the biological sense of the term, history cannot accept this view. If we agree, as most do, that Jacob is the father of the Jewish people, how are we to understand that of the two sons of Isaac and Rebecca, only Jacob is held to be Jewish, while Esau, his twin brother, is held to be a non-Jew, and even the representative of nations considered enemies of the Jews (Edom)? Jacob and Esau were born to the same father and mother, but Jacob believed in the God of Abraham and took on himself the way of life of his forefathers, whereas Esau clearly dis-associated himself from this faith and way of life, preferring hun-ting and aggression and seeing no point or meaning in human life. His attitude, understanding, and conduct were not those of a Jew. The opposite is also true; we know that King David himself was a descendent of Ruth, a Moabite woman. In terms of race, in its most basic meaning, Ruth was alien to the Jewish people, yet her affection for her mother-in-law, her devotion, her heart, and her feeling for a person in trouble were such that she is considered a Jew. In effect, she represents a special case of a sincere proselyte, that is, a person who becomes part of the Jewish people by unreserved and unfal-tering devotion to Jewish values, not only in thought, but in deed as well. [. . .]

Nonetheless, it is still very difficult for a non-Jew to become a Jew. In other religions, it is sufficient to accept a system of beliefs in order to become a member. For example, it is quite easy to become a Christian, as Christianity facilitates the process of con-version and operates spiritedly to increase its ranks in this manner. The situation is very different in Judaism, however. Not only has it been reluctant to convert gentiles and almost entirely refrained from forced conversion, unlike Christianity and Islam, but it also places very serious obstacles in the paths of converts. This attitude stems from the fact that Jewish law is not satisfied with the acceptance or declaration of tenets, but aims for Jews to maintain a whole way of life, down to the very last detail. For Jews, the value of actions is greater than the value of declarations; in fact, actions are the only translation of faith. Thoughts and their implementation in practice are one and the same, and cannot be separated, as this unity is the organizing factor in Jewish life. From this perspective, it is very difficult to be a Jew. It demands lengthy preparation, the most advanced study, and meticulous practice for a person to accustom himself to profound habits both in thought and in lifestyle. [. . .]

These facts are all indications that Judaism is much more than a religion, in the sense in which the word is generally understood, that is, as a set of obligatory beliefs, and that Judaism is truly an organic cell in which the spiritual and the material merge into a single entity. Here faith has become part of the body of the nation, as well as of the physical body. It is not an arbitrary symbol that Abraham's covenant is marked in the flesh, for, as has often been said, a Jew thinks and acts with all his organs, so that the spiritual and the physical are inseparable. [. . .]

Without attempting to sum up Judaism in a few principles, as Maimonides did, I nevertheless believe it is necessary to stress the specific most characteristic features of Jewish civilization in order to demonstrate not only what it has already contributed to humanity, but also what it is obliged to realize in the future, as the purpose of life is the primary factor that gives life to individuals and nations.

1. *The Abolishment of Human Sacrifice; Moral Responsibility and the Concept of Justice*

From the time of Abraham, the Jewish people abolished the practice of human sacrifice and replaced it with animal sacrifice, thereby laying the foundations of human responsibility and justice. [. . .] Denying a moral consciousness not only leads to a frightening increase in crime, but also to a faulty system of justice. [. . .] Justice assumes true faith; it must be carried out before God, the Supreme Judge who protects the innocent. This is because justice assumes an unreserved love for the truth. [. . .] It is this love of authentic justice that represents the deepest meaning of Judaism. [. . .]

2. *Justice and the Worship of God as Opposed to Idolatry*

[. . .] Responsibility, judgment according to good and evil, the rulings of the unbiased incorruptible Supreme Judge who is not swayed by everyday affairs and protects the innocent—this is the concept which humanity fears and cannot tolerate. What is wished for by a large force opposing any attempt for real reform and seeking to spoil any such effort is tolerance for contemptible exploiters who live off their brothers and advocate the Roman ethic of "*homo hominus lupus.*" All attempts to strengthen the morality of mankind incur the appalling loathing of this force, a circumstance with which the Jewish people is very familiar. [. . .] Paganism, submission to blind fate, to the stars, to destiny, can all lead to the corruption of virtue, especially in sexual matters, and can spread swiftly. [. . .] A proper Jew does not give in to paganism and the perversions associated with it. He leads a holy life and defends it and its meaning enthusiastically. True human happiness is a product of the value of deeds and the undying hope for a better constellation of life on earth, in a covenant between man and the laws of nature handed down to him by God. Such happiness can never come from the misguided sanctification of the human being, which is often no more than a mere arrogant response meant to compensate for helplessness, despair, and abandonment. [. . .]

3. *The Sabbath*

[. . .] The seventh day rest is stated and reiterated in every text and appears at the head of the list of commandments as one of the most important rules. [. . .] The Jewish people is, in fact, defined as the nation charged with preserving the Sabbath. Without the Sabbath, Jewish civilization could not exist. It is, above all, a reminder of the Creation, as the Lord rested on the seventh day. But it is also a symbol and guarantee of the freedom of man and of human social organization. [. . .]

4. *Respect for the Sources*

[. . .] Pious and meticulous respect for the sources is a basic pillar of Judaism. It is reflected in honoring one's parents, honoring those from whom one learns anything, honoring one's elders, [. . .] and through these forms of respect, honoring the Lord who created man. Thus Jewish monotheism represents a single indivisible entity. [. . .]

This belief is dictated by the principle of the unity of theory and practice. This is not a blind principle relegated to "the heavens and beyond the sea" in order to avoid putting it into practice, but rather a living fact so real that it is an essential part of daily life. [. . .]

5. *The 613 Commandments and Application of the Torah*

[. . .] The many commandments of the Torah are extremely difficult to comprehend for anyone with a Western orientation accustomed to dividing everything into categories, sectors, compartments, or specialties. From this perspective, it is obviously a simple matter to separate medicine from sociology, political economics, the martial arts, dietetics, morality, cosmology, the natural sciences, philosophy, theology, etc. [. . .] The Torah can be divided however one likes, but such decomposition gravely alters it and distorts historical truth. This is because the Torah is all those sciences at once; it is all those sciences merged into a single unalterable unity. [. . .]

What is a Jew?

1. It can be understood that the Jewish people has served as living support for the most profound civilization for hundreds of years, which must be preserved in practice and by adapting to the conditions of each century in anticipation of the Messianic period. From this perspective, the nation must also take care not to be flooded by a mass of new members. On the other hand, the practice of Jewish civilization demands long years of acquisition of habits passed on in the family from generation to generation, and to a certain extent also by heredity. In contrast to the imperialist conception of the universality of conquering souls, Judaism and the conception of Abraham respect the personality of individuals and nations and do not attempt to convert them. Rather, they wish to create a sort of federation of different peoples in which each nation preserves its own character but all are united by awareness of the basic moral principle directing humanity and the world. [. . .] The effort for improvement in Judaism does not impose itself on others in order to justify their conquest, but on the Jew himself so that he may more deeply study the Torah and apply it. The universal preoccupations of Judaism are very great, but they exist only as a model of realization and not as propaganda. [. . .]

2. Judaism has never refused to accept new members so long as this acceptance was limited and conditioned on unequivocal guarantees. The commentaries of the Midrash and Rashi explain that when Abraham left Ur and moved to Canaan with all his belongings and all those under his authority, there were already believers who adopted his monotheistic faith. Similar commentaries deal with Jacob. Thus, the convert, the non-Jewish foreigner who became a Jew out of conviction, was always accepted, and it can be said that such spontaneous unimposed conversions played an important role in the history of the Jewish people. This situation served as a filter preventing the entrance of weak self-interested parties. In several cases we see the phenomenon of "sincere proselytes," that is, foreigners who left behind a fine secure status in order to join the Jews and stand beside them during the persecutions, accepting a law much stricter than those common in other nations. [. . .]

3. Jews by birth, that is, who are born to Jewish parents, may benefit from a legacy of practice and the profound education of genera-

tions, but only if they maintain the Jewish faith and its virtues. However, Jews by birth are not shielded from assimilation. On the contrary, particularly in this age of extreme anti-religion, the Jews, like other peoples, are subject to the influence of doctrines and lifestyles alien to their traditions, and an extreme active neo-paganism is evolving. [. . .] In addition, some Jews by birth regret the fact that they are Jewish and the object of persecution, especially if they lack a Jewish education, and are attracted to the ways of life of other nations which they might easily consider superior and successful. They are influenced by the ostensibly triumphant religions, and are liable to make serious efforts to become assimilated, to abandon Judaism and identify with non-Jews. Such efforts often encounter the opposition of their collective subconscious, shaped by Jewish customs that have existed for thousands of years. The result is severe psychological consternation, which generally leads these Jews by birth to become anti-Semitic, to exhibit a willingness for shameful submission, or finally, to suffer particular mental illness. [. . .] Without going into what are very important psychiatric details, I would only mention that the confusion that turns Jews into anti-Semites has far-reaching implications. [. . .]

The quality of being Jewish cannot be associated exclusively with the racial factor. Heredity is not enough, as the Jewish people does not constitute a racial group but a group formed by its connection to a faith, a civilization, and a way of life; a group supported by family and heredity but one that can not be divorced from the spiritual faith that molded it, that in effect created it, since it is faith that led Abraham to leave his country in order to build a special nation, "a nation of priests" devoted to one God. Anyone forgetting this origin and its significance not only denies the whole of the Jewish tradition, but also supports a doctrine that is alien to Judaism, a doctrine that is to be considered an abomination, a manifestation of paganism. [. . .]

Some rabbinical groups distinguish [in respect to the conversion of the children of mixed marriages] between the children of Jewish mothers, whom they consider Jewish, and children whose father alone is Jewish, whom they find it difficult to recognize as Jews. This distinction has its source in Deuteronomy, which gives the names of the mothers of kings. However, this indication of the mother might be explained by the fact that all of them already bore the names of their fathers, so that in order to note the name of the second parent, the mother's name had to be mentioned. This does not imply that only descent from the mother counts.

On this subject, it is worth noting that while the laws of the Torah represent eternal law, the writings of the rabbis are prescriptions determined by circumstances and can be altered. Furthermore, the customs of a time have often led to certain changes in the laws of the Torah that were of major importance. Thus, animal sacrifice replaced human sacrifice, and the law of the red heifer and certain laws of uncleanness lost their validity. We cannot, however, predict that these laws will not be reinstated when Judaism returns to thrive in the Land of Israel. Conversely, rabbinical prescriptions formulated at certain times may lose their validity, particularly those that relate to maternal or paternal heredity. It should be mentioned here that Moses himself was married to a non-Jew, and yet his children were considered Jewish; Joseph married an Egyptian woman and his two sons, Ephraim and Menashe, became the two leaders of the Jewish tribes. [. . .] On the other hand, on the return to the Land of Israel from Babylon, in the time of Ezra and Nehemiah, a harsh battle was waged against Jews married to foreign woman for fear that they would lead their husbands and children to idolatry. Yet even in these struggles we see that the motive was to preserve religious faith and was not racial or biological. [. . .] Obviously, the numerous mixed marriages jeopardized the survival of the Jewish nation among other nations, and therefore after lengthy exile and the return to Zion, it was necessary to take precautions to ward off this danger. In fact, within mixed marriages it is the stronger conviction that holds sway. If the Jewish spouse is weaker in his or her faith, the other spouse will pull them toward their spirituality. Thus it is the spiritual aspect that counts, and not blood. [. . .]

The Government of Israel, like any government, has the right to study the situation of each candidate for citizenship in order to decide whether or not to grant it. Citizenship is a matter for the country, for the government, and requires no religious intervention; it can be equal for all, whatever their origin and religion. The Torah itself commands that the same law apply to Jews and non-Jews, and that foreigners receive the same treatment as all citizens. Every Jew must remember that he was a stranger in Egypt. The State of Israel is not only the center for the ingathering of the exiles, but must also be the center of living Judaism. As in the days of antiquity, Judaism must shine on the world and bring the spirit of the Torah alive. Naturally, in granting citizenship, the State of Israel may take into consideration the rights of each candidate, his connection with Judaism, his family, his wishes, the enquiries he was submitted to, etc. In view of all of these, it can grant citizenship with greater or lesser alacrity. Such an approach, applied in a just and unbiased manner, is preferable to the automatic granting of citizenship, and will make it more highly appreciated.

4. SHMUEL HUGO BERGMANN

A philosopher, Bergmann (1883–1975) was born in Czechoslovakia and studied in Prague. He was strongly influenced by the ideas of Martin Buber, Aharon David Gordon, and Ahad Ha-am. Arriving in Israel in 1920, he was one of the founders of the Histadrut Labor Federation, representing Hashomer Ha-Tza'ir. He went on to help found the Hebrew University in Jerusalem, where he was a lecturer in philosophy (1928), a full professor (1935), and rector of the university (1936–1938). He was awarded the Israel Prize in 1954 for his writings in philosophy, and again in 1974 for his contribution to society and the country. Bergmann preached reconciliation between Jews and Arabs, and was a member of the Brit Shalom movement.

14 December 1958

Honorable Sir,

With the greatest reverence, I hereby offer my response to your letter of 27 October 1958. I believe in the special sanctity of the Jewish people as a "holy nation" in which nationality and religion are one and the same. The act of being born in holiness is the foundation of the existence of our nation-religion. Franz Rosenzweig once said, making a German pun, that for the Jews, unlike other religions, birth (*zweigung*) came instead of faith (*uberzweigung*), and I accept that view and therefore fully comprehend the position of the ultra-Orthodox toward any attempt at modification in this respect.

On the other hand, however, I cannot ignore the historical situation in Israel created by the establishment of a secular Jewish state and the influx of immigrants who have been detached from the historical-religious basis of our existence. In the situation that has emerged, I can understand the decision of the Government that "the religion or nationality of adults will be listed as 'Jewish' if they declare themselves in good faith to be Jewish and not a member of another religion." However, this creates a concept of "Jewish" that is in no way in accord with the halakhic concept of "Jew." To phrase it in the terms of the science of logic: it creates two concepts of "Jew," both of which are given the same equivocal name. If we do not wish to delude ourselves, we must distinguish between the concepts of "Jews by halakha" and "Jews by declaration who are not Jews by halakha." There are also Jews by halakha who are not Jews by declaration. Edith Stein, for example, a nun who died in a concentration camp and the daughter of a Jewish family in Breslau, was a Jew by religious law and died as a Jew. Yet according to the decision of the Government, she was not Jewish because she was a member of another religion.

Following this decision of the Government, we must therefore accept the fact that there are two concepts of "Jew," and that the State of Israel is founded on principles that can not be accepted by halakha. We do not have the right to cover up this tragic conflict, but must await the decision of history that will demonstrate whether the Jewish nation wishes to remain faithful to its religious foundations or to be a nation like any other. No equivocal formulation will be of any use. We must face the reality of the tragic situation courageously.

As for the concrete question you posed concerning the registration of the children of mixed marriages, I see two possibilities:
1. Such children can be registered as "Jews by parents' declaration" similarly to adults.
2. The indication of religion can be eliminated altogether. While among the arguments contained in your letter, I find important reasons for noting the nationality of every citizen, I can find no convincing argument for indicating religion. Thus I believe the best solution would be to eliminate the notation of religion. The religious authorities can conduct their own registration according to the demands of halakha, but this is not a matter for the state, which is secular and whose secular needs require that—as in the case of the registration of adults by declaration—it acts in ways other than halakhic.

We can only hope that this situation of two authorities—secular and religious—is a transitional one, and that the development of both halakha and secular concepts will one day reunite them once again.

Respectfully and with best wishes,

S.H. Bergmann

5. ISAIAH BERLIN

A philosopher and political scientist, Berlin (1909–1997) was born in Latvia and emigrated to England as a child. He studied at Oxford, where he later became a lecturer in philosophy (1932). The first Jew admitted to All Souls College (1938), Berlin was conscripted into British intelligence in World War II and served in Washington and Moscow. In 1957 he was appointed professor of social and political theory, and in 1966 became president of Wolfson College at Oxford. He also served as vice president of the British Academy from 1959-1961 and as its president from 1974. Berlin was awarded the Jerusalem Prize in 1978, and was a member of the Board of Trustees of the Hebrew University in Jerusalem. His work reveals a consistently liberal approach to social and political questions. *Four Essays on Liberty* (1969) is one of his many published works.

Oxford, 23 January 1959

Dear Mr. Prime Minister,

I must begin with a number of apologies. The first for delaying for so many weeks in answering your enquiry (which I received towards the end of last year, about a month after the letter was dated), with regard to the definition of Jews in Israel, and with special regard to the problem of the children of a certain type of mixed marriage. I must apologize also for not replying to you in Hebrew, a language which I love so much more deeply than I know it, that it may be that I have not perfectly understood the sense of your letter, and for this too I must ask to be forgiven; and finally, for the observations that I am about to make.

I was naturally greatly honored by the fact that you should have considered me worthy of being consulted on a matter of such importance; and it is not only because of the intrinsic interest and urgency of the matter, but, far more, because of the deep respect (as you must know) and admiration which I feel towards yourself and the principles for which you stand, that I have done my best to produce an answer. At the same time, I should not be wholly candid if I did not add that your letter placed me in a somewhat embarrassing, not to say false, position: for I do not believe that much good can be done by consulting anyone outside the frontiers of the State of Israel on a matter which is not only ultimately, but immediately, the administrative responsibility of the Israel Government itself, and can be settled only by it and the Knesset. You speak, unanswerably, of the bonds that unite the Jews of Israel with the Jewish community in the rest of the world: nevertheless a minute examination of these bonds is bound to bring up issues concerning which there may be profound disagreement, not merely between Israel and the Diaspora, but within Israel itself, and the Diaspora itself. Insofar as Israel is a sovereign State founded to give full political and social expression to the Jewish nation, it must (and does), whenever critical issues present themselves, act on its own responsibility as a sovereign State, and on behalf of what it conceives to be the interests of the nation of which it is the political expression, without responsibility to, and without being obliged to seek the advice of Jews beyond its borders. It cannot (and would not wish to) escape the judgment of public opinion among the Jews of the world, any more than a British Government could escape the judgment of many men of British race in other parts of the world. But it cannot be guided by such opinion directly. If, of course, the Jews are to be conceived as principally a religious establishment—a kind of church— then nothing is more natural than to seek the expression of the views of the members of the church before an important decision by the leaders of the church is made. But I cannot believe that you hold this view. It appears to me, and I am sure you will agree, that the status of the Jews is unique and anomalous, composed of national, cultural, religious strands inextricably intertwined. It seems to me that unless and until it becomes imperative, as it may one day, to face Jews with so crucial an issue, little advantage is to be gained from doing so. It does not seem to me that the case concerning which you have formulated your enquiry is crucial in this extreme sense, and that therefore little good and perhaps some harm could result from forcing an alignment on it, i.e., by getting various individual Jews to state their cut-and-dried opinion on the subject, declare themselves, and fly a flag.

If, of course, you think that a "Kulturkampf" is, in any case, inevitable, that the civil status of the State of Israel must be sharply and definitively divided from Judaism as an established religion (a point of view with which I have some sympathy), and that this is the moment to establish once and for all the principle that a modern liberal State is, and must be, secular in character, and that the religion of its citizens is, in so far as it is a State and nothing else, indifferent to it, then you may be right to issue such a questionnaire. I myself feel qualms before adding even my own minute drop of fuel to what is not yet a major conflagration. I was much tempted to follow the example of my illustrious friend Justice Felix Frankfurter, and refrain from giving a definite reply to your questions. But I have not his protection of judicial neutrality in political matters; and I therefore do append an answer (which does not satisfy me, but is the best that I can produce) because my regard for your person is greater than my wish to preserve myself from error by refusing to commit myself, where factors are so precariously balanced and in a field where I am (and am known to be) an ignoramus, and the issue so dubious. This is my only reason for sending a reply. I have shown it to Sir Leon Simon, and find that while I share some of his views, I do not share others. I am neither a rabbi, nor a lawyer, nor a specialist in Jewish history or sociology: my opinion is not, you must believe me, worth much: but I cannot bear to be so self-regarding or self-important as to decline to give it because it is not weighty enough, or may expose me to justified (or unjustified) criticisms.

I hope profoundly that it will not be necessary to advertise the results of this great enquiry in any way—not only that individual replies will be treated as confidential; and that when the Government finally acts it will do so without too much regard for, and too much open debate with, its outside advisers. I hope you will forgive me for all this gratuitous advice in your uniquely responsible and historic predicament. It is not meant to be officious or immodest.

I should like to say once more how deeply I appreciate the fact that you have done me the honor of asking for my views.

Yours sincerely,

Isaiah Berlin

Memorandum to the Prime Minister of Israel

1. I assume that the main problem before the State of Israel is of the attitude that it should take towards the children of Jewish fathers

and non-Jewish mothers, where the mother has not been converted to Judaism, and both parents desire the child to be registered as a Jew in Israel. There is also the related question created by whether or not the religious authorities can accept as Jews persons who for their own reasons do not desire to belong to any religious denomination, or avail themselves of facilities provided by religious bodies. The two classes may of course overlap.

2. Should children of such mixed marriages be regarded and registered as Jews in Israel? Should persons who declare themselves atheists or belong to some religion other than Jewish, but who nevertheless claim to be Jews by nationality, be permitted to register as (say) atheists or Christians by religion, and Jews by nationality? What would this latter category connote, and what privileges and rights would it carry or forfeit?

3. In connection with this it seems to me not a merely academic fact that most words in common use are susceptible to at least two types of definition: (a) a precise but somewhat artificial definition necessitated by legal or theological or scientific requirements; and (b) the loose definition entailed by the use of words in everyday speech. The word "Jew" has, so far as I can tell, this narrower or tighter meaning as defined by Halakha—namely the son of a Jewess or a convert to Judaism; but equally it has a looser connotation in common speech. A Jew in this looser sense is anyone whom a normal person, acquainted with the customary use of the term, would, without too much reflection, describe as a Jew (just as a table is what most people agree to be a table, even though, e.g. for certain commercial or legal purposes, the meaning of the word "table" may have to be artificially tightened up). In this normal sense we can speak of "atheistic Jews" without any sense of contradiction; for we should make a man to be a Jew, if he were in most respects identified with a Jewish community, despite the fact that his mother may be an unconverted non-Jewess, and that the rabbis may therefore quite correctly reject his claims to be a Jew in the religious—narrower—sense of the word.

4. The practice of the State of Israel, inasmuch as it involves the ascription to Jews of certain rights and duties which may not necessarily also be ascribed to non-Jews, creates the need for a legally precise definition of the term "Jew." How should it be defined?

5. It seems clear to me that inasmuch as the State of Israel claims to be (as I think it does—and with justice) a liberal state and not a theocracy, it cannot define the status of its citizens or even of its

residents in purely religious terms. If Israel is not to be a theocracy or impose religious tests of civil rights, it cannot withhold such rights as marriage, divorce, burial, etc. from persons who proclaim themselves avowed atheists, or from those who do not profess a religion recognized as such by the State, simply on those grounds alone. If there is to be no religious coercion, as your letter so properly states, it must be possible for any resident of Israel to be married and divorced without recourse to a religious ceremony of any kind. If this is at present not politically feasible, owing to the strength of Israeli or Jewish opinion against it, this makes for some, if not a very high degree, of religious discrimination, and the problem of how to guarantee the civil liberties of the entire Israeli population, as civil freedom is understood in modern states today, seems to me, so long as this persists, in principle not soluble. This may, in view of the small number of persons affected by the absence of the civil institutions of marriage, divorce, etc., not be an urgent problem at present. But the existence of this situation is nevertheless a blemish; and grave though the moral and spiritual problems its solution may pose, nothing is gained by denying its existence.

6. If Israel is to be in the full sense a modern liberal State, the question of religious affiliation should make no difference to its laws of citizenship, or the civil and political rights enjoyed by its inhabitants. On the other hand, it is clear that there would have come into being no State of Israel if Judaism were merely a religion, and not, in some sense, a nationality as well. I assume that, for reasons of security, if none other, the inhabitants of Israel may at any rate for some time be required to register as either Jews or non-Jews of various categories. Should persons who are recognized (by members of their society, Jewish or non-Jewish) as Jews in the common sense of the word, but are not recognized as Jews by the rabbis interpreting the Halakha in the traditionally accepted manner, be regarded as politically and legally Jews or not? There can be no clearcut or ready-made solution to this problem. If we are to rule out religious coercion even of the mildest kind—by the pressure of custom and public opinion—as being incompatible with the minimum of requirements of individual liberty (and I cannot see how Israel can morally fail to do so—it was not denial of religious liberties that created Zionism) then there must exist a category of persons who will be entitled to register themselves as Jews by nationality, but not by religion. What criterion can be used in determining who these persons

are? I must admit that the common sense criterion, according to which anyone is a Jew who is taken to be a Jew, particularly by his Gentile neighbors in the countries of the Dispersion, seems to be near the mark but somewhat fluid and vague. We can invent one, e.g., the criterion already proposed by some in Israel, including, I believe, yourself, of a declaration that one belongs to no other religion and therefore desires to be a Jew. Against that, some may argue that this definition is too wide—it could include persons not normally thought of as Jews by anyone (say an ex-Nazi pagan)—and too narrow, for it should in principle be possible—however few persons will follow this in practice or however anomalous this may seem-, for a man to be nationally a Jew and by religion a Christian, a Moslem or whatever he pleases. To say that the national categories of Jew, Arab, Armenian, etc., may be retained, but that if a man is a Christian, he is automatically deprived of some political rights does seem to me—even if it is politically unavoidable and demanded by Jewish public opinion—a form of religious discrimination. You may call this academic, since it is not, at present, an important practical issue, since the number of eccentrics who desire to live as Jews in Israel and yet practice some non-Jewish religion, does not at present seem likely to become at all significant. Nevertheless, the issue of principle is there, and might one day (if, for example, Christian missions succeed in making converts) become important. Perhaps therefore the best solution to this problem, so long as the Law of Return operates, is to determine the nationality of such queer borderline cases (and it is only about them that this issue revolves) by means of *ad hoc* machinery: to establish a Commission, whether as part of an existing Ministry, or as a special institution consisting of qualified experts, to determine with regard to potential immigrants, and to those already resident in Israel, both children and adults, who should and who should not be qualified to register as (politically) a Jew.[1] I should have thought that (a) someone who has lived the life of a Jew outside Israel, e.g., by being identified with the Jewish community in some clear sense, even though his mother may be a non-Jewess, would be cruelly punished if he were excluded from Jewish nationality—and not only from the Jewish religious community—

[1] No clear directives could in the nature of the case be given to this body. They will have to be guided by the light of reason and common sense.

on religious grounds. Such persons may of course choose to go through the rite of formal conversion (as, for example, I am told that the late Lord Melchett in England did), but even if they do not, to exclude them from the (politically) Jewish community unless they do so seems to me gratuitous and harsh; (b) similarly, children of mixed marriages whose Jewish fathers desire them to be brought up as Jews should in my view be allowed to be registered as Jews, in the expectation that the mere process of being brought up with other Jews in Israel will surely do its work of adequate assimilation.

7. Since the rabbinical authorities will of necessity, and quite properly, not regard such classes of persons as Jews, there will be a certain inevitable social pressure upon them, whatever steps may be taken to prevent this from becoming a form of coercion, to leap over the final fence which stands between them and full membership of the Jewish community everywhere, i.e., accept actual conversion to the Jewish religion. It may well be that most such persons will have little objection to accepting and practicing the Jewish religion, at any rate the minimum required by Halakha. But some may choose not to do so, and they may, when they leave Israel, find themselves debarred from being accepted as members of Jewish communities in lands outside Israel. This is a necessary consequence of the structure of any organized religion, which rightly makes certain minimum demands of its members, and cannot relax them for political or legal or moral or any non-religious reasons. But the number of such persons is likely to be exceedingly small, nor, it seems to me, will the bonds which unite Israel to the Diaspora be likely to be snapped or even strained by the existence of such persons, and by their necessarily anomalous status. To repeat my earlier point again, I see no way of finally determining the status of these persons except by means of a Commission which judges each particular case whether or not he or she satisfies a sufficient number of the clearly felt, but often indefinable, conditions of being a member of the (politically) Jewish community in Israel.

8. If it is felt that public opinion in Israel is not yet ripe for such a solution, and may indeed be outraged by it, that it may lead to a ferocious Kulturkampf within Israel, and indeed to a schism between Israel and the Jewish community beyond its borders, then, if it is desired to avoid an early head-on crash with painful consequence, I think that some kind of interim status could be created for these

problematical cases. The children of unconverted non-Jewesses, the unconverted wives of Jews in Israel (who desire to play their full part in the Jewish community) and similar persons could be registered not as "Jews" politically, but as "of Jewish origin: father a Jew" or "wife of a Jew," "paternal grandfather and maternal grandfather Jews," or the like, simply recording the facts; and a special status would then have to be created for such cases in anticipation that this will itself lead to crystallization of the issue, that the persons placed in this no-man's land would either ultimately become assimilated wholly into the Jewish community, or drop out of it, or at worst continue indefinitely as borderline cases until such time as a more liberal legislation is politically feasible and they can be freely absorbed into the Jewish texture without too much protest by anyone. This is not a satisfactory solution, but in the circumstances assumed above, the most painless that I can think of. This situation must on no account be allowed to be more than temporary; nothing could be more iniquitous or ruinous than to permit the emergence of a permanent category of citizens of inferior status—half-Jews, with incomplete civil and political rights; an abominable inverted caricature of antisemitic persecution in other countries. If religious resistance to the free integration of such persons is really too slow to be overcome by the authority of the State at present, it would be better not to allow such persons to immigrate than to expose them to the horrors of minority status.

9. I must admit that I find it hard to believe that the acceptance into the Jewish community of persons who would normally be regarded as Jews (at any rate by those who, for whatever reason, are interested in such matters—persons conscious of what it is to be a Jew) even if they do not fully qualify under the rules of rigorously applied Halakha, would cause a deep rift either within Israel or between Israel and the Jews of the outside world. But about this I may well be mistaken; on this issue I should not like to volunteer a view. Historically, the Jewish religion, the Jewish race, and all the factors which combine into Jewish culture, have combined into a single, persistent entity, incapable of being neatly fitted into the political pattern of a modern state of a Western type. The rise of the State of Israel can "normalize" the Jewish population only by allowing—not necessarily encouraging—each of these factors to pursue a separate career. This seems to be neither avoidable or necessarily

undesirable: one must hope that it will upset as few Jewish convictions and loyalties as possible; but I doubt whether it is realistic to hope that it will offend against none. I feel this the more strongly, since I am not happy about this "solution" myself.

Isaiah Berlin

6. YEHUDA BOURLA

Bourla (1886–1969), a Hebrew writer, was born in Jerusalem to a family of Turkish extraction who settled in the Land of Israel in the 18th century. After graduating from a teachers seminary in Jerusalem, he was conscripted into the Turkish army in World War I. After the war, he ran several Hebrew schools in Damascus, and then worked in the Arab Department of the Histadrut Labor Federation. In 1948 he was appointed head of the Arab Department of the Office for Minority Affairs. A noted author, Bourla served as president of the Hebrew Writers' Association. His many books focus on the Sephardic communities of Jerusalem, Sefad and Hebron. *Luna* (1911) and *His Despised Wife* (1928), written early in his literary career, established his status as a major figure in Hebrew literature.

Haifa, 12 December 1958

Dear Sir,

When I replied to your letter in respect to the registration of a child as Jewish, I believed that the matter was of some urgency and I thus wrote a short, almost cryptic, response. After reconsidering, I feel I should explain my position a bit more, and so I am sending you the enclosed opinion and would ask that you disregard the first, as it is included in this second letter with the addition of a short explanation.

Respectfully,

Yehuda Bourla

1. In my opinion, a single ceremony is required for the registration of any child as a Jew: circumcision. This rite, the first of the ancient commandments handed down to Abraham, has been sanctified by the Jewish people as identical with the very fact of a child's Judaism. Being Jewish is first of all being circumcised.
   2. Accordingly, this ceremony does not constitute a form of religious coercion (for any child, whether born to two Jewish parents

or to a mixed marriage), as becoming a Jew is inseparable from circumcision and circumcision is inseparable from becoming a Jew.

What is more, this ritual (the surgical procedure) causes no harm whatsoever to the child; on the contrary, it provides (according to medical science) effective immunity against certain diseases. Thus there is no need for any other rite in addition to this ceremony—ritual circumcision. Later, when the child grows up, he can choose to be observant or liberal.

3. The rabbis' demand for some other ceremony would presumably apply to the (non-Jewish) mother. If such a ceremony constitutes religious coercion of the mother, then it is forbidden by law, which bans religious and anti-religious coercion in Israel. We value this law very highly and must do all we can to uphold it.

4. If the rabbis' demand for an additional ritual is based on religious law, they should find a way to ensure that the humane law of the land does not clash with religious law.

5. We are highly cognizant of the attitude of the rabbis to sacred halakha which has been sealed for generations (from the time of the Talmud and by the authority of the Sages, from the first to the very last), but they are also well aware that there have been moments in our history when religious authorities felt it necessary and inescapable to adapt the laws of the Torah to the realities of life. They sought an equivalent for the laws of damages demanding an eye for an eye, etc., and set monetary compensation for physical damage. By doing so, the Sages overturned a Biblical law (which was undoubtedly carried out to the letter in ancient times). Similarly, the Bible states: "he shall not dun his fellow or kinsman" [Deut. 15:2], and yet the rabbinical court duns and collects debts. And not only in the first generations of the Talmudic period, but in later generations as well, Rabbi Gershom ben-Judah, "The Light of the Exile," found it in the power of his wisdom to overturn a Biblical law and forbid polygamy in "Rabbi Gershom's ban" (at least among Ashkenazi Jews).

6. Thus it is not impossible for the rabbis to acknowledge the fact that at this time as well there has been a conspicuous upheaval in our way of life in all areas of finance, society, politics, and especially religion. It is a fact (rather than a theory or estimation) that the majority of the Jews in Israel, to say nothing of the Diaspora, are not observant, and no matter how hard the rabbis try to impose their authority on them, they will not succeed. It is also worth noting that if in the past the leadership of the nation was in the hands of

the rabbis, it is because the nation wanted them as leaders, as its life was characterized by the stamp of religion, so that more than the rabbis wished to be leaders, the nation wished to be led by them. But when the majority of the nation has ceased to desire this, what is the point of their insistence on leading? After all, without a cause there is no effect.

7. Now, if there is in the hearts of the rabbis a true and natural national sense, as strong as in the hearts of the people, and if they do indeed wish for the growth, prosperity, and strengthening of the state and for the absorption of a large part of the existing nation in its homeland, they must make every effort to compromise between religious law and the law of the land for the sake of peace, unity, and the survival of religion itself within the nation. The glory of the rabbis in our generation will not be found in the stressing and exacerbation of conflicts and difficulties between national life and religious law, but in the very opposite: in their efforts to adapt religious law, to the greatest possible extent, to the evolving laws of life.

8. If they do not do this because they cannot find the spiritual capacity or religious authority, they must not then blame the nation for abandoning the commandments, but should examine their own actions. They will then realize that the nation will willingly take on itself the laws and commandments when they fulfill the condition "to live by them and not die by them."

Yehuda Bourla

7. HAIM HERMANN COHN

A jurist and Supreme Court justice, Cohn (1911–2002) was born in Germany and studied law at the University of Munich, the Hebrew University in Jerusalem, and Merkaz Harav yeshiva in Jerusalem. Before being appointed to the Supreme Court, he served as Attorney General of Israel and Director General of the Ministry of Justice (1948–1950), and as legal advisor to the Government (1952–1960). He is the author of numerous books and articles on a variety of legal subjects, including foreign laws of marriage and divorce, Jewish law, criminal law and criminology, and judicial policy in Israel.

10 February 1959

Dear Mr. Prime Minister,

I would like to beg your forgiveness for not having replied to your letter of October 27 until today. Lack of time and official business prevented me from researching the issue, and I am afraid that even now I have not managed to discover more than a small part of what could be found.

As far back as 20 February 1958 I wrote to the Director General of the Ministry of the Interior stating, *inter alia*:

> When both parents declare that their child is a Jew, their declaration is seen as if it were the legal declaration of the child himself. According to the Equal Rights for Women Act, 1951, both are the guardians of the child and speak for him. This too, of course, is contingent on the condition of good faith, but the mere fact that one of the parents is not Jewish and declares so cannot be considered evidence of bad faith. For the registrar, it is of no consequence that according to the law of the Torah the child follows the mother. It is possible that some other law than the law of the Torah applies to the child, and according to the applicable personal law he may follow the father and not the mother. These are issues that the registrar is neither authorized nor competent to investigate. In order for him to register the child as a Jew, the declaration of the parents that the child is Jewish is sufficient. But what if one of the parents declares that the child is a Jew and the other declares that he is not? In my opinion, the religion and nationality of the child should then be registered as unknown.

When you honored me with your letter and I perused the books, I became even more convinced of the opinion I had expressed in my letter to the Ministry of the Interior. As I did then, I still believe that there is no better way for the State to act than to indicate the religion and nationality of the child in the population registry by the declaration of the parents. This is the only way to comply with the law. Even though it ostensibly contradicts the rule of religious law that states that a child born to a non-Jewish mother is designated according to the mother and not the father, this appears to me the solution most fitting to the finest legal and moral traditions of Israel.

1. *The Law*

The meaning of "Jew" in Knesset legislation is not identical to its meaning in religious law. The country's religious authorities are not charged with carrying out the Law of Return, Citizenship Act, or Population Registry Act. It is the Minister of the Interior who is charged with their implementation, and it is not reasonable to assume that by so instructing, the Knesset meant to grant him the authority to rule on whether or not an individual is a Jew according to religious law. In certain cases, the question of whether a person is a Jew may arise, by law, in reference to religious proscriptions and prescriptions, such as in matters of marriage or divorce, and here the law grants exclusive jurisdiction to the religious authorities, that is, the rabbinical courts. This is not the case, however, when the question of whether a person is a Jew arises not in reference to marriage or divorce or any other religious matter recognized as such by the law, but in connection to a clearly administrative or political matter, such as entrance into the country, residence or citizenship. In such matters, a person's religious definition as a Jew, that is, his status according to religious law, is not applicable and cannot be relevant, not only because the administrative agencies implementing the laws are not, by nature and competency, either qualified or authorized to rule on religious law, but also because the boundaries between administrative and religious authorities are clearly defined. The religious authorities are in no way bound, in respect to the matters legally within their jurisdiction, by anything an administrative agency may decide or do in order to implement administrative laws.

Religious rulings may differ in content and nature from administrative rulings. The fact that according to religious law a person is
considered a non-Jew does not preclude or contradict his being considered a Jew for purposes of the Law of Return, and vice versa.
Even the fact that a certain woman is considered to be married
according to religious law does not preclude or contradict the possibility of her being considered divorced for purposes of civil laws,
such as the Inheritance Act. The same sort of inconsistency may
occur within the district court itself: the same judge ruling according to religious law, such as in a matter of maintenance, may regard
the woman to be married, and when ruling according to civil law,
as in a matter of inheritance, may be compelled to judge the same
woman to be divorced from the man who is still maintaining her.
Such inconsistencies may arise in any case and in relation to any
man or woman. They stem unavoidably from our system of justice
and the splitting of jurisdiction between rabbinical and civil courts
and the splitting of the law into religious and secular laws. So long
as this distinction remains in force, we have no choice but to accept
its woes willingly and must not be deterred from reaching any decision, whatever judicial or administrative distress it may generate.

With all due recognition of religious jurisdiction and all due respect
for it to the extent that the law instructs, the executive authorities
do not have the right to extend its boundaries. Aside from matters
of marriage and divorce, religious laws are not binding in this country. Anyone wishing to extend them to other areas must convince
the legislature to do so, but cannot raise claims to the Executive.
For the Authorities, the borderlines between binding law and non-
binding religious precepts are the boundaries on which the entire
country is founded and which underlie the basic rights of its citizens.

The Government resolution that "the religion or nationality of
adults will be listed as 'Jewish' if they declare themselves in good
faith to be Jewish and not a member of another religion," leads, in
my opinion, to the conclusion that the religion or nationality of a
minor will be listed as 'Jewish' if both parents declare in good faith
that he is Jewish and not a member of another religion. The parents are the guardians of their child, not only by nature and custom, but also by the explicit provisions of the Equal Rights for
Women Act, 1951. By virtue of their authority and role as guardians,
it is their right and duty to act for and on behalf of the child as
they do on behalf of themselves as qualified adults. Their hand is

the hand of the child and their declaration is his declaration. This declaration of the parents in his name is tantamount to the declaration of the child himself, except that the law requires the declaration of the guardians and will not accept the declaration of the child in view of the child's status as a minor and his lack of understanding.

The following analogy from the citizenship laws might be drawn. If the parents declare on behalf of their child that he does not wish to acquire Israeli citizenship by virtue of the Law of Return, the child does not acquire citizenship (section 2 (c) (3) of the Citizenship Act, 1952). If they do no so declare, the child acquires Israeli citizenship together with his parents, just as he immigrated together with his parents according to the Law of Return. Thus, for the purposes of immigration and citizenship, the child follows his parents. If they receive an immigration permit in the wake of their declaration that they are Jews, the child also receives a permit; if they immigrate and become Israeli citizens in the wake of their declaration that they are Jews, the child immigrates with them and becomes an Israeli citizen. Why should his rights be curtailed and his parents' declaration deemed invalid solely for the purposes of registration in the population registry?

It is true that the question of religious affiliation, as opposed to the question of national affiliation, is by nature a "religious" issue. Nevertheless, I believe that the matter of registration in the population registry does not require a solution that complies with religious law. When the law provides that a person's religion is to be listed, this alone does not authorize or require the registrar to investigate and determine, in religious terms, the individual's religion. The law imposes the obligation to register on the resident, not on the registrar. The resident fulfills this duty by telling the registrar what his religion is, just as he fulfills his duty by telling the registrar what his address is. The registrar is entitled, but not required, to ask the applicant for documents and other evidence, and will do so only in those cases in which he has reason to suspect that the applicant's statements were not made in "good faith." However, when the applicant's statements do not arouse any suspicion, there is no reason and no need to demand evidence. Should the evidence requested reveal that an individual's statement was not made in good faith, his religion or that of his child will not be listed as declared. But the registrar is neither a judge nor a codifier; he is merely a registry clerk and only writes down what the citizen required to register tells him to write down. Even in those cases in which the registrar demands evidence to confirm a certain particular, his conviction one way or the other in no way prevents the court or some other administrative agency from rejecting the same evidence and judging it unconvincing. The decisions of the registrar are valid and binding only for purposes of implementing the Population Registry Act. They have no legal force for purposes of implementing any other law. Thus registration of a person's religion as Jewish in the population registry is not binding on any court, rabbinical court, or religious or administrative body. It does not even constitute prima facie evidence, as if the burden of proof were on anyone claiming it to be false. The only thing it proves is that the person asked the registrar to indicate his religion in the population registry as Jewish. In other words, the registration is evidence of the statement made to the registrar regarding the applicant's religion, and that the registrar found no reason to doubt that the statement was made in good faith.

The same applies to a minor: whatever appears in the population registry regarding a minor is merely what his parents, as his legal and natural guardians, told the registrar to indicate. If his religion is registered as Jewish, this does not imply or prove that he is Jewish according to religious law or even according to civil law, but is evidence that his parents declared him to be a Jew and that the registrar found no reason to doubt their good faith.

Registering religion in any other way would, in my opinion, overstep the authority of the registrar. He is not entitled to indicate anything the applicant (or his guardians) do not ask him to indicate, and is certainly not entitled—nor is he qualified or competent—to rule on the law, whether religious or civil, regarding the attribution of the child to one or the other of his parents, or even on the more basic question in need of a solution regarding the personal law applicable to the child—whether religious, the law of another country, or secular Israeli law.

If we were to require or authorize the registrar to examine these questions and rule on them, we would be thrusting him into a vicious circle. If the child is not Jewish, then the laws of the Torah do not apply to him, but it is these same laws that do not apply to him that deprive him of his status as a Jew! On the other hand, if a secular law or some other sort of law were to determine that the child follows his father and is therefore Jewish, the laws of the Torah, which do not recognize him as a Jew, would apply to him! It is best to leave such problems to the civil and rabbinical courts whose job it is to unravel difficult problems. The civil court, in regard to matters within its jurisdiction, might consider him to be a Jew, while the rabbinical court, in regard to matters within its jurisdiction, might not recognize him as a Jew. And it is also possible that he will not apply to either. Attributing the child to the mother has indubitably legal ramifications for complex and intricate legal issues, and what qualifications does a registry clerk have to decide such questions?

To conclude: The registrar may not register the religion of a child except in keeping with what he is told by the parents.

2. *Jewish Tradition*

a. The rule that the son of a heathen is like his mother, without taking the father into consideration,[1] comes from the interpretation of Scriptures: "You shall not intermarry with them: do not give your daughters to their sons or take their daughters for your sons. For they will turn your children away from Me to worship other gods."[2] From this it is deduced that the son of your daughter from a heathen man is called your son, but a son, your son, from a heathen woman is not called your son but her son;[3] for if the intent was that if your daughter had a son from a heathen man it would turn the child away from God, the Hebrew text would have employed the feminine as well as the masculine form [of the word for "turn"].[4] A further source for this rule was found in the verse: "If a man has two wives . . . and both . . . have borne him sons."[5] When a woman can be legally married, she can bear him sons, but if she cannot be his lawful wife, the sons are not his, but hers.[6]

The theory that this interpretation is actually an afterthought, and that the real reason for attributing children to their non-Jewish mothers is the fear or experience that children follow their mothers' ways and are a bad influence in general, relies on the fact that when the heathen women were expelled at the time of Ezra, their children

---

[1] Maimonides, *Issurei Bi'ah*, 15, 4.
[2] Deut. 7:3–4.
[3] Kiddushin 68b.
[4] Rashi, Deuteronomy, ibid.
[5] Deut. 21:15.
[6] Kiddushin 68b.

were expelled along with them.[7] The intention was not to be rid of
the women per se, even for being non-Jewish, but to be rid of "their
abhorrent ways that they, in their impurity, have filled [the land]
from one end to the other."[8] The expulsion was designed to bring
about the purification of the nation and its isolation from the other
nations and thus avoid the danger of total assimilation, both in the
cultural and religious sense and in the ethnic sense—a familiar
phenomenon. Under those circumstances, it was decided that the
children would go with their mothers. This was a purely political
decision. The Books of Ezra and Nehemiah contain no hint of any
religious or legal reason for it. Although the words of Shehania, son
of Yehiel of Elam, that the expulsion of the women and their children was done "according to the Torah" were later taken as evidence that attributing the children of heathen women to their mothers
was a law from the Torah,[9] the truth is that Shehania simply meant
what he said, that by expelling the non-Jewish women the nation
would repair the wrong of not obeying the Torah and would from
now on conduct themselves according to the Torah.

Although no one now disputes the rule that the child of a non-
Jewish woman follows the mother, among the early codifiers there
were those who ruled that the child of a Jewish man and a non-
Jewish woman was a Jewish bastard and could be lawfully married
to a Jewish woman. This opinion is based on the words of Rabbi
Judah in the name of Rabbi Assi that if a heathen married a Jewish
woman at that time the legality of his marriage was suspect lest he
was from the ten tribes.[10] Rashi explains that the men of the ten
tribes wed Cuthite women, and he was of the opinion that the child
of a Jewish man and Cuthite woman was a bastard and the legality
of the marriage of a bastard was suspect.[11] There is thus evidence
that the early codifiers, at least, held different views regarding this
rule.

b. Even assuming that the law holds unequivocally that the child
of a non-Jewish woman follows the mother, this does not provide a
solution for all the problems raised by the issue at hand. It is incum-

---

[7] Ezra 10:2–3.
[8] Ezra 9:11.
[9] Yerushalmi, Yebamot, 2, 6.
[10] Ibid., 17b.
[11] Rashi, ibid.

bent upon us to remember that we are talking about a husband and wife and their sons and daughters, people who immigrated to Israel on the basis of the Law of Return and are fulfilling their duty to register in the population registry and declaring that they are Jews, or at least the father declares himself and his sons and daughters to be Jewish.

We might consider the case of the man who came to Rabbi Judah and said he had converted himself to Judaism (i.e., without applying to a rabbinical court; converting oneself does not make one a Jew). Rabbi Judah asked if he had witnesses. The man replied that he did not. Do you have sons?, he was asked. He replied that he did. Rabbi Judah then told him: you are competent to disqualify yourself as a Jew, but you are not competent to disqualify your sons.[12]

The Talmudic source of this case does not mention whether the children's mother was a Jew, a non-Jew, or a convert. Apparently, this was of no concern to Rabbi Judah. It was enough for him that the children were qualified as Jews, and their father was not competent to disqualify them.[13]

Maimonides followed the lead of Rabbi Judah, although he altered the formulation of the rule: A man who is married to a Jewish woman or a convert and who has sons and says I converted myself to Judaism is competent to disqualify himself and is not competent to disqualify his sons."[14] The commentators wonder what Rabbi Judah sought to teach here, since if the mother was a Jew or a convert, the sons were Jewish in any case, and the fact that the father was non-Jewish would not disqualify them.[15] Thus, if the mother was a non-Jew the sons were automatically disqualified, and if the mother was a Jew, they were automatically Jews.[16] As usual, the commentators found various pretexts on which to hang an explanation: perhaps the woman was a convert who was not properly converted, or perhaps the disqualification related only to the issue of whether or not they were bastards. For myself, I see no reason to seek out a pretext, and I believe it would be best to adopt Rabbi Judah's view as written.

---

[12] Yebamot 47a.
[13] Rashi, ibid.
[14] *Issurei Bi'ah*, 13, 8.
[15] *Maggid Mishne*, ibid., *Bet Yossef* on *Tur Yoreh Deah*, 24b.
[16] Tosafot, Yebamot 47a.

Indeed, Maimonides' addition was deleted from Shulkhan Arukh, which rules: a man thought to be a Jew who says I converted myself and who has sons is not competent to disqualify his sons, but is competent to disqualify himself,[17] and the sons remain qualified.[18]

The father is not competent to disqualify his sons because, by his own admission, he is not a Jew, and non-Jews can not bear witness. This is even more conspicuously true of a non-Jewish mother. She is not competent to disqualify her sons as she is both a non-Jew and a woman, two facts each of which make her incompetent to bear witness. Thus, according to the law of the Torah, children in Israel are presumed to be qualified Jews, and can only be deprived of this status on the testimony of two competent witnesses before an authorized rabbinical court. Until such time as they are duly deprived of their status, they are considered to be Jews.

c. We have not yet sufficiently stressed the fact that the issue under discussion has arisen in Israel, most of whose residents are Jewish, so that every ordinary citizen is held to be a proper Jew. Certainly, the claim of anyone who asserts that he is Jewish is not investigated.[19] This is evidenced by the non-Jew who came to Jerusalem and ate of the paschal offering as if he were a Jew, although it is said "No foreigner shall eat of it."[20] According to the Tosafists, this does not constitute a reason to believe anyone who claims to be Jew. However, the situation is different here, since the majority of the people are Jews, and we follow majority rule.[21] Elsewhere, the Tosafists even go so far as to say that when someone claims to be a Jew he is to be believed even where Jews are not in the majority, since the majority of people claiming to be Jews are indeed Jews,[22] so that in this sense, at least, there is a majority. Even if there are a few who falsely claim to be Jews, we follow the majority who speak the truth and consider them to be among them as well.

In Sefer Mitzvot Hagadol from the 13th century we find the following illuminating evidence: "it happens every day that strangers come to us and we do not investigate them, but drink wine with

---

17 *Yoreh Deah.*
18 *Bet Yossef* on *Tur Eben ha-Ezer*, 2.
19 *Maggid Mishne* on *Hilkhot Issurei Bi'ah*, 13, 10.
20 Ex. 12:43; Pesachim 3b.
21 Tosafot, Yebamot 47a.
22 Tosafot, Yebamot 47b.

them and share our food with them and eat from the animals they have slaughtered."[23]

It follows that if a person claims that he has converted according to the law, and he is not known to be a non-Jew, his words are to be considered reliable. He could have said that he was a Jew and he would have been believed, so why should he not be believed when he says he was properly converted.[24] Maimonides added a reservation of his own to this rule: "If a person says he was converted before a rabbinical court—he is to be believed, for the same mouth that disqualified him now qualifies him; this applies only to the Land of Israel and the time when everyone there is presumed to be Jewish; but outside the Land of Israel evidence must be brought."[25]

This appears to me to be clear authority for acting in this manner in the Land of Israel today, where once again everyone is presumed to be Jewish, as opposed to the situation abroad. If the rabbis outside of Israel feel it proper to be stricter and demand conclusive evidence of any claim that a person is Jewish or was properly converted, there is no need or justification for doing so in the Land of Israel and the Jewish state. Here everyone is presumed to be Jewish. Anyone who claims to be a Jew is believed, and if anyone claims to have been a non-Jew and to have converted according to the law, he is not investigated and no evidence is required for him to be accepted as a Jew in every sense. This is not the case abroad, where the majority are non-Jews. There he will not be allowed to marry a Jewish woman unless he can provide evidence that he was properly converted. (It goes without saying that there are also some who are more lenient in respect to this issue abroad, particularly among the later codifiers. Habayit Hadash states that it is customary to be lenient and believe him, and even allow him to marry a Jewish woman and that Maimonides may also have accepted strangers who come and say they are Jews, believing them even now when most people are non-Jews, and even allowing them to marry Jewish women.).[26] Consequently, there are no grounds for the argument that

---

[23] *Sefer Mitzvot Hagadol*, 116.
[24] Ibid., note 22.
[25] *Issurei Bi'ah*, 13, 10.
[26] *Siftei Cohen on Yoreh Deah*, 268, 10.

the same procedures must be followed in Israel and abroad. There has always been one law for the Land of Isarel and another, different, and more stringent law for the Diaspora. The consistency between them is that we both follow the majority, but our majority is Jewish, while theirs is not.

d. Another issue has not yet been sufficiently stressed, and that is that we are not talking about non-Jewish women who will turn their husbands and children away from Judaism and Israel and lure them into idolatry, but about non-Jewish women who, of their own free will, have joined their husbands in immigrating to Isarel and brought their children with them to live a Jewish life in the State of Israel. These are non-Jewish women most of whom (and why should we not follow the majority here too?) were persecuted, incarcerated, and tortured by the Nazis during the Holocaust, some of whom risked their lives to save Jews, hiding and feeding them and becoming their wives in the most desperate of times. These women sincerely believed that they were coming to Israel by right, not by sufferance, and that the children they bore their Jewish husbands were the children and builders of Israel returning to their homeland as the remnant of the survivors.

In the name of the law of the Torah, we are being asked constantly by our rabbis to keep ourselves apart from them and their children, not to recognize them as Jews and not to love them as resident converts until such time as they provide convincing evidence to the rabbinate that they have been circumcised and immersed according to the law. In my opinion, in the name of the law of the Torah, the exact opposite should be asked of us. It is established in religious law that non-Jewish men or women who are always seen to conduct themselves as Jews are to be presumed to be sincere proselytes, even when there are no witnesses to testify to their having converted.[27] Admittedly, Maimonides explains that conducting oneself as a Jew means observing all of the practical commandments. However, the conduct of Jews in the past is no longer the conduct of Jews today. It stands to reason that the test of the non-Jewish woman today should be whether or not she conducts herself in the same manner as all, or the large majority, of Jewish women now-

---

[27] Maimonides, *Issurei Bi'ah*, 13,9; *Shulkhan Arukh, Yoreh Deah*, 268, 10.

adays, and not whether she conducts herself as the very few most righteous of them do.

According to the Midrash, in the eyes of God, strangers who voluntarily attach themselves to Israel are greater than Jews themselves. In the same breath it is said: "Then the Levite . . . and the stranger . . . shall come and eat their fill."[28] Moses asked God: Is the stranger the same as the Levite for you? He said: he is greater for Me, for he came to Me of his own free will. It is like the deer who grew up in the desert and came of his own free will to join the sheep. The shepherd would feed him and water him and cherish him more than his sheep. If they asked, why do you cherish this deer more than the sheep? He would answer, how hard I worked with my sheep, taking them out in the morning and bringing them back in the evening, until they grew. But this one who grew up in the deserts and forests came of his own free will to be among my sheep—should I not cherish him for that?[29]

These gracious notions in our sources have been silenced and forgotten. Our world has been overtaken by an outlook expressed in the famous saying that "proselytes are as bad to Israel as a sore in the skin";[30] the official religious approach to the issue can be explained only in terms of this outlook. The fact is, however, that this is not the spirit of Judaism, as evidenced by the attempts of the greatest commentators and codifiers to explain it away. Maimonides states: go and learn what happened in the desert in the story of the golden calf and the lack of self-restraint. In most instances, it was the mob that started it.[31] In other words, it was only a lesson to be learned from the past, a fact of ancient history that the "mob" (the foreigners) started the trouble. The Tosafists go even further, with one explaining that they were like a sore on the skin because they were so well-versed in the commandments and meticulous in their observance, and thereby reminded God of the sins of the Jews when they did not obey Him. Another Tosafist maintains that proselytes are as bad to Israel as a sore on the skin because God admonishes the Jews twenty-four different times not to cheat them, and it is impossible

---

[28] Deut. 14:29.
[29] *Midrash Devarim Zuta*, ibid.
[30] Kiddushin 70b.
[31] *Issurei Bi'ah*, 13, 18.

not to disappoint him! A third offers the interpretation that the proselytes were the reason for the exile of the Jews, for it says:[32] Why
was Israel dispersed among the lands more than other nations? So
that proselytes would join them![33]

Proselytes joined us in the harshest and most bitter of exiles. When
they join us now in our free country, they are not bad and are not
a sore on the skin. Nor is there reason, from the perspective of the
laws of the Torah, to fear they will bring the unqualified into Jewish
families and defile the purity of the race, as it were. According to
religious law, all bastards and foreigners (from among the Gibeonites)
will be pure in the future.[34] Thus a family into which an unqualified
person may have married need not expel him, for they will all be
pure in the future.[35] The author of Bet Yossef ruled that "It follows
that even at this time that a family that has absorbed a non-Jew
has absorbed him; that is to say, anyone who knows of the impro-
priety is not entitled to reveal it, but must allow it to remain to be
presumed a pure family, and in the future, even if the fact should
be learned, it will be pure."[36] In the words of the prophet: "He shall
act like a smelter and purger of silver; and he shall purify the descendents of Levi and refine them like gold and silver, so that they shall
present offerings in righteousness."[37] Maimonides regards this as an
indication that at the time of the Messiah, when his kingdom is
established and the whole nation gathers, all will conduct themselves
as he does in the holy spirit of God that will imbue him.[38] And what
are the "offerings in righteousness"? According to Rabbi Isaac,
"Righteousness is what God did unto Israel, that a family that has
absorbed, has absorbed."[39] This is the spirit of the Torah and Jewish
tradition: God does not reject any creature, but accepts them all.
The gates are open at all times, and anybody wishing to enter may
enter. As the prophet said: "Open the gates, and let a righteous

---

[32] Rabbi Eliezer in Pesachim 87b.
[33] Tosafot Kiddushin 70b.
[34] Kiddushin 72b.
[35] *Tur Eben ha-Ezer* 2.
[36] *Bet Yossef* on *Tur Even ha-Ezer*, ibid.
[37] Mal. 3:3.
[38] *Hilkhot Malakhim*, 12, 3.
[39] Kiddushin 71a.

nation enter, [a nation] that keeps faith."[40] He did not say, "and let priests, Levites, and Israelites enter," but "let the righteous of all nations enter."[41]

Yours as ever,

Haim Cohn

---

[40] Is. 26:2.
[41] *Shemot Rabbah* 13.

8. LOUIS ELIEZER HALEVI FINKELSTEIN

The son of an Orthodox rabbi and he himself a Conservative rabbi, Finkelstein (1895–1991) was born in Cincinnati, USA. He received a B.A. from City College of New York (1915) and a Ph.D. from Columbia University (1918), as well as rabbinical ordination from the Jewish Theological Seminary of America. Finkelstein served as a rabbi in New York for ten years, and was a member of the Jewish Theological Seminary faculty—Professor of Theology (1931), Vice-President (1934), President (1940), and Chancellor (1951–72). As one of the most prominent leaders of Conservative Judaism in America, he was appointed Advisor to the President of the United States for Jewish Affairs by Franklin D. Roosevelt (1940). One of the many books he wrote and edited is The Jews: Their History, Culture and Religion (1949, 1960). In addition, he published numerous articles and collections of textual interpretations of rabbinical and liturgical literature.

15 December 1958

The Honorable Mr. David Ben-Gurion,

In reply to your letter of 13 Heshvan, I would like first of all to note that it is not my habit to remark on issues of halakhic ruling. There are many experts greater than myself in this field, and I am not competent to rule. I therefore relate here only to the practical aspects of the problem.

The question before us is a matter of definition. It is quite difficult to change definitions accepted by the nation without generating confusion in related issues. As soon as one begins to consider one definition, problems arise regarding all the other definitions, such as: why should the Sabbath in Israel begin in the evening and not in the morning; why should we employ the lunar year and not the solar year, and so on. Many definitions have come down to us from our forefathers, and what they all have in common is that they are marks of the character of the nation. The canon of the Scriptures, the status of an ancient language for us, and even the place of the Land of Israel in our ideas and outlook cannot be explained save by the historical tradition; and all these are included among the definitions we have inherited from our forefathers. We must not alter such definitions. Even those who do not approach these problems from a positive attitude to religion and tradition per se are well aware of the disaster that awaits us as a unique nation if we start to debate the aspects of these issues that were already decided in ancient times.

In particular, we must beware of introducing confusion into a definition whose history and rationale are well-known. Our forefathers thought long and hard before concluding that a Jew is a person born in sanctity, that is, whose mother is a Jewess or a convert, or who himself is converted, and that the father's family is not to be taken into consideration. On the other hand, our forefathers saw no reason to be more lenient in the case of a Jewish man who married a non-Jewish woman, as in most mixed marriages since the time of Ezra and to today, it is the wife who is not Jewish. Ezra realized that by such nuptials the entire nation might become assimilated among the non-Jews. The children's primary approach to life, their spiritual attitudes, basic outlook, and conscience would be formed by the education they received from a non-Jew, who is neither familiar with nor has adopted the Jewish outlook. Our Sages realized that a child's decisive education is that which he receives in the cradle, even before he can speak. As a rule, he gets this education mainly from his mother. Therefore, she must be born of our people or have adopted Judaism. Obviously, if she accepts the Jewish tradition and religion, she becomes a full-fledged Jew, as did Ruth, and is worthy of giving birth to kings and leaders of Israel.

In this period of time, particularly in the Diaspora, Ezra's wisdom and deep understanding can be learned from reality. Mixed marriages are increasing in number, to the extent that in some cities here on the West coast, in over half of the marriages the women are non-Jews. Although a son is often named after the father and his family, it is crucial not to disregard halakha, according to which the children are not recognized as Jews if they do not take on our tradition in the accepted formal manner. They must be made aware that they have the choice of remaining non-Jews or converting. If they opt for Judaism, they take on themselves a weighty commitment toward the tradition and the Jewish people.

The greatest danger here is that the problem and its solution will be put off from day to day, and no clear decision will be taken as to whether or not they are Jewish. Given their doubtful status, they will choose the easy path, to enjoy the rights of Jews, becoming integrated among us and our public, and to remain non-Jewish because of the obligation to study and learn the nature of Judaism, and convey it to their children.

You are familiar with my view, which I explained to you when I was in Israel six years ago, that we have only one spiritual center and that is Jerusalem. We do not have two traditions or two nations. I thus applaud you for consulting Jewish intellectuals in the Diaspora in this matter, as it is clear that the decision taken in the issue at hand will have a considerable effect on the communities in the Diaspora as well.

There is no question that we must consider the difficulties arising from this conclusion because of the children who, unaware of the traditional approach to the issue, have regarded themselves as Jews and will be astonished to learn that we do not recognize them as such. Here, too, there are cases of this sort, and I have encountered circumstances in which I was compelled to explain to the children of mixed marriages how they are regarded by Jewish tradition. Once these youngsters learned that in Judaism the mother is responsible for all spiritual matters, so that the answer to the question of whether or not they were born Jewish depends on the status of their mother, they understood and agreed to officially convert according to Jewish law.

Obviously, we must treat these children sympathetically, whether or not they officially adopt the Jewish religion. If they do, they become converts, and the Torah commands us to love them dearly forty-six times. If they do not wish to become merged with our nation, they are, after all, among the righteous gentiles, or at least the wise gentiles, and we must love them as well, for as the Sages said, we always reject them with the right hand and draw them near with the left. We must hope that they will recognize the value of our Torah and tradition, and will cleave to them and to the nation. Although as a rule we do not seek out proselytes, these children, whose fathers are Jewish, are connected to us. In order to remedy the situation, we must surely make every effort to convince them to cleave to us.

With great respect and friendship,

Louis Eliezer Halevi Finkelstein

9. FELIX FRANKFURTER

A U.S. Supreme Court justice, Frankfurter (1882–1965) was born in Vienna and moved to the United States with his family at the age of 12. After graduating with distinction from the Harvard University School of Law in 1906, he was hired by the Federal Attorney General's Office and later became legal advisor to the War Office. In 1914, he joined the Harvard faculty as a Professor of Law, and in 1939 was elected to the Supreme Court. Frankfurter, noted for his rulings on sensitive cases, was among the founders of the American Civil Liberties Union and a legal advisor to several public bodies, as well as being involved in Zionist activities. In 1962, he was awarded the president's Medal of Freedom. Among his books are: Of law and Men (1956) and Of law and Life (1965).

July 28, 1959

My dear B-G,

Your letter, inviting my opinion regarding "the registration of children of mixed marriages" in Israel, reached here while I was hospitalized for what the doctors called a mild heart attack, but as a result I did not see it for a considerable stretch of time after its arrival. On my return to work, the business of the Court was so exacting that everything else had to be shunted to one side. This accounts for my delay in acknowledging your letter and I crave indulgence for this delay.

Happily, nothing was lost by this delay, for I should not in any event have been able to deal with the problem which you put to me. Even assuming that I were equipped to deal with it, the question concerns action on the part of the Government of Israel. One in my position must keep aloof from all participation in governmental problems in this country, except in so far as they come for adjudication before the Supreme Court. All the more reason is there for abstention in the expression of any views affecting the affairs of another Government, close as what happens in Israel lies to my interest.

I follow your doings and the course of events in Israel as much
as I can. How often I wish we could have talk again—you and I.
With warm regards and good wishes,

Very sincerely yours,

Felix Frankfurter

10. SOLOMON B. FREEHOF

A Reform rabbi, Freehof (1892–1990)was born in London and moved with his family to Baltimore, MD, U.S.A. in 1903. He received a B.A. from the University of Cincinnati in 1914, and one year later was ordained a rabbi by the Hebrew Union College and became a member of the faculty. After serving as an army chaplain in Europe during World War I, Freehof became a Professor of Liturgy at the Hebrew Union College and rabbi of communities in Chicago (1924) and Pittsburgh (1934). In 1930 he was named head of the Reform Liturgical Committee, which published the movement's prayer books, Union Prayer Book (1940–45) and Union Home Prayer Book (1951). In addition, he was the author of numerous articles on the literature of responsa.

11 December 1958

Dear Mr. Ben-Gurion,

I have your most interesting and important letter of the 27th of October, 1958, indicating that you are asking a number of Jewish religious leaders their opinion of the problem of accepting as Jews the children of a mixed marriage in which the mother is an unconverted non-Jewess.

Since I presume you are asking me as Chairman of the Responsa Committee of the Central Conference of American Rabbis and, therefore, want the opinion, among others, of a liberal interpretation of Jewish law and practice in this regard, and since I am sure you know the problem is much more complicated than a mere statement of the Orthodox law would indicate, it was somewhat necessary for me to make a systematic and, therefore, elaborate reply. Please forgive, therefore, the length of my answer that is enclosed.

With best wishes, Sincerely,

Solomon B. Freehof

Question:

The security of the State of Israel requires that every citizen carries an identity card recording nationality (or origin) and religious affiliation. This recording of religious affiliation has created considerable dispute between Orthodox religious leaders and the registration office of the State of Israel. The dispute becomes clear in the case of a child born of a Jewish father and an unconverted Gentile mother. The parents desire to have this child registered as Jewish. This, the State is ready to do, on the ground that religious affiliation is free choice of the individual and that in the case of an infant, the parents, as guardians of the child, may make the choice for the child. However, the religious leaders object from the point of view of Orthodox law. A child born of an unconverted mother is a Gentile, and a Gentile cannot become a Jew except by specific ceremony, Mikva [immersion] for a girl, and Mikva-and-circumcision for a boy. To allow affiliation merely on the basis of choice, as the State proposes, is declared to be a violation of the requirements of Jewish law and would dilute the identity of Jewry as a religious community. What is to be done in this situation?

Answer:

The laws involving the reception of proselytes into Judaism seem on the surface to be absolutely clear and unmistakable. However, this is not entirely the case. As in the case of other laws, also, the emotional attitude of the scholars of the various generations reflect themselves in their decisions on this question. When from time to time the rabbis have felt that the circumstances of their day require extra cautionary prohibitions, they applied them and then [the law] becomes stricter. Unfortunately, these restrictive actions tend to become permanent, and the longer the law lasts, the longer do these times of restrictiveness accumulate, and the law grows further and further away from actual life.

The present attitude of the Orthodox Rabbinate towards the reception of infant proselytes reveals this tendency towards cumulative restrictiveness. Basically, the law was generous about receiving infants into Judaism. The Talmud (b. Ketubot 11a) says simply that the Bet Din [rabbinical court] may bathe an infant as [a] proselyte. The discussion that follows indicates that although the infant cannot be aware of all that is implied in its adherence to Judaism, nevertheless, to accept the child as a Jew is a favor to the child, and we can always do a favor to someone without that person's knowledge. Furthermore, the Talmud (b. Yebamot 47b) considers the acceptance of proselytes to be a Mitzvah [a positive commandment]. While it is true that under varying circumstances they disliked to accept proselytes, while at other times they were willing to do so, it seems clear that with regard to an infant, whose soul is still pure (see Ketubot 11a) they were always hospitable.

However, about a century ago, a different mood came over Jewish scholars. There was an increasing amount of intermarriage, and many men asked the Jewish community to circumcise the children born of their Gentile wives because they wanted the children to be Jewish. Here a great objection arose. Solomon Kutno wrote a two volume work, "Let the Law be Obeyed," emphasizing the great dangers to Judaism in accepting such children. On the other hand, the Chief Rabbi of the British Empire indicated that his uncle, Tevele Schiff, permitted the circumcision of such children in California and Australia (i.e., under frontier conditions) and, of course, with the understanding that later, if possible, if the family moves to a more settled place, the child should be taken to the Mikva. A similar mood of friendliness is recorded in the responsa of Marcus Horowitz, the Orthodox Rabbi of Frankfurt seventy-five years ago (see his Matteh Levi, Volume 2). There he finally decides not to be too strict, but to permit such children to be circumcised, however exacting the promise that at some future time the Gentile mother will convert to Judaism. In other words, there is a noticeable difference in attitude, one more receptive and the other more prohibitive.

The fact is that Orthodox law is not objective. There is a large subjective element involved. Although with regard to a child of a Gentile mother even the Shulkhan Arukh implies that he should be circumcised, but says that he should not be circumcised on the Sabbath (Yore Deah 266:13). Nevertheless, if the rabbis feel that it is necessary to be strict, they will rely upon the law in the Shulkhan Arukh (Yore Deah 334:6) where Isserles says that in the case of a man under the ban, the court may refuse to let his children be circumcised.

It is clear, then, that the law is not absolutely fixed. If the rabbis today felt it proper to be liberal, they would encourage rather than fear the reception of these children as Jews. They would, of course, ask for the ceremonial requirements, but their attitude would be friendly and not hostile to the entire situation.

In this regard, it is important to note the decision of the Central Conference of American Rabbis, which is the official organization of the Reform Movement in America (see Yearbook, 1947). Such a child is welcome to enter the school of a Reform congregation, and if the child completes the school courses, we consider this education to be the full equivalent of a ritual ceremonial of conversion. In other words, in Reform, while the ceremonials are not disregarded, the education in ethics and in Jewish history and literature is considered the more important element. That is also why, in our reception of converts, we are not content merely with the ceremonies, but take a month or more in instruction.

Basically, then, one of the sources of difficulty in the situation is not so much what the law is, but the attitude of the Rabbis. There is only one form of Jewish religion in Israel, and that form, for reasons which seem adequate to itself, is afraid of the whole situation confronting the Jewish religion in the present world (including Israel) and reacts vigorously against a liberal attitude in the reception of proselytes. There are also in Israel many moods among Jews, but only one type of religious organization. In America, for example, where there are more than one type of religious organization, the mood between traditional and modern has become mutually tolerant.

But what is to be done under the present circumstances? The State can do no other than to make religion a matter of choice, and Orthodoxy can do no other than express its mood of suspicion in the matter and demand the full ceremonial of bathing and circumcision as an indispensable preliminary. In fact, it may even demand the formal conversion of the mother, on the ground that the child, even if converted, yet being raised by a Christian mother, would not be truly a Jew. All this constitutes a sharp conflict in which a solution must be found.

May I suggest that a solution is possible? The State can make clear that it is not deciding for the Jewish religion what is a Jew. It is making only a civic or political decision as to which of the three communities, Christian, Mohammedan, or Jewish the citizen belongs. The religious tests remain. When this child grows up and is about to marry, it will be the duty of the religious authority to inquire whether this child is born of a Jewish or a Gentile mother. It should have such a questionnaire for all who come to be married. If the religious authorities find that the person was born of a Christian mother, then they may demand that certain ceremonials be observed before the marriage is permitted. All that the State now says is that this child is politically or civically Jewish. Whether or not it is religiously Jewish is left to the religious authorities to decide whenever the matter will come before them, in such individual cases as in marriage or divorce.

Of course, this involves, in effect, the creation of a group of what may be called half-proselytes to Judaism. They will be people who have full Jewish rights civically, but only tentative Jewish rights religiously. Is this possible? Is there a precedent for it? There is, indeed! Besides the full proselytes [ger zedek] which Orthodoxy now demands, there was, also, during the time of the Jewish State, a status of half-proselytes [ger toshav]. This is based upon the Talmud (Abodah Zarah 64b) and codified by Maimonides (Issurei Bi'ah XV, 7–8). But such half-proselytes could only be accepted while the Jewish State existed. The technical phrase for that being, "while the Jubilees were being observed." But after the Jewish State ceased to exist, it was not safe or permitted to welcome such half-proselytes (cf. Maimonides, ibid., 8). However, now there is a Jewish State. Without going into the complex question of the State's status in Jewish religion, the human fact is clear, as you indicate in your letter, that whatever assimilation there is, it will be towards Judaism and not away from it. Therefore, it is again possible to have "gere toshav," half-proselytes.

Actually, this is all that the government of the State of Israel wants. The present difficulty with the religious groups has arisen chiefly because of a confusion between "ger zedek," the full proselyte, and "ger toshav," the half or tentative proselyte. If the State will now declare that it does not proclaim these children "gere zedek" (This gerut—type of convert—will be a matter for religion to decide, when the problem of the status of the child will come before the religious authorities at marriage, etc.) the State is only making a "ger toshav" decision affirming the civic right to choose to belong to the Jewish community rather than to the Christian or Mohammedan. It is with this clear distinction that I believe a solution can be arrived at.

Solomon B. Freehof

11. SHLOMO GOREN

Chief Ashkenazi Rabbi of Israel, Goren (1917–1994) was born in Poland and arrived in Israel with his family in 1925. His father was among the founders of Kfar Hasidim. Goren attended Hebron Yeshiva in Jerusalem, and published his first work, *Netzach Ha-Kodesh*, on Maimonides' *Mishne Torah*, in 1935. In 1936 he joined the Hagana, becoming the Chief Army Chaplain during the War of Independence, a position he held throughout several of Israel's wars as an officer with the rank of colonel. Goren was the first rabbi to conduct a prayer service at the Western Wall in June 1967. Awarded the Israel Prize in 1961 for his work *Yerushalmi Ha-Meforash*, he was appointed Chief Ashkenazi Rabbi of Tel Aviv in 1968 and Chief Ashkenazi Rabbi of Israel in 1972.

19 February 1959

Mr. Prime Minister,

I am writing in reference to the request in your letter of 17 Oct. 1958 for my "opinion as to how we should act in the matter of registering the children of mixed marriages both of whose parents, the Jewish father and the non-Jewish mother, wish them to be registered as Jews." Although I am unworthy of this appeal, out of a sense of respect and esteem for the Government of Israel, and in view of the rule that one does not refuse a respected person, I will embolden my soul to stand where the great should stand and address this complex and emotional issue, in the hope and prayer that I do not err in the ways of halakha, and do not cause others to err, and the proper spirit will light you from above to guide you on the right path and to direct your actions according to the spirit of the Torah and the visions of the prophets.

I have divided my comments into two parts: the first part addresses the theoretical-historical aspect of the problem, and the second is a practical proposal for regulating the problem of registering the children of mixed marriages in the population registry and on identity cards.

I. *Theoretical Discussion*

Three fundamental problems are raised by this enquiry: 1) the status of children born to mixed marriages in halakha and Jewish history; 2) the accepted and established procedure for conversion in Israel in light of halakha and history (including the conversion of minors); 3) is it possible to convert to Jewish nationality and not to the Jewish religion, in view of which secular procedures might be established for accepting a non-Jew into the Jewish nation.

(1) *The Status of Children Born to Mixed Marriages in Halakha and Jewish History*

The definition of the status of children of mixed marriages, in which the father is Jewish and the mother is a non-Jew, can be found in the Mishnah of Kiddushin (Ch. III, 61b), which states: "and whatever (woman) who cannot contract kiddushin [sanctified marriage] with that particular person or with others, the infant follows her status. This is the case with the infant of a bond-maid or a Gentile woman." Rashi explains that the offspring assumes her status, i.e., "the offspring of a gentile is a gentile and, if he was converted, he is a fit convert." In the Talmud (ibid., 68b), this rule is derived from the verse: "You shall not intermarry with them" (Deut. 7:3). The Gemara asks: "Since the betrothal was not valid, why does the offspring assume her status? Rabbi Johanan, in the name of Rabbi Simon Ben Yohai, replies: we read in Scripture, "For they will turn away thy son from following me." Thy son, of a Jewish mother, is called thy son; but thy son, from an idol worshipper, is not called thy son but her son."

Another ruling of this sort can be found in the Mishnah of Yebamot (Ch. II, 21a): "He counts as his brother in every respect, unless he was the son of a bond-maid or of a gentile woman." Maimonides thus rules in Yad Ha-Hazakah, Chapt. XV (Issurei Bi'ah), Halakha 4 (first edition, printed in Rome in 5240): "This is the general rule— the status of an offspring from a slave or a gentile, or from a bond-maid or from a gentile woman, is the same as his mother's; we disregard the father." In Chapt. I of Yebamot ve-Halitzha (Halakha 4) Maimonides states: ". . . the children of a bond-maid are slaves, and from a gentile woman—gentiles, without any status . . . as obvious in the Scriptural text: 'For they will turn away thy son from following me—turn him away as an integral part of the community, etc." A similar interpretation appears in Shulkhan Arukh (Eben Ha-ezer section VIII, paragraph 5): "The offspring of a bond-maid and a gentile woman acquire their status, irrespective of whether the father is Jewish or not."

From the story of the blasphemer as well (Lev. 24:10–11), it can be seen that in the case of mixed marriages, the son assumes the status of the mother, so that if the mother is a gentile, the children are also gentiles. The words "from among the Israelites" indicate that the son of the Israelite was considered a son of Israel. However, in Torat Kohanim (as well as in Rashi) it says "we assume that he was converted." The commentators are in disagreement as to this interpretation (see the commentaries of Nahmanides on the Torah and Rabbi Shimon on Torat Kohanim).

A more explicit Biblical source for this Talmudic law that the children of mixed marriages are defined by the mother, and if the mother is a gentile the children are gentiles as well, can be found in Ezra 10:2–3: "Then Shecaniah son of Jehiel of the family of Elam spoke up and said to Ezra, 'We have trespassed against our God by bringing into our homes foreign women from the people of the land; but there is still hope for Israel despite this. Now then, let us make a covenant with our God to expel all these women and those who have been born to them, in accordance with the bidding of the Lord and of all who are concerned over the commandment of our God, and let the Teaching be obeyed'."

From this we learn that the children of the gentile women were considered gentiles, and thus when the Jews vowed to expel the gentile women from the congregation of Israel, their children were expelled along with them, for it says: "and those who have been born to them." The same meaning can also be understood from the end of the chapter at the conclusion of the list of marriages to foreign women: "All these had married foreign women, among whom were some women who had borne children." As Rashi states in reference to this verse: "The minority who married pagan women, and had children from them, all sent away their wives and children."

This Biblical evidence for the halakhic ruling for the generations that the son of a gentile woman is also a gentile was already presented by the Sages of the Jerusalem Talmud and the Midrash, [Kiddushin (Jerusalem), Ch. III, 12 and Midrash Rabbah Numbers, Hukat Ch. XIX]: Rabbi Hagai forbid the circumcision on the Sabbath of the son of a gentile mother and a Jewish father because the infant was considered a gentile. He further decreed that Jacob of Naburaya be flogged for legalizing circumcision for such an offspring on the Sabbath. When Jacob of Naburaya challenged his ruling, he replied: It is written "Now therefore let us make a covenant with our God."

A further source in the Bible from which we may learn that the son of an Israelite from a foreign woman does not follow the father relates to Amnon and Tamar (II Sam. 13:13): "Please, speak to the king; he will not refuse me to you," although it is unthinkable that David would have approved the marriage of a brother to a sister. The reason, however, is that Tamar was the daughter of a gentile woman, for she was her sister from the mother of Absalom (ibid., 20–21), and Absalom was the son of Maacah, daughter of King Talmai of Geshur (ibid., 3:3). The Sages thus explain (Sanhedrin 21a): "Tamar was the daughter of a captive beauty", and Rashi elaborates: "Before Maacah became a true convert, she engendered Tamar to David. She was [thus] (to David) a captive beauty." This notion, substantiated by the Biblical commentators, explains why the text relates Tamar to her brother Absalom rather than to her father David. As Tamar was born before her mother Maacah converted, she was considered a convert assuming the status of her mother and not that of her father. Thus the phrase "He will not refuse you to me," as Tamar was eligible to marry Amnon, the son of David.

From the Book of Malachi as well we can derive the ruling that the children of a gentile mother and Jewish father do not belong to the congregation of Israel, an eventuality the prophet views as betrayal of the nation: "Judah has broken faith; abhorrent things have been done in Israel and in Jerusalem. For Judah has profaned what is holy to the Lord—what He desires—and espoused daughters of alien gods. May the Lord leave to him who does this no descendants dwelling in the tents of Jacob, etc." (Mal. 2:11–12). It is perfectly clear that the reference is to his children who should be removed from the tents of Jacob, that is, expelled from the congregation of Israel.

A different approach can be found in the commentary of Rabbi Moshe Isserlish on Shulkhan Arukh (Eben ha-Ezer, section XV, paragraph 10), which states: "Some are in doubt; it may be that only according to the Biblical enactment the offspring derives its status from the bondmaid and the gentile woman; but according to the Rabbinical enactment the status is that of the father. Therefore the severity of the interpretation must be assumed at the outset." The same approach appears in the notations of "Darkei Moshe" on

Tur Eben ha-Ezer. At the beginning of Yebamot he speculates that: "the son from a bondmaid or from a Samaritan [gentile] woman is his son; according to the rabbinical law, he is not his son." All the commentators were astonished by this opinion, for the accepted law in Israel is that the child of a gentile assumes her status and not that of the father. Indeed, the Gaon Rabbi Eliyahu of Vilna expresses his wonder at it in his commentary of Shulkhan Arukh. Nonetheless, he provides the correct source for this approach, Tractate Derekh Eretz Rabba [Ch. I, and Yalkut Shimon (section Ki Tetzeh, reference 9310)], where it is said: "One who cohabits with a Samaritan woman is guilty of fourteen prohibitions, among them are the prohibitions of [cohabitation with] the 'wife of his father' and 'the wife of his brother'." This is clarified by the Zayit Raanon in his comprehensive commentary, as cited in the commentary Nakhalot Ya'akov on Tractate Derekh Eretz: "according to the rabbinical law, the son acquires the status of the father." The Gaon, however, takes issue with this interpretation and refutes the evidence. Moreover, this approach does not alter the status of the children of gentile mothers and Jewish fathers; rather it places further rabbinical constraints on them that are not imposed on non-Jews.

Another approach in Knesset Hagedola, (Hoshen Mishpat, Section VII) suggests that after the conversion of the son of a gentile mother and Jewish father, the child reverts to the status of the father and is considered a Jew born of Israel and not a convert, and not only by the rabbis but by the Torah as well, he is considered as if he came "from among his brothers." He is even eligible to marry the daughter of a priest like any other Jew. This view, however, is also a minority opinion and not accepted by halakha.

Thus we learn from the Torah, the Prophets, and the Writings that the child of a gentile mother and a Jewish father is considered a non-Jew and does not assume the status of the father. Therefore, he is subject to full conversion in order to become a member of the Jewish congregation. (There are those who contend that after conversion he reverts to the status of the father, according to rabbinical interpretation, or to certain laws in the Torah as well.) This law has been accepted throughout Jewish history, and has been followed in theory and practice in every generation.

(2) *The Procedure for Conversion in Light of Halakha and History (and the conversion of minors)*

Three things are required for the conversion of a male: acceptance of the commandments before three Jews, circumcision, and immersion. Two are required for a female: acceptance of the commandments before three Jews and immersion. We learn this from the Sages of the Talmud who had received the convention and tradition passed on from generation to generation to insist on these three elements in the conversion procedure, as explained in the Talmud (Yebamot 41–47; Yerushalmi Kiddushin, Ch. III, Halakha 13; Keritot IX-1, and Gerim, Ch. 1–II).

Accepting the commandments is the first condition and the essence of conversion. The motive for doing so must be spiritual recognition of the Jewish religion and the meaning of conversion according to the Torah and halakha: entrance into the religious covenant of the Jewish people. In the words of Maimonides (first edition of the year 5230, Ch. XIII, Issurei Bi'ah, Halakha 4): "In future generations, too, if a gentile will seek admission to the Covenant, to be sheltered by the Shekhina, through the acceptance of the authority of the Torah, he will require circumcision, immersion and the offering of a sacrifice. If the proselyte is a female the requirement will be immersion and a sacrificial offering, as it is said 'You and the stranger shall be alike'—your requirements are circumcision, immersion and a sacrificial offering."

The Sages learned the procedure of accepting the authority of the commandments from Ruth the Moabite (Ruth 1:16): "'Do not urge me to leave you, to turn back and not follow you. For wherever you go, I will go . . . your people shall be my people and your God my God'." These verses teach us the strong bond between nationality and religion at the time of conversion, as Ruth explicitly accepted both, and stressed this by saying "your people shall be my people and your God my God." We also learn of this essential combination of accepting nationality together with religion at the time of conversion from the verses (Ruth 2:11–12): "Boaz said in reply, 'I have been told of all that you did for your mother-in-law after the death of your husband . . . and came to a people you had not known before. May the Lord reward your deeds. May you have a full recompense from the Lord, the God of Israel, under whose wings you have sought refuge." Again we find the two elements: a people you had not known before—that is nationality; under whose wings you have sought refuge—that is faith and religion.

Acceptance of the commandments must be before a court of three, as explained in (Yebamot 46b). In the same place it is stated: "The initiation of a proselyte requires the presence of three men, for law has been written in his case." Also (ibid., 47a): "And judge righteously between a man and his brother, and the proselyte that is with him." From this, Rabbi Judah deduced that he who is converted by a rabbinical court is a true proselyte, while he who does so privately is not. The reference is to the acceptance of the burden of the commandments, as explained in Tosafot (ibid.) and established in Shulkhan Arukh (Yoreh Deah, section 268, paragraph 3): "except when disqualified by non-acceptance of the commandments."

Despite these rulings, if in retrospect it is learned that a proselyte was not asked and was not informed of the nature and substance of the commandments, or even if we know that he wishes to convert for some material reason and not for motives of religious faith, so long as he was accepted by a court of three, was circumcised and immersed, he is considered to have converted, as stated in the Talmud (Yebamot 24b): "The halakha is in accordance with the opinion of him who maintains that they are all proper proselytes." Maimonides adds: (ibid., Ch. XIII:17): "A proselyte who was not examined or was not informed about the commandments and their penalties but was circumcised and performed ablution before three laymen, is considered a proselyte. [This applies] even though it was known that he became a proselyte for a non-religious reason. Since he was circumcised and immersed, he is no longer a gentile. We are apprehensive about him until his intentions are verified; even if he returned to idolatry, he is regarded like a Jewish apostate . . . Because he was immersed, he is regarded as a Jew."

Indeed, there have been many cases of this sort in Jewish history in which people converted for some material benefit, such as those during the time of Solomon and his wives, the wives of Shimshon, and so on, as Maimonides explains. While in retrospect they were considered converts, the consequences demonstrated the inception, for not only did they not become integrated into the nation, but they brought down trouble and suffering upon it by remaining faithful to their original religion and people. The Edomites also illustrate this, as does the "mixed multitude" that went up with Israel out of Egypt and caused most of the Israelites' hardships in the desert. This gave rise to the typical Jewish reluctance to accept converts, for as the Sages say "proselytes are as bad to Israel as a sore in the skin," since most proved that they did not join with Israel for spiritual reasons, but for material considerations existing at the time. Nevertheless, as a general vision of Israel, the Sages also saw conversion as a positive event, for it is said (Pesahim 87b): "The Holy One, blessed be He, exiled Israel among the nations only in order that proselytes might join them." And in Tractate Gerim (Ch. IV:3): "The proselytes are beloved, for everywhere He identifies them with Israel: Love is mentioned in regard to Israel, and also in regard to proselytes, etc. Acceptance is recorded with regard to Israel and likewise used with regard to proselytes, etc." The Sages further say: "All these will become [self made] true converts, as it is said, 'For then will I turn to the people a pure language, that they may call upon the name of the Lord'" (Zeph. 3:9). Although according to halakha, converts will not be a party to the Messianic era, as stated in Yebamot cited above, if they have converted for reasons of personal benefit and convenience, they will still chose to convert of their own free will, even without being accepted, as Rashi explains in Abodah Zarah (ibid.), and are known as "self-made proselytes."

All this applies only when the proselyte does not declare himself unwilling to accept the Torah and commandments. Although we may be aware that he is not motivated by devotion to the Jewish religion, we are entitled to regard his formal request for conversion as consent to accept the commandments. However, if someone explicitly proclaims that he is unwilling to take on the Jewish religion, but wishes only to join the Jewish people and nation, his proselytism is totally invalid and he is not even considered a "self-made proselyte." This is because the primary intent of conversion is acceptance of Jewish faith and religion, as it is the soul of Judaism and its fundamental element, and there is no Jewish nationality without the Jewish religion.

We therefore learn from Tosefta, Demai, Ch. II and Bekorot 30b that "we must not receive (as an Israelite) a proselyte who accepted the teaching of the Torah, except one law." Similarly, Maimonides rules (loc. cit., Ch. XIV, Halakha 8): "But in this age, even if he accepted the entire Torah, excepting one law, he is not accepted."

Our entire history in the First and Second Temple periods demonstrates the failure of mass converts to become integrated into the nation. This is illustrated by the fate of the Samaritans (II Kings 16) and the security and religious problems they provoked, which reverberate throughout Talmudic literature and history books. This occurred because they were not sincere in their loyalty to the Jewish faith. The same situation applies to the Edomites at the end of the Second Temple period. Nevertheless, they are not to be rejected retroactively, but are to be given the opportunity to prove themselves. In the words of Maimonides (ibid.): "It is an historical fact that many proselytes were converted during the reigns of Kings David and Solomon in the presence of laymen. Although the Great Beth Din was apprehensive about them, they were not rejected after immersion, but they were likewise not encouraged, until their sincerity was firmly established."

The Immersion of a Proselyte
The requirement for the immersion of a proselyte, in addition to its being a tradition passed down from generation to generation since the time of Moses on Mt. Sinai, was deduced by the Sages from several Biblical sources. In Keritot (9a) we learn that it derives from the verse: "You and the stranger shall be alike" (Nu. 15:15). "You"— as your forefathers. As your forefathers did not enter the covenant except by circumcision and immersion and sacrificial offering, so they will not enter the covenant save by circumcision and immersion and sacrificial offering. In Yebamot (46b) we find that the obligation of immersion for the proselyte derives from the text concerning the time when Israel received the Torah and entered the covenant: "Go to the people and warn them to stay pure today and tomorrow. Let them wash their clothes" (Ex. 19:10), which refers to immersion as well. It may also derive from: "Moses took the blood and dashed it on the people" (Ex. 24:8), and we know that there can be no "dashing of blood" without immersion.

Similarly, in Gerim (I; 5) we find: "In the same manner that the Israelites entered into the covenant by virtue of three precepts, so do proselytes enter into the covenant by means of circumcision, immersion and a sacrifice. The omission of two disqualify; the omission of one does not," and in Maimonides (loc. cit., XII:1): "Israel entered into the covenant by means of three qualifications: Circumcision, immersion and a sacrifice." Circumcision was practiced in Egypt, according to the verse: "But no uncircumcised person may eat of it" (Ex. 12:48). Moses himself circumcised them, as everyone, with the exception of the tribe of Levi, had abolished circumcision in

Egypt, as it says: "And kept your covenant" (Deut. 33:9). Immersion was also practiced in the desert before the receiving of the Torah on Mt. Sinai, as is says: "stay pure today and tomorrow. Let them wash their clothes, etc." And so for all generations, if a gentile wishes to enter the covenant and be sheltered by the Divine Presence and accept the commandments, he requires circumcision, immersion, and a sacrificial offering. If it is a female, she requires immersion and sacrificial offering, as it is said: "You and the stranger shall be alike"— as you require circumcision, immersion and a sacrificial offering, so for all generations the convert shall require circumcision, immersion and a sacrificial offering. In our time, when there are no sacrifices, he requires circumcision and immersion, and when the Temple is rebuilt, he will bring the offering.

Immersion, which the Sages learned from our forefathers in the desert before the receiving of the Torah, can be deduced from the Bible "to stay pure," which refers, according to the interpretation of Ibn Ezra, to immersion: "The intention of 'to stay pure' is to cleanse themselves with water, as obvious from the sequence 'and wash their clothes,' as paraphrased, 'but if he wash them not nor bathe his flesh'." Others deduce this from the washing of clothes in the Bible, which is explained in Mekhilta: "there can be no washing of clothing without immersion," so that in all Scriptural references to the washing of clothes it is accompanied by immersion. Furthermore, as the Israelites were warned to abstain from women at the time of the receiving of the Torah, it is clear that immersion is required in order to stay pure, as it says: "He shall bathe his whole body in water and remain clean until evening" (Lev. 15:16). It is thus clear that the start of the entrance of the Israelites into the covenant was accompanied by sanctification by means of immersion.

Numerous non-Jewish sources from the Second Temple period bear witness to the fact that for the Jews, the procedure for conversion was associated with immersion, an expression of the purity of both body and soul which leads to spiritual uplifting, as it was at the time of the revelation of the Torah on Mt. Sinai. I do not wish to cite alien sources on this subject. However, our own history demonstrates the great importance that Jews attribute to immersion itself. Conversion or the transition from one sect to another or one religious stage to another have always involved immersion. In History of the Jewish War (Vol. II, 8:7), Josephus Flavius relates that initiation into the sect of Essenes also involved immersion in purifying water.

It may be assumed that the seven immersions of Naaman in the Jordan, as directed by Elisha, stemmed from Naaman's conversion to the Jewish religion, as it is written: "For thy servant will never again offer up burnt offering or sacrifice to any god, except the Lord" (II Kings 5:17). It would appear from this that Naaman, at the time of his cure, accepted the Jewish faith following immersion. The Sages, however, consider him a "resident alien," as stated in Gittin (57b), since he did not take on the rest of the commandments, but only renounced idolatry, as it says "thy servant will never again offer up burnt offering, etc." According to halakha, there is no need for a resident alien to undergo immersion in order to convert, but only to accept, in the presence of three associates, the seven precepts obligatory for all men.

Procedure for the Conversion of Minors
Three possibilities can be found in halakha for the conversion of minors: (1) They are converted together with their parents; (2) Their parents request their conversion but do not themselves convert; (3) They request conversion for themselves.

The first circumstance is a simple matter evident from Ketubot 11a: "a proselyte whose sons and daughters were converted with him and are content with their father's actions." However, according to Shulkhan Arukh, even here the child has the right to protest his conversion when he grows older, and it is then invalidated retroactively. Others disagree, contending that whoever was converted together with his father as a minor has no independent right to invalidate the conversion when he comes of age.

In respect to the second circumstance, we find in Shita Mekubezet on Ketubot (in the name of Rashi and his associates, who were among the first codifiers), that when the father and mother request the conversion of their child without converting with him, he is converted by the authority of the rabbinical court. This derives from Ketubot 11a: "A minor proselyte is immersed by the direction of the court," as a man may be granted a privilege in his absence. Since a minor does not have the right of independent decision, the court is authorized to convert him with the consent of his parents. Others maintain that if both parents request his conversion, although they themselves do not convert, the intentions of his parents suffice and the "authority of the court" is not required. Only if the child is fatherless and his mother alone requests his conversion, without converting herself, is he then converted by the authority of the court.

In the event that the child is thus converted by the authority of the court, he may, of course, protest his conversion and invalidate it retroactively when he comes of age. At such time, he reverts to being a gentile in every sense, as explained in the Talmud, in Maimonides (Hilkot Melachim: Ch. X, Halakha 3), and in Shulkhan Arukh (Yoreh Deah, Section 268, par. 7).

The third circumstance, where the minor has no father or mother and requests conversion for himself, appears explicitly in Shulkhan Arukh (ibid.), and can be derived from Maimonides and from Shita Mekubezet (Bet ha-Raah): "If he comes before us to be converted, on his own accord, we accept him by the direction of the court." This implies that even when he has parents, he is entitled to be converted by the authority of the court, although the same principle cannot be deduced from the codifiers. In this event, as well, the child has the right to revoke his decision and protest his conversion when he comes of age, at which time it is invalidated retroactively and he reverts to his previous status of gentile. This applies only if the minor did not practice Judaism as an adult; if he did practice Judaism as an adult, he cannot protest his conversion.

In all these circumstances for the conversion of a minor, there is no need for the procedure of accepting the commandments or informing him of them. As he undergoes immersion by the authority of the court, not accepting the commandments does not disqualify him; he is required only to undergo the conversion rituals of circumcision and immersion.

(3) *The Third Problem*
Here the question arises of whether it is possible to convert to Jewish nationality and not to the Jewish religion, in view of which secular procedures might be established for accepting a non-Jew into the Jewish nation.

The answer is: not only is there no such possibility in Jewish reality according to the Torah and Oral Law, as can be seen from the impassioned words of Ruth the Moabite, imbued with the flame of true faith, when she chooses to convert—"Your people shall be my people and your God my God"—but the whole of Jewish history teaches us that it is impossible to separate or divide between Jewish nationality and religion, as the religion is the first element and fundamental basis on which the nation was established and the source of the sense of brotherhood and singularity of the Jewish people. The Jewish religion and nationality are like a soul and a body whose separation from each other necessarily leads to the death of the individual.

If we attempt to discover at least one typical feature common to all members of the Jewish people, we will find it nowhere else but in the Torah and the Prophets, which unite and sustain the nation throughout the world. In the First Temple Period, numerous attempts were made to abandon true Jewish religion and faith and endeavor to consolidate a Jewish nationality in their stead, and we see what happened to the Kings of Israel who championed this view. Bitter experience led to the loss of many of the Israelite tribes "for our nation exists only by virtue of the Torah," in the words of Rabbi Sa'adia Gaon.

Establishing a secular procedure for membership in the Jewish people would constitute a blow to the unity of the Jewish people and its singularity, and would sow the seed of divisiveness, controversy and strife among the tribes of Israel, and would throw up a wall between one Jew and another.

Such a procedure is liable to create a unique androgynous creature: a Jew by nationality and a gentile by religion. Such an odd commixture would eventually rebel against the nation itself and lead to the destruction of Jewish unity and the ability to survive as a nation in and of itself.

Numerous facts from contemporary history serve as clear evidence for the concerns expressed here, and they should suffice to deter us from undertaking new efforts of this sort that might lead to further rifts in the nation and erect an unbreachable wall between Jew and Jew and between tribe and tribe.

What government or regime, be it of the highest level and authority in the Jewish nation, would dare to be responsible for obliterating substance and changing procedures that have been sanctified for over three thousand years, ever since we stood on Mount Sinai, and that concern the very heart and soul of the nation.

It is well known that the gravest danger for the future of the Jewish people in the Diaspora is intermarriage, which leads to assimilation, from which there is no return or possibility of independent life. The only constraint curbing mixed marriages is the Jewish tradition and religion engraved upon and sacred to the heart of the nation. Therefore, any deviation from this tradition in the State of

Israel, which serves as a model for Jews in the Diaspora, any justification for mixed marriages in any way, shape, or form, or any de facto recognition of the Judaism of the children of gentile women on the part of the Government of Israel, is liable to undermine the last spiritual link on which Judaism depends. Under no circumstances is it feasible that the masses of Jewish people in the Diaspora will accept a situation in which what is forbidden for them is ostensibly permitted and justified in the State of Israel.

Finally, I am surprised that the question you raise concerns only the registration of minors born to mixed marriages. The Government's decision regarding the registration of adults, as presented in your letter, that they "will be listed as 'Jewish' if they declare themselves in good faith to be Jewish and not a member of another religion," is equally in contradiction to Jewish tradition. If a gentile should come and declare "in good faith" that he is a Jew and not a member of another religion, will that make him a Jew? This can only be said to open the door to the blurring of the lines of demarcation between Israel and the other nations, and we are in danger of encouraging a multitude of gentiles to instantly become Jews with the sanction of the State of Israel.

(4) Conclusion

In view of my comments above, based on the sources of the Talmud, halakha, and history, we may arrive at the following conclusions:

(1) The Jewish religious law we follow, which establishes that the children of mixed marriages invariably acquire the status of the mother, has always been accepted by the Jewish people. We find at the time of King David, the Prophets, and Ezra in the Second Temple Period that the children of foreign women born to Jewish fathers were considered foreign in every sense and required full conversion.

(2) According to halakhic opinion, after proper conversion the child reverts to the status of the father and is considered the same as if he had been born Jewish.

(3) The accepted halakhic procedure for conversion, based on the three principles of accepting the commandments, circumcision and immersion, has its source in the revelation on Mt. Sinai when Israel first entered the covenant, and it has been consecrated and accepted by the Jewish people ever since.

(4) Our history reveals that the immersion of the proselyte was

fully sanctified and accepted by the Jewish people, and served as a fundamental means of transition to acceptance of and loyalty to the Jewish religion.

(5) According to halakha, it is possible for the rabbinical court to convert minors at the request of the parents, even if they themselves do not convert. Similarly, the court is entitled to convert the children of mixed marriages when the mother is a non-Jew and the father is Jewish, even if the mother herself does not convert along with them. However, in every instance of the conversion of minors without the conversion of the parents, the conversion is conditioned on the consent of the minor when he comes of age, that is, the child does not protest his conversion upon reaching majority. If he is opposed to it upon reaching majority, the conversion is invalidated retroactively.

(6) No agency, government or regime is legally or morally entitled to or justified in abolishing a tradition that has stood for thousands of years and establishing a secular procedure for accepting converts that does not follow halakha, not even for the sole purpose of registering nationality. By doing so, a commixture would be created in the form of a Jew by nationality and a non-Jew by Jewish religion and halakha. This strange commixture would constitute a constant plague on the Jewish nation even in the State of Israel.

(7) The registration of the children of mixed marriages as Jews by the State of Israel in contradiction to tradition, even if only by nationality, would be seen by the entire Jewish world as if the Government of Israel were sanctioning assimilation.

(8) The decision of the Government regarding the registration of adults on the basis of a "declaration in good faith" is similarly contrary to halakha and Jewish tradition, and opens the door to the entrance into the Jewish nation of a nameless multitude.

In view of these remarks, the Government of Israel must ensure and establish that the regulations for the registration of citizens, both adults and minors, conform to halakha and Jewish tradition, so that no adult will be registered as a Jew on the basis of a declaration alone, but that whenever there is doubt as to the Jewish affiliation of an individual, it will have to be confirmed by means of incontrovertible evidence or reliable documents recognized by halakha. All conversions must be performed solely according to halakha before a rabbinical court alone.

A Practical Proposal for Regulating the Registration of Children of Mixed Marriages

(1) A special category of "professing Judaism" [mityahed] should be created in the population registry (taken from the verse: "And many of the people of the land professed to be Jews," Esth. 8:17). This status would include all minors who require conversion and cannot yet be immersed, but are in the process of conversion with the consent of their parents.

(2) In the case of the child of a mixed marriage where the father is Jewish and the mother is not Jewish, and both wish to register the child as a Jew, the child will have to undergo a process of conversion according to halakha, save for acceptance of the commandments which is not required.

(3) In such cases, if for some reason it is not possible to fully carry out the procedure of conversion, including immersion, as in the case of an infant, the child will be registered in the population registry as "professing Judaism" until he grows older and completes the conversion process according to halakha, at which time he will be registered as a Jew.

(4) As for the identity card, the child can be listed in the father's identity card, indicating below the "identification number" and in the same box the notation "professing Judaism." Alternatively, a numerical symbol or some sort of other symbol can be allotted for the special status of "professing Judaism" in the box for "identification number."

This practical proposal for regulating the problem of registering minors born to mixed marriages can, in my opinion, solve the problem in the best possible way, both in terms of halakha and in humane and practical terms, and all will be properly arranged, with the grace of God.

Respectfully and sincerely,

S. Goren

12. ARYEH LEIB GROSSNASS, MEIR LEW, ABRAHAM RAPPOPORT, MEIR HALEVY STEINBERG AND MORRIS SWIFT

All respondents were members of the rabbinical court of London.
Aryeh Leib Grossnass (1912–1996) was born in Poland and emigrated to England where he was the director of a college of Talmudic studies from 1949.
Meir Lew (1907–1990) was born in Poland and emigrated to England where he earned a Ph.D. in addition to his rabbinical studies and published several books on the subject of Polish Jewry.
Abraham Rappoport (1908–1983) was born in Russia and served for many years as the rabbi in charge of kashrut inspection and a teacher at Etz Haim Yeshiva.
Meir Halevy Steinberg (1891–1975) moved from Dvinsk in Russia to Heidelberg, Germany, where he received a doctorate in law. After settling in England, he was active in the Jewish community and became a member of the executive committee of the World Jewish Congress.
Morris Swift (1907–1983) was a professor of philosophy who collaborated with the historian Simon Dubnov. He was born in England, served as the chief rabbi of the London Federation of Synagogues and filled a variety of rabbinical posts in the Los Angeles youth movements and the Jewish community of Johannesburg, South Africa.

14 Tebet 5719

Dear Prime Minister,

We received your letter of 13 Heshvan 5719 addressed to the Chief Rabbi, Dr. Israel Brodie on Friday, 23 Kislev 5719, the day he departed London for South Africa for reasons of health.

The members of the London Rabbinical Court are serving temporarily as a Chief Rabbinate Commission, and thus your letter—after it was read by the Chief Rabbi—was conveyed by him to the Commission for consideration and response. We hereby wish to thank you for your letter and are honored to present our opinion.

1. First, we would like to express our deepest regret that this issue is still of concern in the State of Israel after the Chief Rabbinate of

Israel has already openly expressed its learned and decisive opinion regarding this dangerous measure which is so treacherous for the nation. It is well known that all of the rabbinical scholars in Israel and the Diaspora have protested harshly against the Government's proposal for the registration of the children of non-Jewish women.

Nor can we ignore the fact that you have found it appropriate to address your enquiry on what is without doubt an essentially halakhic matter to people who are neither qualified to pronounce on religious law nor familiar with the Jewish tradition, a step unprecedented in Jewish history.

2. Halakha on this matter has never been in doubt. Anyone born to a non-Jewish mother, whether a child or an adult, is a non-Jew and can not be considered or registered as a Jew by religion or nationality without being converted according to religious law by a recognized and authorized rabbinical court. In the State of Israel, this is, of course, only a court authorized by the Chief Rabbinate of Israel. No political or civil authority is entitled to distort this fact and register as a Jew a person who was born to a non-Jewish mother and did not convert according to halakha.

3. We read with pleasure your remarks concerning the sense of unity and identity with world Jewry of the Jewish community in Israel. Precisely because of this sentiment, which is also the ardent wish of tens of thousands of Jews in the Diaspora, whose rabbis and spiritual leaders are making every effort to instill and deepen it, we, as the representatives of the Chief Rabbinate of Britain and the Rabbinical Court of London and the country, a central rabbinical institution servicing Jewish communities the world over, would be remiss in our duty if we did not warn against the grave danger of a rift in the House of Israel that would not heal for generations and an irreparable schism in the nation that would necessarily result from any deviation—in the laws of the State of Israel—from the time-honored precepts of halakha in matters of personal status, descent and family.

The position of the Government of Israel and its proposal regarding registration can only horrifyingly encourage the processes of integration, assimilation and intermarriage that are playing havoc with the Jewish communities in the Diaspora, and are of grave concern to every Jew anxious for the survival and unity of the nation.

The Jewish communities in the Diaspora, the overwhelming majority of whose organized public Jewish life centers around religious communities and synagogues and is grounded on the Torah, and who look to the Holy Land as a spiritual and religious center to shed its light and influence their way of life, view the proposal of the Government as a danger and tragedy for the personal and family life of Jews throughout the world.

We pray that the Government of Israel, over which you preside, will withdraw the proposal which would destroy the sanctity of the Jewish people and family and the unity of the nation, and may there be peace on Israel.

Sincerely and with the blessings of the Torah,

A.L. Grossnass, dayan
A. Rappoport, dayan
M. Lew, dayan
M. Steinberg, dayan
M. Swift, dayan

13. ZECHARYA HACOHEN

A rabbi, Hacohen (d. 1967) was born to a family of weavers in Para, an outlying town in Yemen, at the end of the 19th century, and studied with instructors and rabbis from an early age. One Saturday in 1911, his family welcomed into their home Shmuel Yavnieli, who had come to encourage the Jews of Yemen to immigrate to Palestine. Hacohen came to Palestine in 1919 with his wife and young son and settled in Nes Ziona, where he worked as a laborer. He later moved to Nahalal where he served as the ritual slaughterer, moshav rabbi, and regional rabbi. Rejecting invitations to join any religious party, Hacohen revealed an open and tolerant attitude toward the secular. In his later years he served as head of the religious affairs department of the moshav movement, became a member of Mapai (the social democrat party), and was active in the Histadrut Labor Union. Many of his articles and homilies addressed the subject of the attitude to socialist Zionism.

5 Shevat 5719

Dear Sir,

I hereby convey to you my response to your enquiry regarding the children of mixed marriages (minors). . . .

Response
"For you are a people consecrated to the Lord your God: of all the peoples on earth the Lord your God chose you to be His treasured people" [Deut. 7:6]. Before the title "consecrated" there was the command—"When the Lord your God brings you to the land that you are about to enter and possess, and He dislodges many nations before you—the Hittites, Girgashites, Amorites, Canaanites, Perizzites, Hivites, and Jebusites, seven nations much larger than you—and the Lord your God delivers them to you and you defeat them, you must doom them to destruction: grant them no terms and give them no quarter. You shall not intermarry with them: do not give your daughters to their sons or take their daughters for your sons" [ibid., 1–3]. And the reason for this is "For they will turn your children away

from Me to worship other gods, and the Lord's anger will blaze forth against you and He will promptly wipe you out" [ibid., 4]. The commandment and the warning come to ensure that there be no reason for the Lord's anger. They were, instead, to "tear down their alters, smash their pillars, etc." [ibid., 5]. "You are a people consecrated to the Lord your God"—unlike the other seven nations who were idolaters, for if they were not idolatrous there would have been no need for the admonition and commandment—and we would say that this prohibition does not exist. But because the reason is given alongside the prohibition and because "they will turn your children away from Me," we cannot but acknowledge that the law-giver was the father of the wise and the first of the prophets. This is the basis for the law that prohibits a Jew from marrying a hea-then woman. According to Maimonides (Issurei Bi'ah, XII): "An Israelite who takes a heathen woman of the other nations as his wife, or an Israelite woman who marries an idolater are liable to the biblical penalty of stripes, as it is stated: 'You shall not inter-marry with them: do not give your daughters to their sons or take their daughters for your sons'." He adds: "Though the prohibition of the Torah applies only to the seven nations of Canaan, the Sages extended it to other nations." To emphasize the apprehension that they will turn the children away from the God of Israel, Maimonides explains: "This practice leads one to cleave to idolatry, from which the Holy One, blessed be He, separated us; it weans us away from the Lord and causes us to trespass against Him." The prohibition is thus accompanied by its reasoning and justification. We are then told that the ban against marrying a proselyte from the seven nations does not appear in the Torah (but that the Sages feared to allow it lest it turns the children away). Having seen the proscription and warning and the reason for the prohibition, it might be argued that at the time it was issued it was clear and understandable. However, if those nations no longer exist—and idolatry no longer exists—and as Maimonides states, when Sennecherib King of Assyria rose he mixed the nations together and exiled them from their land, then it might be said that if there is no effect then the cause is invalid and the prohibition is automatically canceled. But we cannot contend thus and therefore permit intermarriage, for the Torah was not given provisionally. Its laws are eternal as the nation of Israel is eternal. The Torah and commandments are for all times, and we must do all we can to uphold them. The Sages were well aware of the intermingling of the nations—and the abolishment of idolatry—and that the nations believe in the one Creator, and yet they still established limitations and restrictions lest the holy seed of Israel be defiled. They ruled that the child of a handmaiden and a gentile woman follow the mother—whether or not the father is Jewish (Eben ha-Ezer, 60:5). Maimonides (Ishut, 4:15) states that if one betroths a non-Jewess, his union is not valid; it is if nothing had been contracted. We are told in the Mishnah (Kiddushin 66b) that no Jew can contract a marriage with a non-Jewess, and that the child born of such a union follows the mother. Rashi, however, adds that if the child is converted, he is a proper Jew and not a bastard. And just as the Torah forbids intermarriage with the seven nations and provides the reason for it, so too does it forbid intermarriage with Ammon and Moab, and similarly provides the reason: "No Ammonite or Moabite shall be admitted into the congregation of the Lord, none of their descendants, even in the tenth generation, shall ever be admitted into the congregation of the Lord" [Deut. 23:4]. And why? The reason is given: "Because they did not meet you with food and water on your journey after you left Egypt, and because they hired Balaam son of Beor . . . to curse you . . . You shall never concern yourself with their welfare or benefit as long as you live" [ibid., 5–7]. This seems to imply that if they had welcomed the Israelites with bread and water, there would have been no prohibition against them entering the congregation of the Lord and this commandment would not have been written of them as it was of the seven nations. However, if we consider other reasons, we cannot ignore their efforts to lead the Israelites astray, as is written: "They are the very one who, at the bidding of Balaam, induced the Israelites to trespass against the Lord in the matter of Peor" [Nu. 31:13], nor the warning not to be led astray by them: "Beware of being lured into their ways . . . Do not inquire about their gods, saying . . . I too will follow those practices" [Deut. 12:30]. The daughters of these nations were dangerous and capable of luring the Israelites, they "invited the people to the sacrifices for their god. The people partook of them and worshipped that god," and immediately afterwards it says: "Thus Israel attached itself to Baal-peor" [Nu. 25:2–3].

In every generation, there are means of temptation, and in our times, there are but a few who resist. The celebration of Christmas and the Christian new year is one example in our nation, and we can only regret this offensive custom, for it will turn your children away. What response can be given to the instruction of the lawgiver that says "But if your heart turns away and you give no heed [Deut. 30:17]" and warns of the consequences and then admonishes the nation to distinguish between the unclean and the clean. Just as we are warned in eating to distinguish between the unclean and the clean, so we are warned in another matter in the same terms for "He paid attention to nothing save the food that he ate" [Gen. 39:6]. The Torah cautions us "You shall be holy to me, for I the Lord am holy, and I have set you apart from other peoples to be Mine" [Lev. 20:26]. All this, in my humble opinion, clarifies the law, of which the Torah instructs us "Do not turn aside to the right or to the left" [Deut. 5:29].

Now for the bitter reality of all that has been inflicted upon and befallen the Diaspora of European Jewry under the persecutors of the Jews in the days of the inhuman Hitler, the Jews were transported from place to place, shunted from encampment to encampment, from one extermination camp to another, as they were by the intermingling of nations by Sennecherib. They could not avoid the hurdles by which many Jews, some unknowingly, were caught up, and in many cases it is difficult to uncover the truth. Who can know whether Jewish blood flows in the veins of the gentiles in mixed marriages and vice versa. The books of responsa are filled with such instances. Several couples in mixed marriages are now arriving in Israel with the non-Jewish fruit of their womb, and the vineyard of the House of Israel is being intermingled with alien plantings. Some perpetrate frauds in order to escape the Diaspora and find refuge in Israel, and others are evil saboteurs who cloak themselves in the guise of Judaism to further their mission of enfeebling and distressing Israel, and these things are actually happening. We find ourselves in an uncomfortable position. Are these people being truthful when they say I am a Jew or a Jewess, or are they lying? In my opinion, the truth should be discovered by established Jewish examinations by those well-versed in Judaism, and a mere declaration should not be relied upon. Thus the Aramite who came to Jerusalem to eat of the Paschal lamb was examined, for he would have enjoyed it and defiled the sacrifice as he knew that an uncircumcised foreigner should not partake of it. His deception appeared in his query before Rabbi Judah ben Batira.

If the investigation reveals that he is indeed a Jew, even if he is not circumcised but can give an adequate explanation for the fact, such as coming from Russia or other countries where circumcision placed people in jeopardy and therefore was not performed, then we circumcise him as a proper Jew. Because he was coerced he is like those whose brothers died as a result of circumcision, and many such brothers indeed died abroad because of circumcision. Otherwise, he is adjudged like a gentile who requests conversion, and all the rules must be followed. If one of them is not a Jew and they have a son and do not wish to accept conversion for the son, then he is a non-Jew and should be converted without them, for he is not the child of a Jewish marriage.

He alone has the right to be converted by circumcision and immersion. Without this, he cannot be called a Jew, for he is the product of the total ban on intermarrying with them. By circumcision and immersion, he becomes a Jew in every way.

Things are very different in the period in which we live, and people are very far from being called "sincere proselytes." A proselyte who wishes to convert is asked for the reason for his desire to do so and he is questioned and told do you not know that Jews are such and such to see if he will withdraw his request to convert.

I do not believe that this question and informing him that the Jews are persecuted and so on is appropriate today. If we examine the situation, we find that we have been privileged to see the enhancement of Israel's prestige in many nations and the Jews are no longer a disgraceful nation. Today we are among the respected nations, and recognized as the seed blessed by God and many more will wish to shelter under the wings of the Divine Presence.

Although it has been said that "proselytes are as bad to Israel as a sore in the skin," we have no choice but to accept them. The words of the Prophet Zechariah (Chap. 8 and following) reflect the reality, and most specifically verses 20 and onward: "Thus said the Lord of Hosts: In those days ten men from nations of every tongue will take hold—they will take hold of every Jew by a corner of his cloak and say, 'Let us go with you, for we have heard that God is with you'." We cannot contradict the words of the prophet which have come to life here before us and happy are we in our good fate. Everything appropriate must be done to bring these people as close as possible to the State of Israel for the welfare of the state— to be lenient where the rules and the law permit and to be strict where we must in the measure that derives from the Jewish position.

I have already mentioned above the changes in accepting converts and in the observation of the commandments in actual Jewish life. Can we demand that the proselyte observe all the 613 commandments at a time when the majority of those among whom he will be integrated are far from observing even a small number of them. In times of revolution and upheaval even in daily life, even the faithful may err in view of the innovations in the world that is not as it was in the past.

However, the Jews in Israel today should not be seen as through a dark mirror, Heaven forbid. The House of Israel is not devoid of good deeds, but is as full of them as a pomegranate, although alongside the virtues there are also failings, as in any accounting of life. How can we demand that the proselyte observes the Sabbath and laws of kashrut and so on as commanded. That would be like saying "Do as I say, not as I do." If he adopts the failings he finds in daily life, then immersion is nothing but a rite of transition [. . .].

But this is Jewish law and cannot be ignored. Law is law. Time will do the rest in the soul of the converts who receive Jewish culture and instruction, especially for the minors who will learn with Jewish children in Israeli schools and will absorb the laws of the Torah and commandments and the way of life in Israel. There is no doubt that they will become integrated and will be good Jews no less virtuous than the rest of the nation in religion and nationality, sharing the rights and duties in the state they will come to regard as their homeland. And there can be no doubt that the children will influence their parents and bring them closer to Judaism and they will accept the law and religion of Israel and will also convert for reasons of conscience or otherwise. In many places in Israel there have already been such instances of the children influencing the parents, who have converted and are good Jews. We must embrace them according to the commandment to love the convert. Circumcision and immersion are no different for those who are lax in their daily life or those who observe the laws and commandments of the Torah in every way possible. There is one Torah and one law for you, for the convert and the citizen of the land.

However, a convert is not a convert without circumcision and immersion. The Sages ruled that he must immerse before three religious authorities. And the law of Israel states that he is not a convert until he has been circumcised and immersed, as Maimonides says: "A proselyte who was circumcised and did not immerse or

immersed and was not circumcised is not a proselyte until he is circumcised and immerses" (Issurei Bi'ah, XIII, 6).

Although our forefathers began as idolaters, and the tribes married Canaanite women, Jacob asks that only his sons and not their
sons bear his body when he dies.

I have hereby presented my humble opinion. The wise man plans
ahead.

Rabbi Zecharya Hacohen

14. SHALOM YITZHAK HALEVI

Rabbi Halevi (1891–1973) was born in Yemen and came to Israel in 1935, where he received a traditional education at the Rabbi Amiel Yeshiva as well as a master's degree in law and published numerous works on Jewish law and halakha. He later served as the rabbi of the Yemenite community and a member of the Tel Aviv-Jaffa rabbinical court.

2 February 1959

To the honorable Prime Minister of Israel,

May his welfare be enhanced,

I hereby acknowledge receipt of your letter from 27 October 1958 (which I received late) regarding the registration of minors from mixed marriages. I respectfully offer my reply.

The request of the Government for the opinion of rabbis is to be congratulated. I hope and pray that the Government will not only listen to these opinions but will also accept them, for they are the stance of our holy Torah. It would, however, have been preferable had the Government relied only upon the response of the Chief Rabbinate of Israel which has supreme authority to decide in these matters and the like even for the Diaspora.

As for the question itself, I would like to consider the problem as I understand it because of its critical importance to the very existence of the Jewish people. The fate of the nation in general and the State in particular hangs on its solution.

The critical question before us is whether Judaism allows for a distinction between religion and nationality as exists in other nations.

It is well-known that the Jewish religion preceded the Jewish people. Abraham, the father of the nation, was the first to introduce into the world the element of belief in one God. He instilled this belief in his sons after him.

The tribes of Israel received the Torah on Mount Sinai before they came into possession of the Land of Israel and became a special nation distinct from all other nations in essence and outlook, as it says: "You shall be my treasured possession among all the peoples" (Ex. 19:5). And it says too: "There is a people that dwells apart, not reckoned among the nations" (Nu. 23:9). That is our legacy from the Patriarchs Abraham, Isaac, and Jacob. When the people sinned against God and broke the covenant of the forefathers, even though they preserved their nationality, they were sent away from the land and scattered to the four corners of the world. This is a well-known fact that cannot be denied, nor can it be called a mere accident. Reliable evidence is provided by the pronouncements of all the prophets, from Moses the first to Malachi the last, who said at the end of his prophecy: "Be mindful of the Teaching of My servant Moses" (Mal. 3:22).

The Jewish people repented their deeds and remained faithful to its tradition throughout the Diaspora, giving their lives the world over in the name of the Lord rather than breaking the covenant of the Patriarchs. Especially now when we have returned to our homeland and are rebuilding our country, we much construct it on the foundations of Jewish tradition, for our Holy Torah is the law of the Land of Israel. Allow me to offer one example from the war of Sennecherib, who transferred nations from country to country and brought the Cutheans to the Land of Israel. These people did not observe the laws of the God of Israel and broke the proscriptions of the Ten Commandments. Consequently, they were set upon by lions. The King of Assyria then ordered that a priest be brought "and let him teach them the practices of the God of the land" (II Ki. 17:23–28).

The Jewish religion preserved the Jewish people throughout the thousands of years of their wanderings among the nations the world over. It served, and continues to serve, the Jewish people not only as a philosophy and way of life, but also as a means of uniting and unifying the different sectors of the nation. Jews have come together in the State of Israel after being separated and cut off from one another for thousands of years of exile, after each and every diaspora adopted its own ways of life, and still, when they meet, they do not seem like strangers to each other. The reason for this is simple: religion served as an instrument of unity for them all, not only for the pious who observe the ways of religion, but also for the liberals. For the Jewish religion, unlike others, contains three elements: love for God and His commandments, love for the Jewish people, and love for the Land of Israel, as the Sages say: "God, the Torah and Israel are one."

Yemenite Jewry can serve as a concrete example of how religion and nationality are intertwined. In their unfortunate history, neither religious persecution on the one hand nor the temptations offered them in exchange for assimilation on the other were successful. Night and day they dreamt of Zion and of returning to it, even though there, in Yemen, there were no nationalist movements or any other movement that might have influenced them. It was simply the pure messianic faith that maintained them until the time of redemption and they were able to immigrate in mass numbers to the land they had yearned for. None of the attempts thus far to separate religion from nationality have born fruit. Suffice it to mention that the "Canaanites" and similar groups who estrange themselves from the nation and everything sacred to it are the product of liberalism and the separation of religion and nationality. So as not to overly elaborate on this subject, I will address myself to the specific question at hand—mixed marriages and their offspring.

It would seem to me that we are not the first to encounter this problem. It arose as far back as the time of Ezra and Nehemiah, who issued an appalling cry to the people: "All the men of Judah and Benjamin assembled in Jerusalem in three days . . . Then Ezra the priest got up and said to them, 'You have trespassed by bringing home foreign women, thus aggravating the guilt of Israel. So now, make confession to the Lord . . . and separate yourselves from the peoples of the land and from the foreign women'" (Ez. 10:9–11). And: "Those of the stock of Israel separated themselves from all foreigners and stood and confessed their sins" (Neh. 9:2).

We might ask what was all this anxiety about? The answer is that intermarriage does serious injury to the purity of the Jewish nation and leads to children who estrange themselves from the people and its holy traditions, as explained in the Talmud Yebamot 17 and in Maimonides' Issurei Bi'ah, Ch. XIII. Of this the prophet Hosea says: "Because they have broken faith with the Lord, because they have begotten alien children" (5:7). This teaches us how deeply the leaders of Israel are concerned for the purity of the nation and that they should not become assimilated into mixed marriages, as it is written: "You shall not intermarry with them: do not give your daughters to their sons or take their daughters for your sons" (Deut. 7:3), and "For they will turn your children away from Me, etc." (ibid., 4). It follows, therefore, that the phenomenon of intermarriages that we are encountering now is not new to our history. As we have seen, Ezra and Nehemiah faced the same situation. And if they stood firm and curbed assimilation in order to obey the word of the Lord, it means that it is not in keeping with the life of the nation returning to its homeland.

The Jewish people is not eager to accept converts. As the Sages say: "proselytes are as bad to Israel as a sore in the skin" (Yebamot 16). This is certainly true in both religious and national terms, save for those who choose to convert from a sense of sympathy with the Jewish people and its tradition. I would cite one of the most positive and outstanding examples in the history of our nation from the Bible. Ruth the Moabite, determined to convert and become a Jewess out of sincere desire, said to her mother-in-law Naomi "Your people shall be my people [relating to nationality] and your God my God [relating to religion]" (Ruth 1:16). In other words, Ruth thought it was enough to accept the nationality, but Naomi did not consent until she also accepted the religion. Ruth holds a position of honor in the history of the Jewish people and is a symbol of those wishing heart and soul to convert.

Therefore, if the non-Jewish women who married Jews in the Diaspora (contrary to religious law) sincerely wish to be part of the Jewish people, nothing prevents them from becoming an integral part of the nation by converting according to accepted Jewish tradition when they come to Israel. If they do so, it will prove that such a non-Jewish woman has decided to become integrated into our nation and to turn her back on her foreignness (and this is not only a question of religion or religious coercion). But if a non-Jewish woman continues to maintain her foreign characteristics, then even from a national perspective it is very doubtful whether the nation can include her and her sort. There is also considerable doubt as to the type of education she would give her children who are growing up in the State of Israel.

If one should ask whether any Jew who does not observe the Torah and tradition thereby cuts himself off from the Jewish people, the answer is, certainly not! A born Jew remains a Jew even when he transgresses against the Jewish religion. He is like the son who disobeys his father and yet remains his son. This essence cannot be altered and even a Jew who sins is a Jew. This does not apply to a person who is not a Jew because he was born to non-Jewish parents. Naturally, he is not more privileged than the rest of the Jewish people who only become Jews after they are circumcised, immerse, and offer a sacrifice, as stated in Yebamot 47, Keritot 9, and in Maimonides' Issurei Bi'ah (Ch. XIII). All this was done after the Israelites were informed that they would receive the word of God: "Thus shall you say to the house of Jacob and declare to the children of Israel: 'You have seen what I did to the Egyptians . . . Now then, if you will obey me faithfully and keep My covenant . . . All the people answered as one, saying 'All that the Lord has spoken we will do!' . . . Moses came down from the mountain to the people and warned the people to stay pure and they washed their clothes" (Ex. 19:3–14). Only after all these preparations did the Lord reveal himself to Moses on Mount Sinai and did they receive the Torah.

Belief in the revelation on Mount Sinai is engraved on the heart of the Jewish people to this very day. And it has always been ordained for every non-Jew or non-Jewess and their non-Jewish children who wish to shelter under the wings of the Divine Presence and the Israeli nation and become Jews. They must, before all else, accept the Jewish religion and all that it entails. And this includes circumcision and immersion. Only in this way can they be considered part of the Jewish people, as explained in Yebamot 23, Maimonides' Issurei Bi'ah (Ch. XIV), and elsewhere.

In the fourth consideration contained in your letter, you state: "On the other hand, the Israeli nation does not see itself as separate from Diaspora Jewry." Since the State of Israel and its leaders are conscious of the unity of the nation and encourage it, how then can this unity be undermined by registering a child as a Jew when by religious law he is, without question, a non-Jew, as explained in Mekhilta, Exodus 21:4, Sifri Deuteronomy 7:3–5, Kiddushin 65, Yebamot 23, Maimonides' Issurei Bi'ah (Ch. XII) and Hilkhot Yibum (Ch. I Halakha 8), and so on? And how could this child ever marry a Jew?

As mentioned in your letter, by law, marriage and divorce in Israel are governed by religious law. Imagine what would happen if the Government were to decide that any man or woman (including the children of a non-Jewish mother) who declared in good faith that he or she was a Jew was to be registered in the population registry as a Jew. When in the course of time they should wish to marry a Jew and appeared at the marriage bureau they would learn that they are not Jewish and the rabbinical court would not consent to the marriage. Would this not be a terrible emotional shock for them? Would there not be two government authorities (the Office of the

Population Registry and the Rabbinical Court) that contradict each other? And what would the attitude of that man or woman be in respect to the marriage? Under these circumstances, the non-Jewish man or woman might agree to convert according to the precepts accepted by the Jewish people. If so, why should this not be done in advance before the individual finds himself in this unfortunate and uncertain situation? Alternatively, if he does not wish to convert, he will undoubtedly protest to the Government. Will the Government then consider enacting a law of civil marriage specifically for this category?

Is it advisable to cause upheavals in the Jewish people for a very small number of non-Jews? We would again be facing a rift in the nation, contrary to the conscience and wishes of your Excellency, the Prime Minister, in particular, and to the regret of the Jewish people in general.

It is thus advisable and desirable to seek ways that lead to the unity of the nation, to which all those involved in solving the problems of the people and the State aspire. May it be God's will that the heads of state succeed in finding a way to achieve this much desired goal.

With all due respect,

Shalom Yitzhak Halevi

15. HAYIM HAZAZ

An author and playwright, Hazaz (1898–1973) was born in the Ukraine and received both a secular and a religious education. As a young man, he moved from place to place in Russia during and following the October Revolution of 1917, and worked as a journalist for the Jewish paper Ha'Am in Moscow. In 1921 he arrived in Constantinople, and a year later traveled to Paris and London. He immigrated to Palestine in 1931, settling in Jerusalem. After 1967, Hazaz was active in the Movement for a Greater Israel. His essays, books, and plays include Rekhayim Shevorim [Broken Millstone], (1942), Be-ketz Ha-yamim [At the End of Days], (1950), and Delatot Nekhoshet [Copper Doors], (1963). He was awarded the Israel Prize for Literature in 1953, and twice won the Bialik Prize.

1st day of Hannukah, 5719

Dear Mr. D. Ben-Gurion,

I thank you for the honor you have bestowed upon me by counting me among the Jewish Sages. I shall attempt to reply to your question of "Who is a Jew?" as briefly as possible.

In halakha the answer has been clear, tried and tested for thousands of years, and in practice it is equally clear and has already created a certain reality. It is to be regretted that two contradictory responses cannot be given to this single question.

In the past, when the nation was in exile and was not in fact a nation but a people, religious communities scattered throughout the world, religion had the power to maintain its singularity and national existence. In the meanwhile, times changed, human conduct changed, people became free-thinkers, and the devastation of the Diaspora in our era led people to abandon religion. All this is well known. The Jewish community in Israel triumphed over its enemies and established a state. It was established as a secular state in which religion has no ruling power, but is an option available to the individual if he so wishes.

It therefore appears to me that halakha has no power over the population registry, which is within the exclusive authority of the law of the State.

Particularly today, when there are hundreds of mixed couples among us, the last surviving remnants of the nation, and when tomorrow the gates open and thousands or tens of thousands of mixed couples arrive, what should we do about them? Should we impose on them the religion according to halakha? Or should we turn them away?

Hence, if the father and the non-Jewish mother wish to have their son circumcised in order to be registered as a Jew, they should be accepted. For there is no greater virtue than a mother who gives her most prized possession, her son, to a nation that is not hers.

I do not know whether the mothers of all the converts in history also converted. The grandmothers of Shemaya and Abtalion, of Rabbi Akiva and Rabbi Meir and all the other great figures of the nation throughout the generations were descendents of converts and were a blessing for the Jewish people.

With regards,

H. Hazaz

16. YITZHAK ISAAC HALEVI HERZOG

Chief Rabbi of Israel, Herzog (1888–1959) was born in Poland and moved to England with his family in 1897. Ordained a rabbi in 1908, he went on to study mathematics, classical languages and literature in London and Paris, receiving a Ph.D. in Literature from London University in 1916. In 1925, he was appointed Chief Rabbi of Ireland. Herzog, who was active in the Zionist movement in Ireland and among the founders of the Mizrachi movement in the country, attended several Zionist Congresses. In 1936 he was elected Chief Ashkenazi Rabbi of Palestine.

24 Tebet 5719

Honorable Prime Minister,

I received the query you sent to various figures concerning the law for a child born to a non-Jewish woman.

The author of the *Kusari* has already stated that the Torah did not leave us its commandments to do with as we like. Even the greatest Torah scholars do not have the authority to determine the law as they see it, but only on the basis of the Torah that they teach. As the Sages said, the Torah and commandments shield us and are the source of our existence: "When the end of the redemption is at hand, God will say to Israel: 'My children, I am surprised at your patience in waiting for me all these years'. They will then reply: 'Master of the world, were it not for your Torah which You gave us, we should long have perished among the nations'." The very essence of Judaism is its Torah.

I now appeal to you: as you announced the suspension of the guidelines regarding the registration of the children of non-Jewish women—which are in total contradiction to the law of our Torah—so should you now announce the revoking of all the new guidelines. By doing so, you will save the nation in Israel and the Diaspora from the scourge of a schism and the blurring of the lines of descent, without which the foundations on which the whole of the House of Israel stands will be undermined.

By this action, may we soon be blessed with true and lasting peace at home and abroad and to the coming of righteous redemption when Israel will dwell tranquilly and safely on the land of its forefathers. Amen.

With the blessing of the Torah and Zion, Respectfully and in appreciation of your great worth,

Yitzhak Isaac Halevi Herzog

17. ABRAHAM JOSHUA HESCHEL

A scholar and philosopher, Heshel (1907–1972) was born in Warsaw, a descendent of Dov Baer of Messeritz and Levi Yitzhak of Berdichev. After earning a Ph.D. in philosophy from the University of Berlin in 1933, he taught at the Graduate School of Jewish Studies. In 1937 he was selected by Martin Buber to succeed him at the Jewish Institute for Adult Education in Frankfurt am Main. The following year, he was deported by the Germans to Poland, from which he fled to England where he founded the Institute for Jewish Studies in London. In 1940, he moved to the USA, teaching philosophy and Judaism in Cincinnati, and serving from 1945 as a professor of ethics and Jewish mysticism at the Jewish Theological Seminary of America. Heschel's books on Sa'adia Gaon, Ibn Gvirol, Maimonides, Abarbanel, the Kabbala, Hasidism, and the philosophy of religion earned him the respect of Jewish and Christian circles alike.

18 December 1958

Dear Mr. Ben-Gurion,

I received your letter concerning the registration of the population in Israel several days ago. I have considered the issue, taking into account both halakha and reality. In what way reality? It is a fact that there have been those in the national movement who have sought to establish Jewish existence on nationality alone and to distinguish between the people and the religion. I thoroughly understand the sentiment of those who honestly cannot say of themselves: we are not Jews in the religious sense, and yet they feel a connection to the people, the state, and the Hebrew language.

You have done well to stress that "the Israeli nation does not see itself as separate from Diaspora Jewry." I know how deeply you are concerned for the fate of the nation in the Diaspora. Our existence as a people is like a mountain suspended by a hair, and this concern hangs over us like a double-edged sword. However, in my opinion, the Government decision may be injurious. I am referring to the decision that "the religion or nationality of adults will be listed as 'Jewish' if they declare themselves in good faith to be Jewish and not a member of another religion."

It is generally accepted in our life that the Jewish people and the Torah (I shall use the word "religion") are inseparable. The Government decision separates the inseparable and creates two authorities: the nation, on the one hand, and religion, on the other. This approach, which determines that there is a Jewish people without religion, also implies that there is a Jewish religion without a people. Such a distinction is liable to cause a rift between the sectors of the nation, as well as a fundamental change in the nature of the essence of the nation and of the Torah. The nation will be like any other, and the Torah like any other religion. The first change will lead to denial of the existence of a Jewish people, and the second will turn the Jewish religion into a denomination or sect. Such a rift would also open the door to the possibility that even a Jew who converted to Christianity could remain a Jew.

It is a fact that many Jews not longer believe in the God of Abraham and His Torah. But it is also a fact that many have ceased to believe in the existence of the nation, just as the belief in the return to Zion has disappeared in the modern age. Many were convinced that the end was near. Without faith, there could be no visionaries. Just as there is a bad angel who releases a single drop that leads to destruction, so there is a good angel who releases a single drop of faith. It is on this drop that we live. The last word has not yet been written in the chapter of faith. Our children are drawing closer to us every day. I do not believe in the decline of faith, but in its reawakening.

Reason and daily experience both demonstrate that there is no possibility of establishing Jewish existence in the Diaspora on a secular Jewish culture. All the aspirations of writers in the Diaspora to create a secular culture have been trodden under and ridiculed. Nothing remains save the Torah and soulful yearning for a way of life given meaning by eternal life. You are of the opinion that in the State of Israel "there is no fear that the Jews will become assimilated among the non-Jews." I believe that the danger of spiritual assimilation can be expected anywhere, and not even the holiness of the Land of Israel and the endeavor to rebuild it can obviate this danger.

I am not ignoring the difficulties. I understand the distress of those who claim that the world of halakha is too narrow for them. The problem is that some see all of Judaism through the mirror of the finest point of religious law and disregard the Jewish spark. They make the fence more important than what it contains. Extremism and punctiliousness are not to our advantage. Even the Lord, who wished at first to create the world by the quality of justice, saw that it could not exist thus and added to it the quality of mercy. Flexibility is a virtue, not fanaticism.

Faith can not be imposed. Coerced faith is worse than heresy. But deference can be planted in the heart of the generation. Like the wicks of a candle waiting to be lit, many wait to hear the tidings that the spirit of God is hovering over the face of the deep, to see the beauty of that spirit. The trouble is that they do not know of the light that is in Judaism. Many of us who recoil from the shadows have never seen the light.

Some of those who deny God in public believe in secret. But as we have yet to find a way to express ourselves to those who reject the faith they have learned by rote, they wander confusedly in alien worlds.

May I be allowed to remark that now that the State of Israel is firmly established, the time has come to examine the national movement carefully and to ask whether there is justification in viewing religion as merely a means to an end or a device for ensuring the survival of the nation. This approach rests on ignorant assumptions. The nation is eternal. And the end itself is basically a religious one. Moreover, the mission of the Torah is to seek answers for problems of paramount importance in private and public life.

Every definition distorts. "Jew" is both a religious and a national concept. As a religious concept, it has an immutable definition. As a national term, it is vague. In such a situation, it is advisable to say: better not to define than to define and thereby uproot what has been planted. If for reasons of national security there is a need for legal residents of Israel to identify themselves by means of some document, those who cannot call themselves "Jews" might be registered as "Hebrews." As for the Law of Return, "do not ask questions."

Respectfully and with heartfelt greetings,

Abraham Joshua Heschel

18. JOSEPH SHLOMO KAHANEMAN

Rabbi Kahaneman (1888–1969), head of the Ponevez Yeshiva, studied at the yeshivot of Telz, Novogrodek and Radin. In 1919 he was appointed rabbi of Ponevez, where he founded a new yeshiva. A leader of Agudath Israel, Kahaneman also served as a member of the Lithuanian parliament (the Seimas; 1923–25). He moved to Palestine in 1940, and in 1943 founded the Ponevez Yeshiva in Bnei Brak as the center of a complex of schools, making it the largest educational institution of its kind in Israel. He then established similar campuses in Ashdod and other places around the country. Kahaneman also revived the custom of yarkhei kala, weekend seminars on religious subjects that became popular among secular circles as well.

27 Tevet 5719

Dear Mr. Prime Minister,

I received your letter of 13 Mar-Heshvan of this year late, and am replying with due respect.

I read the letter, although the questions it contains are not addressed to me. Rulings on matters of religious law properly belong only to issues that may be interpreted in more than one way. To my regret, in respect to almost all the matters under discussion, explicit laws can be found in the holy Torah, leaving it to us to comply with them or, Heaven forbid, to disobey them. One of these is the issue of a child born to a non-Jewish mother who is not a Jew until he is converted, which is a simple and accepted law of our people in our holy written and oral law, undisputed anywhere in the Babylonian Talmud. Admittedly, in the Jerusalem Talmud, in Yebamot 2 and Kiddushin 3, we are told of the case of Jacob of Naburaya who raised the question of whether the son of a non-Jewish mother could be circumcised on the Sabbath, believing that he could. However, even this Jacob of Naburaya, after hearing the response of Rabbi Hagi, admitted his mistake.

The same story is referred to several times in midrashic literature: in Bereshit Rabbah, Chap. 7; Bamidbar Rabbah 19; Kohelet Rabbah 7; Pesikta Rabbah, Parashat Parah. Each time, two rulings of Jacob of Naburaya appear together: that fish require ritual slaughter, and that the son of a Jewish man and non-Jewish woman may be circumcised on the Sabbath. The juxtaposition of these two rulings, together with the unparalleled response of Rabbi Hagi, highlights their absurdity and repugnance (and both are specifically attributed to Jacob of Naburaya).

I am, however, certain that your questions are the result of an attempt to find a solution to the very serious problem of the arrival in Israel of tens of thousands of immigrants from Eastern Europe and their integration in our holy land, when, to our great sorrow, some are the products of mixed marriages.

In respect to these applicants for registration, the answer appears explicitly in the holy Torah.

This is not a new problem in the history of our people. It arose as early as the start of the patriarchs' settlement of the land, at the time of Joshua. These are his words for the future and survival of Israel in his vision and testament: "For should you turn away and attach yourselves to the remnant of those nations—to those that are left among you—and intermarry with them, you joining them and they joining you, know for certain the Lord your God will not continue to drive these nations out before you; they shall become a snare and a trap for you, a scourge to your sides and thorns in your eyes, until you perish from this good land that the Lord your God has given you" (Josh. 23:12–13). Joshua stood up and warned of the utter destruction that would be brought about by intermarriage in our holy land.

The problem recurred even more acutely in the period of the return to Zion at the time of Ezra. Seventy years after the destruction of the Temple, when for forty years before the return no bird had chirped in the land. Only a very few exiles returned, while the majority of the people were reluctant to do so, as the memory of the horrible scenes of destruction and the image of the wasteland awaiting them were still fresh in their minds. It seemed that the salvation of the nation and the land demanded a temporary departure from the law regarding non-Jewish women and their children. Certain leaders of the nation indeed adopted this stance, as is written: "It is the officers and prefects who have taken the lead in this trespass" [Ez. 9:2]. The use of the word "officers" indicates that this national faithlessness was encouraged and supported by some sort of policy. After all, the return to Zion was of a decidedly religious character, with the Temple as the center of the nation's spiritual life. Thus at first glance there would seem to be no danger involved in accepting the non-Jewish women and their children. Religious life and the Temple would be a melting pot for the foreigners, forging everyone into a single nation.

Nevertheless, Ezra, with his pure spirit, considered these children of non-Jews and their mothers to be the seed of terrible destruction. He envisioned that the nation might, Heaven forbid, collapse from within because of the foreigners and heathens. "And when I heard this, I rent my garment and robe . . . and I sat desolate. . . . But now, for a short while, there has been a reprieve from the Lord our God, who has granted us a surviving remnant and given us a stake in His holy place. . . . Shall we once again violate Your commandments by intermarrying with these peoples who follow such abhorrent practices? Will You not rage against us till we are destroyed without remnant or survivor?" [Ez. 9:3–14]. With his greatness of soul and ardent faith, Ezra succeeded in instilling this awareness in the returning exiles until they agreed to act as they were commanded.

Again we confront the same problem. But, as we have said, its solution is set down and established in our sacred books.

Particularly at the time of this third settlement of Zion, in the current spiritual environment with the return of the lost and estranged, the real danger represented by non-Jewish women and their non-Jewish children is great. Although we do not seek out proselytes, we will welcome with love, as we are commanded to do, all those who wish to attach themselves to us, to convert to Judaism and share in our legacy from God in the hallowed tradition of halakha. Only through halakha are the purity and singularity of the people, are its wholeness, unity and eternal existence, ensured.

With respect and esteem,

Rabbi Joseph Sh. Kahaneman

Dear Mr. Prime Minister,

Please permit me to add a few words from the depths of my heart.

I see in the return to Zion in our generation a sign of the light of Divine Providence taking our hand and leading us through the hostile waters threatening to engulf us. I see God in every aspect of the people dwelling in Zion. I am certain that you too see this, for who better than you, the captain steering the ship of state, is aware of the miracles taking place at every moment. We are the people of God and our land is divine, as the Seforno says on the verse "The heavens belong to the Lord, but the earth He gave over to man" [Ps. 115:16]: "This land is the heaven of the Lord." Let us go out to meet the Lord, let us receive Him and draw closer to the hand of Divine Providence reaching out to us, let us meet with all our brethren, the children of Israel, on the eternal paths of our nation, Torah, and commandments, so that full redemption may soon be ours.

With respect and esteem,

Rabbi Joseph Sh. Kahaneman

19. YOSSEF KAPPAH

A rabbi and researcher of Yemenite Jewry, Kappah (b. 1917) was born in San'a, Yemen. In 1943 he immigrated to Palestine, where he studied at the Merkaz Harav Yeshiva in Jerusalem. In 1950, he was named a member of the Rabbinical Court of Tel-Aviv-Jaffa, and in 1951 of the Rabbinical Court of Jerusalem. He was elected to the Chief Rabbinate Council in 1968, and in 1970 was appointed to the High Rabbinical Court. Winner of the Israel Prize in 1969, Kappah authored books on Yemenite leaders, translated Yemenite works into Hebrew, and produced new translations of Maimonides and Sa'adia Gaon.

21 December 1958

Dear Mr. Prime Minister,

As you have granted me the title of "intellectual, I am obliged to proffer a 'proper reply'" (Avot, 5:7). It would be utterly superfluous to copy the law from the Gemara or Maimonides and Shulkhan Arukh. The sources of the law are undoubtedly as obvious to you as they are to me. Furthermore, as I understand it, the question is not what halakha has to say, as that is perfectly clear, but a more general perspective of the problem. I shall therefore attempt to present my view on the subject in brief.

1. What is the meaning of the term "Jew"? It must be stated that the term does not denote a certain race. Perhaps it is wrong to use the word "race" so as not to mimic the modern-day racists and their associates, as according to the perception of the Torah, there are no different races in the world. In order to uproot this theory, the Torah felt compelled to provide extensive details of the lineage of all the people in the world so as to attribute them to a single father and a single mother. Thus it might be more proper to say that the term "Jew" does not denote a certain tribe, or in other words, does not indicate the descendants of Abraham, Isaac, and Jacob in the limited sense of the phrase. We know beyond any doubt that throughout the generations, many people of different nations became intermixed with the Israelites. Beginning from the time they were in Egypt and "a mixed multitude went up with them" (Ex. 12:38), followed

by the Gibeonites (Josh. 9) who eventually became absorbed into the nation, and onward to include the many generations when they lived on their land under the great kings of Israel and Judah (II Chron. 2:16). Particularly during the period of the nation's exile and dispersion, with no difference between East and West, North and South, there was also a two-way movement, with individuals and groups converting to Judaism and abandoning Judaism (I do not wish to go into detail about the later periods, since some people of certain origins might consider it libelous). This is apparent to anyone with even the slightest knowledge of the upheavals in world history, assuming he is willing to face facts. Admittedly, there are fables that claim that all insincere proselytes will eventually be screened out and return to their origins in one generation or another. Indeed, there was a common saying in Yemen that "anyone from them goes back to them." However, fables and folktales should not be taken as the absolute truth. This being the case, it is therefore clear that the term does not denote a certain tribe.

Nor does the term denote a certain geographical unit, since people who live in England, Barbary, China, Yemen, Spain, and Germany, even if they and their fathers and grandfathers have been born there for thousands of years, are still called Jews. It is not inconceivable that while the Israelites were still in Egypt, certain families and households among them went off to other lands (although this is not the place to elaborate on this point). Nevertheless, they remained connected to the body of the nation, and the granting of the Torah and all the stages in the nation's consolidation and development reached them one after the other. Thus despite their distance and seeming detachment from the beginnings of the consolidation of the nation, and despite their residence in a certain geographical unit, they were not absorbed into that unit but remained separate and were called by the special name "Jews."

Nor can we say that "Judaism" is a religion and not a nationality, Heaven forbid. There are no such accepted terms as "Jewish Arab" as there is "Christian Arab" or "Moslem Arab" or "Druze Arab." Nor are there "Jewish Englishmen" or "Jewish Portuguese." Rather, there are "Yemenite Jews" or "French Jews." The adjective describes the noun in the same way that there are Jerusalem Jews and Tel Aviv Jews. Consequently, the name does not denote only religion and not nationality, but refers to a much broader concept. It is also a nationality. And how did this nationality take shape? By acceptance of a certain religion. In other words, the core of the nation is a certain tribe, or if you wish, the descendents of a certain person. However, anyone who accepts a certain religion becomes an interwoven part of the fabric of this tribe until he is indistinguishable, "for I make you the father of a multitude of nations" (Gen. 17:5; see also: Jerusalem Talmud, Bikkurim 1:4). To emphasize this principle, the Torah refers to the Jewish people as a "nation" with all that implies in terms of those it absorbs and who attach themselves to it. Maimonides wrote the following to the convert Rabbi Obadiah:

"Re your inquiry about blessings and prayers, whether you may say 'our God and the God of our fathers, Who sanctified us with His commandments, Who distinguished us, Who hath chosen us, Who caused our ancestors to possess, Who has taken us out of Egypt, Who performed miracles to our ancestors', and similar benedictions that have reference to our ancestors, I assure that you have the religious right to utter all those phrases in their accepted form, without any change . . . the reason for this is that Abraham instructed the whole of the nation and informed them of the true religion and the one and only God. . . . He brought many sons under the wings of the Divine Presence and taught them and commanded his sons and the sons of his household to walk in His ways. . . . Therefore all who convert to the Jewish religion, even unto numberless generations, become the disciples of Abraham and are like his descendants. Abraham is the father of all his proper descendants who walk in his ways and father of his disciples and they are all who convert. Thus you are granted the right to say in your prayers 'our God, the God of our fathers', since Abraham is also your ancestor. Likewise, you may say that 'Thou hast caused our ancestors to possess', [. . .] since you have adopted our religious belief and our Torah-guided ways; there is no difference between us [. . .] 'And let not the foreigner say, who has attached himself to the Lord, the Lord will keep me apart from His people' (Is. 56:3) [. . . .] The Torah was given to us and to you. You are assured of the privilege to recite the biblical words: 'That Thou has promised to our fathers, for Abraham is your ancestor as well as ours.'"

This principle, that "Jew" refers to a nation that was shaped by a certain religion and not to a "religion" alone, was a guiding principle for the Sages of all generations, and the basis for the precept: "A Jew even if he transgresses remains a Jew" (Sanhedrin 44a). Even the marriage of an Jew who converts to Christianity remains valid, even though he has already left and abandoned the Jewish religion entirely (see Yebamot 47b). In terms of the national meaning he remains a "Jew" since, as I have said, this concept does not refer only to religion. We therefore hold that those who are not religious and do not observe the commandments are still part of the concept "Jew" and do not have the capacity to withdraw from it, whatever their attitude to this fact.

We are familiar with the decree "Be sure to set as king over yourself one of your own people" (Deut. 17:15), and the Sages added: "All your appointments shall be from your own people; this one, since his mother was a Jewess, we consider from your own people" (Yebamot 45b). Maimonides ruled in the same manner in Hilkhot Melakhim 1, 4. The reason for this prescription, in addition to what the early codifiers explain, may be that it was intended to hasten the integration of the convert and his swift and utter assimilation among the Jews, making him a tiny particle within the body of Israel. If for some self-serving reasons he did not yet wish to integrate fully into the nation despite the feelings that led him to convert, the Torah prevents him from holding office unless he does, so that converts concerned for the future of their offspring would marry Jewish men and women. Thus there could be no status of the Jewish-born alone and the converts from one nation or another alone, who in the course of world events might become a liability to the nation, as indeed happened more than once (see Neh. 3:34).

Hence, when a non-Jew comes and declares his desire to be called a "Jew" without entering through the front door known as "conversion according to halakha," or in other words "acceptance of Judaism according to the laws of Judaism," how can he be granted this name? I am certain that none believes that we should accede to the request of a non-Jewish adult who states that he wishes to be called a Jew and asks to be so registered. There is no doubt in my mind that the registrars would categorically refuse until such time as he undergoes the accepted procedure. Can it therefore be possible that something a person cannot and does not have the right to do for himself can be done by his guardians, who are merely acting on his behalf in order to ensure his legal rights? Can the agent have greater power than the principal?

2. In respect to the Government decision that a person will be registered as a Jew if he declares in good faith to be Jewish, I assume

the phrase "in good faith" to refer to a person who is regarded as a Jew and who knows himself, his parents, and his grandparents to be Jews. If he declares that he is a Jew, this is a declaration "in good faith," and there is no need for him to provide evidence or proof. However, if a person knows that an individual is not a Jew by the law from which the title "Jew" derives, and yet states that he wishes that individual to be registered as a Jew, there is, without question, no good faith here. Mere desire is not good faith, and I am afraid that anyone who claims that such a declaration is an instance of the good faith mentioned in the Government decision is not arguing in good faith.

3. In response to those who advocate registering as a "Jew" the child of a mixed marriage about whom a "good faith" declaration is made, I would insist that such an act is only possible for those wiling to overlook deception and falsification if it is not blatant. However, falsification will inevitably result indirectly because the person who was misled was not sufficiently careful and alert. Jewish ethics do not permit this. We find that our ancestors differed as to whether a man could marry the wife of his deceased brother, with the school of Shamai allowing it and the school of Hillel forbidding it. Nevertheless, they did not prevent the adherents of one school from marrying into the other. The Gemara (Yebamot 14) explains that the reason for this is that the adherents of the school of Hillel would be informed of all details that might be of significance from their standpoint, even though the adherents of the school of Shamai did not consider them to be of any importance. Why should we not act according to the same high moral principle as our forefathers and not conceal any detail that might be of benefit or harm to another person from his standpoint. Although unfortunately we occasionally find cracks in the moral standards of individuals, the Government and its institutions are obliged to act in a way that will not deceive or mislead any person from his standpoint. Clearly, such a form of registration, even if it is not relied upon by religious entities, might be misleading to many, and even very many. If only for this reason alone, we must avoid registering anyone as a Jew who is not a Jew according to Jewish law.

4. I doubt whether the advocates of improper registration have considered the tragedies and mental anguish that might be caused to the children of mixed marriages by concealing from them their true status. Let us assume, and this is not a far-fetched assumption,

that such a boy or girl grow up knowing themselves to be Jewish as the registrars misled them to believe. In the course of time, as these things go, they might form a connection with an observant man or woman, and when they ask "in good faith" to be married, they are informed by the clerks at the Marriage Bureau that they are not Jews and cannot be married to the person of their choice. Have the advocates of such registration considered the terrible emotional blow they will be dealing to both sides, particularly to the one who was born of a mixed marriage. Even if the other side is not observant, they cannot be married (according to the Law of Marriage and Divorce). Furthermore, today there are many marriages between people of different ethnic communities, and many of the Eastern communities are unacquainted with the phenomenon of conversion. Thus for reasons of long-established practice, they are emotionally unprepared to accept the idea of marriage to a woman who has converted. As soon as the future husband is made aware of this fact, the marriage is likely to be called off, whether for emotional reasons or because of pressure from other people. Without a doubt, this will engender a deep mental crisis for the couple that might last their entire lives because it will come as such a surprise to them. Have the advocates of misleading registration considered this? In my opinion, for this reason alone, as well, we must avoid such a circumstance.

I do not hesitate to invoke the words of the servants of Naaman: "'Sir', they said, 'if the prophet told you to do something difficult, would you not do it'? How much more when he has only said to you, 'Bathe and be clean'" (II Ki. 5:13). This is not "good faith" but cruel bad faith. I must repeat here the familiar story of the Jew who asked for advice as to how to register his son's age. If he registered him as younger than he actually was, he would be subject to conscription, and if he registered him as older, he would be subject to taxes and other levies. The advisor suggested that he might register the correct age. The man was amazed at the wisdom of this marvelous suggestion that had never occurred to him. Let us follow the same wonderful advice and indicate the facts precisely as they are, recording neither "Jew" nor "Arab," "Catholic" nor "Protestant," but simply the mere truth: "The father is Jewish, the mother is not Jewish, and he has not been converted."

I shall conclude with a few words about the four considerations. 1) I believe it goes without saying that stating the simple truth is in no way a form of coercion, whether religious or anti-religious. Neither does it constitute discrimination of any sort. 2) I fail to understand how this item is relevant to the issue at hand. I assume it refers to the various ethnic communities in Israel and not to non-Jews. 3) and 4) These are one and the same. In this respect, I would like to relate an incident that occurred during my childhood and left me with certain memories. One of the members of our congregation used to cover his face during the service and doze off, sometimes actually falling asleep for a while. His son saw this and did the same. Once when the father woke up, he found his son sleeping and scolded him angrily, slapping his face. I remember how the congregation responded contemptuously toward the father, and rightfully so. How could he be permitted to do something and his son be forbidden to do the same thing? He could, of course, have claimed that he was only covering his face or just resting his eyes in unimportant places, or some such. Here, too, one wonders whether the "philosophical" arguments that have been raised in the course of the debate can justify doing what we demand that others refrain from doing. This is beyond my comprehension.

My dear Prime Minister, please act as you always do to promote the harmony and unity of the nation. May you be guided by the prophecy of Isaiah: "But the Lord will pardon Jacob, and will again choose Israel, and will settle them on their own soil. And strangers shall join them and shall cleave to the House of Jacob" (Is. 14:1).

With all due respect,

Yossef Kappah

20. JACOB KAPLAN

A philosopher and Chief Rabbi of France, Kaplan (1895–1994) was born in Paris and was a decorated soldier in World War I. In 1919, he received a B.A. from the Sorbonne, and in 1921 was ordained a rabbi by the Rabbinical College of France, after which he served as rabbi of Mulhouse in France. Kaplan joined the French Resistance during World War II. In 1950, he was appointed rabbi of Paris, and in 1955 became Chief Rabbi of France. A professor at the Institut de Sciences Politiques and member of the Academy of Ethics and Political Sciences from 1967, his works include Le Judaïsme et la justice sociale (1937), Racisme et judaïsme (1940), French Jewry under the Occupation (1945), and Les temps d'épreuve (1952).

2 January 1959

Dear Mr. Prime Minister,

I hereby reply to your letter of 27 Kislev, written in the wake of the decision taken by the Government of Israel on 17 July 1958 establishing a committee of the Prime Minister, Minister of Justice and Minister of the Interior, etc. Your letter states that "the Government has determined that the religion or nationality of adults will be listed as 'Jewish' if they declare themselves in good faith to be Jewish and not a member of another religion," etc. A question has arisen, however, in respect to the registration in the population registry of the children of mixed marriages when the mother is not Jewish and did not convert, but both she and the father agree that their child is Jewish. Should the child be registered as a Jew on the basis of the parents' wishes and their good-faith declaration that he is not a member of another religion, or is some other ceremony required in addition to the parents' consent and declaration?

Answer

The very fact that this question is being addressed to people outside Israel seems quite odd to me, as it should be decided according to halakha, and the Chief Rabbinate of Israel is authorized and qualified to make this determination.

The Council of the Chief Rabbinate of Israel has already rendered its opinion on the basis of the Torah that "the registration guidelines strike at the foundations and roots of Judaism and constitute a danger to the existence and singularity of the nation. They distort the image of Judaism and undermine the foundations of the Jewish law that has been hallowed for generations." Let there not be the slightest doubt whatsoever that I concur with this opinion.

I am deeply saddened not only by the posing of the question regarding the registration of children, but even more so by the Government decision concerning the registration of adults. May I be allowed to say, with all the respect in which I hold the Government of Israel, that a secular government does not have the authority to determine "who is a Jew." No such decision has ever been taken by the government of any free country in the world. Those who are entitled to rule in such matters are the religious leaders, and in our case, the Chief Rabbis of Israel. It is the Government's responsibility to decide who is a citizen of the State of Israel.

In your letter you note that all forms of religious or anti-religious coercion are prohibited in the State of Israel. I do not find any religious coercion in the fact that the Chief Rabbinate of Israel does not agree to register the child of a non-Jewish mother as a "Jew" if he has not been converted. This is because the term Jew on this document, which indicates "religion" and "nationality," is purely a religious concept, and the Rabbinate does not force anyone to convert. Thus this is not a case of religious coercion.

In the third consideration, you state that "whereas mixed marriages abroad," etc. It is true that in many countries, such marriages are increasing in number. But we are fighting against mixed marriages with everything in our power, as they are a grave danger to the survival of the community in the Diaspora. I therefore regret to inform you that as Chief Rabbi I will be compelled to fight for the rescinding of these regulations if they remain in force.

You further state in consideration four that "the Israeli nation does not see itself as separate from Diaspora Jewry; on the contrary," etc. For this reason, I believe that notwithstanding the many factors that maintain the connection between Israel and the Diaspora, the strongest link is religious. I am therefore obliged to inform the Prime Minister of Israel that these guidelines are contrary to the religion. The consequences of these regulations are dangerous and will lead to a severing of this link and a rift in the unity between Israel and Diaspora Jewry.

I am certain that you, who have had the honor of leading the ingathering of the exiles and whose name will be recorded among the greatest and most eminent figures in Jewish history, will take the lead in convincing the members of the Israeli Government to rescind these guidelines so as to ensure Jewish unity.

With all due respect and with a Cohen's blessing of peace,

Jacob Kaplan

21. MORDECAI MENAHEM KAPLAN

A rabbi and founder of the Reconstructionist movement in the United States, Kaplan (1891–1993) was born in Lithuania and moved to the U.S. with his family at the age of nine. Although he received an Orthodox education, he was later drawn to non-Orthodox ideas. Kaplan served as the Orthodox rabbi of a congregation in New York, and in 1909 was named dean of the Teachers College of the Jewish Theological Seminary, where he taught philosophy and midrash. From 1917–1922, he served as the rabbi of a congregation he himself established. In 1935 he founded the Society for Reconstructivist Judaism and its journal, Reconstructivist Magazine. While a Zionist, Kaplan also advocated the continued existence of Diaspora Jewry. His works include: The Greater Judaism in the Making (1960), and The Meaning and Purpose of Jewish Existence (1964).

2 December 1958

Greetings,

On my return yesterday from the west coast, I found your letter asking for my opinion on how to register the children of mixed marriages whose parents, both the Jewish father and the non-Jewish mother, wish to have them registered as Jews.

In order to understand this problem properly, we must consider it in the full context from which it derives. This context is alluded to in the first paragraph of the letter: [the purpose is to] "formulate registration guidelines that accord with the tradition accepted by all circles of Judaism, the Orthodox and liberals of all trends, and with the special circumstances of Israel as a sovereign Jewish nation ensuring freedom of conscience and religion and as the center for the ingathering of the exiles." This sentence is the frame of reference for our understanding of the problem. However, when I examine this frame of reference, I find it fraught with contradictions, such as the following:

1) The assumption that there is a "tradition accepted by all circles of Judaism, the Orthodox and liberals of all trends" is baseless, both in ideological terms and in respect to way of life.

2) The assumption that "freedom of conscience and religion" are ensured in Israel is disproved by the fact that the Government has granted the rabbinate the right to compel all Jews in Israel to accept its jurisdiction in matters of personal status, inheritance, etc. Moreover, the Government itself is obligated to consider the opinion of the rabbinate in respect to the issue of who to recognize as a Jew.

3) The basic assumption that the State of Israel is a Jewish state is itself open to question. As I shall explain below, there is in fact an alternative to this assumption that in no way detracts from the Jewish character or Jewish value of the establishment of the State. These flaws in the frame of reference of the question under discussion are not accidental. Rather, they result from the complexity of human life in general caused by the emergence of modern nations which emancipated the Jews and are absorbing them, and by the intellectual revolution in the approach to all religious traditions. In the interim, we were beset by afflictions and persecutions that delayed our normal adaptation to the new material and spiritual environment. It is therefore not surprising that we did not pay sufficient attention to basic questions of our existence, our future, and most especially our nature as a social unit and the status of that unit. The poet J.L. Gordon protested in vain that we are nothing but a flock. The truth is that we are nothing but an aggregate group or population.

Had the Zionist Movement not arisen, we would have forgotten that we are members of the same nation, and that our forefathers were once "a unique nation on earth" [II Sam. 7:23], and we would not have sought to reestablish ourselves as a social entity, the reality of whose existence is not in question. In view of these facts, it is now possible to formulate a frame of reference in which we can understand the problem at hand properly and find an appropriate solution.

1) It was the Jewish Agency which enabled the establishment of the State of Israel as a modern country. Its modernity is reflected first in the very fact of its creation, and secondly in its nature.

In terms of its creation, the State did not take into consideration the traditional belief that we must await the coming of the Messiah, but went ahead aforetime despite the traditional warnings against acting in this premature fashion.

In terms of its nature, the State is utterly different, in respect to both religion and nationality, from the two earlier states of the First and Second Temple periods. The structure and status of the Jewish population throughout the centuries preceding the French Revolution do not apply, as a matter of course, to world Jewry today. The appropriate structure and status for our generation has yet to be devised either in Israel or in the Diaspora.

2) The Jewish Agency conveyed to the Government of the State of Israel the fiat or mandate to create in the Land of Israel the conditions suitable for a Jewish community that would forever constitute the decisive majority in the country, and serve as the center of a world Jewish body which would perpetuate the previous existence of the Jewish people and breathe new life into the tradition of that people.

In view of these facts, the Government took it upon itself to enact the Law of Return, which bestows on Jews abroad the special privilege of immigrating to Israel, whereby "immediately upon arrival in Israel, and after expressing a desire to settle here, they automatically and instantly become Israeli citizens." Accordingly, the Government must determine who is a Jew before their arrival in Israel in light of the authority it has been granted by the Jewish Agency, and not in light of religious tradition, as it is the function of the Government to establish a modern state and not a Jewish state, an Israeli state and not a Jewish state.

I therefore conclude that if the Government of Israel considers that recognizing the child of a non-Jewish mother as a Jew, should the parents wish to register him as a Jew, will help to increase and enhance the decisive majority of Jews in Israel, it is then permitted to do so.

However, if I am not mistaken, while this conclusion is, in my opinion, thoroughly consistent and based on factual assumptions, it is liable to be of more harm than good should an attempt be made to put it into practice at this time. This is a time of transition. Hardly a day goes by that does not bring with it new surprises and threats. We must therefore be as cautious as possible in asking the Jewish community, growing in numbers and strength in Israel, to agree to regulations whose benefit they doubt and which they view with suspicion. Consequently, I would suggest a compromise, that is, to distinguish between "Jew" and "Jewish resident." The child of a non-Jewish mother would be registered as a "Jewish resident," and then, when he comes of age, should he undergo circumcision and formally agree to observe religious rituals, he would be registered as a "Jew" with no qualifying terms. In this manner, the Government will fulfill its obligation without infringing on traditional religious practices and issues.

Respectfully,

Mordecai Menahem Kaplan

22. YEKHEZKEL KAUFMANN

A Biblical scholar and philosopher, Kaufmann (1889–1963) was born in Podolie, Ukraine and received a religious education. He then studied Philosophy and Semitic Languages at Bern University, graduating in 1918, after which he worked on the publication of the Encyclopedia Judaica in Berlin. In 1929, Kaufmann moved to Palestine, where he taught at the Reali School in Haifa and became a Professor of Bible Studies at the Hebrew University in 1939. He was the author of major works in Jewish philosophy, including Exile and Foreign Lands (4 volumes, 1929–30), The History of Israeli Art (8 volumes, 1937–57), and The Biblical Story of the Conquest of the Land of Israel (1956).

27 Kislev 1959

Dear Sir,

1. The guidelines for the registration of residents and immigrants of 10 March 1958, sent to the district directors by the Deputy Director General for Immigration and Registration, are based on the opinion of the Attorney General of 20 February 1958, parts of which are cited in the guidelines for purposes of explanation. However, this opinion, and particularly the sections on the designation "Jew" (paragraphs 17–18 of the regulations), confuses issues and includes irrelevant arguments, a flaw which makes the regulations confusing and contradictory.

2. It is a well-known fact that Judaism is not merely a system of beliefs and precepts, but also a covenant that unites a community and turns it into a congregation of brethren. Affiliation with Judaism (like affiliation with Christianity or Islam) is not always dependent on the individual's beliefs or actions. Judaism is an inherited religion, so that a Jew becomes affiliated with it by birth. Every Jewish-born child is a Jew by birth, a member of the Jewish community, regardless of the beliefs, actions, or wishes of his parents or of himself when he reaches majority.

This notwithstanding, Judaism is not a "racial" religion. A person of any other nation or tongue can join Judaism by means of the ritual of conversion. Conversion turns a non-Jew into a full-fledged Jew.

In other words, the basic connection with the Jewish religion derives from an inherited covenant or from the covenant of conversion.

The question we are debating (i.e., "Who is a Jew?") is therefore not a question of a personal credo. It denotes: Who can be regarded as a member of the Jewish community by virtue of heredity or conversion? Registering a person as a "Jew" defines neither his outlook nor his racial or national origins, but rather establishes the fact that he belongs to the Jewish community in this sense. The religion draws its own conclusions from the religious definition. The secular government may choose to use it as the basis for its decisions, but the definition itself has a single essence: it is a religious definition.

3. Since the day of its inception, the State of Israel has declared itself to be a "secular and not theocratic state." This means that it has no "authorized religion" and no religious coercion. However, the State did not alter the definition of "Judaism." In political terms, Jew is the same as Christian or Muslim. In the laws and regulations of the State of Israel, "Jew" is not a racial or national term, but a religious one. The Law of Return applies not only to members of the Jewish race, but to converts as well, who are Jewish only by religion. The Government excludes only converts to other religions from the Law of Return, although they are Jewish by birth.

This decision is, without any doubt, in line with the religious conception of apostasy. Although according to halakha, the apostate is a "Jew," he is a "Jew" only in the sense that he is still bound by the obligations of the Torah. He does not, however, share the rights of a Jew. Thus Tosafot states that Jews are not required to support or ransom "the apostates of today," etc. (Abodah Zarah 26b, s.v. "Ani shonay").

Apostasy at this time involves joining another religious community by means of a religious ceremony that establishes affiliation in that community according to its own laws. A Jew who converts to another religion in Israel is not registered as a Jew. Thus the religious ritual alone determines the definition of the personal status of converts to and from Judaism. According to the laws of the State of Israel, matters of the marriage and divorce of Jews are under the exclusive jurisdiction of the religious rabbinical courts. Parallel laws apply to Christians and Muslims. In these laws, therefore, Jews are simply those citizens with a religious affiliation, by birth or conversion, with the Jewish community.

4. In the population registry as well, the definition of a resident as a "Jew" is a religious definition. According to the Prime Minister's letter, people are registered "as 'Jewish' if they declare themselves in good faith to be Jewish and not a member of another religion." Although the reservation "and not a member of another religion" is phrased in the negative, it has a positive meaning: the applicant claims that he is a member of the Jewish religion. This is not meant to refer to the applicant's personal credo or to his express desire to be considered a Jew.

The declaration is evidence of a fact. The applicant testifies that he has the right to be regarded as a member of the Jewish community according to its accepted practice, that is, that he is the child of Jews, or a convert, or the child of converts, and has not changed his Jewish religion. The guidelines offer an explanation for this provision: "It may be assumed that a person knows whether or not he is a Jew." The reservation in the guidelines, that registration does not determine "who is a Jew according to religious law" means that a rabbinical court may choose not to believe the applicant. Registration, however, is based on a declaration that implies that it is evidence of membership in the Jewish religious community as consistent with its practices and concepts.

5. The paragraph concerning the regulations for the "registration of a Jewish minor" is obscure and ambiguous. It presents the opinion of the Attorney General that "when both parents declare that their child is a Jew, their declaration is regarded as if it were the legal declaration of the child itself," and the child is registered as a Jew. The paragraph goes on to relate expressly to mixed marriages, and its intent is to establish that the law applies equally to all categories of children, who are registered as Jews on the basis of their parents' declaration. The only reservation is the matter of "good faith." The opinion further explains that the fact that "one of the parents" is not Jewish does not impinge upon the condition of good faith. Accordingly, the children of mixed marriages are also to be registered as Jews on the basis of their parents' declaration. This ignores the fact that the issue of the children of mixed marriages has absolutely nothing to do with good faith. It ignores the fact that the argument against registering the children of mixed marriages as Jews is not based on doubts regarding the parents' good faith, but on a religious precept. To make matters even more obscure, the explanation speaks vaguely of one of the parents, as if there were

any objection to registering as a Jew the child of a non-Jewish father and a Jewish mother. The clarification that the fact that "one of the parents" is not Jewish does not impinge on good faith is irrelevant. It serves as a specious foundation for equating all categories of children.

Indeed, the opinion underlines the fact that there are no real grounds for the guideline, and it therefore looks elsewhere for further support. It goes on to say that although according to the law of the Torah, the child of a non-Jewish woman is not Jewish, this has no bearing on the matter at hand. The reason given is that "it is possible that another law rather than the law of the Torah applies to the personal status of the child, and according to that law it follows the father and not the mother." Thus not only is "good faith" required, but "another law" as well. What this "other law" might be is not explained. Nor is it explained how "another law" of any kind could determine religious affiliation in a community against that community's own religious law. Furthermore, there is no explanation of the status according to "another law" of a child born to a non-Jewish father and a Jewish mother, who is a Jew according to the law of the Torah. The opinion states that racial affiliation alone is the crucial factor. Therefore, since "another law" provides that the child follows the father, the child of a non-Jewish father is not Jewish. Consequently, if "another law" is found to apply, then the question we are grappling with will merely be transferred from one category of children to another, but will not be solved. Unless, of course, there are two "other laws"?

A regulation based on such explanations is groundless.

6. In contrast, the question as phrased in the Prime Minister's letter is quite clear: Should the child of a Jewish father and non-Jewish mother be registered as a Jew "on the basis of the parents' wishes and their good-faith declaration that he or she is not a member of another religion"? Here the good-faith declaration relates only to the fact that the child "is not a member of another religion." However, it is proposed that his registration as a Jew be based in this case on the parents' wishes. Since according to halakha the child of a Jewish father and non-Jewish mother is a non-Jew who requires conversion, the proposal seeks to overturn the religious law and establish a new one whereby the expression of the parents' wishes has the authority in this special case to make the child a Jew by birth without any rite of conversion. The registry may indeed serve civil purposes; how-

ever, as it determines religious status, the proposal encroaches on the domain of religion.

The fact that it is a registry of religion is also clear from the reservation (which this time relates to a minor who is not legally responsible!): "is not a member of another religion." Here, too, religion is the determining factor. Again it is not made clear whether this reservation also applies to the child of a non-Jewish father and Jewish mother. If it does not, it can only be because the child of a Jewish woman has a different status according to halakha. Thus the proposal both conforms with halakha and deviates from it. If the reservation applies to both categories of children of mixed marriages, we must ask, what is their status? Is the true intention of the proposal that all the children of mixed marriages who are members "of another religion" should require conversion? If so, then it is suggesting a muddled religious law, as there is no connection between conversion and adopting "another religion." A Jewish convert to Christianity can change his mind and become a repentant Jew, but does not require "conversion." Conversion applies only to a person who is not Jewish by birth. Thus the child of a Jewish mother does not require conversion, even if he is "a member of another religion," whereas the child of a non-Jewish mother does require conversion, even if he is not "a member of another religion." Making the demand for conversion dependent on affiliation with "another religion" is liable to create a clumsy hybrid law. In order to avoid this, the regulation would have to state that the child of a Jewish woman is to be registered as a Jew when he becomes a penitent, and the child of a non-Jewish woman when he is converted. Clearly, this whole argument is untenable.

The population registry should therefore be consistent with halakha, not for the general reason (which applies only to Jews) that it is impossible to separate "religion" and "nationality," but for the specific reason that it is, in effect, a registry of religious status.

7. The fact that the registration of civil citizenship alone is not sufficient in the State of Israel is made abundantly clear in the Prime Minister's letter. Theoretically, it might seemingly be content with the registration of "nationality," except that nationality in the ethnographic sense is not distinctly immutable and canot serve as the basis for a precise definition of personal status. Nationality might be defined according to mother tongue, but this is not the criterion for Jews. The enduring hallmark of Jewish nationality is religious affiliation.

While the Jewish religion is essentially universal, certain historical factors consolidated it into the Jewish people and turned this universal religion into the legacy of the Jewish people alone. (Conversion was only a sporadic phenomenon.) As a result, the term "Jew" denotes both religious and national affiliation. This is true not only in Hebrew, but in all languages. The definition of an individual's personal status as "Jew" is understood everywhere as a religious designation. These circumstances prompted the State—whether by force or desire— to base the registration of the personal status of Jews on religion. As a result, registration must be consistent with religious concepts. Otherwise, there is a danger that a controversy will erupt within the Jewish people, in Israel and abroad, whose consequences are unforeseeable. In actuality, the problem has arisen only in respect to the children of a Jewish father and non-Jewish woman, and this problem can be solved by conversion.

8. It is rumored that the rabbinate in Israel tends to be strict in accepting converts from among the children of mixed marriages, and imposes the condition that the mother also converts. Such rigidity might put paid to the only possible solution provided by halakha.

It cannot be denied that the question of conversion is a difficult one for religious Jewry today. Judaism has not always adopted a consistent attitude toward conversion. However, Judaism itself created the possibility of religious conversion, and to this day prays that all people will one day embrace the Jewish religion. It longs for "sincere proselytes" who will convert for the "proper impulse," out of conviction and a desire to observe the commandments of the Torah. It does not wish for converts who will be "like a sore on the skin." Obviously, it cannot expect sincere proselytes who convert for the "proper impulse" from the circumstance of a mixed marriage. This is not a new phenomenon, however. The question was already asked of the ancient authorities: what is the status of those proselytes who did not convert out of a love of God, and halakha rules that they are all proselytes (Yebamot 24b). A further ruling states that a proselyte who was not informed of the commandments, but who was circumcised and immersed before three laymen, is also a proselyte (Maimonides, Mishne Torah, Issurei Bi'ah 13, 17). Thus, according to halakha, conversion is valid even if it was not performed for the proper impulse or before a rabbinical court. Moreover, it was ruled that a minor can be converted by the authority of a rabbinical court, although he can revoke the decision when he comes of age

(Maimonides, op. cit., Melakhim 10, 3). Surely, this type of conversion can also be performed before a court of three laymen (Maimonides, op. cit., Kesef Mishne, s.v. "Ve-im haya katan"). Therefore, without a doubt, religious Jewry can find a way to be more lenient and thereby eliminate the threat of impending controversy.

With the hope of peace for Israel,

Yekhezkel Kaufmann

23. AARON KOTLER

The head of a yeshiva, Kotler (1892–1962) was born to a family of rabbis from Sislowitz. An outstanding student, he was admitted to a yeshiva at the age of 13, and at 14 was already studying at the Slobodka yeshiva. After his father-in-law, Rabbi Isser Zalman Meltzer, immigrated to Palestine in 1921, Kotler was named head of the Etz Chaim Yeshiva in Sluzk, and was also active in Agudath Israel. During World War II, he fled through Japan to the United States, where he settled in Lakewood, New Jersey and founded the Beth-Medrash Govoha of America. In 1954 he was elected president of the High Council of Agudath Israel. Kotler was also Honorary Chairman of the Etz Chaim Yeshiva in Jerusalem.

17 Tebet 5719

Dear Sir,

In reply to your letter, I am amazed at the fact that a question concerning the purity and integrity of the Jewish people, whose preservation is the basis of our existence, should be posed as if it required some other solution or opinion from me. The question has a simple and explicit answer in the Holy Torah and for the Jewish people throughout the generations ever since it became a nation.

1) It is clear that a Jew is only someone who is Jewish according to the law of the Holy Torah. A Jew according to the law of the Torah is thoroughly explained in a clear ruling. Halakha determines and shapes reality, and so it has been since Israel became a nation. No individual or public body has the power or capability to alter this, just as it is impossible to alter reality itself. Any change is nothing but falsification and the nullification of the form and essence of our people.

Conversion itself, which is the only way in which to enter the Jewish people, is in essence entrance into a covenant with God, like the covenant forged on Mount Sinai by which we became a nation, and according to the provisions of halakha, as laid out in the Gemara and Maimonides (naturally, even if the mother converts according to religious law after giving birth, this does not alter the status of the child born prior to her conversion).

2) There is no difference whatsoever between the terms "religion" and "nationality," as no such distinction exists in Judaism—neither in halakha nor in reality.

3) The registration of non-Jews as Jews would be disastrous for the nation, and would place huge obstacles in the way of many people, mainly because of the danger of assimilation into the Jewish people by marriage. This would result in future generations being cut off from the nation. (Maimonides, Issurei Bi'ah Chap. 2, states: "Although this sin does not carry the death penalty, let us not treat it lightly, as it incurs a loss that is not in any other forbidden union— that the son from a non-Jewish woman is not his son, as it says 'for they will turn thy children away from Me' [Deut. 7:4], will turn them away from following God, and this will cause them to join the idol worshippers from whom God set us apart, and they will turn away from God and will betray Him").

As a result of this intermingling, the Jewish people would inevitably be beset by rift and division.

4) I feel compelled to respond also to the statement in your letter that "the Government has determined that the religion or nationality of adults will be listed as 'Jewish' if they declare themselves in good faith to be Jewish and not a member of another religion." This too, without question, contains the danger of assimilation and confusion, with all that entails as explained above.

Unless a person was born a Jew and there is proof of this from documents or compatriots—or even from him alone—if there are compatriots from whom it is learned that this is a case of "the lips that forbid are the lips that permit," or even if it is rumored to be so, then even if he claims to have been converted according to the law by a rabbinical court, his claim is not credible unless there are competent witnesses. Otherwise, he must now be converted by a rabbinical court.

It goes without saying that if he does not claim to have been converted according to the law, but merely makes a "declaration," it is worthless.

Even if none has knowledge of his personal history and he presents himself as a Jew, he will need witnesses to his lineage in order to marry a Jewish woman, particularly if there is any cause for suspicion. This being the case, registering a person of unknown lineage as a Jew is liable to mislead and deceive.

There is certainly reason to suspect that a non-Jewish man or woman would fraudulently declare to be Jewish, especially given the circumstances in Israel. Who can determine whether the declaration is made "in good faith," in Your Excellency's words, or in bad faith. Only the Lord can see into the heart.

5) I must add that conversion according to the law is a complicated matter and demands deliberations in respect to every detail (the character of the individual, his religious beliefs, etc.), including certain conditions that require investigation by a qualified rabbinical court. In the case of minors as well, whose conversion is based on the principle that one can do a favor for a person without his knowledge, there are details that require halakhic clarification by rabbis. The Book of Ezra (9;10) relates at length that it was decided to expel the non-Jewish women and their children, and this was indeed done, proving that they were not accepted as proselytes.

In view of the above, there is no need to add further reasons beyond what is stated explicitly in the Holy Torah. Nevertheless, I must note that from all perspectives, any change or departure from accepted form would constitute a grave danger to the very existence of our people.

1) It has been clearly proven that the nation has survived to this day only by virtue of the written and oral Torah, which are one and the same thing. All the sects and streams that appeared in different periods as separate entities, who sought to establish their Judaism on other systems that deviated from the beliefs accepted throughout the generations, whether we were in the Land of Israel or in the Diaspora, have faded into oblivion. (What is more, any group of Jews who became cut off from the Torah, whether through neglect or for other reasons, no longer exists. The different parts of our people survived only if they maintained contact with those who follow the Torah and are rooted in it).

2) In addition to the reasons stated above, there is no substitute for the Holy Torah, and no meaning or purpose capable of filling the void if the sanctity of the Torah and faith in the eternity of the human soul are abandoned. (All the new ideals that recent generations were misled into adopting have cracked like a poorly made harp when faced with reality). There is, in fact, no other way to sustain the human spirit in this generation or in the future, as the Lord created no other purpose, so that no other purpose can exist. No negative purposes can be of any use whatsoever, nor can they

provide any stability or joy to the nation, to say nothing of the strength to withstand the trials and overcome the difficulties and obstacles that invariably arise. (The present sorry states of morality whose consequences are unforeseeable are ample confirmation.)

3) In regard to the unity of the nation, it is perfectly clear that the Torah alone unites the Jewish people, distinguishes it from other nations, and makes it a single entity in the world.

"There is a people that dwells apart, not reckoned among the nations" [Num. 23:9]; the Jewish people cannot exist as a nation like any other. As an individual can not become assimilated and thereby remove himself from the Jewish people (see Maimonides, Letter to Yemen: "This is the Torah and none can escape it, nor can his children or his children's children for all time"), so even more so the entire nation cannot become assimilated and assume a different form, as explained in the Torah and the Prophets. (Nor would the persecution of the other nations cease even then, as we have seen in the case of individuals and groups, as well as in the case of the nation as a whole.) Any attempt to alter the face of the nation is a denial of who we are to the extent of actually nullifying our existence. Indeed, we know that the Jews who adopted Greek ways constituted a greater threat to our people than the Greeks themselves.

Thus the sole basis for the unity of the nation and the fusion of its parts is through the link to our shared roots and common purpose. "Israel encamped there in front of the mountain" [Ex. 19:2], as one individual, in unanimity.

To conclude, I would like to express my amazement at the addressing of a fundamental matter of Jewish sanctity to people who are not scholars of the Torah, some of whom are not even religious, as well as to people who have severed almost every link with the Jewish people. The solution has been given by the Lord in the Holy Torah and the words of the Sages.

It is my hope that the Government will settle this whole matter according to halakha and the opinion of the rabbis, the scholars of the Torah in the Holy Land.

With the blessings of the Torah, Respectfully,

Aaron Kotler

24. DANTE LATTES

An author, journalist and educator, Lattes (1876–1965) worked for the Corriere Israelitico in Trieste from 1896. In 1915, he founded the weekly Israel in Florence, and later La Rassegna Mensile di Israel, serving as editor-in-chief until his death. Lattes translated classic Zionist texts into Italian and taught Hebrew language and literature at the Institute of Eastern Languages in Rome. He was the author of interpretations of the scriptures and numerous other works, including L'Appologia dell'Ebraismo (1923) and Il Sionismo (1928).

25 January 1959

Dear Sir,

Your letter of 27 October 1958, sent from Jerusalem by official post on 2 December 1958, reached me only on 22 January 1959. I beg your forgiveness for the delay in responding, which was not of my doing.

In the matter of the registration of the children of mixed marriages whose parents—both the father and the mother—express the desire for them to be registered as Jews, I believe it is beneficial and desirable not to reject them and push them away, but to accept them into the Jewish people.

Given that the registration has no relation to religion and does not serve religious purposes, its aim and substance being to indicate that the registered person is not a Christian or a Muslim and there is thus no reason to fear that he might constitute a danger to the state or disturbance to the community, there is no doubt in my mind that it would be unjustified to deprive him of the right and honor of belonging to the Jewish people. Such a person is not a member of any other religion or nation; he is a citizen of Israel together with his parents; he attends or will attend Jewish schools, will speak Hebrew, and his entire upbringing and education will come from Israeli sources and its thousands-of-years-old history, from the time of Abraham to the present.

The rabbis, teachers, and national leaders will bear the responsibility for bringing the child of a non-Jewish mother closer to full genuine Judaism. The Government should announce publicly, or print on the margins or rear of the identity card, that the term "Jew" indicated under nationality has no religious significance and in no way detracts from the law of jurisdiction of the rabbinical courts or from customary Jewish tradition or law. It is no more than a regulation demanded by contemporary circumstances for the benefit of the people and the peace of the country.

Mr. Prime Minister, please accept my respect and loyal friendship. Dante Lattes

25. SAUL LIEBERMAN

A Talmudic scholar, Lieberman (1898–1983) was born in Byelorussia and studied at the yeshivot of Malcz and Slobodka. During the 1920's he attended universities in Kiev and France, moving to Palestine in 1928 where he settled in Jerusalem. There he studied Talmudic and Greek philology at the Hebrew University, becoming a professor of Talmud in 1931. In 1935 he was named dean of the Fischel Institute for the Study of the Talmud in Jerusalem. From 1940, he was a professor of the history of Hebrew Literature at the Jewish Theological Seminary in New York, becoming faculty dean in 1949 and rector of the institution in 1958. An expert on the Jerusalem Talmud, his many works include Tosefet Rishonim (4 volumes, 1938–39), Sifrei Zuta (1968), and studies of the influence of Hellenistic culture on Judaism in the first centuries A.D. Lieberman served as president of the American Academy of Jewish Studies, and was an honorary member of the National Academy of the Hebrew Language, and a member of the Israeli Academy of Arts and Sciences. In 1971 he was awarded the Israel Prize for Jewish studies.

25 Kislev 5719

Your Excellency, the Prime Minister of Israel,

On my return from the mountains outside the city, I found your letter, and I hasten to reply. In the matter of your query as to whether the son of a Jewish father and non-Jewish mother can be called a Jew, the answer is clear and simple. Undisputedly, the child is a non-Jew in every sense. No sort of statement, declaration or promise, whether by the father or the mother, can alter that fact. The child is subject to conversion according to the law, and this question needs no further explanation. Similarly, it is clear that the rabbinical court of Israel will never agree to convert minors when it is obvious from the start that their parents will not give them a religious upbringing. Whatever the personal tragedy of the parents, it cannot justify making a mockery of conversion.

I must however consider the case of a person whose father is Jewish and whose mother is not Jewish, yet stands and proclaims: I regard myself as a full-fledged Jew from birth. Can he be prevented from doing so? Here too it is clear that he is entitled to regard himself as a full-fledged Jew. A non-Jew who considers himself a Jew and does not conceal his true origins is still obliged to meticulously observe the seven commandments required of all human beings in order to be called a pious gentile. We should not heed the claims of the casuists and pedants that this non-Jew's arrogance is a violation of one of the seven universal laws. What is more, if he displays love and devotion for the Jewish people, we are commanded to love and esteem him, and he can be called a friend of the Jews, a devotee of the Jews, a companion of the Jews, or some such. However, just as we are not entitled to impose on him our will that he not consider himself a Jew, so he is not entitled to impose on us his will that we recognize him as a Jew. If he really loves the Jewish people that much, the gates are open to him: he can agree to be bound by the Torah and commandments and convert. Conversion will in no way affect virtually any of his rights, as we harbor no prejudice against converts. When Jewish children study the stories of the destruction in tractate Gittin, they learn as a matter of course that some of the greatest men and teachers of Israel were the descendents of converts. Elsewhere we find the story of the high priest who left the Temple and all the people followed behind him. But the moment they caught sight of Shemaya and Abtalion, the sons of proselytes, they abandoned the man with the most distinguished lineage and flocked after the descendents of converts. We see, therefore, that the Jewish people welcomed proselytes not only in theory, but in practice as well. The same applies to a non-Jewish woman who bears a son to a Jewish man and requests conversion for her minor child. If she accepts the Torah and commandments according to law, her child will immediately be converted together with her. If she is unwilling to do so, she can allow her son to be a pious gentile, and when he comes of age and wishes to join the holy people, he can convert of his own free will. This is the prevailing Jewish law. I turn now to the form of the discussion.

The Sages established the rule that one must reply to a person only in his own terms and not employ arguments to which he does not subscribe. As the principles of the Government of Israel are only known to us from sources upon which we are forbidden by law to rely, in fact, are instructed to suspect, let us, for the sake of a sound argument, approach the issue from a premise to which everyone undoubtedly subscribes—the unity of the Jewish people. Any departure from halakha in respect to mixed marriages and the children of mixed marriages will cause confusion and chaos in the minds of the Jews in the Diaspora. The overwhelming majority of Jews in America, including those who do not even observe Yom Kippur, flinch from intermarriage. To the last moment, the parents do everything in their power to prevent their sons and daughters from marrying non-Jews. The sincere grief of the parents often tips the scales. Any leniency in Israel regarding the children of mixed marriages will be disastrous for the Jews in the Diaspora. It will affect the heart and soul of the entire nation. Parents will not be able to call on attorneys to explain to their sons and daughters that circumstances are different in Israel. The children can claim, and rightfully so, that what is permissible in Israel must certainly be permissible in America. Let us not create a situation for ourselves whereby people can say: if you want to get rid of your non-Jewish wife, go to Nevada. If you want to marry a non-Jewish woman and have her bear Jewish children, go to the holy city of Jerusalem.

As this issue has been imposed on us against our will, let us denounce unreservedly those who denigrate the Government of Israel by claiming that it is using the issue at hand to attack religion with the malicious intent of encouraging Jews to become non-religious. We do not know the intent of the Government, as there is only One who can tell what is in the heart. The same voice that said on Mt. Sinai: "You shall not intermarry with them, etc." also said: "Do not deal basely with your countrymen," and "You must not carry false rumors." We are forbidden to admit slander, and are commanded by the Torah and Oral Law to deal mercifully with all people. One cannot make compromises with the commandments, declaring that we accept some and reject others. In the words of the Sages, if anyone does so, his blessings are mere abuse. Thus, it is enough for us to condemn actions that cause us pain and leave the question of thoughts to He who can divine them. I am convinced that the words of brothers who come from the heart will be heard by the heart.

The man called Jacob of Neburaya who tried to issue instructions in violation of the law preceded the Government of Israel by some seventeen hundred years when he ruled that the son of a Jewish father and non-Jewish mother was a Jew, and he earned immortality by being mentioned in the Jerusalem Talmud and Midrashic literature because he admitted his error and complied with the law. By doing so, he displayed his greatness, or in the words of Judah

II in his letter of honor: "A great person . . . what is his greatness—that he is not ashamed to say I was wrong." There are many wise people among the nations of the world, but there are also many great people among the Jews. The Government of Israel has already displayed its greatness on more than one occasion, and I trust that here too it will prove its greatness and courage and will follow the practice of the greatest Jews who did not refrain from declaring: What I said before was wrong. The Government too should not be ashamed to say: We were wrong, and now we understand and admit our error. The arrows its enemies are readying for it will thus be turned into straw and dust.

I would like to conclude with the blessing that the Lord guide you in the proper path and grant you a good and long life.

With the blessings of the least of Israel,

Saul Lieberman

26. YEHUDA LEIB HAKOHEN MAIMON

Rabbi Maimon (1875–1962), a leader of the religious Zionist movement, was born in Bessarabia and studied at Lithuanian yeshivot. After
receiving his ordination, he served as a rabbi in his hometown of
Marcolsi, and from 1905–1913 in Onega. One of the founders of the
Mizrakhi religious Zionist movement, he attended the Zionist Congresses
starting with the second, and in 1935 was the Mizrakhi representative
and co-chairman of the Zionist Executive Committee. He also served
as head of the Trades and Business Department and the Religious
Affairs Department. In 1913, he moved to Palestine, where he was
among the founders of the Mizrakhi school system. Expelled by the
Turks during World War I, Maimon went to the United States but
returned after the war, when he became acquainted with Rabbi Kook
and collaborated in the establishment of the Chief Rabbinate in Israel.
Associated with the underground movements Etzel and Lehi, Maimon
was imprisoned by the British Mandate authorities in June 1946. Named
Minister of Religious Affairs in the Provisional Government, he was
elected to the first Knesset. Maimon advocated rooting the state in
the spirit of Jewish law, and sought to reconstitute the Sanhedrin as
the supreme spiritual body. He was the author of numerous works on
halakha, history, and politics.

Jerusalem, 26 Kislev 5719

My dear friend,

I also received the form letter you sent to "Jewish intellectuals,"
although I have no relation to some of those intellectuals and I do
not trust their intellect. I read the whole letter, and despite the considerable heartache, sorrow, and pain you have caused me in particular by your grave error regarding the question of "Who is a
Jew?" (I believe it is the greatest mistake you have ever made)—I
feel it proper nevertheless to reply because of our mutual respect
and friendship.

The question "Who is a Jew?" has been answered for thousands
of years, ever since we became a distinct nation. According to our
eternal Torah and tradition, a Jew is only a person who was born,
at the very least, to a Jewish mother. No power in the world can

or is entitled to revoke this ruling, which is the primary foundation of the whole of Judaism.

I shall cite here only one ruling from the Talmud (Yebamot, 47a) in reference to a proselyte who was converted: "A proselyte who was converted by a rabbinical court is a convert, if he converted himself he is not a convert. The case of a person who came before Rabbi Judah and said to him: I converted myself. Rabbi Judah asked: do you have witnesses? He said: no. Do you have sons? He said: yes. He said to him: you are competent to disqualify yourself as a Jew, but you are not competent to disqualify your sons." In other words, a person who says I converted myself cannot be relied upon. It follows even more strongly that we cannot rely upon a person who says "I am a Jew" without any evidence or witnesses.

If, for some reason, there should ever arise any doubt as to this traditional ruling, one must request the opinion of the Chief Rabbinate, which alone has the authority to rule on matters of halakha. The Chief Rabbinate was established not only by Bentwich—as you recently stated—but by Rabbi Kook of blessed memory and myself. It was my suggestion to establish a Chief Rabbinate, and when Rabbi Kook gave his consent, we both approached Herbert Samuel. After receiving his approval, we convened a convention that was attended by dignitaries such as David Yellin, Dr. Klausner, and Dr. Pen, in addition to rabbis. Together we founded the Chief Rabbinate in unanimous agreement that this religious halakhic institution would have supreme authority over all Jewish questions, and that is my short and decisive reply.

As a friend, I advise and wish you that like the other great figures of Isarel, you too can rise above your personal honor and admit the truth, declaring in public "I was wrong." That will be your greatness and glory.

In sincere friendship and the blessing of Zion and Jerusalem,

Yehuda Leib Hakohen Maimon

27. MOSHE MAISELS

A journalist, philosopher and translator, Maisels (1901–1984) was born in Warsaw, where he was an editor of the Hebrew papers Ha-yom and Ha-tsfira. He moved to the United States in 1930, and in 1932 became an editor of the Hebrew paper Ha-doar, and soon afterwards was named editor-in-chief. After immigrating to Israel in 1959, he became a senior editor and later chief editor at the Bialik Institute. In addition to his most noted work, Mahkshava ve-Emet (Thought and Truth; 1939), a tome on Jewish philosophy, Maisels translated numerous books from English to Hebrew under various pen names.

9 December 1958

Dear Mr. Prime Minister,

I have never imagined myself worthy of being asked for my opinion on this matter, neither by virtue of my knowledge of halakha nor by virtue of my familiarity with the subject. However, the eminent esteem of the inquirer obliges me to make the effort to respond. I shall therefore attempt to make my comments as brief as possible so as to limit, at least, the trouble of reading them.

1) The problem should not be regarded in terms of "eternity," but as a temporary situation necessitated by current circumstances. In ordinary times and places in which Jews live a permanent stable life, one does not investigate anyone claiming to be a Jew. It is indeed impossible to investigate every instance of the restriction of marriage rights. The ineligibility of a bastard to marry a Jew remains in force for all time (except where a bastard marries a non-Jewish woman, in which case their children, who follow the mother, are entitled to convert and become members of the Jewish community), and a family's lineage cannot be investigated back to the first generation. Furthermore, it is said that Elijah, who will erase all doubts, will come to declare what is unclean and what is clean, to divide and unite (in respect to those ineligible for marriage), but "a family that was assimilated was assimilated" (Kiddushin 71a). And "Rabbi Isaac said: Righteousness is what God did unto Israel, that a family that was assimilated, was assimilated" (ibid.). Rabbi Eliezer said of

the bastard, whose illegitimacy remains in force for all time, "give me the third generation and I will purify it" (Yebamot 78b; although the Gemara explains the reason for this to be that "a bastard does not survive," the simpler reason would seem to be that after three generations the family becomes one that "is assimilated").

2) The question has only arisen in the special circumstances of the State of Israel, that is, the return to Zion and ingathering of the exiles. The exact same question arose at the time of the first return to Zion, after the Babylonian exile. Chapter 7 of the Book of Nehemiah lists all the families of pure ancestry, as well as "the people of the province who came up from among the captive exiles" (7:6), and "those who came up from Tel-melah, Tel-harsha, Cherub, Addon, and Immer—[and who] were unable to tell whether their father's house and descent were Israelite" (7:61). The Mishna (Kiddushin 5:1) states: "Ten family lines came up from Babylon, the priestly, the Levite, the Israelite, the impaired priestly, the proselytes and freed men, the bastards, the Gabaonite, the descendants of unknown fathers, and the descendents of foundlings." And Ezra was not ashamed to include them among the builders of the land in his time. Hundreds of years later, the authors of the Aggadah revealed a difference in attitude toward the illegitimate lines among those who returned from Babylon. In reference to the above verse in the Book of Nehemiah, the Gemara (Kiddushin 70a) explains: "Tel-melah . . . Cherub, Addon and Immer. Rabbi Abbahu said: The Lord [Addon] said, I thought Israel would be like a cherub to me but they behaved like a tiger. Others say: Rabbi Abbahu said: The Lord said, although they behaved like a tiger they are to me like a cherub" (Rashi: Addon—the Lord, like a cherub—holy, as the cherubs of God, like a tiger—like this animal which is not scrupulous in its choice of mate). Incidentally, the people from these places, who "were unable to tell whether their father's house and descent were Israelite," are immortalized in the Bible, sacred to the Jews and to the world, while others of pure Israelite descent who remained in Babylon have been forgotten.

3) The question, therefore, is: how should we act at this time, a great moment in the life of the nation, in certain instances we encounter in the course of immigration and the ingathering of the exiles. Obviously, the relevant religious law, which has evolved among the Jews for many generations and has ancient roots, can make no concessions. According to halakha, the child of a Jewish man and a non-Jewish woman follows the mother and is not a Jew. The ques-

tion is whether we should accede to halakha and formulate the present guidelines accordingly. The State of Israel has already gone in
this direction, even going so far as to place all legal matters of personal status in the hands of the rabbinate and the rulings of halakha,
and this is not a temporary measure, but a permanent decision.
Seemingly, the determination of an Israeli's Jewish identity belongs
essentially to the area of personal status, which determines the identity of the Jewish family, and why should this be an exception to
the rule? If the Government institutes separate registries, one for civil
purposes and one for religious purposes, it will create a new type of
individual who is half Jewish and half non-Jewish. This will solve
nothing. On the contrary, whenever a civil Jew of this sort, who
already considers himself Jewish and is thought to be Jewish by
others, comes before a rabbinical court on a matter of personal status, he will be subject to demands and investigations that will generate
considerable offense, anger and bitterness, in many cases much more
than would be created by a single universal guideline, properly
explained, requiring that the child of a non-Jewish mother undergoes
a certain ceremony in order to be accepted into the Jewish people
due to its four thousand-year-old ancestry. Incidentally, the existing
law is not sufficiently consistent either. Adults are registered as Jews
"if they declare themselves in good faith to be Jewish and not a
member of another religion." Why is it impossible for a person to
be a Jew and a member of another religion, as customary for all
other nationalities? Thus even the existing law establishes a connection between religion and nationality in Judaism, a connection
we cannot sever in this generation, a generation that is itself torn
between the past and future of the Jewish people.

   4) As for the national aspect of the issue, what is evolving before
our eyes in Isarel is amazingly unprecedented in the two thousand
years of our history, in human, social, spiritual and material terms.
The change is incomparably greater than it was at the time of the
first return to Zion. The Babylonian exile lasted only two generations or less, and even then the return generated a total departure
from the nation's past history in terms of spirit and culture. The
present-day return to Zion comes after two thousand years of wanderings throughout the world—and the whole of Western civilization today is not two thousand years old. Consequently, the break
is deeper and the change more extreme—appearing almost to have
been created ex nihilo. But every new creation entails some danger.

The nature of something new made out of existing materials may be deduced, but the nature of a creation ex nihilo can never be known for certain. What can be better than light, yet it says: "God saw that the light was good" [Gen. 1:4]. Until He saw it, he did not know whether or not it would be good. We must, therefore, reduce to the minimum the nihilo from which the wonderful new reality in Israel is springing, rather than enlarging or deepening it. This too is a temporary circumstance: the new reality will grow bigger and stronger as a matter of course, in accordance with its wondrous nature. This generation, the father of the new reality born out of the past, must incorporate as much existing Jewish content into Israel as possible in order to reduce the danger involved in creating something out of nothing. The aforementioned link between Jewish religion and nationality, whether natural or spiritual allegiance, is the basic element of the Jewish essence we inherited from our forefathers. Let us leave it to future generations, and to the new Jewish reality that will emerge with them, to define their nationality and religion and the link between them as they see fit.

5) Your letter stresses that "efforts must be made to increase shared and unifying properties and eliminate as far as possible those that separate and divide" the different communities arriving in Israel, and "to enhance its [Israeli youth's] moral commitment to world Jewry." Without a doubt, this need obligates us to concede to the opinion of halakha on this issue, as it has been accepted for generations by the majority of the nation in all communities and countries. Contemporary Diaspora Jewry will undoubtedly lay greater stress on the religious element of the Jewish identity of its members.

I do not mean my remarks to indicate a disregard of the difficulties involved in the matter under discussion. They do not presume that there is no problem and that everything is clear and elucidated, as the extremists on both sides might claim. Our generation has spurned tradition, and had it not we would not have achieved what we have in Israel and most of its present citizens would have remained where six million of this generation of Jews were left. Yet just as the State of Israel is not a mere continuation of "Zionism," but a wondrous new Jewish entity in our history, so our desire for spiritual renewal need not be a mere continuation of the tradition-spurning of the first generation of pioneers. With our face and heart to the future, we must incorporate as much as possible of the present Jewish essence, which draws on the past, for the sake of this future.

My comments have not been as brief as I first thought and wished. I apologize.

Respectfully and sincerely,

Moshe Maisels

28. ANDRÉ NEHER

A scholar and researcher, Neher (1914–1988) was born in Obernai, France. Before and after World War II, he taught German in high school. During the war, in hiding with his father and brothers, he turned to Jewish studies, becoming one of the spiritual leaders of French Jewry once the war was over. Devoting himself to the study of the Scriptures, he was named Professor of Jewish Studies at the University of Strasbourg, and succeeded to bring about the introduction of Hebrew in the French school system as an optional foreign language. He founded the Hebrew Institute, which he ran until immigrating to Israel in 1974. Settling in Jerusalem, he divided his time between Israel and Strasbourg. Neher's works on the prophets and the essence of Jewish philosophy include: L'essence du prophétisme (1955), Moïse et la vocation juive (1955), and Histoire biblique du peuple d'Israël (1962).

22 January 1959

Dear Mr. Prime Minister,

I confirmed receipt of your letter of 13 Heshvan on the first day of Hanukkah, when I stressed that I viewed your appeal to Jewish intellectuals as an historic event displaying your devotion to the unity of our people and capable of building a bridge across the widening gap between Israel and the Diaspora, between the Jewish state and the Jewish religion.

At this time, I shall attempt to present my opinion on the question itself.

1) The religious nature of the definition of Jewish identity can not be denied. There is no way to enter Judaism save in the manner recognized by the religion (being born to a Jewish mother or converting). Obviously, the degree of piety, faith, and observance of the commandments in no way detracts from the Jewish identity of anyone who is already a Jew, as once the shawl of Judaism has been acquired it can not be removed. However, it can only be acquired through religion.

This aspect, which distinguishes the Jewish people from other nations in the world, is the very basis of its distinctive essence and

is the foundation on which the House of Israel is constructed and
the "covenant" is based. This principle affords the State of Israel its
Jewish status and Jewish value. You yourself have often stressed (particularly in your letters to Prof. Simon Rawidowicz recently published
in the late author's *Babylon and Jerusalem*) that Israel is a Jewish
state and in this way differs from all other countries in the world.
This dual face of Israel stems from the fact that it is rooted in the
religious destiny of the Jewish people. In this sense, there is no
difference between the Biblical period, the periods of halakhic rule,
and the present time. In relation to Judaism, separating nationality
and religion means separating the spirit and the flesh, elements that
cannot be divided in a living organism. Such a separation destroys
the monism that is characteristic of the Jewish approach on which
Jewish life in all communities, past and present, is based. It invali-
dates the Jewish significance of the State of Israel.

2) It therefore follows that:

a) no government committee has the authority to decide who is a
   Jew and who is not a Jew.
b) this decision comes under the authority of the rabbinate.

However, this very conclusion creates a state of confusion.

On the one hand, the Government has no de jure authority to
define who is a Jew, yet on the other hand the rabbinate has no de
facto authority in the matter. Rabbinical rulings are not accepted
by non-religious Jews, and if they are it is only because of coercion
and not wholeheartedly or out of conviction.

Over time, this situation is liable to have very damaging consequences. It will dishonor both the secular government, which also
takes part in, sanctions, and approves religious ceremonies, without
acknowledging their religious value, and religion, whose authority
will be stripped of spiritual substance, leaving it to issue mere formal statements and encouraging hypocrisy.

How can we find a way out of this impasse?

3) One way to solve the problem would be a separation of state
and religion. "When two men grasp hold of a prayer shawl, and
one says I found it and the other says I found it, one says it is all
mine and the other says it is all mine . . . let them divide it!" This
is the sort of separation proposed by Prof. Yeshayahu Leibowitz, a
positive productive separation that places the burden of responsibility on both the state and religion for the values crucial to each.

However, such separation not only conflicts with the essential demands of Judaism, but is also unreasonable in the psychological circumstances now prevailing in Israel and the Diaspora. Today it would push the parts of the nation farther apart instead of bringing them closer together.

4) I therefore suggest:

As a solution to the problem at hand and similar problems that have arisen or may arise, an assembly can be convened, composed as follows:

a) One-third of the participants: government representatives who will introduce the problem and explain its various implications.

b) One-third of the participants: men and women invited more or less by the same criterion you employed in sending out your letter (rabbis and secularists, scholars, men of letters, jurists, doctors, psychologists, sociologists, authors, poets, artists . . . and last but not least, laborers, farmers, the "man in the street" (as it was customary in Mishnaic times for the wool carriers from the Dung Gate in Jerusalem to enter the house of study of the great figures Shamai and Hillel). This third of the assemble will debate the issue from various perspectives, including the most subjective, each according to his or her own feelings and life experience.

c) One-third of the participants: rabbis who will formulate a solution to the problem after active participation in the assembly's deliberations.

5) In my opinion, this solution has the following advantages:

a) De jure responsibility for religious matters will remain in the hands of the rabbis who alone have the authority to rule on them.

b) On the other hand, a decision will not be made without personal, face-to-face contact between the rabbis and the representatives of the Jewish people.

c) Contact between the religious and secular sectors of the people will be established through constructive efforts, encouraging dialogue between them.

d) The Government will be able to convene the assembly whenever needed and to submit to it problems for a public debate conducted in an atmosphere of mutual respect and responsibility.

It goes without saying that many of the details involved in instituting such an assembly can be altered. The main point is not to view it as a "Sanhedrin" (composed solely of rabbis and sages), as a rabbinical court (in which there is an organic distinction between the judges on the one hand and the litigants and witnesses on the other), or as a Ministry for Religious Affairs (which has only administrative authority). The basic feature of the assembly is that it is adapted to its purpose and intent. In other words, while the Government initiates the deliberations and the rabbis issue the ruling, its aim is to prevent academic discussion, that is, discussion without a foundation in reality, and to generate a debate based on the widest possible human contact.

I am certain that if such an assembly were to function regularly, it would produce not only favorable decisions in specific matters, but would also develop the practical principles needed for our life today. Moreover, it would succeed in creating a psychological and moral climate that might convince the affected parties to willingly and consciously accept the religious ruling, whatever it may be, as they will have participated in the debate not as anonymous individuals, litigants, or subjects of a regime, but as members of the Jewish people as befits anyone who bears that exalted title.

In conclusion, I would like to state that my proposal may be seen as the fruit of your devoted efforts to promote the state and the nation, both materially and spiritually. I would like to convey to you my blessings and deepest gratitude for this.

In respect and esteem,

André Neher

P.S. I shall not publish this letter without your consent, and I will ask that you inform me of your consent to do so. For my part, I have no objection to the publication of my letter by your office should you feel it to be of benefit.

29. SALOMON RODRIGUES PEREIRA

The Chief Rabbi of the Portuguese Jewish Community of The Hague (Holland) before World War II, Pereira (1887–1969) moved to London during the war, where he was named Chief Rabbi of the Dutch army-in-exile and Honorary Chairman of the Association of Dutch Immigrants in England. On the liberation of Holland, he returned to his country and served as Chief Sephardic Rabbi of Amsterdam and Holland. He devoted considerable efforts to encouraging assimilated Jews to return to the fold.

27 Kislev 5719

Dear Sir,

I received the letter you sent me about children born to mixed marriages. I was amazed and astonished when I read it.

First, I was surprised that you should address an enquiry regarding a question of halakha to rabbis outside Israel, despite the existence of a Chief Rabbinate for Ashkenazi and Sephardic Jews, whose members are rabbis expert in religious law and have vast knowledge of every detail of halakha.

Furthermore, I learned that you also addressed these inquiries to non-religious individuals, leaders of the "reform" who call themselves rabbis. It is obvious to every rabbi and halakhic authority that in a matter as weighty as preserving our lineage, no heed whatsoever should be paid the opinions of reform Jews that are contrary to our holy religion.

For these reasons, I do not wish to rule on the law, nor is there any need for me to do so, as I concur heart and soul with the Chief Rabbinate who alone has the authority to rule on this matter. As they have rendered the decision that it is absolutely forbidden to call the children born of mixed marriages Jews if their mothers are not Jewish, I cannot comprehend the need to address the question to others. The Chief Rabbis are worthy of being relied upon and having all their decisions obeyed.

Respectfully,

Salomon Rodrigues Pereira

30. CHAIM PERELMAN

A scholar of the philosophy of law, Perelman (1912–1984) was born in Warsaw, Poland and moved to Belgium, where he studied at the Free University of Brussels, and later joined its faculty as a Professor of Logics and Metaphysics in 1944. He served as dean of the Faculty of the Humanities and director of the School of Education. Many of his works deal with mathematical logic and the concepts of justice and wisdom. Perelman was the General Secretary of the International Association of Philosophy and of the Belgian Society of Logic and Philosophy of Science. A member of the Board of Trustees of the Hebrew University of Jerusalem, he was knighted by the King of Belgium. His works include Rhétorique et philosophie (1952), Traité de l'argumentation (1958), and Justice et raison (1963).

10 January 1958

Dear Mr. Prime Minister,

I received your inquiry regarding the meaning of Judaism according to the resolution of the Government of Israel of 15 July 1958. I am conscious of the honor you have afforded me by asking my advice on this subject, and I thank you sincerely.

After giving it considerable thought, I would hereby like to address the following comments to you:

1. The question of the registration of the children of mixed marriages in which the mother is not Jewish raises a problem when one is asked to provide a solution in respect to Jews for the rubrics of "nationality" and "religion."

However, if the parents are entitled to rights under the Law of Return, and they were received as Jews in Israel, it would appear to me to be difficult and even contrary to humanitarian sentiments, as well as to the Law of Return, not to respect their wish to register their child as a Jew under the rubric "nationality." The same does not apply to the rubric "religion." Here, only the religious authorities are entitled, in my opinion, to determine the conditions for membership in the Jewish religion.

2. I myself, as a non-religious Jew, believe it would be much sim-

pler, and would conform with the development we are witnessing in civilized nations, to separate the two rubrics, "nationality" and "religion." It goes without saying that such separation should lead to the increasing secularity of the State of Israel, in a manner that would allow its residents, should they so desire, to see all matters concerning their personal status administered exclusively by the law of the land and the secular authorities.

There will, of course, be those who claim that Judaism, in accord with a tradition thousands of years old, does not distinguish between religion and nationality, that the Jewish community should be viewed as a large family practicing rituals that manifest its allegiance to the God of Israel and the Torah, and that to create a distinction between the concept of the Jewish people and the religious element and model the Jewish religion on universal conceptions, like Christianity, would falsify the spirit of Judaism. Indeed, the leaders of the State of Israel have agreed that such a division between the religious and national viewpoints would have dire consequences, and have presumed that not belonging to another religion than the Jewish religion is a condition for registering a person as a Jew under the rubric "nationality.

This family, then, has the right to determine its destiny, the right to formulate the code of laws appropriate to it. Its members can not all be required to live under the authority of 3,000 year-old laws which, for over 1000 years, have not been adapted by their interpreters to the changing conditions of social and political life. So long as those who were not content with the law were free to escape it, it could remain rigid, as it was only applied voluntarily. However, when it becomes compulsory, even for non-believers, it must adapt itself so as not to tolerate abuses that might appear scandalous to the modern conscience, those, for example, which allow for prescriptions regarding the Levites.

In any case, it is impossible in the modern conception of a democratic state for an essential aspect of the life of its citizens to remain outside its jurisdiction. If for purposes of determining the nature of a Jew, making it possible to apply the laws of the State of Israel which employ this term, the two rubrics of "religion" and "nationality" cannot be separated, then the State of Israel cannot be denied all rights in this respect, which links it a priori with religious tradition.

If one wishes the national and religious viewpoints to be compatible without being coordinated, one must expect conflicts of interpretation to arise.

In order to avoid such conflicts, which may be injurious to the State of Israel, it is desirable to establish a mixed court which will be composed of judges appointed, for example, by the Israeli parliament, the Jewish Agency, and Jewish religious authorities, and which will rule sovereignly on all disputes.

So long as no such court is constituted, the Supreme Court must rule on the subject, as it does on any matter concerning the interpretation of Israeli law, without its decision having any religious significance.

I hope that these remarks will be of some benefit to you, and please accept, Mr. Prime Minister, the assurance of my highest respect.

Chaim Perelman

31. SIMON H. RIFKIND

An attorney and prominent jurist, Rifkind (1901–1994) was born in Russia and came to the United States with his family in 1910. After receiving his law degree from Columbia University, he was appointed a district judge in New York. Rifkind served as the chairman of numerous public committees and societies, and performed special duties delegated him by the Supreme Court. In addition, from 1947 he was a member of the Executive Board of the American Theological Seminary, from 1949 Vice President of the United Jewish Appeal, and in the 1950s Chairman of the American Jewish Committee.

19 January 1959

Dear Mr. Ben-Gurion,

Please forgive my delay in responding to your inquiry of October 27th, concerning the registration of children of mixed marriages. After much reflection I have concluded that I am not qualified to express an opinion deserving of consideration. I have been immersed for these many years in practice under a system of law in which the question you propose would be regarded as irrelevant. Consequently I have never had occasion to evaluate the considerations which should have a substantial weight in arriving at a judgment in this matter. In short, I lack confidence in the views which superficially appear to me right, and under these circumstances I am sure that what I would say would not contribute to the solution of your problem.

Respectfully and sincerely yours,

Simon H. Rifkind

32. YECHESKIEL SARNE

A rabbi and Talmudic authority, Sarne (1889–1969) was born in Gorodok, Lithuania. His father, Jacob Chaim Sarne, was known as the Maggid of Slonim, and was closely associated with Chaim Soloveitchik. From an early age, Sarne studied at Epstein's Slobodka yeshiva in Kovno. A branch of the yeshiva was founded in Hebron in 1924, and in 1927, on the death of Epstein, by now Sarne's father-in-law, Sarne became the head of the institution. During the riot's of 1929, he moved the yeshiva, with its 265 students, to Jerusalem, and renamed it Hebron Yeshiva. Sarne was a member of the Agudat Israel's Council of Sages and a familiar and respected figure among the secular public. He was the author of numerous works of commentary on the writings of the Sages.

25 Adar 5719

Dear Mr. Prime Minister,

I am honored to confirm receipt of your letter of 13 Heshvan of this year concerning the registration of the religion of children born to mixed marriages in the population registry. I hereby proffer my reply.

The registration of the Jewish religion or nationality of both children and adults must be guided in the State of Israel, and everywhere in the world, solely by the laws and precepts of the Torah, which are clear and established. The teachers of the Torah, sitting as judges, are the ones who must show us the path to follow in order to act in accordance with the Torah.

Our Torah is a Torah of life, and is as eternal as its giver. The Master of the Universe handed it down to us with love and favor. He—who knew all generations from the beginning and sees to the end of all generations—knew that there could be no situation which was incapable of a solution by means of the good judgments and laws of the Torah, and therefore no consideration in the world can detract from even one iota of God's Torah and His commandments, written and oral. One of the articles of faith (as listed by Maimonides) is that "this Torah will not be replaced and there will be no other Torah from the Blessed Creator."

Together with all true Jewish believers, I believe in perfect faith that the day will soon come when the entire Jewish people will return to its Creator and His Torah. Recognizing a non-Jew as a Jew will seal shut the gates of repentance, since these adults and children, who are not Jewish, will become indistinguishably intermingled with our people and will create, Heaven forbid, a situation in which "the crooked can not be made straight."

I would like to express my confidence that this obstacle will not be created by Your Excellency's hand. May God be with you.

I apologize for the lateness of my reply, which was caused by ill health.

Respectfully and with the blessing of the Torah,

Yecheskiel Sarne

33. JOSEPH SCHECTER*

December, 1958

Dear Mr. Prime Minister,

I was quite surprised to receive your letter of 27 October. While I
have acquired a certain amount of general knowledge, I have little
Jewish learning. I shall therefore not presume to express my opinion
on the question itself, but I can, perhaps, make a small contribution in respect to a matter to which I have devoted many years of
my life. I am referring here to the issue of the proper approach to
problem solving. I believe I may be able to offer a few helpful comments in this regard. When a researcher approaches a problem, he
first peruses all the material that has already been published about
it and related issues. He studies the approach, methodology, and
conclusions of other scholars, and finds out how these conclusions
were received. The researcher generally tends to accept as reliable
the information that has accumulated, and to erect his new construction upon it, unless he finds reason to doubt its reliability as a
result of its containing inconsistencies, being contrary to empirical
fact, and so on.

The fundamental questions of our people have been debated by
generations of scholars who examined and analyzed every single
detail, including their most remote implications, in what may be an
unmatched intellectual effort. The difference between this approach
and the manner in which the Government has resolved to study the
question at hand is glaringly apparent. Not only is the approach of
our scholars estimable in the eyes of anyone who values the devotion and sense of responsibility of national leaders, but the result as
well is wondrous and unique: the survival of a small persecuted
nation for hundreds of generations and preservation of its strength

---

* Ben-Gurion's letter to the philosopher and educator Dr. Joseph Schecter mistakenly reached a physician of the same name. This is evident both from the let-
terhead and from the opening paragraph. It is presented here nevertheless because
of his intrinsic interest.

and robustness to the extent that it was able to rise up again out of the ruins. If our scholars chose such a protracted and exhausting method, then it would seem that the same result could not have been achieved in any other way, but that a rash decision is liable to jeopardize the very existence of the nation. Although it is true that thanks to the greatly refined tools available today, we can arrive at results much more quickly than previous generations, and this applies, naturally, to those areas of life which are based on empirical material. The solution of spiritual problems relies on thought, not experimentation. Indeed, there is not, nor can there ever be, a tool capable of hastening human thought. On the contrary, anyone examining the situation objectively will realize that civilization has dulled human senses and diminished our intellectual faculties.

There will undoubtedly be those who claim that ancient rulings do not suit the spirit of our times. Again, there is no call for a probing investigation to prove that our times are among the darkest of ages and most likely the darkest in all history—a period in which the sins of humanity brought it to the brink of annihilation, much like the generation of the flood and the people of Sodom. Can anyone seriously argue that the Torah itself, which bears the imprint of divinity, should be adapted to the spirit of this time?

Respectfully,

Dr. J. Schecter

34. MENACHEM MENDEL SCHNEERSON

The Lubavitcher rebbe, Schneerson (1902–1994) was born in southern Russia, the direct descendent of Shneur Zalman of Lyady, the founder of Habad Hassidism. He received an education in both religious and secular subjects. In 1936, after marrying the daughter of the Habad leader Joseph Isaac Schneerson, he went to France to study Philosophy and Electrical Engineering at the Sorbonne. He then returned to Poland, but in 1941 fled from Warsaw to the United States, where he served in the U.S. Navy as an electrical engineer. After fulfilling various functions in the Habad movement, he was chosen to succeed his father-in-law upon the latter's death. Under his leadership, the movement expanded throughout the Jewish world.

9 Adar 5719

Greetings,

I hereby reply to your letter requesting my opinion on the subject of the registration of the children of mixed marriages when the father is Jewish and the mother is not Jewish and did not convert prior to the birth of the child. The reference—according to the wording of the resolution cited in your letter—is to formulate regulations "that accord with the tradition accepted by all circles of Judaism, the Orthodox and liberals of all trends, and with the special circumstances of Israel as a sovereign Jewish nation ensuring freedom of conscience and religion and as the center for the ingathering of the exiles."

My opinion is absolutely clear, in line with the Torah and the tradition accepted for generations, that in such matters a verbal declaration of the desire to be registered as a Jew has no validity. A declaration does not have the power to alter reality.

According to the Torah and the tradition that has existed for generation and is still alive and well today a Jew or—to phrase it differently but with the same meaning—a member of the Jewish people, is only a person who was born to a Jewish mother, or a convert who converted according to the precise procedure, whose details are explicated in the books of rulings of our people, the House of Israel, from generation to generation until Shulkhan Arukh.

This applies in full not only to children whose parents or some other person declare their desire to register them as Jews, but also to anyone who declares that he wishes to change his status and condition in order to enter the Jewish people. Such a declaration is of no value unless he actually performs, or has already performed, the proper conversion procedure according to tradition, as detailed in Shulkhan Arukh, as above.

Respectfully and wish best wishes,

Menachem Mendel Schneerson

35. SH. (SHALOM JOSEPH SHAPIRA) SHALOM

A poet, novelist, playwright, essayist, and translator, Shalom (1904–1990) was born in Poland, the son of Abraham Jacob Shapira, the head of a Hassidic dynasty. On the eve of World War I, he moved with his family to Vienna, and in 1922 they immigrated to Palestine, settling in Jerusalem. After studying at the Mizrachi Teachers Seminary, in 1926 he joined a group of rabbis from his family in establishing the village of Kfar Hassidim, where he taught Hebrew. In 1928, he moved to Rosh Pina before going to Germany to study at the University of Erlangen from 1930–31. On his return, he took up residence in Jerusalem, later moving to Rehovoth, and finally making his home in Haifa in 1954. Shalom served as head of the Israel Authors Society in 1968. His many works include: Panim el Panim (Face to Face; 1941), a collection of poetry, the novel Yoman be-Galil (Journal in the Galilee; 1932), Ha-ner lo Kava (The Candle did not Go Out; 1942), and the play Shabbat Olam (World Sabbath, 1945).

Haifa, 30 November 1958

Most esteemed Mr. Ben-Gurion,

With profound respect and a deep sense of responsibility, I hereby respond to your inquiry of 27 October 1958 on behalf of the Israeli Government's Committee of Three for my opinion on the subject of the "regulations regarding the registration of children of mixed marriages both of whose parents wish to have them registered as Jews."

The State of Israel arose out of the ashes of the cremation of Diaspora Jewry. For generations, the Jewish people bore terrible torments for its loyalty to Judaism. By virtue of that loyalty, the link with the land of the Patriarchs, the Holy Land, was maintained, and the remnant of our people was finally able to achieve independence. This history, fraught with suffering and abounding in heroism, obliges anyone wishing to join, or to have his children join, our nation, to accept, at least symbolically, the "yoke of Judaism" in a traditional ceremony. This traditional ritual is not sacred in the religious sense alone, but has also become a national symbol accepted by all generations of Jews who sacrificed themselves for their faith. Its performance links the Jews in Israel and world Jewry; its abolishment would break this fateful link, at least with a large part of world Jewry.

Performing this ceremony does not contradict "the principle of freedom of conscience and religion," nor the rule that "a Jew may live either an observant or secular life," laid down as one of the foundations of the Declaration of Independence. So long as an individual does not declare his Judaism, he enjoys the equal rights of other religions in the country. When he declares that he is Jewish and wishes to enjoy the right to "live either an observant or secular life," he must first accept the commitment of "being Jewish," and the traditional ritual is obligatory and has been sanctified by the generations as part of acceptance of this commitment.

The fact that the ritual is performed by religious officials does not detract from its value for all Jews. As long as we agree and accept that responsibility for the rite of circumcision of every boy born in Israel should not be taken away from the religious authorities—who are the agents of the State in this matter—we must also understand and accept that another ceremony is required "in the case of a mother who is not Jewish and has not converted."

My considered opinion regarding the registration of the children of mixed marriages, which I arrived at after a great deal of study and in a deep sense of responsibility, is therefore as follows:

1) "Religious criteria [which are criteria accepted by Jews throughout the world, Sh.S.] should indeed by used for registering both nationality and religion."

2) "In the case of a mother who is not Jewish and has not converted," in addition to circumcision, "an additional ceremony" which complies with tradition is required in order to make the child a full-fledged Jew.

3) The ritual must, as stated, be performed according to tradition, but in a proper manner and at a government institution and should be aesthetic and dignified. For example, the two witnesses required for immersion may be doctors, and the entire ritual may be performed by a hygienic medical body before which a woman is not loathe to disrobe, in coordination with a religious authority, similar to a circumcision which is performed these days in a maternity hospital by a doctor.

4) Proper and persuasive explanations should be provided—in the

form of a leaflet or orally—to discount all the fabrications that have been spread about the ritual and enable the "mother who has not converted" to clearly understand the profound meaning of the symbolic sacrifice she is being asked to make for her child.

5) It should be explained, among other things, that in order for a Jew to enjoy "freedom of conscience and a ban on religious coercion," he must first become a member of this "brotherhood" called Judaism. Just as there are initiation rites in other brotherhoods, some of which are quite unpleasant (such as baptism in the Jordan for the early Christians or the Baptists today, or, on a lighter note, the wig adopted by academics in England and many other rituals in that country), but which are endowed with a halo of time-hallowed significance, so entrance into the "brotherhood" known as Judaism can not be effected without this ritual. Fundamentally, it is a symbol of the cleansing of bodily sin and purification of the spirit, and has been sanctified by all Jews throughout the generations.

Faithfully and with my esteem,

Sh. Shalom

36. MOSHE SILBERG

A Supreme Court justice, Silberg (1900–1975) was born in Lithuania and studied in the great yeshivot of Mir, Slobodka, and Novorodk, as well as at the universities of Hamburg and Frankfurt. In 1929 he moved to Palestine where he taught Talmud, and then practiced law from 1934–1948. From 1950–70, he served as a Supreme Court justice, holding the position of deputy president of the court from 1965. Silberg also taught in the Hebrew University Faculty of Law and published numerous articles on personal status in Israel and other subjects. In 1964 he was awarded the Israel Prize for Law Studies. His works include Personal Status in Israel (1961) and This is the Way of the Talmud (1962).

4 December 1958

My Dear Sir, the Honorable Prime Minister,

I have the honor, Sir, to hereby offer my reply to the query in your above letter. I would ask that you view the following as the sincere response of an ordinary jurist, without any additional authority that might accrue to a judge in Israel.

Before examining the question, allow me to comment on the task placed on the respondents in accordance with the Government decision cited at the end of the first section of your letter. I am doubtful whether any person, even the wisest of men, could formulate registration guidelines that—as stated therein—"accord with the tradition accepted by all circles of Judaism, the Orthodox and liberals of all trends." In my humble opinion, and with all due respect, these terms are contradictory, as there is no tradition or shared view of this sort. After receiving the replies of the respondents, the Government may certainly reach a practical conclusion that would appear to it to represent the "golden mean" between all the opinions expressed, but even that conclusion, because of its very nature as a compromise, will not constitute the *omnis doctorum opinio* of all the streams in Judaism. If indeed—and I will state my reservations in this regard below—we, the respondents, must first examine the general abstract question of "Who is a Jew?", it is not difficult to predict the three types of replies that will be given, namely:

(a) biological Jewish origin (at least on the maternal side), or conversion according to every detail of religious law—the "Orthodox" view;
(b) inclusion of all non-Jews who wish heart and soul to share the fate and culture of the Jewish people—the "liberal" view;
(c) a third Reform-religious view, that proposes a "modified" conversion ceremony that will not weigh too heavily on them and on the conscience of those who wish to acquire citizenship in the Jewish nation without undue difficulty.

It is also conceivable that within the first type of response some may suggest, as a minor concession, certain dispensations and allowances, relying on several of the more lenient rulings, particularly in respect to the immersion of women (see, for example, Yebamot 45b and Tos. ibid., "mi lo tavla"; Maimonides, Issurei Bi'ah 13:9; Ba'h and Bet Joseph on Tur Y.D. 268: Mordecai, Yebamot, and Haholetz). In any case, full, or even not-so-full, agreement between the "Orthodox" and the "liberals" on the fundamental question of "Who is a Jew?" is not possible. The fierce controversy that was sparked by the question and has been raging for over half a year in the Jewish press in Israel and abroad is ample evidence of this.

I therefore believe that in order to find a practical solution to the question of registration guidelines, it would be better to bring the issue down from the Olympian heights of ideology and confront it face to face in the valley of Israeli reality as shaped by the laws of the land. Our country—the Prime Minister has said—is a country of law and not a country of the Torah. In other words, it is a secular state and not a theocracy. I applaud you, for this is quite true! However—and certain circles will say "to our good fortune" while others will cry "That's the problem"—the secular state itself has given authority to a most important body of religious law and made it (for Jews) an integral part of the legal code. This was either the result of the mandatory laws we inherited, such as His Majesty's orders-in-council, or of new legislation enacted by the Israeli legislators, such as the Rabbinical Court Jurisdiction Act (Marriage and Divorce) of 1953. We must therefore consider the mutual effect of the existing laws and the guidelines and how they will operate or impose themselves on one another. They are intimately connected, and no chisel, however sharp, can ever force them apart. I would reprimand the "ayes" and "nays" on the question of the guidelines for not sufficiently baring this side of the problem.

Let me make this clear. I admit, as no one can dispute, that registration on an identity card does not alter an individual's status, but serves merely as apparent evidence of his status, which can be disproved or refuted by any other form of credible legal evidence. However—and this is the sting in the tail—although registering the child of a mixed marriage as a Jew in no way changes his true legal standing, it does, as a matter of course, determine his recognized status in society, making him a full-fledged Jew in his own eyes and those of others. He will remember this "detail" even more clearly than the date of his birth, and will be reminded of it in all his dealings with schools and official or unofficial bodies. It will be engraved deeply on his soul, both consciously and unconsciously, and he will not be aware of any difference between himself and his Jewish-born friends and acquaintances. This formal "non-binding" registration will become a formidable factor in his education, directing and guiding his spiritual development and creating in him a Jewish consciousness.

What is the lesson to be learned from this? That we must ensure that when granting the title "Jew" to a person in his infancy, he will not lose this "Judaism" later in life, and that all official authorities, including the religious authorities operating on behalf of the state, recognize the designation in all circumstances. Without a guarantee that this will be so, it would be better not to grant him the title in the first place, since it will determine his spiritual life and status in society. A young Israeli born to a Jewish father and non-Jewish mother and registered as a Jew at the request of his parents will suffer terrible and bitter disappointment, indeed his whole world will be destroyed, if, when he reaches majority and wishes to marry a Jewish girl, he suddenly "finds out" that he is not a Jew at all and never was.

The question, therefore, is whether this disappointment is what awaits such a young man. My answer is yes; it is most certainly what awaits him, almost inevitably! The reason for this lies in the laws of the secular state, which stipulate that for Jews in Israel, matters of personal status come under religious law. When that young man wishes to marry a young Jewish woman, he will apply—as he is required to do—to the Rabbinate, and once the rabbis become aware of his origins, they will refuse to grant the couple a marriage license on the grounds that according to Jewish law, the son of a non-Jewish mother is not a Jew but a gentile, for "a gentile woman and her child like her" (Mishnah Kiddushin 66b; Maimonides, Issurei Bi'ah 15, 4; Shulkhan Arukh, Eben ha-Ezer 8, 4), and marriage between a gentile and a Jewish woman is not valid (Yebamot 45a; Rashi, ibid., "Ha-yevei Lavin"; Maimonides, Ishut 4, 15; Tur Eben ha-Ezer 42 and comm.; Shulkhan Arukh, Eben ha-Ezer 44, 8).

Nor will the High Court of Justice intervene to order the marriage of that young man for the simple reason that this "proselyte-for-sincere reasons" does not have the marriageable status of a "sincere proselyte" or a Jew. Even if this civil court should adopt a purely "civil" approach and consider both partners to be "Jews," it does not have the power to override the provisions of section 2 of the Rabbinical Court Jurisdiction Act which states explicitly that: "The marriage and divorce of Jews shall be performed in Israel according to the law of the Torah."

According to the law of the Torah, this couple is, in fact, not entitled to form the legal bond of husband and wife.

Furthermore—and this is what is so curious about the existing legal situation—even if it were possible to find an Israeli rabbi who, in view of the tragic circumstances of the case, was willing to ignore the young man's "birth defect" and officiate at the couple's wedding, if at some time (after a family quarrel) one of the partners should appeal to a civil court—in this case the district court—it would annul the marriage. Justice knows no mercy, and the court, after reviewing the legal code and meticulously examining the husband's bloodline, would have no choice but to rule that the marriage was not legal.

The fact that the wedding ceremony had been performed by a rabbi would be of no avail to the defendant for two reasons:

(a) A Jewish wedding is, as you know, a private legal act between the partners and not a ruling of the rabbinical court, as the rabbi is not acting as a court but merely overseeing the correctness of the procedure as a "religious agent." This court has already recognized the validity of marriages that were not performed by rabbis (see: 208/53, 8 Rulings 833).

(b) Even if someone were inclined to view the marriage certificate issued by the Rabbinate following the performance of the couple's wedding ceremony as a "court ruling"—and a precedent for such an opinion might ostensibly be found in the decision of the mandatory courts (see: 158/37, 2 Levanon 201)—the "ruling" would be tainted by lack of jurisdiction and would be overturned by the authorized court. Even now, after enactment of the Rabbinical Court Jurisdiction Act, the rabbinical court does not have jurisdiction in matters of marriage if one of the partners is not Jewish.

Thus, if the rabbi who officiates at the wedding should disregard one of the basic rulings of Jewish law, the secular civil court will demand that it be honored. In other words, both religious law and the laws of the State of Israel will repudiate the legality of this marriage. What remedy will these young men have? Their "remedy" will be either a life of celibacy or legal marriage to non-Jewish women! Few of them will opt for the ultra-modern institution of open marriage.

My dear Mr. Prime Minister, it appears to me that as long as there is no form of civil marriage in the country, and the marriages of Jews must—by law—be performed according to religious law, we must not create a dichotomy or difference between the meaning of the title "Jew" on the identity card and its legal meaning in Jewish law. My reply to the question I have been asked is that the child of a mixed marriage, born to a Jewish father and non-Jewish mother, should not be registered as a Jew on any official document. Otherwise, that is, if he is registered as a Jew, not only will his integration into the life of Jewish society not be made easier in the long run, but we will actually be setting a trap for him in his future life. There is no such thing as a half-Jew or temporary Jew. "Going up requires going down" is, as anyone familiar with Kabbala knows, a concept that has come down to us from the context of "exile." The sons and daughters of a non-Jewish mother ultimately have no choice but to become reintegrated into non-Jewish society in the wake of their marriage to non-Jewish men and women. We do not open the gates of the house of Israel to strangers so that it may serve them as a temporary home.

Respectfully,

Dr. Moses Silberg

37. AKIVA ERNST SIMON

An educator and man of letters, Simon (1899–1988) was born in Berlin to an assimilated family. He became a Zionist in his youth, and after receiving a Ph.D. in Philosophy was hired as editorial assistant to Martin Buber on Der Jude. Simon moved to Palestine in 1928, where he first taught high school and filled the post of vice-principal, and later became a Professor of Philosophy and History of Education at the Hebrew University in Jerusalem (1935), and head of the School of Education. Active in politics, he was among the leaders of the Brit Shalom Movement. His works include Goethe and the Modern Age (1949), The Theory of Pestalozzi (1962), and Are We Still Jews? (1985).

7 January 1959

Dear Mr. Prime Minister,

I thank you for the faith you placed in me by addressing me as well your form letter of 13 Heshvan 5719. My reply is divided into four parts: a) the difficulty of providing an answer; b) the problem of registration; c) the problem of converting minors; d) the problem of freedom of conscience.

The difficulty of providing an answer

The Government decision that serves as the basis for the work of the committee of three ministers stipulates four conditions that the future registration guidelines must fulfill, as follows:

1. Compatibility with Jewish tradition, both the Orthodox and the various branches of non-Orthodox;
2. Compatibility with Israel as a Jewish state;
3. Compatibility with it as a democratic country that does not impose any religious attitude or practice on its citizens;
4. Compatibility with it as the center of the ingathering of the exiles.

One wonders whether this formulation is not so inclusive as to create an insoluble problem, like trying to fit a square peg in a round hole. There does not seem to be any possibility of fulfilling all four conditions at one and the same time. Nonetheless, I shall attempt to take each of them and all four together into account insofar as possible.

The letter concludes with "four considerations." The first two are essentially identical to the third and fourth conditions above, but the last two together add a fifth condition: although the registration guidelines will only be binding on an Israeli citizen, the Israeli legislator must consider the far-reaching consequences of his directives on the Jewish Diaspora. Our faith in the Diaspora is today in the throes of a harsh struggle for the religious, national, and even biological survival of the nation, and is entitled to expect the whole-hearted moral assistance of the State of Israel in this struggle. Anyone who bears responsibility for the whole of the Jewish people wherever they may be, can not be relieved of the need to take into consideration the effect of certain arrangements in Israel on the struggle for the survival of Diaspora Jewry.

The problem of registration

The letter attributes the need for a population registry to three factors: reasons of security, the Law of Return, and the Law of Marriage and Divorce.

Even someone totally unfamiliar with security matters can understand the reason for the existence of a registry and the opportunity it affords to issue identity cards so that "legal residents of Israel [may] be able to identify themselves at all times by means of a document issued them by an official body." While, the Prime Minister does not specify the advantage for security of indicating "nationality" and "religion" on that document, we may assume that he believes this internal classification of the legal residents of Israel to be one of the primary functions of the identity card. Otherwise, the value to security of including these items on the card is quite incomprehensible. In my opinion, this consideration is untenable, as in view of the relative ease of deceiving the registry clerks and even falsifying the card, there is no question that the doubtful value to security is overridden by the injury to democratic life in Israel. Who among our people does not know that indicating national, ethnic, or religious affiliation on official documents is an open invitation to discrimination? All of us regard the absence of these items on an

American passport, for example, as one of the most conspicuous hallmarks of active democracy that is not content with formal equality. The Arab citizens of the State of Israel are also entitled to rest assured that the Government of Israel is doing all it can to prevent an official document from serving as a potential instrument of discrimination.

Nor can indicating "religion" and "nationality" on the identity card be of any help in implementing the Law of Return, as it can be performed only after the immigrant has arrived in Israel under the terms of the law. However, although there is no connection whatsoever between the Law of Return and the problem of registration, it touches directly on the question of "Who is a Jew?" as Israeli agents abroad must know who is entitled to immigration under the law and who is not. In this regard, I believe it would be best to adopt the Government proposal that anyone declaring in good faith that he is a Jew and not a member of another religion is to be considered a Jew. In respect to mixed marriages performed in the Diaspora, I feel the practice should be continued whereby the Law of Return applies to the couple, even if only one of them, either the husband or the wife, is Jewish, and they should therefore have the right to immigrate to Israel. However, the immigration official should be charged with the duty of cautioning them before immigration and informing them that should they have reason to apply to a rabbinical court, it, and not the State, will rule on whether or not they are Jewish. While as a rule, one does not seek out defects, as the Sages said: "Whoever finds fault is at fault and does not speak in praise of the world," and Samuel added: "He faults for his own fault" (Kiddushin 70a). Accordingly, Maimonides rules: "All families are presumed fit and one may marry into them from the first" (Issurei Bi'ah, 19:17).

The letter states that determining the religion of Israeli residents is essential because existing law places matters of marriage and divorce exclusively within the jurisdiction of the various religious courts. While this is true in and of itself, the problem of who will make this determination remains. I believe there is no doubt that by giving judicial authority for matters of personal status to the religious courts, the State has also waived the right to determine who will be judged by them. It is inconceivable for a court to judge a person to whom its laws do not apply. Furthermore, the non-Jewish religions in the country will never agree to waive their right to determine for themselves, by means of whatever criteria they deem appropriate, who is a Christian, a Muslim, and so on. The Government is not entitled to rescind or limit this fundamental right. Can a Jewish State, however it defines its Jewishness, discriminate only against the Jewish religion in respect to self-definition?

There is, therefore, no critical need for the indication of "nationality" and "religion," neither for security reasons nor for purposes of the Law of Return and the Law of Marriage and Divorce. On the other hand, the damage that might be caused by indicating religion appears to be grave.

When the question of "religion" appears separately from the question of "nationality," the very distinction constitutes a ruling on one of the sharpest and deepest controversies between Jews of different persuasions, namely, the issue of the relationship between the Jewish religion and the Jewish people.

The State has not succeeded in framing a law in its first decade of existence, and the major reason for this delay would seem to be the desire to avoid making decisions at this early stage on such basic questions. This desire—which is shared by the majority of Israeli citizens—stems from recognition of the need, in the words of the letter, "to increase shared and unifying properties and eliminate as far as possible those that separate and divide." Whatever our position regarding the specific issue of legislation, it would be a serious mistake to slip into an administrative guideline a specious solution to a fundamental problem which we are unable or unwilling to deal with directly through legislation.

In addition, separate registration of "religion" and "nationality" allows for the unwished-for possibility that a national Jew professing Christianity will be able to indicate both of these facts side by side on an official Israeli document. While I myself support an attitude of utmost tolerance, for such people as well, I do not believe that their ideas should be officially sanctioned by the State of Israel.

The problem of converting minors

Although I am not competent to discuss matters of halakha, as I have been asked I shall attempt to reply to the best of my understanding and conscience, since the issue is not, in fact, the sole concern of halakhic scholars. Their reply would be clear and largely unequivocal, save perhaps for the question of the right of a non-Jewish mother, who is unwilling to convert, to request that her children be converted. On this issue too there are those who take a more lenient stance, and I would hope that their opinion hold sway. The problem, however, goes beyond the four walls of halakha in that it concerns the deepest feelings of the people and occupies the mind even of those who do not recognize the binding authority of halakha. Not all these religious-national feelings can be explained rationally. It is worth noting that it is precisely those commandments whose rational explanation is the most forced that are most strictly observed: the eating of matzo on Passover, the Yom Kippur fast, and circumcision. A very large number of Jews, including those who are not at all religious, continue to view the observance of these three commandments as a sort of "sign of the covenant," and this is true of circumcision even more than of the other two.

This last fact might be explained—ex post facto—in two ways: by means of a historical explanation and a theoretical one.

The historical explanation. In the modern history of the Jewish people, if memory serves, there has been only one organized attempt to do away with circumcision. By this, of course, I mean an attempt by people who wished to remain members of the Jewish people, excluding Communist assimilationists who sought to abolish Judaism as a unique entity. I am referring to the efforts of the Frankfort Reform Association founded in 1842 by the scholar Theodore Kreuzner (who, in fact, later converted to Christianity). Dubnow, who cannot be suspected of being ultra-Orthodox, sums up the subject as follows:

> The association published a radical program which contained three sections: a) We regard the Mosaic law as capable of infinite development; b) The hodge-podge of debates, disquisitions and decrees going by the name of the Talmud is not binding on us, neither as far as doctrine or practice; c) We neither wait nor yearn for a Messiah to restore the Jews to the Land of Israel; for we do not recognize any other homeland than the one we are citizens of.

Dubnow continues:

> These three negative assumptions which the association proclaimed without a definition of its positive program were received by the public as the charter of atheism. In particular, bitterness welled up against the association when it became known that, apart from these three publicized sections, there was yet another secret one—that of the abrogation of circumcision. The storm that arose in Frankfort as a result of the abrogation of an explicit Biblical precept immediately spread

through all the communities of Germany. The question was posed as follows: Was it possible for a father who had not circumcised his son and for the son himself when he reached maturity to be considered members of the Jewish community? . . . This controversy was the only result of the activity of the Frankfort association. The association dissolved without accomplishing anything, because its program lacked any positive element (History of the Jews, Vol. 4).

David Einhorn adopted a similarly extreme stance, but he, too, had no real influence (ibid.). The Liberal Synod, convened in 1871 at Augsburg, took a much more moderate stand toward the question of circumcision, acknowledging "the importance of this commandment," yet at the same time resolved that "even a child who was not circumcised is a Jew," referring, of course, to a child born a Jew (ibid.).

Reform Judaism in America and other countries overseas also developed in the same direction. The Reform rabbi of the Liberal Synagogue in Sydney, Australia, Dr. R. Brasch, describes the situation in his country as follows: "The Melbourne community demands from a woman convert immersion in a mikva, whilst the Sydney congregation makes the acceptance of male converts dependent on circumcision" (The Synagogue Review, cited in Temple David Review, Durban: Progressive Jewish Congregation, November 1958, p. 8).

Apparently, even the liberal congregation of Melbourne, which demands immersion in a mikva from a woman convert, is unwilling to forego circumcision for males.

The same trend can be found in the United States. I recall a poll of religious practices taken among the members of Reform congregations a few years ago. According to their responses, observance of the rite of circumcision was in first place, and if I am not mistaken, was indicated by nearly one hundred percent of the respondents.

The situation in Israel is even more conspicuously unambiguous. Circumcision is accepted by virtually all circles of the Jewish population, to the extent that its continued practice is not even an issue on the agenda.

We may, therefore, conclude that requiring circumcision for male converts, both adults and minors, is not only demanded by halakha, but is also in line with the Government resolution that future guidelines should "accord with the tradition accepted by all circles of Judaism, the Orthodox and liberals of all trends."

The theoretical explanation. Every human society has boundaries. One boundary or another might be the subject of debate and might be modified under certain circumstances, but the society cannot exist if it is deprived of its right to set boundaries. This view is universally accepted in respect to the State of Israel, and is equally valid in respect to the Jewish religion. The boundary is sensed when there is an attempt to overstep it, whether with permission or in violation of a prohibition. The unquestioned boundary of Judaism which cannot be crossed without permission is "the sign of the covenant." The elimination of that borderline by the "Jewish State" would strip it of the ability to influence the Diaspora, just as the "violators of the covenant" in the Hellenistic Land of Israel were unable to maintain a link with the Jewish diaspora of their time, not even with the Hellenistic diaspora itself.

Your letter states that in Israel "there is no fear that the Jews will become assimilated among the non-Jews." There is, however, good reason to fear the collective assimilation of the entire nation if it should, Heaven forbid, be gutted of its minimal Jewish substance.

I therefore arrive at the conclusion that mere registration does not suffice to convert minors in Israel to Judaism. A religious ceremony must be instituted, with the details determined by halakhic authorities. The question is whether this constitutes a form of religious coercion?

The problem of freedom of conscience

There can be no doubt that this is a very grave problem. Some parents may wish their children to be registered as Jews, in terms of religion as well, but will be opposed to circumcision, immersion, or any type of religious ceremony. As I stated above, all four conditions in the Government resolution cannot be fulfilled at one and the same time. However, just as the country does not renounce its borders and imposes military service on its citizens in order to defend them, so the people and its tradition are entitled, and even required, to defend their borders if they wish to survive. There is here a conflict, at times a tragic one, between two rights, that of the public and that of the individual, and it does not lend itself to a simple solution.

The conflict will become more acute particularly if the children of mixed marriages, whose mothers are not Jewish, are not converted by their parents as minors, but reach maturity without converting, and then may not wish to convert at all, creating boys and girls "of no faith." Under such circumstances, it will be impossible for them to marry in Israel, as at present there is no civil marriage in the country. I have felt it my duty to raise this question as well, although I have no solution for it except for the institution of civil marriage, at least for special cases of this kind. A civil marriage will not, of course, be the equivalent of Jewish religious nuptials. Inevitably, we are confronted here with a conflict between the "Jewish" and the "democratic" character of the State of Israel. Perhaps it is not the task of our generation to decide this issue, but we must not ignore the acuteness of it or try to gloss over it by means of vague formulations of a false synthesis between them.

For the moment, it may perhaps be assumed that the gravity of the problem will serve as a further motivation for the conversion of minors. Their parents chose to come to Israel. Some of them may see it as no more than a stopping-off point for emigration to other countries where it is easier to avoid the need to struggle with the problems of Judaism. But those who choose to remain here and make Israel their permanent home must be willing to accept an education in "Jewish consciousness" which will introduce them and their children to historical and modern Judaism.

Immigration to Israel involves considerable sacrifices deriving from the need to adjust to a society, economy, culture, language, and climate that are more or less unfamiliar. It would seem that despite our justified reluctance to impose any form of coercion, whether of religion or conscience, we are entitled to demand from a few immigrants, for whom the problem exists, the additional sacrifice of acknowledging in practice the right of the Jewish people to ensure its historical continuity and internal unity.

Respectfully and with my best wishes,

E. Simon

38. LEON (ARYE) SIMON

A Hebrew writer and public official, Simon (1881–1965) was born in Southampton and received a Jewish education from his father, a rabbi in Manchester. In 1904 he began working for the Post Office, rising to the position of director of the Telegraph and Telephone Department (1931–1935) and director of its Savings Bank Services (1935–1944). He was knighted in 1944. One of the founders of the Zionist Movement in England, Simon was a follower of Ahad Ha'Am. He visited Palestine in 1918, and supported the establishment of the Hebrew University in Jerusalem, later serving as a member of the University's Executive Board (1946–49) and Board of Trustees (1950–53). Simon lived in Israel from 1946 to 1953, receiving the Tchernichowsky Prize for his translation of Plato into Hebrew. His works include an anthology edited together with Simon Heller, Aspects of the Hebrew Genius: Essays on Jewish Literature and Thought (1910), and Ahad Ha-Am: Asher Ginzburg (Hebrew ed. 1955; English ed. 1960).

20 January 1959

Dear Mr. Ben-Gurion,

I am hereby honored to convey to you a memorandum on the question on which I was asked to express an opinion in your letter of 27 October 1958. To make it a bit easier for myself, I have written the memorandum in English, and I beg your forgiveness.

Two weeks ago, I had a conversation with Prof. Isaiah Berlin on the subject, and showed him a version of my reply. Yesterday I received a version of his reply, which deals almost exclusively with the general problem that I deliberately refrained from addressing. In respect to that problem, although my stance is closer to that of Prof. Berlin than to the Orthodox, I can not subscribe to the approach which apparently underlies his view, that it is possible and desirable for the term "Jew," insofar as it applies to Jews resident in the State of Israel, to at any time be divorced from its vital link to historical Judaism.

Respectfully,

Arye (Leon) Simon

Memorandum

It is stated more than once in Mr. Ben-Gurion's letter that the question on which opinions are being asked is that of the registration as Jews of children of non-Jewish mothers whose parents both wish them to be registered as Jews. It is nowhere stated that these parents object to the conversion of their children to Judaism in accordance with halakhic requirements (including circumcision in the case of boys); but it must be assumed that that is in fact the case, because if it were not the case there would seem to be no problem. The first question for consideration is, therefore, whether it would be right or expedient for the Government of Israel to insist on registering as Jews children whom the rabbinical authorities are precluded by the halakha from accepting as Jews.

I am compelled to answer that question in the negative.

It is true that, as stated in Mr. Ben-Gurion's letter, the Government already registers as a Jew any adult who sincerely declares that he is a Jew, and does not profess any other religion than Judaism, and that the rabbinical authorities apparently acquiesce in such registration, though they do not necessarily regard it as binding upon them in the religious sphere. It could be argued, I suppose, that the rabbinical authorities might logically be expected to adopt the same attitude of acquiescence in the case of children accepted as Jews by the Government but not by the halakhic tradition. I do not know what the logical answer to that argument is, if indeed there is one. But the question is not one of logical consistency. The position is, as I understand it, that the representatives of religion have in fact taken strong objection to an official ruling which directed that the children in question should be registered as Jews; that the Government has found it expedient to suspend the operation of that ruling pending further enquiry; and that the matter has become the subject of acute controversy throughout the length and breadth of Jewry. In those circumstances it is probable that insistence by the Government on disregarding the halakha in this matter of the registration of children of non-Jewish mothers would precipitate a conflict between the "religious" and the "secular" conceptions of Judaism. Such a conflict is no doubt always threatening to break out; but from every point of view it seems to be the path of wisdom to hold it in check, if possible, until, with the passage of time, and the psychological adjustment of the Jewish people to the new situation created by the emergence of the State of Israel, an atmosphere less unfavorable to a peaceful solution is created.

Such information as I have been able to obtain suggests that in a conflict with the religious authorities on the particular issue now under discussion, the Government of Israel would be unlikely to have the sympathy, at the present time, of more than a minority even among the non-religious elements of Jewry, in Israel or in the diaspora. And of course the views of the diaspora communities are very important in this matter. Mr. Ben-Gurion's letter rightly stresses the Israel Jewish community's deep sense of unity and identity with the Jewish people as a collective whole; and it is clearly impossible for the Government of Israel, as matters now stand, to give a person the official stamp of a Jew without thereby admitting him not only to Israel citizenship, but also to membership of the Jewish people— a status which is less easily capable of clear definition, but unquestionably carries with it, outside Israel, certain rights and duties which flow from the emphasis inevitably thrown in the diaspora on the religious component of that complex of nationality and religion which is the inheritance of modern Jewry.

While, however, it seems to me that the Government of Israel must in present circumstances avoid running counter to the halakha in this particular matter of the registration of children of non-Jewish mothers, I assume that the religious authorities do not claim—and I certainly do not think that they should be allowed—any right to decide which children should or should not be permitted to attend the Government Hebrew schools and to become integrated into the Hebrew-speaking sector of the population of Israel. I think that, at any rate in the class of cases now in question, it is right to regard the wishes of the parents as decisive in that matter; and if, as I assume, that is the view of the Government, the only problem demanding an immediate solution seems to be that of finding a form of registration for the children of non-Jewish mothers which will satisfy the needs of the State without involving disregard of halakhic law.

It is not clear to me that it is necessary for the Government to take a final decision about the registration of such children as soon as they arrive in Israel. I think that it ought to be possible, given a reasonable measure of good will on all sides, to devise a form of provisional registration which would meet the needs of the case. What I have in mind is that in the cases in question the entry on the identity card under "nationality" and "religion" should in the first instance be some non-committal formula like "his" (or "her") "father is a Jew"—"aviv (or aviha) yehudi". This would sufficiently identify the child as belonging, by the desire of its parents and by the actual circumstances of its upbringing, to the Jewish national-religious group in Israel, but would carry no implication of its being halakhically Jewish. If the law does not at present permit a registration of this indeterminate character, I assume that it would be possible to amend the law.

I would suggest that the provisional registration should be valid originally for a limited period, say three years, Within that time, I imagine, some, perhaps many, of the parents concerned would leave the country with their children. Probably a larger number would succumb to the influences of the environment, and would agree to have their children converted to Judaism in the traditional manner at or before the end of the period of provisional registration (and in some cases a boy on reaching the age of thirteen might opt for conversion to Judaism even if his parents oppose it). There would no doubt remain cases that did not settle themselves in either of these ways. Such cases should not be numerous, and it is perhaps unnecessary at this stage to decide how to deal with a situation which could not arise for two or three years at least, and conceivably might affect only a few individuals, who do not seem to have claims of a very high order on the State of Israel or on the Jewish people.

My suggestion of course presupposes a desire on all sides to find by agreement a way out of the immediate difficulty. It presupposes especially a readiness on the part of the rabbinical authorities, in cases where after a time the unwillingness of the parents to have their child converted is overcome, to interpret the requirements of the halakha in the [compromising] spirit of Hillel rather than in that [uncompromising] of Shamai.

I have deliberately confined my observation to the specific question raised in Mr. Ben-Gurion's letter, and have refrained altogether from entering into the wider and more fundamental question "Who is a Jew?" That question of course underlies the particular problem raised by the registration of the children of non-Jewish mothers who come to Israel under the Law of Return; but in my opinion there is at present no possibility of finding a complete answer to it which would meet with general acceptance, and I do not see that the State of Israel is called upon to deal with it except when it presents itself, in one or other of its aspects, as a practical problem for which a practical solution has to be found.

Leon Simon

39. JOSEPH DOV SOLOVEITCHIK AND CHAIM HELLER

Joseph Dov Soloveitchik (1903–1993), a noted philosopher and halakhic authority, was born to a distinguished family of rabbis in Prozhen, Poland. He grew up in Haslowitz, Byelorussia, where his father was the community rabbi. Until his 20's he studied Talmud, entering Berlin University at the age of 22, and graduating with a degree in philosophy. In 1932, he moved to the United States, becoming the rabbi of the Orthodox community of Boston, where he founded the Maimonides Jewish School and taught Talmud to religious scholars. In 1941, he succeeded his father on the Halakha Committee of the American Rabbinical Council. Soloveitchik's most noted work is Ish Ha-halakha (Man of Halakha; 1944). Associated with the Mizrakhi movement, he was the undisputed leader of Orthodox Jewry, and advocated inter-faith dialogue.

Chaim Heller (1878–1960), a rabbi and halakhic authority, was born in Bialistok, Poland, and served as the rabbi of the Lomza community. In 1917 he moved to Berlin, and in 1922 founded a yeshiva in which Soloveitchik studied. In 1929 he joined the Theological Seminary in New York. Heller spent several years in Israel and then returned to the United States, settling first in Chicago and then in New York.

25 Shevat 5719

Greetings!

Each of the undersigned received the Prime Minister's letter. As we share the same opinion regarding the question it poses, we have decided to employ a single halakhic coin rather than two separate versions, and to reply in this letter that contains our opinion.

The question raised as to the registration of infants born to non-Jewish mothers who have not been properly converted needs no meticulous investigation. Two basic laws that have been accepted since time immemorial and are the pillars of the Jewish tradition provide an unequivocal answer.

The first law states: "The child of a non-Jewess is like her." The second law rules: "A non-Jew who was circumcised and did not immerse or who immersed and was not circumcised is not a convert until he is circumcised and immerses." In other words, the mother determines the sanctity of the child and his membership in the Jewish people, and proper effective conversion requires circumcision and immersion for the male and immersion alone for the female. Hence, neither a child nor an adult can be considered or registered as a Jew if his mother is not Jewish and he was not converted according to religious law. The declaration of the parents or of the adult himself are of no consequence. These laws constitute the foundations of the Torah and commandments, and require no explanation or interpretation.

We therefore will not refer to any citations or sources. Any further comment is superfluous. In respect to such principles of the Torah, the great teacher Maimonides has already written in Mishne Torah (Hilkhot Hobel u-Mazik, 1.6): "Although these words appear clearly in the Written Law and are all explained by Moses at Mount Sinai, for us they are practical matters. According to them our forefathers ruled in the courts of Joshua and Samuel and in every single rabbinical court since the time of Moses and until today."

We are quite puzzled as to why the Government of the State of Israel should now wish to chop down what has been planted and bring down the ancient citadel of Judaism that has been sanctified by the blood and agony of previous generations. Only through them has our uniqueness as a holy people bound by ties of fervent sacred love to the Holy Land been preserved. Will the State of Israel be constructed upon the destruction of all that is holy to Israel? Please heed our words, your Excellency, the Prime Minister, whose name we honor and whose historic contribution to the rebirth of the country we greatly admire!

Warmly and respectfully,

Chaim Heller and Joseph Dov Halevi Soloveitchik

40. ALFREDO SHABTAI TOAFF

Rabbi Shabtai Toaff (1880–1963) was born in Livorno and studied at the local rabbinical college. In 1923 he was appointed the city rabbi, and from 1931 was a member of the Rabbinical Council of Italy, over which he later presided. Toaff served as the head of the Italian Rabbinical College from the time it was reopened in 1955, and as a professor of literature and ancient languages at Florence University. His numerous writings on Biblical, literary and historical subjects include Cenni stricti sulla comunita ebraica e sulla singagoga di Livorno (1955), a history of the Jewish community of Livorno.

14 December 1958

Dear Prime Minister,

You have been granted the great privilege to establish landmarks in Judaism that are of crucial importance for the future character of the Israeli Jew and world Jewry.

Therefore, if you should be responsible for enacting a statute that unintentionally does harm to the sacred laws of Judaism, you will, without desiring to do so, become the abuser of what is sacred to Judaism and will, Heaven forbid, create dangerous precedents for the character of the Jewish nation in Israel and abroad. This will, in the future, be the scourge of the nation, and then the verdict of history will be of no help, as the pure character will have been sullied and the next generation will not have the power to alter this ominous reality.

I therefore protest vigorously against your having turned to all these Jewish intellectuals in Israel and the Diaspora, as, in my opinion, the rabbis of the State of Israel are thoroughly qualified to rule on halakha. In such an area, which is by all logic basically a religious one, the rabbis of Israel would rule faithfully. It is highly offensive to ignore the very important point of acknowledging the opinion of the rabbis of the State of Israel as an authorized judicial body. It is a slap in the face to all the religious institutions the world over to detract from the authority of the Israeli rabbis who are the recognized supreme body of religion and Judaism. You should have addressed such questions to them alone, as it appears quite odd to allow a person considered an "apostate" to rule on religious law, since we know that you addressed your query even to Jews who desecrate the Sabbath and so on.

I am of the opinion that it is unthinkable to determine the future character of the Jew without taking into consideration the Jewish communities in the Diaspora who view the rabbis of Israel as the authorized body to whom the Israeli Government should appeal.

We, the Jews in the Diaspora, wish to maintain an active link to Israeli Jews, and clearly any practice reflected in the way of life of the Israeli Jew will be viewed by us as desirable. Thus, if, Heaven forbid, the Israeli Jew is the first to deviate from the hallowed form of the approach to the meaning of Judaism, the Jews in the Diaspora will have no choice but to follow, as they have done until now, and be led, unavoidably, to assimilation. For example, up to now a Jew who married a non-Jewish woman (of which, sad to say, there are many) would argue with his wife and her relatives that a Jew needs something special, and can not be a Jew and be considered a member of the Jewish people without evidencing the accepted hallmarks sanctified in Judaism. The child grew up and became part of Jewish society without suffering any complexes because he felt no difference between himself and his Jewish friends who were the children of Jewish mothers and fathers. However, if this dangerous option becomes available to anyone who wants it, that is, to be a Jew without the rite of circumcision, according to the proposed guidelines for registering children, this precedent will constitute the greatest possible danger to the future of the nation in the Diaspora. The Jewish father who heretofore saw it as a sacred principle will now become convinced that if in Israel, which both Jews and non-Jews regard as the center of Jewish law from which "instruction shall come forth," the rite consecrated for thousands of years, and which symbolizes that which makes a Jew special, is no longer required, he will be the first to consider it unnecessary for the sake of domestic peace and fewer problems. Not only will the danger increase, but also it will undoubtedly cause the nation to ultimately lose its character. Only those who carried the torch and continue to do so will remain the single foundation of Diaspora Jewry.

Like all Jews in the Diaspora, I believe that a link with the communities abroad is extremely desirable for the State of Israel and its leaders, as expressed in the Government guidelines (despite the increasing Canaanite philosophy of a not inconsiderable number of Israeli-born individuals who seek to deny the vital connection between the Jews in the Diaspora and those in Israel and see the need to demonstrate this at every opportunity). Even more so, the State of Israel is welcome and beloved by the Jews of the world. On this basis, I must state that no law should be enacted which might jeopardize the future of the Jewish nation in Israel and abroad. I therefore believe that you, the leader who has led a nation out of bondage into freedom, who has stood at its head in times of severe crisis, who has taken it a very long way through crises and dangers and established it on the foundations of faith in the destiny of Israel, who has inspired it with a conviction of victory even when the greatest optimists had lost faith, and who has continued to lead it to greater and greater achievements—you will not disappoint us. You will not be the one to help violate the sacred laws of Judaism that I am certain you wish to observe. In debates with various bodies I have demonstrated that upholding the major principles of Judaism is no less a sacred mission to Ben-Gurion than to the religious figures who regard themselves as their guardians, and that the position which maintains that continuing the existing arrangement is crucial to the character of the Jew need not necessarily be advocated by a religious party. I have argued that since this is a matter of our very survival, a person like Ben-Gurion would not impose on the nation a controversy that is inadvisable now and in the future.

Accordingly, in this matter which raises the fundamental issue of religion and nationality and poses the question "who will be called a Jew," the answer is clear and unambiguous even for those considered non-religious. It is "in accordance with halakha." Halakha has decreed who can be a Jew. It was formulated by the Sages who took into account all the situations in which a Jew might be found, sought, debated, found, and formulated guidelines for us that have preserved the fitting Jewish character throughout the generations. To this day, they serve as our guiding principles and light our way.

Hence:

a. a Jew according to the law is a child born to a Jewish mother.
b. a child born to a non-Jewish mother must undergo the following rites to be a Jew:
for a boy: circumcision and immersion
for a girl: immersion

Nothing else will help make him a Jew before he undergoes these procedures. The declaration of a person born to Jewish parents (who has, of course, been circumcised) that he is not religious or does not believe in the Jewish religion, for example, does not exclude him. Though he is termed an apostate, he will forever remain a Jew by nationality and religion. The opposite equally applies to a non-Jewish adult who declares in good faith that he is Jewish and not a member of any other religion. This declaration does not make him a Jew.

The law is no different for adults or minors, as there is no distinction between them on this basic issue. Nor is there any difference if the father is a Jew and the mother a non-Jew. If we consider that mixed marriages are not recognized as marriages, and have no legal validity, then automatically paternity is not recognized. Consequently, the declaration of the parents is of no value and cannot serve as reason to register the child of a non-Jewish mother as a member of the Jewish nation before he has undergone the rites listed above.

In conclusion, it is the desire of world Jewry that the law in Israel be enacted only out of respect for and observance of the sacred principles of Judaism and halakha which have maintained the special character of the Jew.

It is my hope that the heads of the State of Israel will acknowledge this truth and come to a decision that is satisfactory to the entire Jewish nation in Israel and the Diaspora.

Respectfully,

Prof. Dr. Rabbi Shabtai A. Toaff

41. ELIO RAFFAELO TOAFF

The son of Alfredo Shabtai Toaff, E.R. Toaff (b. 1915) was born in
Livorno, Italy, and was the last man to be ordained a rabbi by the
rabbinical college in that city. He studied law at the University of Pisa,
graduating in 1938. During the Second World War, Toaff joined the
partisans in the Livorno region. He served as the rabbi of Ancona
(1941–46), Venice (1946–51), and chief rabbi of Rome (from 1951).
Since 1963 he has been a member of the Rabbinical Council of Italy
and the head of the Italian Rabbinical College. Toaff is the editor of
Annuario di Studi Ebraici and the author of articles on Judaism, the
Bible, and history.

17 December 1958

Dear Mr. David Ben-Gurion,

Permit me, Sir, first of all to protest the scandalous fact, unprecedented in Jewish history, that a basic question of religious law is
being addressed to people who have no authority or competence to
rule on halakha, some of whom even desecrate the Sabbath, and
yet you, Sir, have dubbed them "Jewish sages." For this reason, I
was very hesitant in replying to your letter of Heshvan 13 that only
reached me a few days ago, especially as the Chief Rabbinate of
Israel, which we consider the supreme contemporary religious body,
has expressed its opinion on the question in such a clear and decisive manner. However, so that my silence not be seen, Heaven forbid, as concurrence with the views presented in your letter, and in
order to fulfill the words of the Sages that anyone who leads the
people to virtue does not sin and anyone who leads the people astray
can never do enough to atone for it, I hereby offer my opinion as
follows.

Neither the Government of Israel, nor any other institution, has
the authority to register the children of mixed marriages as Jews at
the request of the parents—a Jewish father and non-Jewish mother.

For the child to be a Jew, circumcision and immersion must be
performed to convert him, according to Jewish law and the rulings
of the Sages and according to halakha, as consecrated for genera-

tions, whose sole interpreters are authorized rabbis. Finally, permit me to express my hope that your Excellency, who has done such wondrous work in establishing the state, not split the nation and create a schism between the State of Israel and the people of Israel the world over by assailing the foundations of our holy Torah.

With all due respect,

E.R. Toaff

42. EPHRAIM A. URBACH

A scholar of the Talmud and rabbinical literature, Urbach (1912–1991) was born in Poland and studied at the rabbinical school in Breslau and at universities in Breslau and Rome. He came to Israel in 1938, where he taught at a high school in Jerusalem and served as a Ministry of Education inspector. He began teaching at the Hebrew University in 1953, where he served as a professor of Talmud (1958), the head of the Institute of Jewish Studies (1956–1960), the head of the Humanities Division of the Israeli National Academy of Sciences and head of the Academy (1990–1986). Urbach published numerous scientific papers, among them The Authors of the Tosefot (1956), which won him the Israel Prize in Science, and The Sages: Beliefs and Opinions (1971). He was also among the founders of the Yehadut Ha-Torah (Torah Judaism) Movement (1966).

17 December 1958

Mr. Prime Minister,

As an observant Jew, I am bound by halakha in all issues relating to the laws of personal status and conversion, and the question you have raised belongs to this realm. Any new decisions or questions arising in respect to these issues, should, in my opinion, be brought before the religious courts authorized to hand down a ruling. The Government decision of 15 July 1958 constitutes not only removing the issue from the realm of halakha and turning it into a public matter, but is also a case of Government intervention in religious affairs. I am therefore opposed to the very act of the Government's raising the question. However, as it has been posed, I would like to respond not as a teacher and halakhic authority, but as a citizen of Israel and a member of the Jewish nation and religion. I shall rely not on the sources of halakha, but solely on public/national considerations, primarily those explained with such praiseworthy objectivity in your letter.

From the statement "the laws of Israel forbid any form of discrimination between individuals on the basis of differences in race, color, nationality, religion, or sex," only one conclusion can be drawn:

it is inappropriate on any document whatsoever issued by the State
of Israel to indicate the "religion" or "nationality" of a citizen,
whether they arrived in Israel under the Law of Return or were
naturalized after residing in the country for two years. Israeli residents who are not citizens should carry documents from their own
countries, and if the state requires further documentation, it will indicate their foreign citizenship in any case. Determining the "religion"
of a citizen can only be a matter for churches, institutions, and organizations for whom "religious affiliation" is relevant, and in a free
state, they and only they have the authority to determine who is
counted among their members and who is not.

I can accept the explanation in your letter that it is impossible to
eliminate the indications of religion and nationality for reasons of
security, which are unlikely to change in the near future. In other
words, the whole question of registration is merely a "temporary
provision" at a time of emergency, a necessity that cannot be condemned. Nevertheless, I believe that those who propose registering
the children of mixed marriages as Jews if their parents so wish it
are ignoring the long-term consequences of such a regulation.

The first of these consequences concerns the registrees themselves
and is not to their advantage. "Existing law places matters of marriage and divorce within the jurisdiction of the religious courts," and
I am certain this law is not a "temporary provision" or the result
of a coalition agreement, but rather the product of "the awareness
of the shared destiny and historical continuity that unite the Jews of
every generation throughout the world wherever they may live," an
awareness which is undoubtedly shared by the large majority of
Israeli Jews and their representatives in the Knesset and Government.

What will be the fate of a youngster registered as a Jew on the
basis of "the parents' wishes" alone when he desires to marry a
Jewish girl and discovers that his Judaism exists solely in the population registry? The appropriate religious authorities will not be able
to take this registration into account. The young man registered as
a Jew will suddenly learn that he is not Jewish and is required to
convert according to religious law.

The second consequence concerns the Jewish people as a whole.
Everyone agrees that mixed marriages abroad are one of the crucial causes of total assimilation and abandonment of Judaism, a fact
confirmed by centuries of sad experience. The claim that "mixed
couples that come here lead to total integration into the Jewish peo-

ple" has yet to be proven. Indeed, as far as I have heard, the lack of integration, and even emigration, of mixed couples that come to Israel is a common phenomenon, especially in families in which the mother is not Jewish and continues to practice another religion. "Transforming" the children of mixed marriages into Jews by means of an empty verbal declaration will not, in my opinion, make their integration any easier. Judaism cannot be acquired through words, and "what you get for nothing is worth nothing." On the other hand, it is quite clear that the decision that the children of mixed marriages will be considered Jewish on the basis of the parents' desire to register them as Jews will have a devastating effect on Diaspora Jewry. How will parents, teachers, educators, rabbis, and leaders be able stem the tide if any youngster in the Diaspora can point to the law of the State of Israel that allows what they wish to forbid? Is this the assistance to be given to those fighting assimilation in the Diaspora, or an expression of the profound feeling of unity and identity with Jews the world over?

The argument that calls up the principle of "freedom of conscience and religion" ensured in the Declaration of Independence and the Government guidelines appears to me to be baseless. The parents in mixed marriages are not being coerced to register their children as Jews. I assume there are cases in which a Christian mother insists on her child being Christian as well, and I am certain that none forces her to do otherwise. The question relates to parents who wish their children to be registered as Jews, and none can demand in the name of "freedom of conscience and religion" that parents should determine the regulations for registration. The Government decision which states that "the religion or nationality of adults will be listed as 'Jewish' if they declare themselves in good faith to be Jewish and not a member of another religion" indicates that even those who believe in separating nationality from religion are willing to admit there is a connection of some sort between Jewish nationality and Jewish religion, if only in the negative.

In my opinion, registering children born to mixed marriages on the basis of the expression of the parents' wishes and their declaration that the child is not a member of another religion has obvious disadvantages and doubtful advantages. Such a regulation, justified as a temporary provision in a state of emergency, will be a scourge for generations to come.

From the Jewish-national perspective as well, children of mixed marriages should be registered solely according to the clear specific stipulations of Jewish law.

Respectfully and with best wishes,

Ephraim A. Urbach

43. YEKHIEL WEINBERG

A rabbi, scholar of Judaism and Talmudic authority, Weinberg (1885–1966) was born in Lithuania and received rabbinical ordination from the Pilwichki yeshiva. In 1914 he moved to Germany, earning a Ph.D. from the University of Giessen. He served as a rabbi in Berlin, and in 1924 taught at the Orthodox Rabbinical Seminary in that city. With the rise of the Nazis, he returned to Eastern Europe. After the war, during which he was incarcerated in a number of camps, he moved to Montreux, Switzerland. Weinberg was the author of four volumes of responsa entitled Sridei Esh (Remnants of Fire; 1961–1969), the last of which was published three years after his death.

12 Shevat 5719

Dear Mr. Prime Minister,

I gratefully acknowledge receipt of your letter of 13 Heshvan 5719 (which reached me at the end of Kislev), and apologize for my delay in replying due to my prolonged illness.

The question addressed to the respondents of how to act in registering the children of mixed marriages both of whose parents wish to register them as Jews occasions two preliminary questions: the question of "Who is a Jew?" and the question of conversion in Israel. Each of these three interrelated questions requires a separate answer.

1) The question "Who is a Jew?", which has suddenly appeared in the Israeli press, has unleashed a storm in the Jewish world. It is not the question itself, but the debate that such a question was capable of generating in the Jewish country established in the land of our forefathers—a debate that appeared quite paradoxical even to the non-Jewish world.

This is a new question, unimagined by preceding generations. A simple Jew, without philosophical predilections or newfound ideologies, would shrug his shoulders at this odd question that has arisen in the very generation of national rebirth and the return to our spiritual homeland. Only confusion and the lack of spiritual underpinnings could have produced this new "Jewish question."

Realizing that the answer to this question of principle would determine the solution to the practical problems that derive from it, I decided to discuss the issue in an article published in the journal Sinai (Heshvan-Kislev 5719 issue). I based my comments on the basic assumption that only Judaism itself can and is entitled to answer the question of who is a Jew. Judaism has already provided an answer that reverberates throughout the thousands of years of Jewish history. A Jew is a person who believes in the God of Israel and keeps his Torah in his heart and soul and observes it in his daily life.

We have no other Judaism than that of the observance of the Torah and commandments. This is the legitimate, historical Judaism. It is this Judaism that shaped the character of the Jewish people and made it a unique national entity with a specific spiritual essence. The gentile world recognizes a Jew as a member of the Jewish faith. This is his hallmark in the eyes of the enlightened non-Jewish world. Only despicable racists and slanderers attribute other characteristics to him. In pre-war Germany and adjacent Western countries, as well as in the United States, an attempt was made to devise a new type of Judaism, a Judaism that denied the basic traditional values and the national character it produced. This Judaism, which dubs itself "liberal" or "progressive," is nothing more than the arbitrary construct of people who have lost their faith and national vigor. The early members of the Reform found meanings in the Torah that are not there, falsified its essence and distorted its nature in a desire to record achievements and gain rights from the ruling gentile nation. In order to earn the gentiles' sympathy and respect for Judaism, they adopted the views and ideas of the Christian religion. They thereby cut out the roots of Judaism, and, ignoring the religious precepts so deeply rooted in the life of the nation, they boisterously declared that following the ethics of the prophets was preferable to observing the practical commandments.

Yet this distortion of Judaism was a dismal failure, and rightfully so. Imitation is a contemptible trait. Distorting the face of Judaism did not help to make the nations of the world like us any better. Ignorant hatred did not cease to exist. This worldwide fatal hostility for the "Chosen People" will endure, and even the establishment of the glorious Jewish state has only succeeded in replacing the attitude of contempt and condemnation with one of envy and antagonism. The nations have not matured. They will do so only by the moral triumph of the true Jewish spirit and the fulfillment of the vision "the earth will be full of the knowledge of the Lord."

Liberal Judaism has not proven itself. As a result of the elimination of the boundaries and the inner weakness of this progressive Judaism, the tide of assimilation has risen and devastated its ranks. This may not have been the desire or intent of its official representatives, but it is certainly a direct product and result of the disregard for the foundations of true Judaism.

Over-emphasis on "the ethics of Judaism" is superfluous and pointless. It is especially grating when it issues from the mouths of people with no religion or religious discipline. There is no question that the lofty morals of the Torah are the very soul of Judaism; the fact that a moral life and spiritual purity are the greatest principle of Judaism is perfectly obvious and does not need to be over-emphasized. A Jew who violates a moral law is unfit and his religious character is flawed. Although for formal legal reasons, the moral offender is not sentenced in court, he is judged by Heaven and his punishment is heavy. It is a well-recognized rule of Judaism that morality exists as an active force only through a religious life and by observing the commandments of the Torah constantly and consistently in one's daily actions and life. It was this fact that instilled religion and morality in the nation as a whole and in the way of life of every Jew.

I do not wish to give the Prime Minister of Israel a lesson in Jewish theology. However, it is obvious that without a religious basis, the laws and precepts of ethics will not be upheld, and are nothing more than noble pipe-dreams in conspicuous conflict with everyday reality.

The moral abandon and sexual depravity that have broken out in the new generation prove that religious observance is the only guarantee of a pure moral life. There is no other restraint on human drives than that of religion. Observance of the practical commandments is the overriding principle and most basic foundation of Judaism, and constitutes the huge distinction between Judaism and Christianity. The Jewish people preserved this great and hallowed principle, and this strict observance of it enabled us to endure throughout the generations, to overcome the innumerable persecutions, hostile edicts, carnages, and conflagrations to which we were subjected, and to sacrifice our lives to ensure the survival of the legacy of our parents and teachers, and all this through faith and anticipation of redemption.

Had we been willing to forego the sacred principle of observance of the Torah and commandments, we could have provided a simple solution to the "Jewish problem." But because of the awareness and conviction that Judaism is the root of our soul and without it our life is not life at all, we were not willing to waive the right to live as Jews. We have no other Judaism, and we have no wish to reshape or alter the form of our Judaism. Traditional Judaism is our national culture, and the name "Jew" is a title of honor for all who bear this culture. This precious name cannot tolerate a different meaning. It has received religious consecration, and nothing is greater than that. We all know how many sacrifices in body, soul and property it has cost us to defend and preserve this hallowed name. We must therefore not dishonor it by offering it to anyone who wishes to gain temporary or permanent residence in our blessed land.

2) As to the question of conversion in Israel: the Prime Minister's letter to a number of people in Israel and abroad gives the impression that he does not intend to concede to the halakhic ruling, as the accepted ruling for generations upon generations is that a child born to a non-Jewish woman is non-Jewish in every sense. The same ruling holds for adults and for minors. The only way for a non-Jew to become a Jew is through conventional conversion. No one has ever cast doubt on this ruling; not even the rebellious sects that have emerged throughout our history went so far as to question it. It has been the foundation of family and personal life, and any attempt to alter it would be a threat to the life of the nation.

Had there been any doubt in this respect, the Prime Minister would surely have addressed the question to the Chief Rabbinate of Israel, which is a public institution, and he would certainly have turned to this only official national body authorized to rule in religious matters. What power do people with no halakhic authority, to say nothing of those who are not religious, to rule on a major religious issue that affects the very soul of the Jewish nation?

The Prime Minister must have been seeking an historical explanation of the form of traditional conversion and the possibility of modifying it and replacing it with a new form that better suits the taste of those who have separated themselves from the Jewish religion and wish to establish a new Judaism founded on the idea of "secular nationalism." This is a fallacious notion in terms of the Torah, refuted by historical tradition and by current Jewish reality.

The statement by Sa'adia Gaon that "our nation is a nation only in its Torah" determines that the Jewish people is different in national essence from the other nations in the world. For them, nationalism is not associated with religion. An Englishman or Frenchman can be Catholic or Protestant, or even Muslim, and can convert from one religion to another any number of times. Religious conversion in no way detracts from his nationality. His "conversion" might engender the grief or protest of his family, but it casts no doubt on his national entitlement. Excluding himself from the official religion does not mean that he is excluding himself from the nation into which he was born.

This is not true in our case. No matter how ardently nationalist a Jew is, and even if he is a permanent resident, pays his taxes, serves in the army and fights in Israel's wars, if he should, Heaven forbid, convert to another religion he is excluded from the Jewish people. Without a doubt, even the most extreme left-wing party would expel the convert from its ranks.

In issuing his amendment to the Minister of the Interior's registration guidelines, whereby an adult who wishes to be accepted as a Jew must declare in good faith that he is Jewish—and also that he is not a member of another religion—the Prime Minister has shown a proper understanding of the essential difference between us and other nations. It is to the Prime Minster's credit that he has recognized and revealed a profound understanding of the national nature of the Jewish people. He has thereby generated the hope that his approach to the Jewish question is not the secular nationalist one that has encroached on the brain of certain circles and confused their minds.

It is, however, this understanding on the part of the Israeli Prime Minster that makes many people wonder why a person who denies all religions and merely declares in good faith that he wishes to belong to the Jewish nation should be so privileged. Why does he have greater rights than a person who also declares in good faith that he wishes to belong to the Jewish nation, but whose religious conscience compels him to remain a Christian or Muslim? Is it only a total denial of faith that qualifies a non-Jew for acceptance into the national framework?

There is no way out of this logical absurdity save recognition of the basic rule that a non-Jew can become a Jew only through religious conversion, that is, acceptance of the Torah and commandments, circumcision, and immersion in the manner prescribed by religious law.

The condition of accepting the Torah and commandments is clear and simple. It requires total assimilation into the spiritual and moral world of the Jewish religious tradition. Circumcision is a biological mark of identification with Judaism. It represents the covenant between the God of Israel and the father of the nation. It is the hallmark of the Jew, and its absence implies total exclusion from the Jewish people.

Immersion is the religious symbol of sanctification and purification. The immersion of a proselyte derives from the declaration of the Sages that when the Israelites stood on Mt. Sinai, they ceased to be unclean. A non-Jew wishing to convert must purify and sanctify himself as instructed by the Torah.

Religious matters do not have a rational explanation. Religion has its own laws and tradition that cannot be subjected to the methods of secular investigation.

The institution of conversion is very ancient, its line reaching back, according to the Sages, to Abraham, who was the first proselyte (Hagigah 3), the father of those who come to shelter under the wings of the Divine Presence of Judaism. For this reason, halakha allows a convert to include in his prayers the words "our God and the God of our fathers." As the Sages explain, "You shall be the father of a multitude of nations (Gen. 17:5);" before Abraham was the father of a person and from this time forward he became the father of all nations (Jerusalem Talmud, Bikkurim and in Maimonides, Bikkurim).

Conversion itself was introduced by Judaism. Other nations are familiar with "religious conversion" but not "national conversion." A person can change his religion as he pleases, but he cannot change his nationality. National affiliation is a matter of inheritance and cannot be replaced. The political regime can grant a person citizenship with full rights in another country, but it cannot imprint on him the stamp of a new nationality.

Goering, the satanic German, proclaimed that he would determine who is an "Aryan," and by doing so became the laughing stock of the whole world.

In democratic countries, the term "nation" has been given the new meaning of political citizenship. This is merely a matter of dressing an old term that has lost its former meaning in new robes. Everyone is aware, however, that nationality is not something determined by a legal constitution, but is determined by racial origin and associated with historical affiliation.

Judaism alone is the exception to this rule. Religious conversion in Judaism means thoroughly becoming a Jew in the national sense as well. No other nation in the world has so devoutly maintained its racial purity and sanctity as the Jewish people. As the prophet said: "Look back to Abraham your father, And to Sarah who brought you forth. For he was only one when I called him, etc." (Is. 51:2), and "But you, Israel, My servant, Jacob, whom I have chosen, Seed of Abraham My friend" (ibid. 41:8). This extraordinary veneration for the national origin stemmed from an understanding of the sanctity of the Jewish race for its spiritual and ethical characteristics. At the age of three, Abraham acknowledged his Creator (Nedarim 32) and he turned evil into good (Jerusalem Talmud, Sotah). Three attributes characterize the nation: mercy, humility, and charity (Yebamot 79). Anyone who is merciful is surely from the seed of the Patriarch Abraham (Betzah 32).

These features shape the character of a person from the seed of Abraham. The spiritual ethical element became supreme in Jewish theology. Biological race took on the form of a spiritual and cultural race. Abraham and Sarah produced this race, as the Sages explain in respect to the verse "And the persons that they had acquired in Haran" (Gen. 12:5): Abraham converted the men and Sarah the women. With this approach to the value of the spiritual, Judaism could open its doors to anyone who desired to belong to the spiritual race of Abraham.

God disqualifies no creature, but receives all. The gates are at all times open and anyone may enter them (Shemot Rabbah).

It is not national origin alone that determines membership in the Jewish people, but spiritual devotion to the legacy of Abraham. For this reason, the Torah sets strict standards for the acceptance of proselytes. It demands total integration into its culture and wholehearted devotion to the spirit of the Jewish people.

Hence, conversion is only possible in the religious manner of accepting the Jewish religion, absorbing the spirit of Judaism heart and soul, and adopting its values and way of life.

No other form of conversion exists. A good-faith declaration that someone is Jewish (and who can tell what is in his heart?) or that he wishes his children to be registered as Jews is meaningless and worthless. Secular national conversion is devoid of all logic and contrary to nature and reality. Anyone born a non-Jew or born to a non-Jewish mother remains a non-Jew, and neither the Government of Israel nor the Knesset can make him a Jew. The laws of Judaism, and they alone, can determine who is a Jew and who is not a Jew. No political regime or legislative body has the power to rule against the judgment of the Torah, and it is inappropriate for the Israeli Government to perjure itself by claiming that a non-Jew is a Jew. The declaration of a person wishing to join the Jewish people is of no value so long as he is unwilling to be bound by the laws of the Torah and devote himself to its spirit. Such lip service carries no weight or commitment. The Sages have even said of proselytes who fulfilled the conditions of conversion in word and deed but did not accept Judaism in their heart and soul that "proselytes are as bad to Israel as a sore in the skin," and that they delay the coming of the Messiah (Nidah 13b).

The Prime Minister's argument that whereas mixed marriages abroad are one of the major factors in assimilation and abandonment of Judaism, the mixed couples who come to Israel encourage total integration in the Jewish people has aroused considerable anxiety in the religious public. Is there anyone with the spark of Judaism still in his heart who will not be appalled by such a statement? We cannot but cry out: we do not wish this sore in the skin of the invasion of a foreign element into the body of the holy nation. Why do we need these "converts" who were crowned Jews by a transitory government?

Everyone here is astounded that the Prime Minister, who is known for his special qualities of love for Israel and its tradition and the determination to defend national unity and harmony at all costs, has chosen to create such a commotion over a handful of people who came to Israel not out of love for Judaism but for unknown personal and private reasons. Does the Prime Minister consider these self-made converts a source of strength and reinforcement for the state? No, Mr. Prime Minister, these converts will ultimately betray us. They will not prove themselves in times of danger and will turn their backs on us.

The State of Israel must steer clear of the utterly fallacious notion of "secularity." Judaism is the combination of two components, its coin: "Who is like your people Israel, a unique nation on earth" [II Sam. 7:23] on the one hand, and "Who chose us from among all the nations and gave us the true Torah," on the other. The Reformers cut the coin in half and discarded one side, making it worthless. Do we really want to scratch out the inscription on the other side and render Judaism a specious currency?

The obvious conclusion is that the Government of Israel is faced with only two alternatives: either it upholds and confirms conversion according to religious law as determined by the law of the Torah, or it does away with the institution of conversion entirely. So-called national conversion has no logical meaning or value of any kind. No Jewish community or institution in the world will accept a self-made Jew because of an identity card issued by a government that did not act in accordance with religious law.

We are deeply concerned for the honor of the Government of Israel which has been established after two thousand years of exile, painful wandering and dispersion. We therefore sincerely advise it to dispense with the guidelines of the law for the registration of both adults and minors born out of conceit, and to have nothing more to do with them.

While I do not consider myself one of the great Jewish figures or scholars, I crave the existence and honor of our country and speak only what is in the heart of every ordinary Jew who loves his nation and his country.

3) The registration of the children of mixed marriages: In respect to the guidelines for the registration of the children of mixed marriages in which the father is Jewish and the mother is not, stating that they are to be registered as Jews if the parents so desire, the same can be said as in the preceding section. The position that maintains that since it is a civil registry that does not serve religious purposes, there is no cause to adopt religious criteria, is rejected and refuted by religious law. According to halakha, the child follows the mother, although we do not know the reasoning behind this precept. Some contend that the reason for it is biological and associated with the creation of the child and his physical and mental make-up, while others claim the reason is moral, as the mother's constant presence and influence are critical for the child's education, as may be suggested in the Torah. Still others consider the reason to lie in the fact that only the maternity of the child can be certain. But whatever the reasons, what is important is not the rational element of scientific investigation, but the religious element, which has been the determining factor in shaping the character of the nation and the Jewish family. It goes without saying that this law is deeply rooted in the soul of the nation and has affected its historical development and the stability of the national consciousness.

Consequently, a Jewish identity card must not be issued to a person who is unquestionably a gentile according to religious law, for it will be a forgery, no different from a counterfeit bill which is invalid.

Secondly, the Sages declare that "a man is not permitted to sell a fringed prayer shawl to a gentile," and the Gemara provides two reasons for this prohibition. The first is that he might attempt to marry a daughter of Israel, and the second, that he might walk beside the Jew and murder him (Minhot 43). We need not fear the latter circumstance in our country at this time. The former, however, is still valid even in Israel, not to mention abroad.

Generally speaking, the nature of the law and what it wishes to achieve are unclear. By an act of the Knesset, approved by the Government, halakha alone has exclusive authority over personal status and all related matters. Is it the intent of the Minister of the Interior to overturn a law passed by the national legislature? So long as this law is in force, there is no room to raise the question in practical terms. Clearly, anyone who is not Jewish according to religious law is not subject to Jewish law, in this case halakha. Undoubtedly, the Government does not wish to create difficulties for the citizens by making someone who is not Jewish according to halakha into a Jew who cannot marry a Jewish woman. And what will be the status in our country of this fake Jew, who in non-religious terms is considered Jewish but in religious terms will be pronounced a non-Jew in every sense?

There can be no question that rabbis abroad will not honor an identity card issued by the Israeli Ministry of the Interior. What is more, they will be forced to forbid the marriage to a Jew of anyone from Israel who cannot produce an identity card issued by a recognized authorized religious body.

The fear expressed by Israeli rabbis that if the registration law is passed it will bring about a rift and internecine division in the nation is in no way exaggerated. Nor is the concern that the law as conceived by the Minister of the Interior will encourage and increase the assimilation that is associated with intermarriage. As rabbis in the Diaspora, we fight determinedly against intermarriage in the clear understanding that it is the crucial factor in total assimilation and abandonment of Judaism. We employ preventive measures to guard against this plague that has broken out in Western countries. We forbid any man married to a non-Jewish woman from participating in any sacred ritual, and forbid the circumcision of a child born to a non-Jewish mother. These safeguards are intimidating, restraining those who might take intermarriage lightly but do not wish to renounce their membership in the Jewish people.

Now, a thoughtless individual will be able to "validate" himself and his children with the sanction of the Government of Israel. All he needs to do is to appear at the Israeli consulate abroad or before the registration clerks in Israel and declare in good faith that he and his children are Jewish. Has the Prime Minister not considered the devastating consequences of this registration bill for Jewry abroad?

Enacting this law will most certainly create a schism from another perspective as well. At this very moment, thoroughly assimilated persons in the United States are preparing a scheme to divide the nation and distinguish between Hebrews and Jews: on the one hand, Hebrews in the Jewish state with all the hallmarks of a nation, language, politics, economy and army, and on the other hand, Jews in the Diaspora as a barely religious entity who adapt to the way of life and culture of the nations in which they reside.

There is no need to spell out the terrible danger to our national unity represented by this notion that is liable to doom our people to utter assimilation.

Does the Government desire such a national division? It is crystal clear that the notion of secular nationality is devoid of all spiritual substance to fire the heart, and there can be no doubt that the secular culture growing stronger in Israel does not have the power to persuade erring Jews in the Diaspora not to become assimilated into foreign nations and tongues.

The Prime Minister's argument that the new registration statute is needed for reasons of security, so as to distinguish between a loyal citizen and an Arab citizen of Israel who may be suspected of criminal espionage and hostility to the state, is not a decisive reason for enacting this perilous law. Some other way to make this distinction must be found, and for this the Government is not in need of my advice. However, you must be aware that we in the Diaspora are also concerned for the survival and security of the state. We are well aware that the young country is surrounded by enemies. Nevertheless, we believe that the greater security and loyalty is that of the loyal Jewish hearts that cling to the tradition of the Torah. We religious Jews were bound heart and soul to the Land of Israel even when it was a ruin and wilderness. No word can cause the heart of an observant Jew to flutter like that name "Land of Israel." Religious Judaism will never cut its ties to the Holy Land. The miracle of the

establishment of the blossoming State of Israel strengthens our faith
in the God of Israel and our love for our Holy Land. All of us stand
ready to make any sacrifice that the security of the state may require
of us.

Why—I must ask—was it necessary to so unthinkingly reject the
unquestioned affection for the state in the Jewish world, to cause
such a shock and create such a storm for religious Jewry unwavering
in its devotion to the Torah and its love for Israel?

Mr. Prime Minister, we all stand in admiration of your achievements in establishing the State and your part in building it and hel-
ping it to flourish. Moreover, we acknowledge your efforts "to deepen
Jewish consciousness among Israeli youth, rooting it in the past and
historical legacy of the Jewish people, and to enhance its moral commitment to world Jewry in the awareness of the shared destiny and
historical continuity that unite the Jews of every generation throughout the world wherever they may live." I will therefore allow myself
to speak to you as one Jewish brother to another, and to express
what is in my heart and the heart of every faithful Jew. None of
these high goals with which you are concerned can exist except
through religion and the strengthening of its influence in education
and in political and social life. No other force can fill the role of
religion in our national life. We have been a thoroughly religious
entity since the time of our creation and birth. The change in the
views and outlook of the new generation growing up in Israel is no
more than a passing morbid crisis, and will not alter the religious
nature that is an integral part of the spiritual essence of every Jew.
Even those whose religious consciousness has been impaired still bear
a vibrant religious sense in their hearts!

Judaism is neither a religious sect nor a national entity in the conventional sense. It is our only national culture. We have no other
culture and never had. Spiritual nationality exists solely in the sphere
of religion, shaping the Jewish experience, the pattern of everyday
life, and the celebration of public and family holidays. It is a Jewish
moral code and a Jewish philosophy of life with a tradition going
back thousands of years and inseparably linked to the Torah given
us on Mt. Sinai.

We see the State of Israel as the first stage in the realization of
the national religious hope of countless generations who suffered,
who were tortured, slaughtered and killed, for their faith and hope
in redemption.

Does the Government of Israel have the right to ignore the philosophy and way of life that the Jewish people have always considered its national singularity and destiny in the world?

Does the Government of Israel have the right to stand by and adopt a stance of neutrality in regard to overriding crucial issues that will determine the human face of the next generation?

No one is asking that a democratic state impose any coercive measures on the life of the individual. There is no question that it has the right—in fact the duty—to afford all of its citizens equal rights without discrimination. This, however, does not lessen the duty of a national government to protect the autonomy of the national culture and to maintain a Jewish way of life as one of the principles of this culture.

The Government of Israel can not ignore its function of leading the nation and educating its children in the spirit of our culture. It is charged with stamping a national spiritual character on the life of the nation, a character that will symbolize Jewish autonomy in all its diversity.

What is it that we ask? Neither dominance nor special privileges. All we ask is that the Jewish State be the State of Judaism. Historical continuity, identification with the great figures of the nation, and promoting the tradition of the forefathers are not strictly religious matters. Rather, they are among the basic elements of any self-respecting culture.

Does it make no difference to the Government of Israel if a secular "gentile" perception prevails in the country and a new type of Hebrew is created that is totally divorced from the national tradition? Heaven forbid this should happen. The Jewish State must uphold the spirit of Judaism, and religious education must be a fundamental part of the official education program. Religious education is the more significant guarantee of the unity of the Jewish people in Israel and its spiritual links to world Jewry.

It is essential that the Jewish religion, the Jewish faith, again becomes an influential factor in our national life. To you, Mr. Prime Minister, who has had the honor of building and establishing the state, goes the task with which history and Divine Providence have charged you: to gather all your strength and concentrate it on a religious reawakening. Your power and influence are great, and you are a thousand times more understanding than the fellow members of your government, some of whom are infused with radical secular notions and some of whom are eager for a material self-interested policy devoid of any spiritual substance or foundation.

Whenever you wish to do so, you can consecrate the name of Heaven and the name of Israel by creating the shining character of the complete and perfect Jew whose way of life and spiritual and moral merit will serve as a living mirror of true Judaism, which, to our misfortune, has become mocked and defiled in the eyes of non-Jews by its distortion at the hands of those who take its name but do not live in its spirit.

"I believe in perfect faith that this Torah will not be altered, nor will there be another Torah from our Creator, blessed be His name" [Maimonides].

With all my blessings and with all due appreciation and respect for the Prime Minister of the State of Israel,

Yekhiel Yaakov Weinberg

44. TSEVI (HARRY A.) WOLFSON

An historian and scholar of the history of philosophy, Wolfson (1887–1974) was born near Vilna and studied at the Slobodka yeshiva. In 1903 he moved to the USA, where he received a Ph.D. in philosophy from Harvard University in 1915 and became a professor of Hebrew literature and philosophy. The winner of numerous prizes and honors, he was a member of the American Academy of Jewish Research and its president from 1935–1937, as well as a member of the American Academy of Arts and Sciences. In 1958 he was awarded the American Council of Scholarly Associations prize. Wolfson's many works include The Philosophy of Spinoza (1934) and The Philosophy of the Church Fathers (1964).

7 January 1959

Dear Mr. Ben-Gurion,

I am honored to reply to your query about the Government of Israel's decision concerning registration guidelines. The ruling for an uncircumcised son born to a non-Jewish mother in a mixed marriage is firmly established in traditional religious law. The Government of Israel, founded on the principle of freedom of conscience and religion, naturally has neither the power, nor, I am certain, the desire, to interfere in religious affairs which are matters of conscience. Just as it does not establish a tribunal to force a father to circumcise his son, so, clearly, it will not take it upon itself to post policemen to prevent pious Jews from excluding from their religious midst those whom they do not consider Jewish. As I can see from your letter, the Knesset resolution regarding registration guidelines does not seek to alter the title Jew in its traditional religious sense. Rather, its intention is merely to add another meaning to the term, a secular political meaning that is needed, according to your letter, for security reasons. Thus the children of mixed marriages who are Jews at heart, but have not entered the covenant of Abraham, will also be registered under the designation Jew in its new meaning. The decision is therefore a political regulation and not a religious one. The question is consequently twofold. First, does halakha permit a person to be called Jewish if he is not a Jew by its standards? Secondly, is it right and proper for the Government of Israel to officially remove the title Jew from its exclusively religious meaning and add to it a secular political meaning?

As to the first question, with all due respect for those with the authority to rule in religious matters, I will allow myself to express an opinion on the matter as "the Torah is bound and placed in a corner" for anyone who wishes to learn from it. The response to this question, while not stated explicitly, can be deduced from the general rule. We know from the Sages that he who calls Abraham Abram is violating a positive or a positive and a negative commandment, but nowhere does it say that he who calls an uncircumcised gentile a Jew is violating either a positive or a negative commandment. On the contrary, from the words of the Sages we learn that we are entitled to call a Jew anyone who has renounced idolatry.

As to the second question, the answer must be in the negative. I say this for the following reasons. First, Jews in every community in the Diaspora are still called Jews in the traditional religious sense of the term. Despite all their differences of opinion on religious matters, to the extent that they are organized, it is on a religious basis. Even the non-religious secular individuals among us in their various forms are still called Jews, yet no new secular meaning has been added to the term as a result. They are called Jews because of their origin and past, whose memory has not been forgotten. Jewish secularism in the Diaspora can be defined only in the negative sense, as an escape or withdrawal. It has no positive content or public cohesiveness. If some secular individuals exist and act as Jews, it is only by virtue of the organized religious communities in which they live, in whose activities they participate, and to whose synagogues they may sometimes belong on whatever pretext they choose. In and of themselves, they are not viable as Jews. Therefore, it would be improper for the Government of Israel to officially remove the title Jew from its specifically religious meaning and turn it into a dubious term with two opposite meanings, religious and secular. There may be a need for a single term to designate adherents of Judaism as one particular group as opposed to the adherents of other faiths, especially now that the term Israel has ceased to be a purely religious title and become a political name. However, there is still Judaism in the world, just as there is Christianity and Islam, and as the name Christian or Muslim has only one meaning, the religious sense, so the name Jew should have only one—religious—meaning. Otherwise, we would have to coin some other name with a single religious meaning to designate adherents of Judaism. Is it not rather late in the history of Judaism to start looking for a new name for its adherents?

Secondly, the question before you is not a personal matter whose answer might be based solely on the nature of the specific case. It has implications for a public issue of interest to many, and there is reason to fear that it might lead to misunderstanding and misperceptions. Thus, as we are cautioned to avoid even the possibility of wrongdoing, so we should avoid the possibility of wrong hearing. While the distinction between a political measure and a religious measure may be correct in and of itself, it appears somewhat artificial, specious, and perhaps even casuistic, and it is doubtful whether those who hear it will understand it correctly and not interpret it in a manner other than was intended. We should be concerned lest the decision on registration guidelines be seen as a bold act on the part of the Government of Israel to high-handedly decide a burning issue that has been a bone of contention for some two thousand of years between us and the Christians, and for about a hundred years within our own camps. We all know the distinction made by the one who called himself the "apostle of the gentiles" between "Israel by flesh" and "Israel of God." We also know that the reform rabbis in America debated the question of accepting converts without requiring circumcision for several years before eventually deciding to allow it for adults, on the assurance of those accepted in this manner that they will perform the ritual of circumcision for any sons born to them in the future.

Therefore, it would not be proper for the Government of Israel to afford those who still consider themselves "Israel of God" the opportunity to proclaim: the man of Tarsus has finally triumphed over them. Neither would it be proper for the Government of Israel to make a decision that might mistakenly be perceived as intervening in a debate between two religious factions and arriving at a conclusion that does not accord with the views of either.

I am cognizant of the fact that you must contend with a practical problem that requires a practical solution. However, in our religious vocabulary there are already several terms for those who are neither thoroughly Jewish nor thoroughly non-Jewish. The visionary

Sages recognized that in the future there would be self-made proselytes, and perhaps they also envisioned the emergence of self-made
Jews. If there is a real need in the State of Israel to invent a single term to denote a person who is not a Muslim or Christian, but
also not a religious Jew, but wishes to be Jewish in the secular
national sense, then the most fitting name for him would be "Hebrew."
Indeed, the secular cultural nationalism that appears to be taking
shape in Israel is founded on the Hebrew language, which is a symbol of its external singularity and internal vitality. However, I do
not wish to propose here the term that should be used in the matter at hand. I have no doubt that the linguistic scholars in Israel
will succeed in introducing the most fitting name. The main thing
is, do not tamper with the name "Jew."

Respectfully,

Tsevi Wolfson

45. AARON ZEITLIN

A poet in Hebrew and Yiddish and philosopher of Jewish aesthetics, Zeitlin (1898–1973) grew up in Gomel, Vilna, and Warsaw. His first collection of poetry was published in 1922, and in 1926 he was named literary editor of a Yiddish daily in Warsaw. He published a play in Yiddish in 1938, before emigrating, the following year, to the United States, where he worked in New York as a Yiddish journalist on the Jewish Morning Journal and a Professor of Hebrew Literature at the Jewish Theological Seminary of America. Zeitlin had a strong influence on the Jewish literary world in America after World War II, and paid frequent visits to Israel. His books include Between Fire and Salvation (Hebrew) and Selected Poems (Yiddish; Vols. 1–2, 1947; Vol. 3, 1957).

10 December 1958

Dear Mr. Prime Minister,

I hereby present my opinion regarding the registration guidelines for the children of mixed marriages in Israel.

I would like to begin by noting that I do not belong to any particular Zionist party, and accordingly not to any religious Zionist party either. My opinion, therefore, is the view of a Jewish individual who reflects on the problems of the nation and responds to them as a writer, and not the view of a person whose ideas are shaped by the prevailing stance of his party.

It should be established that in the State of Israel, the political-civil identity is Israeli, whereas Jew—not only abroad but in Israel as well—is primarily a religious concept which also contains a national meaning by virtue of the fact that Judaism is a national religion. It is national for the simple and obvious reason that only one nation in the entire world represents this religion. No reasonable person would deny this fact, and there is no need for philosophical casuistry to prove it. This evident fact gives rise to a second fact: although the Jews are divided into the religious and the non-religious, there is not one of them who is not Jewish by religion. All Jews, without exception, are Jewish by religion, including those who are non-religious by definition. No Jew can nullify the fact that he is a Jew by religion, even if his views are atheistic, because he was circumcised. We know that even a convert to Christianity, who forfeits his Jewish rights, is not exempt from fulfilling certain Jewish obligations, such as giving a get [a bill of divorce] to his wife who has remained a Jew.

These two interrelated facts—that only the Jewish people represent the Jewish religion, and that every Jew, even a transgressor, is considered a Jew by religion whether he wants to be it or not (there is no choice involved here, as it derives from the inherent structure of historical Judaism)—these two facts are responsible for having preserved our existence, and no political independence can erase or enfeeble them. The concept of Jew cannot be different in the State of Israel than it is in the Diaspora, as then we would become two peoples. What I mean is that its consistency—the single consistent definition of the term "Jew"—is the bridge between the Diaspora and Israel. The only difference is that a second concept, which relates to citizens of various religions, has been added in Israel, and that is the term "Israeli."

This being the case, there is no room for a civil-political Jew. If a person wishes to be called a Jew, rather than simply an Israeli, he cannot do so without becoming a Jew in the religious sense, that is, without converting, or—as you put it your letter—without a "ceremony" (this is not the proper term in respect to religion, as it does not perform "ceremonies" but rather commandments). The principle of freedom of religion and conscience, which are guaranteed in the State of Israel and are precious to us all, do not, to begin with, apply to becoming Jewish or converting, which is unquestionably and essentially a religious concept. Secular-administrative conversion is a contradiction in terms, a total absurdity. The talk of some sort of national conversion—that is, civil-secular conversion—(I am referring here primarily to that non-Jewish Polish journalist who claims to want to have her son "converted" in this way)—and similar ideas are baseless, and threaten to fragment the Jewish people. They constitute a grave danger to the very survival of the nation.

We have had "lion proselytes" [who became Jewish for fear of lions, rather than for reasons of conscience] who became enemies of our people, and in the United States we have had the pleasure of accepting "temporary proselytes." All we need now are registration proselytes or "declaration Jews." Alongside religious Jews and Jews by religion, we will create—if the guidelines are not revoked—

a third type of so-called Jew, "passport Jews," "Jews of convenience," a new version of the "Hebrew-speaking Gentiles" condemned by the late Dr. Klausner, or worse. If the registry is necessary for administrative purposes, there is a perfectly simple solution: the child of a mixed marriage should be registered not as a Jew, but as the child of a Jewish father. This would achieve two things: sufficient information for the evidential purposes of the population registry, and an easing of tensions, as no religious Jew would be averse to a mere statement of fact.

This is a civil registry, and precisely for this reason no government has the right to register a child as a Jew if he is not a Jew in the only true sense of the term—the religious sense as accepted by the nation. Should the Government assume this right, it will be interfering in a domain in which it has no jurisdiction, the domain of religious life, and this would constitute a form of anti-religious coercion. It would be abominable to use the civil-administrative registry in order to create "artificial Jews." The historical structure of an ancient people cannot be altered by force or decree. This is not the proper approach. We may assume that more than one or two of the future "registration Jews" are likely to adopt some faith or another in the course of time, and as they will remain Jews by virtue of the registry, they will be called Jews. We will find we have Christian "Jews," and Muslim "Jews"—and then what will we do? Such a situation is liable to shatter the Jewish people from within and lead not to the ingathering and integration of the exiles, but to an utter rift between the Jews in Israel and Diaspora Jewry, so that eventually we will have two peoples who are not only different from each other, but also—Heaven forbid—hostile to each other. Nor do I believe that "the mixed couples who come here, especially from the countries of Eastern Europe, lead to total integration into the Jewish people." If a non-Jewish mother, like that journalist from Poland, refuses outright to have her son converted according to religious law and categorically demands that he be registered as a Jew on the basis of something that does not exist and never will, something unknown in Jewish tradition or consciousness, that is, non-religious conversion, which, as stated above, is an absurd contradiction in terms—then your diagnosis is overly optimistic. The situation is liable to lead not to "total integration into the Jewish people," but just the opposite.

The agreement of a Jewish father and non-Jewish mother to register their child as a Jew without actually making him a Jew is of no value, as it is merely a private agreement. Halakha, Jewish heritage and Jewish consciousness do not sanction this and never will.

Our generation has seen one case of so-called secular "conversion" that did not succeed and had no chance of success. I am referring here to the Hebrew poet Elisheva Zhirkova, who was mistakenly assumed to be a convert. In an edifying letter which she wrote at the end of her life to the Hebrew writer Rabbi Dr. M.Z. Reisin (which was published by Dr. Reisin in the New York journal Bitzaron), she states candidly that since she never underwent religious conversion she does not regard herself as a Jew—despite the fact that she is a Hebrew author and poet living in Israel.

To sum up:

1) We must not create a new type of "Jew" by guidelines or decrees;

2) Such a scheme would be tantamount to interference in religious life—as "Jew" is a religious term (and consequently also a national one)—and would constitute a form of anti-religious coercion that is prohibited by Israeli law;

3) The child of a mixed marriage should not be registered as a Jew, but as the child of a Jewish father, and no more. This statement of fact in no way limits his rights, and, on the other hand, prevents the creation of a chasm between Israel and the Diaspora.

With the blessing of rebirth, respectfully,

Aaron Zeitlin

46. SHLOMO Y. ZEVIN

A rabbi and religious scholar, Zevin (1885–1978) was born in Broisk, Byelorussia, and studied in the yeshivas of Mir and Broisk. At the age of 18, he began a correspondence with the greatest rabbinical scholars. He served as the rabbi of several communities in Russia, and following the Communist Revolution was elected the Jewish representative to the Ukrainian National Assembly. Although the Soviet regime originally allowed Zevin to publish a monthly journal on halakhic subjects, Yagdil Ha-Torah, it reversed its decision in 1934. Around the same time, Zevin received permission to immigrate to Palestine. From 1936–1945 he published a weekly magazine devoted to halakha, and in 1959 was awarded the Israel Prize for religious literature. Zevin served as a member of the Supreme Rabbinical Council from 1965, and was the editor of The Talmudic Encyclopedia of Halakha. His works include Holidays in Halakha (1944), Hassidic Stories (1955–57), and Authors and Books (1959).

15 Tebet 5719

Dear Mr. Prime Minister,

I am asked in your letter of 13 Heshvan 5719 (which I received somewhat later) to give my opinion on the question of registering the religion and nationality of the children of mixed marriages whose parents wish to register them as Jews. From the explanation of the question, I see that in addition to this issue, there are two further points: a) The responses to the question will be brought before a committee of three ministers appointed by the Government, after which this committee will decide, or make recommendations for a Government decision, on the ultimate solution to the problem; b) the Government has already resolved on a related issue that the religion (the religion!) of an adult will be listed as "Jewish" pursuant to a declaration in good faith that the individual is a Jew and not a member of another religion!

I shall not conceal the fact that the two further points confuse the question of the registration of minors and make it difficult to provide an answer. How can a committee of Government ministers or the

Government itself take upon itself, or be endowed with, the authority to rule on the religion and nationality of an individual? This is
not a political or administrative question. It has been firmly established in halakha since the time of Mount Sinai and to this day,
and has been rooted in the life of the nation in Israel and the
Diaspora for thousands of years, that a Jew is only someone who is
born to Jewish parents, or at least to a Jewish mother, and that a
child born to a non-Jewish mother is a non-Jew in every way, unless
he undergoes conversion according to halakha. This is not as appears
on page 3 of your letter, whether in addition to the consent of the
parents some "additional ceremony" should be required. It is not a
question of a "ceremony," but of conversion—and what does that
have to do with ministerial committees and the Government? Even
if all the "kings of the East and West" and all the "Jewish intellectuals" were to assemble and decide whatever they decided, could
they undo even the smallest detail of reality and make a non-Jew
into a Jew? A non-Jew can be the wisest of the gentiles, or the most
righteous of the gentiles, but he will still be a gentile. The opposite
is also true: a Jew can be utterly wicked and sinful, but he will
always remain a Jew, and his children—from a Jewish mother!—will
be Jews for all generations. And what does the law against "discrimination between individuals on the basis of differences in . . .
nationality [or] religion" (page 2) have to do with this issue? Do
"equal rights" give a non-Jew, who does not wish to convert, the
right to register himself as a Jew? One or the other: the child can
either remain a gentile and enjoy all the civil rights afforded by the
State of Israel to non-Jews as well, or he can be converted and registered as a Jew.

The question would be equally puzzling if it referred to the registration of "nationality" alone, as Judaism does not recognize any
distinction between nationality and religion. It is even more puzzling
as your letter states explicitly that "determining the religion of Israeli
citizens is . . . essential," and the question relates specifically to registration of a child's religion. On an issue of religion, even if there
is doubt as to a certain instance, the Chief Rabbinate of Israel is
the authorized body—recognized by the State as well—to rule. What
have ministers and the Government to do with it? And what authority or jurisdiction do "Jewish intellectuals," to whom the query is
addressed, have in regard to a religious matter? Is any expert in a
particular field, whether a scholar, writer, poet, scientist, or anything

else, authorized to rule on halakha? I would like you to know that the Chief Rabbinate does not rewrite the rulings or enact religious laws, and it is not within its jurisdiction to do so. Rather, it determines what halakha says and is authorized to state what is in halakha and what solution it provides for a given problem.

Furthermore, the very concept of "mixed marriages" does not exist in the Torah, and there is no such thing as a "mixed marriage." Jewish wedding vows are not binding for a non-Jewish man or woman, and a man who takes a non-Jewish wife has done nothing, for without consecrated vows there is no marriage. The term "mixed marriages" is merely a popular phrase to describe a situation existing in reality, a reality that the prophet of the return from exile in the time of Ezra decried: "Judah has broken faith; abhorrent things have been done" [Mal. 2:11]. The only "question" relates to their children, and there is no question here at all, as it has been ruled quite simply that when a non-Jewish man has relations with a Jewish woman, the child is a Jew, and when a Jewish man has relations with a non-Jewish woman, the child is a gentile and subject to conversion like any other non-Jew (Mishnah Kiddushin 66b; Gemara, ibid., 68b and elsewhere; Maimonides, Issurei Bi'ah, 15:3–4; Shulkhan Arukh, Eben ha-Ezer, section 4., par. 19 and section 8, par. 5).

Why, Mr. Prime Minister, have you posed the question only in regard to minors, when "the Government has determined that the religion or nationality of adults will be listed as 'Jewish' if they declare themselves in good faith to be Jewish and not a member of another religion"? This "decision" is in many ways more serious and harmful than the question of minors! The issue is not whether to believe a person who declares that he is a Jew born to Jewish parents. Even from the point of view of halakha it is appropriate to believe him. But it has also been decided that it is enough for a person to declare that he is now a Jew and not a member of another religion, so that even a gentile whose parents, grandparents, and great-grandparents were gentiles can declare that he is a Jew and has no other religion and this makes him a Jew! Just like that, without conversion, merely by making a simple declaration "in good faith"? Even if this decision is taken a thousand times, will it turn a non-Jew into a Jew?

This is no more than a foul attack on the soul of Judaism and on the Jewish people and the State of Israel. It is destined to shake— and is already shaking!—the whole of the Jewish people from one end of the world to the other. It will create terrible confusion and chaos and lead to a huge rift between Jews in Israel and between Israeli Jews and Diaspora Jewry, with unforeseeable consequences.

If the honorable Prime Minister desires the unity of the nation, the honor of the State of Israel, and a bond between Israel and the Diaspora—and I have no doubt that you do—you must revoke the decision regarding adults along with the question of minors, and return the situation to its previous status, as it has stood for generations: no non-Jew, whether an adult or a child, can become a Jew without undergoing proper conversion.

With my greatest esteem.

Respectfully yours,

Shlomo Yossef Zevin

GLOSSARY OF HEBREW WORDS

Agudat-Israel	(lit. the Association of Israel) the political movement of Orthodox allegiance created at the beginning of the 20th century.
Aggadah	narratives found in the Talmud.
Alef	(lit. "a") outlet of the Canaanite movement.
Ashkenazi (plur. *Ashkenazim*)	or Ashenazic (English) refers to individuals who relate to, or originate from, the Yiddish-speaking Eastern European Judaism.
Avoda zarah	(lit. foreign work) designates all forms of cult outside Judaism.
Babylonian Talmud	the rulings of the Oral Law completed by the Scholars of the Babylonian academies, including commentaries, discussions, metaphors and legends.
Bar-mitsva	(lit. son of command) rite de passage of boys taking place at the age of thirteen.
Beshem omro	(lit. In the name of the one who says it) designates the source of the locution.
Beth Din	(lit. the house of judgment) rabbinical court.
Bnei Akiva	(lit. Sons of Akiba) national-religious youth movement.
Baraitha	(plur. braithot) a view expressed in the Talmud opposed to that of the Mishnah.
Brera	(lit. "choice") name of a radical movement in American Judaism.
Brit Shalom	(lit. alliance for peace) designates an organization of intellectuals which, in the 1930s, supported the dialogue of Jews and Palestinians.
Shechinah/shekhina	expression designating the divine presence among men.
Shnat hashemitah	compulsory sabbatical year for cultivated land.
Dam naki	pure/innocent blood.
Dayan (plur. *dayanim*)	judges of a Rabbinical Court.
Dougri/Dugri	(from Arabic, lit. frank) designate direct and laconic speech.
Eda (plur. *edot*)	a ethnic division from within the Jewish nation.
Edim	witnesses in court.
Galut	(lit. exile) the term which expresses the Jewish conception of the condition and feelings of uprootedness from the Biblical homeland.
Gedolei hatorah	(lit. the great men of the Bible) refers to the Sages and Scholars of the Law.

Gemara	the part of the Talmuld which consists of comments of the Mishna.
Ger (plur. *Gerim*)	1. a foreigner in a given society; 2. a converted Jew.
Ger gamoor	a person who has converted by following all the conditions required.
Ger aryot	(lit. foreigner of the lyons) refers to the inhabitants of Cuth who converted to Judaism under the threat of lyons sent by God.
Ger garour	(lit. a foreigner who is pushed) a person who lives among Jews and assimilates to them without formal conversion.
Ger toshav	(lit. a foreigner who resides) a non-Jew who lives among Jews.
Ger tsedek	(lit. a foreigner who [achieved what] is right) a person who has converted to Judaism and has become a Jew.
Gerout/ Gerut	the institution of the conversion to Judaism.
Giour/ Giur	conversion to Judaism.
Gola or galut	(lit. exile) the dispersion of Jews when understood as exile.
Gush Emunim	(lit. Faction of the Faithful) a political-religious movement which was created after the 1967 Six-Day War and aspired to the annexation and colonization of the Palestinian territories occupied by Israel.
Hashomer Hatsair	(lit. the young guard) Zionist-socialist youth movement.
Haggada (of Passover)	(lit. legend) the ritual narration of the exit of the Israelites from Egypt and which is told during the evening of Passover.
Hakham	(lit. intelligent) scholar of the Law.
Halakha	(lit. law) the rulings of the Oral Law committed to writing in the Talmud.
Hamarat dat	religious conversion outside Judaism.
Hanuka/ Khanuka	Jewish holiday celebrating the victory of the Maccabees.
Haskalah	(lit. instruction or knowledge) designates the Englightment movement which emerged among German Jews at the end of the 18th century and later spread over in Eastern Europe.
Hassidim/ Khassidim	followers of Baal Shem Tov who asserted the religious importance of emotional fervor.
Hassidim of Gour (Gur), Habad etc.	various trends which are more or less distinct from each other, within hassidic judaism.

Havoura/ Khavura	(lit. group) designate a model of communitarian religiosity relating to reconstructionist Judaism.
Hillel and *Shamai schools*	two competing schools of study of the oral law which prevailed at the end of the first century B.C. Hillel and his followers showed flexibility where Shamai and his students were more dogmatic.
Hiloula/ Hilula	festivities marking ritual pilgrimages to tombs of holy men.
Irgoun/ Irgun	(lit. organization) a armed Jewish underground which fought against the British mandate in the 1940s.
Ivri	Hebrew.
Kabbalah	the traditional esoteric teachings of Judaism and Jewish mysticism.
Kashrut	the Jewish dietary laws.
Kelal Israel	the community of all Jews in the world as seen as one solidaristic whole.
Khassidé umot haolam	(lit. the faithful to the nations of the world) refers to non-Jews who helped Jews in time of trouble and persecution; often translated as "the Just among the nations".
Kherem derabbénu Guershom	the ostracism ruled by Guershom (960–1028) against bigamy.
Kibbutz (plur. *Kibbutzim*)	collectif settlement.
Kibbutz galuyot	(lit. engathering of the exiles) a principle according to which all Jews of the diaspora should ingather in Israel.
Kidushim	rituals attached to the wedding.
Knesset	Israeli parliament.
Lashon hara	malicious gossip.
Malakhim	angels.
Mamzer	(lit. bastard) a person born from a married woman and a father who is not her husband.
Maskilim	(lit. cultivated persons) refers to the followers of the Haskala movement.
Melakha	work.
Merriba	(lit. quarrel) alludes to Moses when he credited himself for the miracle of the water that sprung from the rock, in the desert.
Mila	circumcision.
Mishna	the text of the Oral Law found in the Talmud, and by extension to the Oral Law itself.
Midrash	designates a kind of rabbinical literature comprising at the same time a compilation of rulings, public speeches, legendary narratives and references to chapters of the Bible.

Mikveh	ritual bath, and by extension, a house or a pool for ritual baths.
Mimuna	an originally Jewish Moroccan custom, it consists in the celebration of bread, at the end of Passover, when it is again allowed for consumption after one week of abstinence.
Minyan	a group of at least ten men that is allowed to hold public prayers.
Mishkan	the Tabernacle which was the principal mobile site of cult before the Temple of Jerusalem was built.
Mitnaggedim (plural of Mitnagged)	(lit. opponents) the followers of the orthodox trend which opposed Hassidism and continued to emphasize the study of holy texts as the principal form of religious experience.
Mitsva	command of the religious law.
Mityahed (plur. *mityahadim*)	a person who is attracted by Judaism but does not convert according to the requirements of the halakha.
Mizug galuyot	(lit. the fusion of exiles) the principle that all exiles should melt into a new homogeneous society.
Mizrakhi (plur. *Mizrakhim*)	(lit. oriental or eastern) a Jew originating from North Africa or the Middle-East, and more generally, of non-Ashkenazi origin.
Mo'etzet Gedolei HaTorah	(lit. Council of Great Torah Scholars) the supreme body of Agudat-Israel consisting of leading spiritual figures.
Moshav (plur. *Moshavim*)	cooperative villages.
Oleh (plur. *Olim*)	(lit. who climbs) Jewish immigrants to Israel.
Omen	educator or provider.
Parah adumah	a red cow the sacrifice of which held special and mystical meanings for Jews.
Perutah	smallest amount of money.
Pessakh	Passover.
Pharisees (or *Prushim*)	as opposed to *Sadducees* (or *Sdukim*) the party which requested, during the Hasmonean regime, devotion to the religious law exclusively, as opposed to the party which firstly favored the interests of the State.
Sai'ir lea-zazel	scapegoat.
Sanhedrin	legislative Assembly of Scholars during the Second Commonwealth.

Seder	(lit. order) the family commemoration of Passover.
Shas	the leading mizrakhi ultra-orthodox party in contemporary Israel.
Shoah	(lit. cataclysm) designates the Nazi genocide against the Jews.
Shtern Group	a Jewish undergound which fought the British mandate over Palestine.
Shulkhan Arukh	(lit. *dressed table*) name of an authoritative Jewish code written by Joseph Caro and first printed in 1565 in Venice.
Tanna (plur. *tannaim*)	compiler of the Talmud.
Tashlikh	a ceremony of purification held on Rosh Ha-Shanah, the New Year celebration.
Talmud of Jerusalem	the work done by Scholars of Judea, parallelly to those of Babylonia.
Tami	a small mizrakhi-ethnic and religious party active in Israel at the end of the 1970s.
Toeva	abomination (in a religious sense).
Torah	(lit. teaching, doctrine or law) refers to the Bible, especially the Pentateuch, but may also be for all the body of Jewish laws.
Tumah	impurity (in a religious sense).
Tsedek	justice.
Yeshiva (plur. yeshivot)	religious academy.
Yehudi toshav (plur. *Yehudim toshavim*)	(lit.: Jew-resident) a non-Jew residing among non-Jews and who tends to assimilate to them.
Yishuv	the pre-State Jewish community of Palestine.
Yom Kippur	the Day of Atonement, marked by fast.
Yored (plur. *Yordim*)	(lit. the one who descends) emigrant from Israel.

REFERENCES

Sources[1]

Ancikolpedia mikrait (Biblical Encyclopedia)
Ancikolpedia ivrit (Hebrew Encyclopedia)
Bible
Hayad hakhazaka, Hilkhot musarei kapara, Hilkhot melakhim ou-milkhamot, Hilkhot issourei bia, Techouvot ha-rambam by Maimonides/Rambam
Michna (Chapters "Yebamot", "Massekhet guerim", "yadim")
Midrachey Halakha: Mekhilta, Safra, Sifri
Babylonian Talmud (Chapters "Avoda zara", "Kritot", "Roch Hachana", "Bekhorot")
Midrachey Agada ("Devarim Raba")
Talmud of Jerusalem (Chapters "Chekalim", "Pessakhim")

Rabbinical literature

Itzchak Ben Reuven Alberzloni, *Azharot*, Livurno: Tartsav
Moshé ben Yakov Mekotsi, *Sefer Mitsvot Gadol*, Jerusalem: Tachka
M.I. Brich, *Khelkat Yacov*, Jérusalem: Tashya
Moché Finchtein, *Igrot Moche*, NY: Tachav
Rai'ah Kook, *Daat Cohen*, Jérusalem, Tachak
Ch. Z. Lipschitz, *Chemdat Cholomo*, Jérusalem: Tachkakh

Bibliography

Abramov, S.Z. (1976) *Perpetual Dilemma—Jewish Religion in a Jewish State*, London: Associate University P.
Abrams, D. & Hogg, M.A. (1990) "An Introduction to the Social Identity Approach", in Abrams, D. & Hogg, M.A. (eds) *Social Identity Theory: Constructive and Critical Advances*, NY: Harvester Wheatsheaf, 1–9
Agassi, J. (1990) *Bein dat le-leom: Likrat zehut leoumit israelit (Religion and nation: toward an Israeli national identity)*, Tel-Aviv: Papyrus
Agassi, J., Buber-Agassi, I., Brant, M. (1991) *Mihou iehoudi? (Who is a Jew?)* Tel-Aviv: Kivunim
Alderman, G. (1989) *London Jewry and London Politics 1889–1986*, London: Routledge
———— (1994) "British Jewry: Religious Community or Ethnic Minority?" in Webber, J. (ed.) *Jewish Identities in the New Europe*, Oxford: Oxford Centre for Hebrew and Jewish Studies and the Littman Library of Jewish Civilization: 189–192
Alon, G. (Tachlaz) *Mekhkarim be-toldot israel (Research in the History of Israel)*, vols. 1 and 2, Tel-Aviv: ha-kibboutz ha-meouchad
———— (Tachlaz) *Toldot ha-iehoudim be-eretz israel be-tekufat ha michana ve-hatalmoud (History of the Jews in the Land of Israel at the time of the Michna and the Talmud)*, Tel-Aviv: ha-kibboutz ha-meoukhad
Amara, M. (1997) *Alimout politit be-kerev ha-aravim be-israel (Political violence among Arabs in Israel)*, Guivat Chaviva: Institute for Peace Research

---

[1] All references to sources concern widely accepted editions of these works in Hebrew.

Anderson, B. (1991) *Imagined Communities: Reflections on the Origins and spread of Nationalism*, London: Verso

Antonowsky, A. & Katz, A.D. (1979) *From the Golden to the Promised Land*, Darby, Pa: Norwood; Jerusalem: Academic Press

Appiah, K.A. (1995) "African Identities", in Nicholson, L. & Seidman, S. (eds) *Social Postmodernism: Beyond Identity Politics*, Cambridge: Cambridge University Press, 103–115

Aptekman, D. (1993) "Jewish emigration from the USSR, 1990–1992: Trends and Motivations" *Jews and Jewish Topics in the Soviet Union and Eastern Europe*, 1 (20), 15–33

Apter, D.E. (1987) *Rethinking Development: Modernization, Dependency and Postmodern Politics*, Newbury Park: Sage Publications

Archer, M.S. (1996) *Culture and Agency: The Place of Culture in Social Theory*, Cambridge: Cambridge UP

Arieli, J. (1986) 'Ha-et ha-khadacha ou-baiat ha-secularizatsia' (Modern times and the problem of secularisation), in J. Gafni, J. Motskin (éditeurs) *Kehouna ve-meloukha, iakhasei dat ou-medina be-israel ou-ba-amim (Clergy and Monarchy: religion and State relations in Israel and among the nations)*, Jerusalem: Shazar Institut, 165–216

Auerbach, J.S. (1990) *Rabbis and Lawyers*, Bloomington, IN.: Indiana University Press

Avineri, S. (1981) *The Making of Modern Zionism: The Intellectual Origins of the Jewish State* NY: Basic Books

Avi-Yona (Tachal) *Be-iemei roma ve-bizantium, historia medinit che iehoudei eretz-israel le-min mered bar-kokhba ve-ad rechit ha-kibouch ha-aravi (In the days of Rome and Byzantium: Jews in the Land of Israel from the Bar-Kokhba Revolt to the Arab Conquest)*, Jerusalem: Bialik Inst

Bachi, R. (1956) 'A Statistical analysis of the revival of Hebrew in Israel' *Scripta Hierosolymitana* 3: 179–247

———— (1974) *The Population of Israel* Jerusalem: The Hebrew University of Jerusalem

Bacon, G.C. (1996) *The Politics of Tradition: Agudat Yisrael in Poland, 1916–1939*, Jerusalem: Magnes Press

Bade, K.J. (1991) "Immigration and Integration in Germany: Historical Background and Present Status" in Troen, I.S. & Bade, K.J. (eds) (1991) *Returning Home: Immigration and Absorption into their Homelands of Germans and Jews from the Former Soviet Union*, Beer Sheva: Humphrey Institute for Social Ecology—Ben-Gurion University of the Negev: 2–10

Bahloul, J. (1990) "What you remember and whose son you are: North African Jewish families and the past" in Fishbane, S. & Lightstone, J.N. *Essays on the Social Scientific Study of Judaism and Jewish Society*, Montreal: Concordia University, 217–230

Balibar, E. (1995) "Culture and Identity" in Rajchman, J. (ed.) *Identity in Question*, NY: Routledge, 173–196

Bamberger, B.J. (1935), *Proselytism, in the Talmudic Period*, New York: Ktav Pub

Banks, M. (1996) *Ethnicity: Anthropological Constructions*, London: Routledge

Banton, M.P. (1983) *Racial and Ethnic Competition* Cambridge: Cambridge U.P.,

Baron, Ch. (Tachkaz) *Historia khevratit ve-datit chel am israel (Social and Religious History of the Peope of Israel)*, vols. 1 et 2, Ramat-Gan: Massada

Bar-On, D., Sela, A. (1991) 'Maagal ha-ksamim: bein hitiachvout le-metsiout ve-hitiakhasout la-choa be-kerev tseirim israeliim' ('The vicious circle: from immigration to reality and the relation to the Holocaust among young Israelis'), *Psichologia*, b/5: 126–138

Barth F. (1969) "Introduction" Barth, F. (ed.) *Ethnic Groups and Boundaries* Boston: Little Brown

———— (1997) "How is the self conceptualized? Variations among cultures" in Neisser, U. and Jopling, D.A. (eds) *The Conceptual Self in Context: Culture, Experience, Self-Understanding*, Cambridge: Cambridge University Press, 75–91

Barth, F. (ed.) (1969) *Ethnic Groups and Boundaries*, Boston: Little Brown
Baubock, R. (1994) *Transnational Citizenship*, UK: Edward Elgar
——— (1998) "The Crossing and Blurring of Boundaries in International Migration: Challenges for Social and Political Theory", in Baubock, R. and Rundell (eds) *Blurred Boundaries: Migration, Ethnicity, Citzenship*, Aldershot (UK): Ashgate, 17–52
Bauman, Z. (1996) "From Pilgrim to tourist—or a short history of identity", in Hall, S. and Du Gay, P. (eds) *Questions of Cultural Identity*, London: Sage, 18–36
——— (1998) "Parvenu and pariah: hereos and victims of modernity" in Good, J. and Velody, I. (eds) *The Politics of Modernity*, Cambridge: Cambridge University Press, 23–35
Beaudrillard, J. (1988) *The Evil Demon of Images*, Sydney: University of Sydney
Bell, D. (1975) 'Ethnicity and Social Change' in Glazer, N., Moynihan, D.P. *Ethnicity: Theory and Experience* Cambridge: Harvard University Press, 141–174
Beller, S. (1989) *Vienna and the Jews, 1867–1938: A Cultural History*, Cambridge: Camb. UP
Beloff, M. (1994) "The Jews of Europe in the Age of a New *Volkerwanderung*", in Webber, J. *op. cit.*: 35–41
Ben Amos, A., Beit El, A. (1996) 'Tekassim, khinoukh ve-historia: iom ha-choa ve-iom ha-zikaron be-beit ha-sefer be-israel' (Rituals, education and history: The Choa Commemoration in Israeli schools) in Ektes, A., Paldakhay, R. (eds) *Khinoukh ve-historia (Education and History)*, Jerusalem: Shazar Centre
Ben Zeev, I. (Tachkav) *Guerim ve-guiour (Converts and Conversion in the past and today)*, Jérusalem: Kook Institute
Ben-Matitiahu, J. (Tachlag) *Kadmoniout ha-iehoudim (The Jews in the Antiquity)*, Jerusalem: Bialik Institute (see also Josephus)
Benoist; J.-M. (1977) "Facettes de l'identité", in Levi-Strauss, C. (ed.) *L'Identité*, Paris: Quadrige PUF: 13–24
Ben-Rafael E. (1994) *Language Identity and Social Division: The Case of Israel*, Oxford: O.U.P./Clarendon.
——— (1996) "Multiculturalism in Sociological Perspective" in Beaubock, R., Heller, A. and Zolberg A. (eds) *The Challenge of Diversity—Integration and Pluralism in Societies of Immigration*, Aldershot, England: Gower/Avebury and European Centre Vienna: 133–154
——— (1997) "Critical' versus non-critical Sociology: An Evaluation" *Israel Studies* vol. 2/1: 174–193
Ben-Rafael, E. and Brosh, H. (1995) "Jews and Arabs in Israel: The cultural convergence of divergent identities" Ron Nettler (ed.) *Medieval and Modern Perspectives on Muslim-Jewish Relations*, London: Harwood Academic Pubs. 18–34
——— (1982) *The Emergence of Ethnicity: Cultural Groups and Social Conflict in Israel.* Westport, Conn: Greenwood Press
Ben-Rafael, E., & Sharot, S. (1991) *Ethnicity, Religion and Class in Israeli Society.* Cambridge: Cambridge UP
Ben-Rafael, E., Geijst, I. (1994) *Ha-oulpan ke-misgueret klita avour olim mi-khever ha-amim ou-me-aratsot ha-maarav (The Hebrew language school as a frame of absorbtion for immigrants of the former USSR and Western countries)*, Tel-Aviv: Institut for Social Research, Tel-Aviv Univ.
Ben-Rafael, E., Olshtain, E., Geijst, I. (1996) "The socio-linguistic insertion of Russian Jews in Israel", in Lewin-Espstein, N. et al. (eds) *Russian Jews in Three Continents—Emigration and Resettlement*, London: Frank Cass: 364–388
Benson, S. (1981) *Ambiguous Ethnicity: Interracial Families in London*, Cambridge, UK: CUP
Berofsky, B. (1993) "The identity of cultural and personal identity" in Godberg, D.T. & Kraucz, M. (eds) *Jewish Identity*, Philadelphia: Temple University Press: 35–49

Birnbaum, P. (1992) *Les fous de la Republique: Histoire politique des Juifs d'Etat de Gambetta a Vichy*, Paris: Fayard

———— (1998) *La France Imaginée*, Paris: Fayard

Birnbaum, S.A. (1967) *Yiddish: A Survey and Gammar*, Manchester: Manchester University Press

Black, E.C. (1988) *The Social Politics of Anglo-Jewry, 1880–1920*, Oxford: Basil Blackwell

Bonacich, E. (1980) "Class Approaches to Ethnicity and Race" *Insurgent Sociologist* X: 9–23

Bourdieu, P. (1979) *La Distinction: Critique Sociale du Jugement* Paris: Les Editions de Minuit

———— (1982) *Ce que parler veut dire*, Paris: Fayard

———— (1987) *Choses Dites* Paris: Les Editions de Minuit

Bourdieu, P., Boltanski, L. (1975) "Le fetichisme de la langue" *Actes de la Recherche en Sciences Sociales*, 4: 2–32

Bourdieu, P., Passeron, J.-C. (1970) *La Reproduction—Elements d'une Theorie du Systeme d'Enseignement* Paris: Les Editions de Minuit

Boyarin, D. & Boyarin, J. (1993) "Diaspora: Generation and the Ground of Jewish Identity", *Critical Inquiry*, 19/4: 693–725

Boyarin, J. (1991) *Polish Jews in Paris: The Ethnography of Memory*, Bloomington: Indiana University Press

———— (1996) *Thinking in Jewish*, Chicago: Chicago University Press

Buber, M. (1973) *On Zion: The History of an Idea* Bath (UK): East and West Library.

Burgess, M.E. (1978) 'The Resurgence of Ethnicity: Myth or Reality' *Ethnic and Racial Studies* 1: 265–285

Calhoun, C. (1994) 'Social theory and the politics of identity', in Calhoun, C. (Ed) *Social Theory and the Politics of Identity*, Oxford: Blackwell: 9–36

———— (1996) *Critical Social Theory*, Oxford: Blackwell

Carmon, A. (1993) "Political education in the midst of a national crisis: the compatibility of Judaism and democracy as a pedagogical theme", in Sprinzak and Diamon, eds, *Israeli Democracy under Stress* Boulder: Lynne Rienner Publishers

Chomsky, W. (1957) *Hebrew: The Eternal Language* Philadelphia: Jewish Pub. Society of America

Cohen, P.S. (1983) "Ethnicity class and political alignment in Israel" *Jewish Journal of Sociology*, 25, 119–130.

Cohen, S.M. & Fein, L. (1985) "From Integration to Survival: American Jewish Anxieties in Transition", *The Annals*, July 1985: 75–88

Cohn-Sherbok, D. (1996) *Modern Judaism*, London & NY: Macmillan & St Martin's Press

Condor, S. (1990) "Social stereotypes and social identity", in Abrams, D. & Hogg, M.A. (eds) *Social Identity Theory: Constructive and Critical Advances*, NY: Harvester Wheatsheaf, 230–249

Connor W. (1978) "A nation is a nation is a state is an ethnic group is . . ." *Ethnic and Racial Studies*, 1, 377–400.

Cooper, H. & Morrison, P. (1991) *A Sense of Belonging: Dilemmas of British Jewish Identity*, London: Weidenfeld and Nicolson

Cooperman, B.D. (1993) "Jewish studies and Jewish identity: some implications of secularizing Torah", *Judaism* Vol. 42

Cronbach, A. (1995) "The issues of Reform Judaism in the USA" in Neusner; J. *Judaism in Modern Times*, Cambridge, Mass, Oxford, UK: Blackwell: 67–72

Dalin, D.G. (1995) "Will Herberg's Path from Marxism to Judaism: A Case Study in the Transformation of Jewish Belief" in Seltzer, R.M. & Cohen, N.J. (eds) *The Americanization of the Jew*, NY: New York UP, 119–132

Dar, I. (1994) 'Tmurot ba-khinoukh ha-kiboutzi' (Changes in kibbutz education) in Ben-Rafael, E., Abrahami, A. (éditors) *Khochvim kiboutz: ha-kiboutz be-mifne ha-*

mea (*Thinking kibbutz: The kibbutz at the turn of the century*), Ramat Efal: Yad Tabenkin, 223–228

David, P. (1998) "Survey: Israel at 50: Tel-Aviv and Jerusalem" *The Economist*, London, April 25

Dawidowicz, L.S. (1981) *The Holocaust and the Historians*, Cambridge, Mass.: Harvard University Press

Dayan, A. (Tachnag) 'Mi-hantsakha kolektivit le-hantsakha individualit: andertaot le-zekher ha-choa be-israel' (From collective commemoration to individual commemoration: the monuments to the Shoa in Israel), *Guesher*, 70–81

De Levita, D.J. (1965) *The Concept of Identity*, NY: Basic Books

DellaPergola, S. (1995) "Changing Cores and Peripheries: Fifty Years in Socio-Demographic Perspective" Wistrich R.S. (ed.) *Terms of Survival: The Jewish World since 1945*, London and NY: Routledge, 13–43

DellaPergola, S. & Shmeltz, U.O. (1989) "Demographic transformations of American Jewry: Marriage and Mixed Marriage in the 1980s" *Studies in Contemporary Jewry* 5: 169–200

DellaPergola, S. & Shmeltz, U.O. (1989a) "American Jewish Marriages: transformation and erosion—a rejoinder to Calvin Goldscheider" *Studies in Contemporary Jewry* 5: 209–214

Derrida, J. *L'Ecriture et la Différence*, Paris, Seuil, 1967, p. 427

Diamond, G. (1993) "Sahibs and Jews" in Godberg, D.T. & Kraucz, M. (Eds) *Jewish Identity*, Philadelphia: Temple University Press: 93–107

Dickens, D.R., Fontana, A. (1994) "Postmodernism in the Social Sciences", in Dickens, D.R., Fontana, A. (eds) *Postmodernism and Social Inquiry*, London: UCL Press, 1–24

Don-Yehiya, E. (1991) "Solidarity and Autonomy in Israel-Diaspora Relations" in Don-Yehiya, E. (ed.) *Israel and Diaspora Jewry: Ideological and Political Perspectives*, *Comparative Jewish Politics*, vol. 3: 9–27

Drai, R. (1995) *Identité juive, Identité humaine* Paris: Armand Colin.

Drummond, L. (1980) "The cultural continuum: A Theory of Intersystems", *Man*, 15/2: 352–374

Dumont, L. (1977) *Homo Hierarchicus—Le Systeme des Castes et ses Implications*, Paris: Gallimard

Edelman, J. (1982) "Soviet Jews in the United States: An Update", *American Jewish Yearbook 1982*, 155–164

Edwards, J. (1988) *Language, Society and Identity*. Oxford: Basil Blackwell.

Eilberg-Schwartz, H. (1995) "This alien thing that is my inheritance" *Judaism*, vol. 44

Eisenstadt, S.N. (1985) "The Israeli political system and the transformation of Israeli society" in Kraucz E. (ed.) *Politics and Society in Israel*, N. Brunswick: Transaction. 415–27

——— (1992) *Jewish Civilization: The Jewish Historical Experience in a Comparative Perspective*, Albany, NY: State University of New York Press

——— (1967) "Israeli identity: Problems in the development of the collective identity of an ideological society" in *Annals of the American Academy of Political and Social Sciences*, 370: 116–123

Eisenstadt, Sh. N. (1983) 'Sikum: baiot moked' (Conclusion: basic problems), in Har-Even, A. (ed.) *Ha-omnam kache lihiot israeli? (Is it really difficult to be an Israeli?)* Jérusalem: Van Leer Institute

Elazer, D. (1978) "The New Sadducees", *Midstream*, Aug-Sept, 20–25

Elias, N. (1994) *The Civilizing Process*, Oxford: Blackwell

Elizur, D. (1980) "Israelis in the United States: Motives, Attitudes and Intentions", *American Jewish Yearbook 1980*: 53–67

Ellenson, D. (1989) Tradition in Transistion: Orthodoxy, Halakhah, and the Boundaries of Modern Jewish Identity, Lanham, MD: University Press of America

——— (1993) "American values and Jewish tradition: Synthesis or Conflict" *Judaism*, vol. 42: 243 (American Jewish Congress)

Elon A. (1971) *The Israeli Founders and Sons*. NY: Holt Rinehart and Winston.

Erickson, E. (1963) "Youth: Fidelity and Diversity" in Erickson, E. (ed.) *Youth: Change and Challenge*, NY: Basic Books: 1–23

Eriksen, T.H. (1991) "The Cultural context of ethnic differences" *Man*, 26/1: 127–144

Etkes, A. (éditeur) (1993) *Ha-dat ve-ha-khaim (Religion and Life)* Jérusalem: Shazar Institute

Ettinger, Ch. (1969) *Toldot israel be-et hakhadasha (Modern History of Israel)*, Tel-Aviv: Dabir

Etzioni-Halevi, Kh, Shapira, R. (1975) *Mi ata ha-stoudent ha-israeli? (Who are you, the Israeli Student?)*, Tel-Aviv: Sifryat Hapoalim

Evron, B. (1988) *Ha-khechbon ha-leoumi (The National Account)*, Tel-Aviv: Dabir

——— (1995) *Jewish State or Israeli Nation*, Bloomington: Indiana University Press

Ezrachi, Y. (1993) "Democratic Politics and Culture in Modern Israel: Recent Trends" in Sprinzak and Diamon (eds) *Israeli Democracy under Stress*, Boulder: Lynne Rienner Publishers)

Fackenheim, E. (1992) *Judaïsme au présent*, Paris: Albin Michel

Farago, U. (1989) "The Jewish identity of Israeli youth, 1965–1985", *Hahadut Zmanenu: Contemporary Jewry*, Jerusalem, vol. 5: 259–285

Fasold, R. (1987) *The Sociolinguistics of Society* Oxford: Basil Blackwell, 335 pp.

Feguson, C.F. (1966) "National sociolinguistic profile formulas", *Sociolinguistics*, ed. Bright W., 309–315, The Hague: Mouton

Feifer, Ch. (1995) *Haskala ve-historia, toldoteia chel hakarat avar iehoudit-modernit (Education and History: The Path of Modern Jewish Conscience)* Jerusalem: Shazar Centre

Fein, L. (1996) "The Future of Yiddish" *Forward*, August 16

Feiner, Sh. (1995) *Haskala ve-historia, toldoteya chel hakarat-avar yehudit-modernit (Enlightment and History: The story of modern awareness of the Jewish past)*, Jerusalem: Shazar Centre

Feingold, H.L. (1995) "From Equality to Liberty: The Changing Political Culture of American Jews", in Seltzer, R.M. & Cohen, N.J. (eds) *The Americanization of the Jew*, NY: New York University Press, 97–118

Feldman, L.-H. (Tachmag) 'Guiour ve-syncrerism' (Conversion and syncretism) in Chtern, M. (éd.) *Ha-historia chel am israel: ha-pzoura ha-iehoudit ba-olam ha-helinisti-romi (The History of the People of Israel: The Jewish diaspora in the Hellenic-Roman world)*, Jerusalem: Shazar Centre

Finkelstein L. (1946), *The Pharisees: The Sociological Background of their Faith*, Philadelphia: Jewish Publication Society

Finkelstein, M. (Tachnad) *Ha-guiour halakha le-maaseh (Conversion from law to pratice)*, Ramat Gan: Bar-Ilan University

Finkielkraut, A. (1980) *Le Juif imaginaire*, Paris: Seuil

Fishbane, S. & Lightstone, J.N. (1990) *Essays on the Social Scientific Study of Judaism and Jewish Society*, Montreal: Concordia University

Fishman, J.A. (1981) "The sociololgy of Jewish Languages from the perspective of the general sociology of languages: A preliminary formulation" *International Journal of the Sociology of Language* 30: 5–16

Fishman, J.A., Cooper, R.L., Conrad, A.W. (eds) *The Spread of English—The Sociology of English as an Additional Language* Rowley (Mass): Newbury, 168–178

Fishman, J. (1989) *Language and Ethnicity in Minority Sociolinguistic Perspective* Clevedon, Philadelphia: Multilingual Matters, 717 pp.

Fontana, A. (eds) *Postmodernism and Social Inquiry*, London: UCL Press, 182–202

Foucault, M. (1972) *The Archeology of Knowledge*, NY: Random House

Franklin, M. (1990) "We must remember the Holocaust" *The Tech*; April 20 Volume 110/20: 4

Friedman, M. (1977) *Khevra ve-hadat: ha-kharedim be-eretz israel, 1918–1936* (Society and Religion: the Non-Zionist Orthodox in Eretz-Israel, 1918–1936) Jerusalem: Yad Ben-Zvi

———— (1982) 'The National Religious Party in Crisis' *State, Government and International Relations* 19–20: 115–120

———— (1986) 'Haredim confront the modern city' *Studies in Contemporary Jewry* 2, 74–96

Friedman, R. (1997) *Michlakhot noar le-polin be-chnot ha-90: teksei zikaron ke-dilemot kolectiviot (Youth delegations in the 1990s: Commemorations and collective dilemmas)*, Tel-Aviv: Tel-Aviv University

Friedmann, G. (1965) *Fin du Peuple Juif?* Paris: Gallimard

Friesel, E. (1994) "The Holocaust as a factor in contemporary Jewish Consciousness" in Webber (ed) *op. cit.*: 228–234

Furman, F.K. (1994) *Beyond Yiddishkeit: The Struggle for Jewish Identity in a Reform Synagogue*, Lanham: University Press of America

Furstenberg, R. (1995) "Israeli culture" *American Jewish Yearbook*, 1995: 448–465

Gans, H.J. (1979) 'Symbolic Ethnicity: The Future of Ethnic Group and Cultures in America' *Ethnic and Racial Studies*, 2: 1–20

Gardinger, M. (1994) "Reflexions on a model of management appropriate to Israelis" *The Israeli culture of Management*, A. Shenhar et A. Yarkoni, A. (eds) Tel-Aviv: Gomeh (Heb), pp. 99–108

Geertz, C. (1965) *Old Societies and New States*, NY: The Free Press

———— (1973) *The Interpretation of Cultures*, NY: Basic Books

Gellner, E. (1983) *Nations and Nationalism*, Ithaca, NY: Cornell University Press

Giddens, A. (1980) The Class Structure of the Advanced Societies London: Hutchinson

———— (1987) 'Structuralism, post-structuralism and the production of culture' in Giddens, A., Turner, J. (eds) *Social Theory Today*, Oxford: Basil Blackwell, 195–223

———— (1991) *Modernity and Self-Identity: Self and Society in the Late Modern Age*, Cambridge: Polity P

Gilad, N. (1995) *Ha-choa ba-michpakha: mekhkar biographi ve-narativi be-chlocha dorot (The Shoa in the family: biographical and narrative research in three generations)*, Tel-Aviv: Université de Tel-Aviv

Gilboa, E. (1986) "Attitudes of American Jews Toward Israel: Trends Over Time" *American Jewish Yearbook* 1986: 110–125

Giles H. (1985) Social Psychology of Language. *Social Science Encyclopedia* (p. 783)

Giles H., & Coupland N. (1991) *Language Contexts and Consequences*. London: Open University Press Milton Keynes. Cambridge: Cambridge University Press, 251–289

Glazer, N. (1987) "New Perspectives in American Jewish Sociology", *American Jewish Yearbook, 1987*

Glinert, L. (1990) 'The historiography of Hebrew and the Negation of the Golah' *The SOAS Language Revival Conference*, London, 7, 8 June

Godberg, D.T. & Kraucz, M. (1993) "Introduction: The Culture of Identity" in Godberg, D.T. & Kraucz, M. (eds) *Jewish Identity*, Philadelphia: Temple University Press: 1–12

Godberg, D.T. & Kraucz, M. (eds) (1993) *Jewish Identity*, Philadelphia: Temple University Press

Gold, S.J. & Phillips, B.A. (1996) "Israelis in the United States," *American Jewish Year Book 1996*

Goldscheider, C. (1986) *Jewish Continuity and Change—Emerging Patterns in America*, Bloomington: Indiana University Press

Goldstein, S. & Goldstein, A. (1996) *Jews on the Move: Implications for Jewish Identity*, NY: SUNY

Goldstein, S. (1992) "Profile of American Jewry: Insights from the 1990 National Jewish Population Survey", *American Jewish Yearbook 1992*: 75–173

Gonzales, N.L. (1989) "Conflict, migration and the expression of ethnicity: Introduction", in Gonzales, N.L. and McCommon C.S. (eds) *Conflict, Migration and the Expression of Ethnicity*, San Francisco: Westview P

Gorni, J. (1986) *Ha-cheela ha-aravit ve-habaia ha-iehoudit* (*The Arab question arabe and the Jewish problem*), Tel-Aviv: Am Oved

———— (1990) *Khipous akharei ha-zehout ha-leoumit* (*The quest for a national identity*), Tel-Aviv: Am Oved

———— (1998) *Bein Ochvitz le-yerouchalayim* (*Between Auschwitz and Jerusalem*), Tel-Aviv: Am Oved

Gourevitch, P. (1995) "What They Saw at the Holocaust Museum" *The Forward* Sunday 12

Graetz, M. (1989) *Les Juifs en France au xix Siècle: de la Revolution Française à l'Alliance Israélite Universelle*, Paris: Seuil

———— (1976) 'Toda'a yehoudit khadasha beréchit hitgabechoutah bedor talmidé Mendelssohn—Chaoul Acher' (The new Jewish conscience at the time of Mendelssohn' followers—Shaul Acher). *Me'hkarim betoledot Israel veérets Israel* (*Studies in the History of Israel and the Land of Israel*) IV. Haïfa, pp. 219–237.

Green, N.L. (1986) *The Pletzl of Paris: Jewish Immigrant Workers in the Belle Epoque*, New York: Holmes and Meier

Grillo, R.D. (1989) *Dominant Languages: Language and Hierarchy in Britain and France*. Cambridge: Cambridge University Press

Guibernau, M. (1996) *Nationalisms: The Nation—State and Nationalism in the Twentieth Century*, Cambridge: Polity Press

Gutenmacher, D. (1991) "Agudath Israel of America and the state of Israel—The case of the Jewish Observer" in Don-Yehiya, E. (ed.) *Israel and Diaspora Jewry: Ideological and Political Perspectives, Comparative Jewish Politics*, vol. 3: 109–126

Haarmann, H. (1986) *Language in Ethnicity—A View of Basic Ecological Relations*. Berlin: Mouton de Gruyter

Halevi, Herzog (Tachma) 'Zekhouiot ha-mioutim lefi ha-halakha' (Minority rights according to the Religious law) *Tkhoumin*, 2, 151–178

Hall, S. (1994) "The question of cultural identity", in *The Polity Reader in Cultural Theory*, Cambridge: The Polity Press, 119–125

———— (1996) "Introduction: Who Needs Identity?" Hall, S. And Du Gay P. (eds) *Questions of Cutural Identity*, London: Sage, 1–17

Hamers, J. & Blanc, M. (1989) *Bilinguality and Bilingualism*. Cambridge: Cambr. U.P.

Heilman, S.C. (1995) "The Ninth Siyum Ha-Shas: A Case Study in Orthodox Contra-Acculturation" in Seltzer, R.M. & Cohen, N.J. (eds) *The Americanization of the Jew*, NY: New York University Press, 311–338

Helfrich, H. (1979) Age markers in speech. Scherer K.R., & Giles H. (eds), *Social Markers in Speech* (pp. 62–107) Cambridge, Paris: Cambridge University Press, Editions de la Maison des Sciences de l'Homme

Heller, A. (1998) "Self-Representation and the Representation of the Other", in Baubock and Rundell (eds) *op. cit.*: 341–354

Herberg, W. (1951) *Judaism and Modern Man*, NY: Farar, Straus and Young

———— (1956) *Protestant-Catholic-Jew*, Garden City, NY: Doubleday

Herman, S.J. (1988), *Jewish Identity: A Social Psychological Perspective*, New Brunswick: Transaction

Herman, S.N. (1970) *American Students in Israel*, Ithaca, NY: Cornell University Press

———— (1970a) *Israelis and Jews: The Continuity of an Identity*, NY: Random House

Hertzberg, A. (1968) *The French Enlightenment and the Jews*, New York: Columbia University Press

Hervieu-Léger, D. (1998) "The Transmission and Formation of Socioreligious Identities in Modernity: An Analytical Essay" *International Sociology*, 13/2, 213–228

Hewitt, J.P. (1989) *Dilemmas of the American Self*, Philadelphia: Temple University Press

Hirsch, S.R. (1984) *The Collected Writings*, NY: Philipp Feldheim

Hobsbawm, E., Ranger, T. (1983) *The Invention of Tradition*, Cambridge: Cambridge University Press

Hoetinck, H. (1972) 'National Identity, Culture and Race in the Carribbeans' in Campbell, E.Q. (ed.) *Racial Tensions and National Identity* Nashville: Vanderbilt UP, 17–44

Hoffman, J.E., Fisherman, H. (1972) 'Language shift and language maintenance in Israel', in J.A. Fishman (ed.) *Advances in the Sociology of Language* 2; The Hague: Mouton, 1972: 342–364

Horowitz, D., & Lissak M. (1978) *Origins of the Israeli Polity—Palestine under the Mandate*. Chicago: University of Chicago Press

——— (1989) *Trouble in Utopia: The Overburdened Polity of Israel*. Albany: State University of New York Press

Horowitz, D.L. (1975) 'Ethnic Identity' in Glazer, N., Moynihan, D.P. (eds) *Ethnicity*, Cambridge, Mass: Harvard University Press, 111–140

Horowitz, T. (1989) *The Soviet Man in an Open Society*, Lantham: UP of America

Hunter, J.D. (1991) *Culture Wars: The Struggle to Define America*, NY: Basic Books

ICBS (Israel. Central Bureau Statistics) (1988; 1989) *Statistical Abstract of Israel*. Jerusalem

Ich Chalom, B. (1990) *Ha-rav kook: bein rationalism le-mistika* (*Rabbi Kook: between rationalism and mysticism*), Tel-Aviv: Am Oved

Inglis, F. (1993) *Cultural Studies*, Oxford: Blackwell

Isaacs, H. (1967) *American Jews in Israel* NY: J Day

Johnson, P. (1987) *A History of the Jews*, London: Weidenfeld and Nicolson

Josephus Flavius (1970) *The antiquities of the Jews*, NY: G. Routledge (see also Ben-Mattiyahu)

——— (1982) *The Jewish war*, Grand Rapids: Mich.: Zondervan Pub. House (see also Ben-Matitiahu)

Josipovic, G. (1993) "Going and Resting", in Godberg, D.T. & Kraucz, M. (eds) *Jewish Identity*, Philadelphia: Temple University Press: 309–321

Kaplan, E.K. (1995) "The American Mission of Abraham Joshua Heshel", in Seltzer, R.M. & Cohen, N.J. (eds) *The Americanization of the Jew*, NY: New York University Press, 355–376

Kaplan, M.M. (1981) *Judaism as a Civilization*, Philadephia: Jewish Publishing Society

Kashti, Y., Levin, M. "Transition and change: biographies of Jewish youth immigrating to Israel 1945–1950" in Kashti Y., Eros F. Schers, Zisenwine, D. (eds) *A Quest for Identity—Post War Jewish Biographies*, Tel-Aviv: Tel-Aviv University, 1996

Katriel, T. (1986) *Talking straight in dugri speech in Israeli Sabra culture* Cambridge: Cambrdige University P.

Katz, J. (1960) *Between Jews and Gentiles*. Jerusalem: Bialik Institute. Heb.

Katz, E. (1997) "Behavioral and Phenomenological Jewishness", in Liebman, C.S. & Katz, E. (eds) *The Jewishness of Israelis: Responses to the Guttman Report*, NY: SUNY: 71–84

Khazan, Kh. (1998) *Kartis halokh ve-chouv le-auschwitz: ideologia ve-zehout collectivit be-kerev michlakhot ha-choa ha-israeliot* (Return ticket for Auschwitz: ideology and identity among Shoa youth delegations), Tel-Aviv: Departement de Sociology, Tel-Aviv University

Kimmel, M.S. (1996) "Tradition as revolt: The moral and political economy of ethnic nationalism" *Current Perspectives in Social Theory*, vol. 16, 71–98

Kimmerling, B. (1985) "Between the Primordial and the civil definition of the collective identity: Eretz-Israel or Medinat Israel" Cohen, E., Lissak, M., and Almagor, U. (eds) *Comparative Dynamic Essays in Honor of S.N. Eisenstadt*, Boulder: Westview Press: 262–283

Kleeblatt, N. (1996) *Too Jewish? Challenging Traditional Identities*, New Brunswick, NJ: The Jewish Museum, NY, and Rutgers University Press

Kleeblatt, N.L. (ed.) (1993) *Too Jewish: Challenging Traditional Identities*, New York, The Jewish Museum of the Jewish Theological Seminary of America, and New Brunswick: Rutgers University Press

Klein, E. (1996) *Lost Jews: The Struggle for Identity Today*, Houndmills: Macmillan

Koestler, A. (1949) *Promise and Fullfilment*, London: Macmillan

Koifman, I. (Tarpat et Tarats) *Galout ve-nekhar (Exile and foreign land)*, vol. 1, Tel-Aviv: Dabir

Kosmin, B. & Schekner, J. (1995), "Jewish Population in the United States, 1994", *American Jewish Yearbook 1995*: 181–205

Kraemer, R. (1978) *Intergroup Contact Between Jews and Arabs in an Israeli High School.* Tel-Aviv: School of Education/Tel-Aviv University

Lafer, G. (1993) "Universalism and particularism in Jewish law" in Godberg, D.T. & Kraucz, M. (eds) *Jewish Identity*, Philadelphia: Temple University Press: 177–211

Lal, B.B. (1983) 'Perspectives on Ethnicity: Old Wine in New Bottles' *Ethnic and Racial Studies* 6: 154–173

Landau, J.M. (1970) The Arabs in Israel: A Political Study. London

Laqueur, W. (1972) *A History of Zionism.* London: Wiedenfeld and Nicolson

Laver, J., & Trudgill, P. (1979) Phonetic and linguistic markers in speech. Scherer K.R., & Giles, H. (eds), *Social Markers in Speech* Cambridge: Camb. U.P. (1–32).

Layish A. (1981) *The Arabs in Israel—Continuity and Change.* Jerusalem: Magnes. heb.

Leibowicz, J. (1976) *Iehadout, am israel ve-medinat israel* (Judaism, the People of Israel and the State of Israel), Jerusalem: Shockan

Lenski, G. (1972) 'Group Involvement, Religious Orientations and Economic Behavior' in Segal, B.E. (ed.) *Racial and Ethnic Relations* NY: Crowell, 154–68

Lévinas, E. (1976) *Difficile Liberté*, Paris: Albin Michel

Lewin-Epstein, N. & Semyonov, M. (1993) *The Arab Minority in Israel's Economy*, Boulder: Westview

Levi-Strauss, C. (1958) *Anthropologie Structurale*, Paris: Plon
——— (1961) *Race et Histoire* Paris: Gonthier

Levy, Sh. & Guttman, L. (1976a) "Zionism and Jewishness of Israelis" *Forum*, 1/24: 39–50

Levy, Sh. (1996) *Values and Jewishness of Israeli Youth*, Jerusalem: Guttman Institute, (mimeograph)

Levy, Ch., Gutman, L. (1976) *Arakhim ve-emdot chel ha-noar ha-israeli (Values and atttitudes of Israeli youth)*, Jérusalem: Institute for Applied Research in the Social Sciences
——— (1981) *Al meouravout hadadit: iehoudei ha-tfoutsot ve-israel be-eynei ha-tsibour* (About reciprocal interference: The Diaspora and Israeli Jews in the eyes of the public), Jerusalem: Institute for Applied Research in the Social Sciences

Levy, Sh., Levinsohn, H. and Katz, E. (1997) "Beliefs, Observances and Social Interaction among Israeli Jews: The Guttman Institute Report", in Liebman, C.S. & Katz, E. (eds) *The Jewishness of Israelis: Responses to the Guttman Report*, NY: SUNY, 1–38

Lewin-Epstein N., & Semyonov M. (1986)Ethnic Group Mobility in the Israeli Labor Market. *American Sociological Review, 51*, 342–351

Liberman, Ch. (Tachana) *Iavanit ve-iavaniout be-eretz israel* (Greek and Greek culture in the Land of Israel), Jerusalem: Bialik Institute

Lichtenstein, A. (Tachla) 'Guerout, leida ve-michpat' (Conversion, birth and law) *Tora che-be-al pet*, vol. 13, pages pei-beit—tsadik-dalet

Liebkind, K. (1989) "Conceptual approaches to ethnic identity" Liebkind, K. (ed.) *New Identities in Europe*, Aldershot UK: Gower, 25–40

Liebman, C.S., Cohen, S.M. (1990) *Two Worlds of Judaism: The Israeli and American Experiences*, New Haven and London: Yale Univeristy Press

Liebman, C.S. & Don Yehiya, E. (1983) *Civil Religion in Israel: Traditional Judaism and Political Culture in the Jewish State*, Berkeley: University of California Press

Liebman, C.S. & Katz, E. (eds) (1997) *The Jewishness of Israelis: Responses to the Guttman Report*, NY: SUNY

Liebman, C.S. (1973) *The Ambivalent American Jew*, Philadelphia: The Jewish Publication Society

——— (1997a) "The Media and the Guttman Report", in Liebman, C.S. & Katz, E. (eds) *op. cit.*: 39–58

——— (1997b) "Academis and Other Intellectuals" in Liebman, C.S. & Katz, E. (eds) *op. cit.*: 59–70

——— (1997c) "Religion and Modernity: The Special Case of Israel" in Liebman, C.S. & Katz, E. (eds) *op. cit.*: 85–102

——— (1997d) "Cultural Conflict in Israeli Society" in Liebman, C.S. & Katz, E. (eds) *op. cit.*: 103–118

Liebman, Ch. (1989) 'Mousag medinat israel ve-tefisotav be-khevra ha-israelit' (The concept of the State of Israel in the Israeli society), *Medina, memchal ve-iakhassim beinleoumit*, 30: 51–60

Lipset, S.M., Raab, E. (1995) *Jews and the New American Scene*, Cambridge, Mass: Harvard University Press

Lissak M. (1981) *The Elites of the Jewish Community in Palestine* T-A: Am Oved. Heb.

——— (1996) " 'Critical' sociology and 'establishment' sociology in the Israeli academic community: Ideological struggles or academic discourse" *Israel Studies*, 1: 247–294

Litvin, B. (1965) *Jewish Identity*, NY: Feldheim

Liwed, I. (Tachikh) *Iemei ezra ve-nekhemia* (The time of Ezra et Nehemia), Jerusalem: sidrat iuounim, vol. 19

Eliav, M. *Ha'hinoukh hayehoudi beguermanya bimé hahaskala vehaémancipatsya (Jewish education in Germany, at the time of the Enlightment and Emancipation)*. Jerusalem, 5721–1961.

Makhou, N. (1982) Changes in the employement structures of Arabs in Israel. *Journal of Palestinian Studies*, *11*, 77–102.

Mandel, A. (1982) 'France', *American Jewish Yearbook 1982*: 196–200

Markowitz, F. (1992) "Community without Organization", *City and Society*, 612: 141–155

——— (1993) *A Community in Spite of Itself: Soviet Jewish Emigres in New York*, Washington: Smithonian Institution Press, 317 pp.

Marouf, N. (1993) "Introduction", in Marouf, N. (ed.) *Identite-Communaute* Paris: L'Harmattan, 11–22

Maxwell, E. (1994) "The Impact of Auschwitz and Vatican II on Christian Perceptions of Jewish Identies", in Webber, J. (ed.) *op. cit.*: 235–245

Mazar, B. (Tacham) '*Canaan ve-israel: Mekhkarim historiim' (Canaan and Israël: Historical Research)*, Jerusalem: Shazar Centre

McClain, E.J. (1996) "Converts: Reinding us what being Jewish is all about", *Moment*, 8–31–1996

Medding P.Y. (1972) *Mapai in Israel*. Cambridge: Cambridge University Press.

——— (1987) "Segmented Ethnicity and the New Jewish Politics" *Studies in Contemporary Jewry* 3, 26–45

Medding, P.Y., Tobin, G.A., Barck Fishman, S., Rimor, M. (1992) "Jewish identity in conversionary and mixed marriages", *American Jewish Yearbook 1992*, 3–74

Meek T.S. (1930), "The Translation of Ger in Hexateuch and its Bearing on the Documentary Theory", *Journal of Biblical literature* 49, p. 172

Memmi, A. (1966) *La Libération du Juif*, Paris: Gallimard

Menahem, G., Geisjt, I. (1996) *Safa, taasouka ve-emdot legabei israel* (Langue, occupation, and attitudes vis-à-vis Israël), Tel-Aviv: Department of Sociology

Menahem, G., Levin-Epstein, N. (1992) *Seker olim* (Survey among immigrants), Tel-Aviv: Institute of Social Research

Miller, S.H. (1994) "Religious Practice and Jewish Identity in a Sample of London Jews" in Webber, J. (ed.) *op. cit.*: 193–204

Misrachi, R. (1963) *La Condition réflexive de l'homme juif*, Paris: Julliard

Mittleman, A.L. (1996) *The Politics of Torah: The Jewish Political Tradition and the Founding of Agudat Israel*, Albany: State University of New York Press

Montefiore, A. (1993) "Structures of Personal Identity", in Godberg, D.T. & Kraucz, M. (eds) *Jewish Identity*, Philadelphia: Temple University Press: 212–244

Moore, D., Kimmerling, B. (1995): "Individual strategies of adopting collective identities: the Israeli case", *International Sociology*, 10/4–387–407

Myers Scotton, C. (1983) "The negotiation of identities in conversation—A theory of markedness and code choice" *Intern. Jrnl. of the Sociology of Language, 44*, 115–136

Nakhleh, K. (1975) "Cultural determinants of collective identity—The case of the Arabs in Israel" *New Outlook*, 18/7, 31–40

Neher, A. (1995) *Un Maillon dans la Chaîne*, Paris: Septentrion

Neuberger, B. (1994) *Dat, medina ve-politika (Religion, State and Politics)*, Tel-Aviv: Open University

Neusner, J. (1989) *Who, What and Where is Israel?*, Lanham, Md: University Press of America

———— (1995) *Judaism in Modern Times*, Cambridge, Mass, Oxford, UK: Blackwell

Niebuhr, G. (1995) "Whose Memory Lives When the Last Survivor Dies?"

Ochana, D. (1996) 'Zarathoustra bi-ierouchalaim' ('Zarathoustra in Jerusalem) dans Ochana, D., Winstrich, R.Ch. (eds) *Mitus ve-zikaron (Myths and Memory)* Jérusalem: Van Leer Institute, 304–269

———— (1998) *Ha-israelim ha-akharonim (The last Israelis)*, Tel-Aviv: Ha-kibboutz ha-meoukhad

Olzak, S. (1983) 'Contemporary Ethnic Mobilization' *Annual Review of Sociology* 9:355–74

Urbach, A.A. (1971) *Hazal—pirkei emounot ve-deot (The Sages of Israel: Chapiters of belief and knowledge)*, Jerusalem: Magnes

Oron, A. (1993) *Zehout iehoudit israelit (The Jewish Israeli identity)*, Tel-Aviv: Sifriat hapoalim

Orr, A. (1994) *Israel: Politics, Myths and Identity Crises*, London: Pluto Press

Parsons, T. (1975) 'Some Theoretical Considerations on the Nature and Trends of Change of Ethnicity' in Glazer, N., Moynihan, D.P. (eds) *op. cit.*: 53–83

Patterson, O. (1975) "Context and choices in ethnic allegiance" Glazer N., & Moynihan D.P. (eds), *Ethnicity*. Cambridge, Mass: Harvard U.P., 305–349

Pedersen, J. (1926), *Israel: Its Life and culture, I/1 & 2*, London: Oxford University Press

Peled, Y. (1997) *Otonomya tarboutit ou-maavak maamadi: hitpatkhout ha-matsa ha-leumi chel ha-bund, 1893–1903 (Cultural autonomy and class struggle: the developpement of the Bund program, 1893–1903)*, Tel-Aviv: Ha-kibboutz ha-méhoukhad

Perotti, A. (1996) *Migrations et Société Pluriculturelle en Europe*, Paris: L'Harmattan

Pinto, D. (1996) *A New Jewish Identity for post-1989 Europe*, London: Institute for Jewish Policy Research

Plant, R. (1998) "Antinomies of modernist political thought: reasoning, context and community", in in Good, J. and Velody, I. (eds.) *op. cit.*: 76–106

Ponzio, A. (1993) *Signs, Dialogue and Ideology*, Philadelphia: John Benjamin Pub.

Raday, F., Bunk, E. (1993) *Integration of Russian Immigrant into the Israeli Labour Market* (Research report), Jerusalem: the Hebrew Unversity, the Harry and Michael Sacher Institute for Legislative Research and Comparative Law, 63 p.

Ragussis, M. (1995) *Figures of Conversion: "The Jewish Question" and English National Identity*, Durham and London: Duke University Press

Raiklin, E. (1993) "On inconsistencies in the modern definition of Jewishness" *International Journal of Sociology and Social Policy*, 13?1–2: 18–63

Ram, U. (1995) *The Changing Agenda of Israeli Sociology: Theory, Ideology and Identity*, Albany: State University of New York

Rex, J. (1996) *Ethnic Minorities in the Modern Nation State*, Warwick: Centre for Research in Ethnic Relations

Ritterband, P. & Cohen, S.M. (1984) "The social characteristics of the New York Area Jewish Community", *American Jewish Yearbook 1984*: 128–139

Ritterband, P. (1995) "Modern Times and Jewish Assimilation" in Seltzer, R.M. & Cohen, N.J. (eds) *The Americanization of the Jew*, NY: New York University Press, 377–394

Rodinson, M. (1981) *Cult, Ghetto, and State*: The Persistence of the Jewish Question, London: Zed Press/Al Saqi Books

Rolland, A. (1994) "Identity, Self and Individualism in a Multicultural Perspective", in Salett, E.P. & Koslow, D.R. (eds) *Race, Ethnicity and Self: Identity in Multicultural Perspective*, Washington, D.C.: NMCI: 11–23

Rosenbaum, Y. (1983) 'Hebrew adoption among new immigrants to Israel: the first three years' *International Journal of the Sociology of Language* 41/1983: 115–130

Rosenbloom J.R. (1978), *Conversion To Judaism: From the Biblical Period to rhe Present*, Cincinati, Ohio: Hebrew Union College

Rosenfeld, H. (1978) "The class situation of the Arab national minority in Israel" *Comparative Studies in Society and History*, 20, 374–407

Rosenzweig, F. (1921) *The Star of Redemption*, London: Routledge and Kegan Paul & Littman Library

Rouhana, N.N. (1997) *Palestinian Citizens in an Ethnic Jewish State*, New Haven: Yale University Press

Rubin, B. (1995) *Assimilation and its Discontents*. NY: Times Books/Random House

Rubinstein, A. (1977) *Lihiot am khofchi (To be a free people)*, Tel-Aviv: Schockan
——— (1980) *Mi-herzl ad gouch emounim (From Herzl to Gush Emunim)*, Jerusalem: Shokan
——— (1997) *Mi-herzl ve-ad rabin ve-halha: mea chnot tsionout* (From Herzl to Rabin and later: 100 years of Zionism), Tel-Aviv: Shockan

Rundell, J. (1998) "Tensions of Citzenship in an Age of Diversity: Reflections on Territoriality, Cosmopolitanism and Symmetrical Reciprocity" in Baubock and Rundell (eds) *op. cit.*: 321–340

Russell, S. (1996) *Jewish Identity and Civilizing Processes*, Houndmills, GB: Macmillan Press; NY: St Martin's Press

Sachar, H.M. (1958) *The Course of Modern Jewish History*, NY: Delta

Sacks, J. (1993) *One People? Tradition, Modernity and Jewish Unity*, London: Littman Library of Jewish Civilization

Safrai, Ch. (Tachal) 'Brikhinot khadachot le-bekhinat maamado chel raban iokhanan ben zakay, leakhar ha-khorban' (New aspects in the study of the status of Yokhanan Ben Zakay after the destruction of the Second Temple) in *Sefer zikaron le-guedalia alon* (In Memorian for Guedalia Alon), Tel-Aviv: Tel-Aviv University

Safrai, Ch. (Tachnad) 'Ha-ichouv ha-iehoudi be-dor iavneh' (The Jewish community at the time of the Yavneh generation) in *Be-iemei ha-bait ou-be-iemei ha-michana, mekhkarim be-toldot israel* (In the Era of the Temple and the Mishna—Studies on the History of Isael) vols. 1 and 2, Jerusalem: Bialik Institute

Said, E. (1985) "Opponents, Audiences, Constituencies and Community", in Foster, H. (ed.) *Postmodern Culture*, London: Pluto Press, 135–159

Said, E.W. (1979) *Orientalism*, New York: Vintage Book

Sarna, J.D. (1995) "The Evolution of the American Synagogue" in Seltzer, R.M. & Cohen, N.J. (eds) *The Americanization of the Jew*, NY: New York University Press, 215–229

Sartre, J.P. (1954) *Réflexions sur la Question Juive*, Paris: Gallimard

Schalit, A. (éditeur) (Tachlag) *Kadmoniout ha-iehoudim* (*The Antiquity of the Jews*), Jerusalem: Bialik Institute

Schatzki, T.R. (1996) *Social Practices: A Wittgensteinian Approach to Human Activity and the Social*, Cambridge: Cambridge University Press

Schiswick, B. (1991) 'Iehoudim sovietim be-artsot ha-brit: nitouakh histagloutam ha-lechonit ve-hakalkalit' (The Soviet Jews in the US: An analysis of their linguistic and economic adjustment), *Rivaon le-kalkala* 148, 138–235

Schmueli, A. (1980) *Sheva tarbouiot Israel* (The Seven cultures of Israel), Tel-Aviv: Bialik Institute

Schnapper, D. & Strudel, S. (1995) "Ethnicity and the Jewish Vote: The French Case" in Wistrich R.S. (ed.) *Terms of Survival: The Jewish World since 1945*, London and NY: Routledge, 231–248

Schnapper, D. (1983) *Jewish Identities in France: An Analysis of Contemporary French Jewry*, Chicago: University of Chicago Press

———— (1993) "Le sens de l'ethno-religieux", *Archives de Sciences Sociales en Religion*, 81: 149–163

———— (1994) "Israelites and Jews: New Jewish identities in France", in Webber, J. (ed.) *op. cit.*: 171–178

———— (1994a) La Communauté des Citoyens: Sur l'Idée moderne de Nation, Paris: NRF—Gallimard

Schtern, M. (Tachkag) 'He-arot la-sipour yosef ben tovia' (Remarks on the story of Yosef Ben Tovia), *Tarbitz lev*, 35–47

Schwarzfuchs, S. (1989) Du Juif à l'Israelite: Histoire d'une mutation 1770–1870 Paris: Fayard

Schweid, E. (1994) "Changing Jewish Identities in the New Europe and the Consequences for Israel" in Webber, J. *op. cit.*: 42–56

Scult, M. (1995) "Americanism and Judaism in the Thought of Modercai M. Kaplan" in Seltzer, R.M. & Cohen, N.J. (eds) *The Americanization of the Jew*, NY: New York University Press, 339–354

Seckbach, F., Cooper, R.L. (1977) 'The maintenance of English in Ramat Eshkol' in Fishman, J.A., Cooper, R.L. and Conrad, A.W. (eds) *The Spread of English: The Sociology of English as an Additional Language*, Rowley, Mass.: Newbury, 168–178

Seguev, T. (1992) *Ha-milion ha-chevii* (The seventh million), Jerusalem: Keter

Seltzer, R.M. & Cohen, N.J. (eds) (1995) *The Americanization of the Jew*, NY: New York University Press

Semyonov M., & Lewin-Epstein N. (1987) *Hewers of Wood and Drawers of Water*. Ithaca NJ: Cornell Institute of Labor Studies.

Shafir, G. (1996) "Israeli society: A counterview", *Israel Studies*, 2

Shalev, M. "Time for theory: Critical notes on Lissak and Sternhell", *Israel Studies*, 2, 1996

Shamir, M. (1970) Pirkei Alik (The stories of Alek), Tel-Aviv: Sifryat Ha-poalim

Shanks, H. (1996) "Can Jewish Life Be Revived In The Former Soviet Union?" *Moment* February 28

Shapira, A. (1997) *iehoudim khadachim, iehoudim iechanim* (New Jews, Old Jews) (New Jews, old Jews), Tel-Aviv: Ofakim, Am Oved

Shapira, Y. (1984) *Elit lelo mamchikhim* (Elite witout continuators), Tel-Aviv: Sifryat Ha-poalim

———— (1996) *Khevra be-chevi ha-politikaim* (A Society jailed by politicians) Tel-Aviv: Sifryat Ha-poalim

Sharot, S. (1998) 'Jewish Ethnicity: Changing Interrelationships and Differentiations in the Diaspora and Israel' in Krausz, E. and Tulea, G. (eds) *Jewish Survival: The Identity Problem at the Close of the Twentieth Century*, New Brunswick, USA: Transaction Publishers: 87–106

———— (1982) *Messianism, Mysticism and Magic: A Sociological Analysis of Jewish Religious Movement*, Chapel Hill, NC: The University of North Carolina Press

Shavit, Y. (1984) *Mi-ivri le-kenaani* (From Hebrew to Canaanean), Jerusalem: Domino

Shokeid, M. (1985) "Cultural ethnicty in Israel: the case of Middle Eastern Jews' religiosity" *AJS Review* 9: 247–271

———— (1988) *Children of Circumstances*, Ithaca, NY: Cornell University Press

Sholem, G. (1971) *Le messianisme juif: Essais sur la spiritualité du judaïsme*, Paris: Calmann-Levy

Shore, C. & Black, A. (1994) "Citzens' Europe and the construction of European identity" Goddard, V.A., Llobera, J.R., Shore, C. (eds) *The Anthropology of Europe*, Oxford: Berg, 275–298

Shusterman, R. (1993) "Next year in Jerusalem?" in Godberg, D.T. & Kraucz, M. (eds) *Jewish Identity*, Philadelphia: Temple University Press: 291–291

Silberstein, L.J. (1996) "Cultural Criticism, Ideology and the Interpretation of Zionism: Toward a Post-Zionist Discourse", in Kepnes, S. (ed.) *Interpreting Judaism in a Postmodern Age*, NY: New York University Press, 325–360

Simmel, G. (1966) *Conflict/The Web of Affiliation*, NY: Free Press, 2nd printing

Simpson, G., Yinger, M. (1958) *Racial and Cultural Minorities* NY: Harper and Row, 775 pp.

Singer, D. (1994) "Jewish renewal in the new Europe: An American Jewish perspective", in Webber, J. (ed) *op. cit.*: 283–290

Singer, S.F. (1996) "In from the Cold: The 'Not Yet' Judaism of the Former Soviet Union", *Moment*, February 28

Sklare, M. & Greenblum, J. (1967) *Jewish Identity on the Suburban Frontier*, NY: Basic Books

Sklare, M. (1971) *America's Jews*, NY: Random House

Sklare, M. and Greenblum, J. (1967) *Jewish Identity on the Suburban Frontier*, NY: Basic Books

Smart, B. (1992) Modern Conditons, Postmodern Controversies, London: Routledge Kegan Paul

Smith, A. (1981) *The Ethnic Revival*. Cambridge: Cambridge University Press

———— (1987) *The Ethnic Origins of Nations*, Oxford: Basil Blackwell

Smith, B. (1994) *Classifying the Universe: The Ancient Indian Varna System and the Origins of Caste*, NY: Oxford University Press

Smolicz, J.J. (1994) *Australian Diversity*, Adelaide: Centre for Intercultural Studies and Multicultural Education—University of Adelaide

Smooha, S. (1972) *Israel Pluralism and Conflict*. London: Routledge and Kegan P.

———— (1976) 'Aravim ve-iehoudim be-iakhassei rov ve miout be-israel' (Arabes et Juifs dans des rapports majorité-minorité en Israël) *Megamot*, 22–4: 397–424

Sokoloff, H. (1996) "Identity Crisis" *Jerusalem Post*, 9–20: 8

Soysal, Y. (1994) *Limits of Citizenship*, Chicago: Chicago University Press

Sperber, D. (1968) 'Le Structuralisme en anthropologie', in Ducrot O., Todorov, T. et al. *Qu'est-ce que le structuralisme?* Paris: Seuil: 167–237

Tabory, E., Lazerwitz, B. (1983) 'Americans in the Israeli Reform and Conservative Denominations: Religiosity under an Ethnic Shield?' *Review of Religious Research* 24: 177–187

Taylor, C. (1985) *Philosophical Papers (vol. 1): Human Agency and Language*, Cambridge: Cambridge University Press

———— (1998) *Les Sources du Moi*, Montreal: Boréal

Temple, B. (1996) "New agendas for research—Time travels: time, oral histories and British-Polish identities", *Time and Society*, vol. 5/1, 85–96

Tiryakian, E.A. (1991) "Modernisation: Exhumetur in Pace (Rethinking Macrosociology in the 1990s)" *International Sociology* 6/2: 165–180

Touraine, A. (1992) *Critique de la Modernité*, Paris: Fayard

Tsabar-Yehoshua, N. (1996) *Kibbutz LA* (Kibuts LA), Tel-Aviv: Am Oved

Urbach, A.A. (1971) *Hazal—pirkei emounot ve-deot* (*The Sages of Israel: Chapters of belief and knowledge*), Jerusalem: Magnes

Weber, M. (1952), *Ancient Judaism*, Glencoe: Free Press

Weingrod, A. (1990) *The Saint of Beersheba* Albany: State University of New York Press

Wertheimer, J. (1993) *A People Divided: Judaism in Contemporary America*, New York: Basic Books

Wiener, M. (1974) *Ha-dat ha-iehoudit be-tkoufat ha-emancipatsia* (*The Jewish religion during the Emancipation*), Jerusalem: Bialik and Leo Beck Institutes

Wieviorka, A. (1994) "Jewish Identity in the First Accounts by Extermination Camp Survivors from France" in *Yale French Studies*, vol. 85: *Discourses of Jewish Identity in Twentieth-Century France*, 135–151

Wieviorka, M. (1996) "Culture, Société et Démocratie" in Wieviorka, M. et al. (eds.) *Une Société Fragmentée: Le Multiculturalisme en Débat*, Paris: La Découverte, 11–60

Wilenski, M. (1978) *Khasidim ve-mitnagdim* (Khassidim and anti-Khassidim) vols. 1 and 2, Jerusalem: Bialik Institute

Wilson, B. (1982) *Religion in Sociological Perspective*, Oxford: Oxford University Press

Wistrich, R. (1990) *Between Redemption and Perdition: Modern Antisemitism and Jewish Identity*, London and NY: Routledge

Wittgenstein, L. (1961) *Tractatus logico-philosophicus*, suivi de *Investigations philosophiques*, traduit de l'allemand par P. Klossowski, Paris: Gallimard

Wolitz, S. (1994) "Imagining the Jew in France: From 1945 to the Present" in *Yale French Studies*, vol. 85: *Discourses of Jewish Identity in Twentieth-Century France*, 119–134

Zakowicz, J. (1990) *Meguilat rout, mikra israel, perouch madai la-mikra* (The Story of Ruth, the Bible, the scientific interpretation of the Bible), Tel-Aviv and Jerusalem: Am Oved and Magnes

Zloti, B. (Tachla) '*Badinou kabalat guerim*' ('*We invented the acceptance of the converted*') *Tora che-be-al-pe*, 13: 3–33

Zohar, Z., Sagui, A. (Tachna) *Guiour ve-zehout iehoudit, ioun be-iesodot ha-halakha* (*Conversion and Jewish identity—Study in the basics of the religious law*), Jerusalem: Hertman Institute and Bialik Institute

INDEX

Abbahu, Rabbi 281
Abraham 230, 249, 338, 339
activists, national-religious 63–64
Agassi, Yosef 75, 76
aggadah 359
Agnon, Shmuel Yossef 47, 151–152
Agudat Israel 14–15, 86–87, 359
Ahad Ha'am (Asher Ginsberg) 22
Alderman, G. 91
Altmann, Rabbi Alexander 40,
    153–157
American Jewry *see* United States,
    Jewish community
Ammonites
    converted 134
    Jews forbidden by Torah to
        intermarry with 131–132, 225,
        244
anti-Semitism 11, 91, 155
anti-Zionism xxii
apostasy 262, 324
Arabic language, use in Israel 73
Arabs, in Israel 66–67, 72–73, 79,
    80, 106, 310
Arter, Yitzhak 21
Ashkenazim 102, 359
assimilation of Jews 163, 241, 271,
    280–281, 314, 324, 330–331, 335
    through intermarriage 340,
        342–343
    in London 91
    in United States 91–92
    in Vienna 91
Australia, Reform Judaism in 313
autonomy, Jewish 25–26

Babylon
    conversion to Judaism during exile
        in 127–129
    return from 131, 281, 282
Baron, Selo xii, xvi
Barth, F. 3
Baruk, Henry 42–43, 158–165
Beller, S. 91
Ben-Gurion, David
    initiating debate with "Sages of
        Israel" xix, xxv–xxvi, 7, 32–36,
        117

query to "Sages of Israel"
    144–147
Ben-Rafael, E. 77
Ben-Zeev, Israel 121 n. 12
Bergmann, Schmuel Hugo 45, 46,
    166–167
Berlin, Isaiah 44, 168–176, 316
Berlin, Rabbi Naphtali Zvi Judah
    140
Bet Yossef (Caro) 192
Biblical Hebrew 21
Biblical texts on intermarriage between
    Jews and non-Jews 124, 132, 164,
    185, 195, 206, 223–224, 244–245,
    357
Biblical times, conversion to Judaism
    in 119–120, 121–127, 129–130,
    132–133, 281
Bnei Akiva youth movement 64, 359
Borowitz, Eugene 93
Bourla, Yehuda 49, 177–179
Brasch, Rabbi R. 313
Buber, M. 23
Bund the 22–23, 24–26, 28, 29–30,
    100, 101, 114
    use of Yiddish 102

Canaanists xxii
Canaanites 74–75, 107, 232
    Jews forbidden by Torah to
        intermarry with 131–132, 225,
        244
    national-territorialist attitude towards
        Jewish identity 109, 114
caste, concept of 10, 41
caste syndrome attitude towards
    Jewish identity xxi, xxii, 10–11, 24,
        37–41, 52, 54, 55, 97, 98, 99, 104,
        105, 109–110, 114
    among Orthodox Jews 103
    among ultra-Orthodox Jews 103,
        107, 108, 109
    place of Yiddish 53
Central Conference of American
    Rabbis 17–18, 202
Chief Rabbinate of Israel, authority of
    254–255, 279, 289, 323–324, 327,
    336, 356–357

Chosen people, religious notion of
155
Christians for Moses 86 n. 6
circumcision
  importance of ritual for Jewish
    identity 49, 50, 177–178,
    312–313
  of mixed parentage children 201,
    206–207, 237
  not related to conversion 126–127
  as part of ritual of converting to
    Judaism 141, 143, 177, 212,
    227, 228–229, 234, 313, 321–322,
    338
  requirement of 128, 227, 237
citizenship, of State of Israel 156,
  164–165, 171–172, 183, 255
Cohen, S.M. 90 n. 8
Cohn, Haim 45–46, 180–193
collective identity
  concept of 3–4, 110
  debate in social sciences xxii–xxiii
  features of 5–6
  Jewish identity as example of xxv,
    6, 9–10
  in post-modernity xxv
  subjective perspective of xxiii–xxiv
colonialism, Zionism seen as form of
  77
commandments
  acceptance of, when converting to
    Judaism 142–143, 209, 210, 211,
    215, 228
  place in Judaism 18–19, 47, 312,
    335
  in Torah 161, 238, 335
Communist movement, Jewish
  participation in 25 n. 3
community of intent 3
congregation
  emphasized by Judaism in United
    States 89–90
  of returning exiles, new perception
    of Judaism 129, 130
Conservative Movement 18–19, 27,
  29–30, 100, 101, 102, 103
  ethno-cultural attitude towards
    Jewish identity 109, 114
  in United States 87–88
  views on conversion 85 n. 5
constructed identity, and modernism
  xxii, xxiii
conversion to Christianity 159
  by Jews 265, 352

conversion to Judaism
  acceptance of the commandments
    142–143, 209, 210, 211, 215,
    228
  attitude of Judaism towards 211,
    226–227, 233, 237, 245, 266,
    339
  in Biblical times 119–120,
    121–127, 129–130, 132–133,
    208, 281
  circumcision as part of 141, 143,
    177, 212, 227, 228–229, 234, 313,
    321–322, 338
  concept of 119, 159, 162, 261,
    268, 338, 352
  Conservative views on 85 n. 5
  during Second Temple Judaism
    133–139
  forced 133–134
  halakhic 48–51, 54, 55, 137, 156,
    217, 218, 250, 266–267, 322,
    336, 337–338
  immersion ritual as part of 141,
    143, 212–214, 217–218, 227,
    228–229, 234, 321–322, 338
  for material benefit 210–211
  of minors 214–215, 218, 228,
    266–267, 270, 274, 311–312
  from Mishnah until modernity
    139–143
  of mixed parentage children 157,
    195–196, 208, 218, 219, 221, 227,
    233, 238–239, 244, 255, 265, 266,
    269, 274, 289, 299, 307, 315,
    319, 325–326, 327–328, 340–341,
    356, 358
  modern Orthodox views on 36,
    40–41, 43
  Orthodox views on 47, 85 n. 5,
    200, 202
  politically motivated 133–134, 139
  Reform movement views on 84,
    85 n. 5, 202, 304, 313
  ritual of 43, 120, 127, 128, 136,
    137, 138–139, 140–141, 209, 210,
    212–213, 227, 228–229, 234, 262,
    300–302, 321–322
  Romans objecting to 135–136
  sacrificial offering as part of
    137, 139, 140, 141, 213
  secular 352, 353, 354
  territorial conception of 125–127
  traditional rules concerning 117,
    279

ultra-Orthodox views on   36, 39,
    41
in United States   84–85
see also 'ger'; proselytes
Cooperman, B.D.   91–92
Cronbach, Abraham   18
cultural communities   3
cultural ethnicity, of Jews in United
    States   94–98, 107
cultural singularity, connected with
    social disadvantage   68, 72
cultural texts   4
culture
    Hebrew   57
    Jewish   25, 82, 90
Cutheans   231

de-Jewishinization of Jews   76
de-Zionization views in Israel   75, 107
deep structures
    in collective identity   5
    of Jewish identity   26–30, 53, 99
definitions of Jewish identity   xi–xii,
    xvi, 36–37, 99–114, 285
    caste syndrome attitude towards
        xxi, xxii, 10–11, 24, 37–41, 52,
        53, 54, 55, 97, 99, 103, 104, 105,
        109–110, 114
    and establishment of Jewish state
        32–33
    ethno-cultural syndrome attitude
        towards   xxi, xxii, 41–46, 52, 53,
        54, 55, 104, 105
    free thinkers views   36
    and Law of Return   32–33, 259,
        262, 290
    modern   xxi, 11–12
    modern Orthodox views   36,
        40–41, 43
    national-territorialist syndrome
        attitude towards   xxi–xxii, 46–54,
        55, 61, 97–98, 104, 105, 106
    non-observant views   41
    non-Orthodox views   36, 41, 47–52
    pre-modern   xxi
    ultra-Orthodox views   36, 37–40,
    52
DellaPergola, S.   57
democracy, and registration of religion
    and nationhood   154
Derrida, Jacques   xxiii, 4
deutero-Isaiah, prophesies of   128
Deuteronomy, names of mothers of
    kings   163–164

Diaspora
    ethno-cultural syndrome attitude
        towards Jewish identity   104
    intermarriages between Jews and
        non-Jews   324
    negative views of Zionism on   52,
        59, 74
    relations with Israel   46–47, 51–52,
        53, 54, 60, 169, 221, 240,
        255–256, 276, 309, 318,
        324–325, 331, 343, 352, 353,
        358
    religious laws different from those in
        Land of Israel   189–190
    "Sages of Israel" in   36, 43–45,
        50–51, 104
    secular Jewish society in   241, 348
diasporism   xi
diasporist Judaism   xxii
Dinour, Ben-Zion   xi–xii, xvi
Dreyfus affair   11 n. 1
Dubnow, Simon   xi, xii, xiii, xvi, 26,
    312–313
Dumont, L.   10

Eastern Europe, Jewish response to
    modernism in   20–26
'eda'   67, 359
    political parties based on   69
Edomites   212
Jews forbidden by Torah to intermarry
    with   131–132, 225, 244
education
    achievements of Jews in United
        States   82–83
    emphasized by Enlightenment
        movement   16–17, 20
    religious   345
Egyptians, Jews forbidden by Torah to
    intermarry with   131–132, 225, 244
Einhorn, David   313
Eliezer, Rabbi   280–281
Eliezer, Rabbi Simon ben   141
Elijah   280
elite groups, Mizrakhi Jews gaining
    access to   68–69
elite status, of native born Israelis
    58–59
Eliyahu, Rabbi of Vilna   208
emancipation of Jews   11
Emden, Jacob   20
English language
    use by American Jews   96
    use in Israel   60

Enlightenment (Haskala) Movement
21, 27, 29–30, 100, 101, 102, 360
    education emphasized by   16–17,
    20
ethnic divisions, in Israel   66–81
ethnic origins
    of Jewish People   124–125, 163
    population registration on basis of
    154
ethno-cultural syndrome attitude
    towards Jewish identity   xxi, xxii,
    41–46, 52, 53, 54, 55, 104, 105
    Conservative Movement   109, 114
    in Diaspora   104
    Humanistic Judaism   109, 114
    Modern Orthodox Judaism   109,
    114
    post-Zionism   xxii, 109
    Reconstructionists   109
    Reform Movement   109, 114
    in United States Judaism   94–98,
    107–108
Ettinger, Shmuel   xii, xvi
Evron, Boaz   74–75
Eybeschütz, Jonathan   20
Ezekiel   123
Ezra   39
    conversion in times of   129–130,
    132–133, 208, 281
    expulsion of foreign women   131,
    132, 164, 185–186, 206, 232, 270
    on intermarriage   132, 195,
    244–245, 357

Fackenheim, Emil   19
'family resemblance', notion of   100,
    111–112
Finkelstein, Rabbi Louis Eliezer Halevi
    40, 194–196
Frankfort Reform Association
    312–313
Frankfurter, Felix   170, 197–198
free thinkers "Sages of Israel"   33,
    35, 51
    on definitions of Jewish identity   36
Freehof, Rabbi Solomon B.   43,
    199–203
fundamentalism   4 n. 1
Furman, F.K.   88

Galut, meaning of   17, 359
Gaon, Rabbi Sa'adia   38, 216, 336
Geiger, Abraham   17
Gellner, E.   5

Gemara   see Talmud
'ger' (convert, stranger)   360
    status during Second Temple
    Judaism   133–135, 138
    status during time of exile in
    Babylon   128
    status in early Biblical times
    119–120, 121–124, 125–127
    see also conversion to Judaism;
    proselytes
'ger aryot' (lion proselytes)   352, 360
'ger gamoor' (proper convert)   140,
    360
'ger toshav' (resident alien, half
    proselyte)   134, 203, 214, 360
'ger tzedek' (sincere proselyte)   133,
    203, 360
Germany
    Orthodox Judaism in   100
    Reform Judaism in   17, 312–313
Gibeonites   121, 122
Gilboa, E.   93
Ginzburg, Louis   19
Glazer, N.   92
God and Torah of Israel
    element of Jewish identity   40–41,
    46, 51, 55, 99, 101, 102, 114
    viewed as cultural and ethical
    concepts   89
    viewed by Jews in modern era   28
    viewed by Jews in United States
    95
Goering, H.W.   338
Goldscheider, C.   84 n. 3
Gordis, Rabbi Robert   85–86
Gordon, David   22
Gordon, J.L.   258
Goren, Rabbi Shlomo   49, 204–219
Gorni, J.   92
Graetz, Heinrich   xi, xii, xv–xvi, 21
Grossnass, Aryeh Leib   37, 220–222
Guenzburg, Mordecai Aaron   20
Gush Emunim movement   64, 360

Ha-Boker (newspaper)   xi
Habad Hassids   38
Habayit Hadash   189
Hacohen, Zekharya   47, 223–229
Hagai, Rabbi   206–207
halakha   37, 360
    constitutional validity of   xx, 329
    conversion according to   48–51, 54,
    55, 137, 156, 217, 218, 250,
    266–267, 322, 336, 337–338

on question who is a Jew 166–167, 171, 283, 325, 356
halakhic Judaism 13
  and Jewish identity 37–39, 47–50, 52, 54, 105, 281
Halevy, Rabbi Yitzhak 39, 230–235
half proselytes 203
Halpern, Benjamin 92–93
Hamaggid (journal) 22
Hameiri, Menachem 143
Hashakhar (journal) 22
Haskala *see* Enlightenment Movement
Hasmonaeans, forced conversions by 133–134, 139
Hassidim 9, 38, 114, 360
Hazaz, Hayim 45, 46, 236–237
Hebrew culture, emergence in Israel 57
Hebrew language
  Biblical 21
  binding element in Israeli society 80–81
  national language in Israel 57–58, 80
  place in ethno-cultural syndrome attitude towards Jewish identity 53
  place in national-territorialist syndrome attitude towards Jewish identity 53–54, 102–103
  replacing Yiddish 23, 62
  as seen by
    Conservative Movement 103
    Orthodox Movement 29, 102
    Reform Movement 103
  spoken by native born Israelis 59
  used by
    American Jews 96, 108
    national-religious community in Israel 63
    ultra-Orthodox communities in Israel 62
  used for
    everyday life 23–24, 29, 80
    literary and secular interests 17, 20–21, 102, 350
    study, prayer and ritual 102
'Hebrews'
  suggested intermediate status of Jewish identity 42, 156, 242, 350
  term used for Jews settled in Israel 74, 107, 343
  see also 'resident Jews'

Hehalutz (newspaper) 21
Heller, Rabbi Chaim 38, 321–322
Herberg, William 94
Hervieu-Léger, Danièle xxv, 6
Herzberg, Arthur 93
Herzog, Rabbi Yitskhak Isaac Halevi 47–48, 238–239
Heschel, Abraham Joshua 42, 240–242
Hinukh Ne-urim (Education of Youth) School 17
Hirsch, Rabbi Richard 92
Hirsch, Samson Raphael 14
Hirschensohn, Haim 14
Hobsbawm, E. 4
Holocaust, as element of Jewish identity xiv–xv
Horowitz, Marcus 201
human sacrifice, abolished by Jews 160
Humanistic Judaism
  ethno-cultural attitude towards Jewish identity 109, 114
  in United States 89

Ibn Ezra, Abraham ben Meir 213
identity
  different versions existing side by side 5
  modern search for 4
  trajectories xxv
  see also collective identity; Jewish identity
identity cards, and registration of religion and nationhood 145, 154
ideology of national integration 58
idolatry, opposed by Judaism 160–161
immersion, as part of ritual of converting to Judaism 141, 143, 212–214, 217–218, 227, 228–229, 234, 321–322, 338
infant proselytes 200–201, 214–215, 228
intermarriages between Jews and non-Jews 131–132, 201, 205, 247–248, 306–307, 357
  Biblical texts on 124, 132, 164, 185, 195, 206, 223–224, 244, 244–245, 357
  in Diaspora 324
  perceived dangers of 216–217, 224, 232, 255, 269, 276, 330, 340, 342–343

Talmud on   205, 206, 232,
    243–244, 281
  in United States   84–85, 86
intermediate status of Jewishness in
    Israel 'Hebrews'   42, 156, 242,
    350
  possibility of   42, 44, 46, 175, 203,
    352–353, 354
  'resident Jews'   43, 259–260, 316
invented tradition   4
Isaac, Rabbi   192, 280
Isaiah   253, 339
Isaiah, deutero   128
Isaiah, tertio   128
Israel
  accepted by Orthodox Judaism
    103
  attitude of American Jews towards
    86–87, 91, 92–94, 95, 107–108
  Chief Rabbinate of   254–255,
    279, 289, 323–324, 327, 336,
    356–357
  citizenship of   156, 164–165,
    171–172, 183, 255
  de-Zionization of   75–76
  establishment of   31
  ethnic divisions in   66–81
  freedom of conscience principle
    146, 156
  Hebrew language in   23–24, 57–58,
    59, 62, 63, 80–81
  Jewish identity in   57–81, 97–98
  Jewish population in   57, 61–66,
    146–147
  Jewish religious center   xiii, xiv,
    46–47, 51–52, 222, 246, 276,
    324
  Jewishness of state   76, 258
  marriage and divorce governed by
    religious law   145, 171–172, 181,
    202–203, 234–235, 252, 262, 282,
    304–306, 310–311, 315, 330, 342
  Mizrakhi integration   67–70
  modernity of   258–259
  multi-culturalization of   66, 80–81
  name of   156
  nation-building in   60, 146,
    156–157
  national allegiance and Jewish
    religion   xv, 32, 44–46,
    48, 50–51, 154
  national-religious community in   63
  pioneers   58–59, 60
  as place of refuge   157

political parties in   69
prestige of native born   58–59,
    60–61
promotion of settlements in
    occupied areas   64
registration of religion and
    nationality   144–146, 154, 172–174,
    180–181, 183–185, 200, 217, 218,
    219, 221, 237, 240, 250–251,
    255, 263, 265, 272, 290, 307,
    309–310, 311, 317, 330, 347
relations with Diaspora   46–47,
    51–52, 53, 54, 60, 169, 221, 240,
    255–256, 276, 309, 318, 324–325,
    331, 343, 352, 353, 358
Russian immigrants in   70–72, 79,
    106, 109
"Sages of Israel" in   36, 45–46,
    47–50
state and religion in   65, 75, 152,
    167, 169–170, 171–172, 181–182,
    184–185, 202, 234–235, 255, 258,
    262, 273, 286–288, 291–292,
    304–307, 310, 315, 317–318, 329,
    345, 353
ultra-Orthodox Judaism in   61–63,
    98, 110
unifying element of Jewish People
    xvi, 92–93
see also Land of Israel; Law of
    Return
Israeli Arabs   72–73, 79, 106, 310
  political strengthening of   66–67
Israeli Judaism   51–52, 53, 106–107,
    114, 146–147
  and new Jewish identity   57–82
Israeli nationalism   106
Israeli society
  divisions within   79–80
  multi-culturalization of   66, 80–81
Isserlish, Rabbi Moshe   207–208

Jabotinsky, Vladimir   59
Jacob of Naburaya   243–244,
    276–277
Jacob, Rabbi Aha bar   140
Jerusalem, sacrificing an offering at
    the Temple as part of conversion
    137, 139, 140, 141
Jewish Agency   258, 259
Jewish autonomy   25–26
Jewish centers, notion of   xiii
Jewish communities, in United States
    82–98

Jewish culture
  promotion of 25
  in United States 82, 90
Jewish identity
  caste syndrome attitude towards
    xxi, xxii, 10–11, 24, 37–41, 52,
    53, 54, 55, 97, 98, 99, 103, 104,
    105, 109–110, 114
  deep structures of 26–30, 53, 99
  definitions of xi–xii, xvi, 36–37,
    99–114, 285
  ethno-cultural syndrome attitude
    towards xxi, xxii, 41–46, 52, 53,
    54, 55, 94–98, 104, 105
  God and Torah of Israel element of
    40–41, 46, 51, 55, 99, 101, 102,
    114
  Holocaust element of xiv–xv
  intermediate status proposed 42,
    43, 44, 46, 156, 203, 242,
    259–260, 316, 350, 352–353, 354
  in Israel 57–81, 97–98
  Jewish People element of 41, 46,
    52–53, 55, 99, 101, 102, 114
  Land of Israel element of 41, 51,
    54, 55, 99, 101, 102, 114
  national-territorialist syndrome
    attitude towards xxi–xxii, 46–54,
    55, 61, 97–98, 104, 105, 106
  pluralism of xvi, 112–114
  self-declared 32, 45, 173, 182, 217,
    218, 226, 250–251, 263, 264,
    269–270, 279, 326, 331, 337,
    339, 350, 352, 357–358
  shared space of identities 6
  in time of exile 127
  Zionism as a new form of 58
Jewish nationalism 22
Jewish People
  element of Jewish identity 41, 46,
    52–53, 55, 99, 101, 102, 114
  ethnic origins of 124–125, 163
  excluding groups from 112
  histories of xi
  Israel as unifying element for xvi,
    92–93
  Jewish religion as unifying element for
    231, 351–352
  role of conversions 162
  versus Israeli Jewish nation 107,
    158
  versus Judaism as a religion 36,
    37, 39, 40, 41, 42, 158, 261–262
  viewed by Jews in modern era 28

  viewed by Jews in United States
    95
Jewish population, in Israel 57,
  61–66, 146–147
Jewish religion
  Israel as center of xiii, xiv, 46–47,
    51–52, 222, 246, 276, 324
  Israeli Jews adhering to symbols of
    65
  and Jewish identity xii, 9, 41–42,
    285
  mixed parentage children following
    status of their mother 180,
    185–187, 195, 205–208, 217, 221,
    225, 243, 264, 274, 276–277, 281,
    289, 306, 321, 322, 325
  and national allegiance xv, 32,
    41–42, 44–46, 48, 50–51, 154
  practised in United States 90
  religious authorities in 9
  trans-territorial xiii
  unifying element for Jewish People
    231, 351–352
  versus Jews as a People 36, 37, 39,
    40, 41, 42, 158, 261–262
  see also Judaism
Jewish socialism 25
Jewish solidarity 78
Jewish state
  calls for end of 76
  and definition who is Jewish 32–33
  establishment of xii–xiii
  possibility to create category of half
    proselytes 203
  and traditional Judaism 14,
    343–344
  see also Israel; Zionism
Jewish studies, in United States
  91–92
Jewish Theological Seminary 19
Jewish world, changes in 56
Jews
  de-Jewishinization of 76
  relations with non-Jews 11
  seen as inferior by others 10–11
Josephus Flavius 213
Joshua, on intermarriage 244
Judah Ha-Nasi, Rabbi 137, 186, 187,
  210, 279
Judah, Rabbi Gershom ben 178
Judaism
  acceptance of proselytes 211–212,
    227–228, 233, 237, 245, 266, 275,
    339, 340

basic principles of 160–161, 257
divisions within 303–304
halakhic 13, 37–39, 47–50, 52, 54, 105, 281
inherited by birth 261
Israeli 51–52, 53, 57–82, 106–107, 114, 146–147
particularism vs universalism xxii, 162, 266
place of commandments 18–19, 47, 312, 335
on question who is a Jew 333–334
religion and nationality in 154–155, 158, 159–160, 166, 169, 172, 175, 209–210, 211, 215–217, 230–232, 236, 240–241, 242, 248–250, 265–266, 269, 271, 282, 283, 286, 290, 291, 311, 318, 331, 336–337, 339, 340, 351, 356
secular perspective of 65, 348
social boundaries of xx, 118, 314
spiritual and physical are inseparable 159–160
territorialization of 23
traditional 13–30, 50, 100, 343–344
Judaism and Modern man (Herberg) 94
Just, Marcus xi
justice, concept of 160

Kahaneman, Rabbi Joseph Shlomo 39, 243–246
Kaplan, Rabbi Jacob 40, 254–256
Kaplan, Rabbi Mordecai Menachem 19, 43, 93, 257–260
Kappah, Rabbi Yossef 48, 247–253
Kaufman, ? 124, 128–129, 131
Kaufmann, Yekhezkel 48, 261–267
Kimmel, M.S. 4 n. 1
Klein, Isaac 87
Knesset Hagedola 208
Kook, Hillel 74
Kosmin, B. 83 n. 2
Kotler, Aaron 37, 268–271
Kreuzner, Theodore 312
The Kusari (HaLevi) 238
Kutno, Solomon 201

Land of Israel
challenges to importance of 106–107
concept of 12, 79, 110

element of Jewish identity 41, 51, 54, 55, 99, 101, 102, 114
emergence of mythical meaning of 64
Jews forbidden by Torah to intermarry with former inhabitants of 131–132, 225, 244
religious laws different from those ruling Diaspora 189–190
Samaria and Judea seen as part of 63–64
tribal nature in Biblical times 122
viewed by Jews in modern era 28
Lattes, Dante 44, 272–273
Law of Return
calls for repeal of xiii, 75
and definition of Jewish identity 32–33, 259, 262, 290
and Israeli citizenship 183
practical implications of xix, 310
privileges afforded by 145
Leibovits, Yeshayahu 64, 286
Levi-Strauss, C. xxiv, 5
Levinsohn, Rabbi Yitzhak Baer 20
Levy, Sh. 65
Lew, Meir 37, 220–222
Liberal Judaism see Reform Movement
Liberal Synod, in Germany 313
liberalism, and religion 94
Lieberman, Saul 40, 274–277
'lion' proselytes ('ger aryot') 352, 360
Lipset, S.M. 82, 83 n. 91
Lissak, M. 76–77
literature in Hebrew 20–21
London, assimilation of Jews in 91
Lowell, Stanley 93

McLain, E.J. 85
Mahler, Raphael xii, xvi
Maimon, Rabbi Jehuda Leib Hakohen 39, 278–279
Maimonides, Moses
on conversion to Judaism 141–142, 187, 188, 189, 209, 249
on (half-)proselytes 140, 203, 210, 211, 212, 228–229
on intermarriage 224, 225, 232
on Jewish religion 9, 190–191, 192, 250, 310, 322, 346
on mixed parentage children following status of their mother 205
Maisels, Moshe 50, 280–284

Marcus, Jacob Rader 18
marriage and divorce
   governed by religious law in Israel
      145, 171–172, 181, 202–203,
      234–235, 252, 262, 282, 304–306,
      310–311, 315, 330, 342
   see also intermarriages between Jews
      and non-Jews
Medding, P.Y. 84–85 n. 4
Medem, Vladimir 25–26
Mekhiltah 138, 213
Mendelssohn, Moses 16
Midrash 138, 162, 191, 213
minors, conversion to Judaism of
   200–201, 214–215, 218, 228,
   266–267, 270, 274, 311–312
Mishnah 205, 225, 281, 362
   see also Talmud
Mitnaggedim 9, 38, 362
mixed marriages *see* intermarriages
   between Jews and non-Jews
mixed parentage children xi, 7, 32,
   40, 48, 163
   accepted into Jewish religious
      communities 174
   circumcision of 201, 206–207,
      237
   concealing true status from them
      251–252, 305
   conversion of 49, 157, 195–196,
      208, 218, 219, 221, 227, 233,
      238–239, 244, 255, 265, 266, 269,
      274, 289, 299, 307, 315, 319,
      325–326, 327–328, 340–341, 356,
      358
   following status of mother 180,
      185–187, 195, 205–208, 217, 221,
      225, 243, 264, 274, 276–277, 281,
      289, 306, 321, 322, 325, 341,
      357
   parental declaration of Jewishness
      xx, 45, 174, 180–181, 182–183,
      187–188, 251, 259, 263–264, 272,
      310, 314–315, 318, 326, 330–331,
      354
   registration as Jewish in Israel 39,
      43–44, 144, 145–146, 151,
      153–154, 155–156, 167, 171, 197,
      200, 217, 218, 219, 221, 237,
      238, 251–252, 264–265, 272,
      290, 301–302, 305, 307, 317,
      318–319, 330, 341–342, 347,
      353, 354
   status in Judaism 205–208

Mizrakhim 67–70, 106, 362
   national-territorialist attitude towards
      Jewish identity 109, 114
Moabites, Jews forbidden by Torah
   to intermarry with 131–132, 225,
   244
modern definition of Jewish identity
   xxi, 11–12
Modern Orthodox Judaism
   ethno-cultural syndrome attitude
      109, 114
   in United States 87
Modern Orthodox "Sages of Israel"
   33–35
   caste syndrome attitude 37
   on definition of Jewish identity 36,
      40–41, 43
   ethno-cultural syndrome attitude
      41–43
modern science, and Judaism 21
modernism
   and constructed identity xxii,
      xxiii
   and duality of collective identity 3
   response of traditional Judaism
      13–30, 50, 100
modernity, of Israel 258–259
Morgenstern, Rabbi Julius 93
mothers
   mixed parentage children
      following status of 180,
      185–187, 195, 205–208, 217,
      221, 225, 243, 264, 274,
      276–277, 281, 289, 306, 321,
      322, 325, 341, 357
   responsible for spiritual matters
      196
multi-culturalism 46
multi-culturalization of Israeli society
   66, 80–81

Naaman, conversion of 126, 127,
   214, 252
nation-building, in Israel 60, 146,
   156–157
national allegiance, and Jewish
   religion xv, 32, 41–42, 44–46, 48,
   50–51, 154
national integration, ideology of 58
national-religious activists 63–64
national-religious community
   in Israel 63
   national-territorialist attitude towards
      Jewish identity 109, 114

national-territorialist syndrome attitude
  towards Jewish identity   xxi–xxii,
  46–54, 55, 61, 97–98, 104, 105,
  106
  Canaanites   109, 114
  Mizrakhim   109, 114
  national-religious Judaism   109,
    114
  place of Hebrew language in
    53–54, 102–103
  Russian immigrants   109
nationalism
  Israeli   106
  Jewish   22
  radical   64
  and religion   19, 66, 336–337
  and Zionism   23
nationality   338
  and religion in Judaism   154–155,
    166, 172, 175, 209–210, 211,
    215–217, 230–232, 236, 240–241,
    242, 248–250, 265–266, 269, 271,
    282, 283, 286, 290, 291, 311,
    318, 331, 336–337, 339, 340,
    351, 356
  spiritual   334–335, 344
native born Israelis, elite status of
  58–59, 60–61
Naturei Karta   xxii
Nehemiah
  book of   281
  conversion in times of   129–130
Neher, André   41–42, 285–288
New York, observing Jewish religious
  practices in   90 n. 8
Nietzchean influence on early Zionism
  59
Nineteen Letters on Judaism (Hirsch)   14
non-Jews
  definition of   117–118
  relations with Jews   11
  see also intermarriages between Jews
    and non-Jews; mixed parentage
    children
non-observant "Sages of Israel",
  definitions of Jewish identity   41
non-Orthodox "Sages of Israel"
  33–35
  definitions of Jewish identity   36,
    41, 47–52
normalization
  general   xiii, xiv
  Jewish   xiv
  particular   xiii, xv

Ochana, David   79
Oron, A.   65
Orthodox Judaism   13–15, 26–27,
  29–30, 41, 42, 100, 101, 102, 304
  acceptance of State of Israel   103
  caste syndrome attitude towards
    Jewish identity   103
  in Germany   100
  views on conversion to Judaism
    47, 85 n. 5, 200, 202
  views on Yiddish language   29
  see also modern Orthodox Judaism;
    traditional Judaism;
    ultra-Orthodox Judaism

particularism vs universalism dilemma
  in Judaism   xxii, 162, 266
Pereira, Rabbi Salomon Rodrigues
  40, 289
Perelman, Chaim   44–45, 290–292
Pharisees, dispute with Sadducees
  139
'Phoenix Generation'   31
pioneers, of Israel   58–59, 60
Pittsburgh Platform   17–18
pluralism, of Jewish identity   xvi,
  112–114
political meaning, of Israel   156
political parties
  established by Russian Jewish
    immigrants in Israel   71, 72
  in Israel   69
politically motivated conversion to
  Judaism   133–134, 139
politics, and religion   15, 47, 65
post-modernity, and identity   xxv
post-Zionism   76–78, 107, 114
  ethno-cultural attitude towards
    Jewish identity   xxii 109
pre-modern definition of Jewish
  identity   xxi
pro-Israeli attitude, versus Zionism
  94
proselytes   191–192, 196, 210
  Abraham   338
  acceptance in Judaism   211–212,
    227–228, 233, 237, 245, 266,
    275, 339, 340
  half   203
  'lion' ('ger aryot')   352, 360
  minors   200–201, 214–215, 228
  'self-made'   211, 279, 350
  sincere   133, 157, 159, 162, 190,
    203, 227, 266

Talmudic rules on 140, 141, 200–201, 203, 210, 212, 214–215, 279
see also conversion to Judaism; 'ger'
proselytizing
by American Jews among Christians 85
prohibited by Romans 135–136
purity, maintenance of 10

Raab, E. 82, 83 n. 1, 91
Rabbinical Court Jurisdiction Act (1953) 304, 306
rabbinical prescriptions, importance of 164
rabbis, role of 178–179
radical nationalism, emergence of 64
Ranger, T. 4
Rappoport, Abraham 37, 220–222
Rashi (Rabbi Solomon bar Isaac) 162, 206, 211
on conversion to Judaism 225
on mixed parentage children following status of the mother 186, 205
on strangers ('gerim') 119, 140–141, 142–143
Ratosh, Yonatan 74
Ratzaby, Shalom 117
Reconstructionists 88
ethno-cultural attitude towards Jewish identity 109
Reconstructivists 19
Reform Movement 16–19, 27, 29–30, 43, 46, 100, 101, 102, 199
in Australia 313
criticism of 334–335
ethno-cultural attitude towards Jewish identity 109, 114
in Germany 17, 312–313
in United States 17–19, 87, 88, 202, 313, 349
views on conversion to Judaism 84, 85 n. 5, 202, 304, 313
views on Hebrew language 103
religion
and Jewish identity xii, 9, 41–42, 285
and liberalism 94
and nationalism 19, 66, 336–337
and nationality in Judaism 154–155, 209–210, 211, 215–217, 230–232, 236, 240–241, 242, 248–250, 265–266, 269, 271, 282,

283, 286, 290, 291, 311, 318, 331, 336–337, 339, 340, 351, 356
and politics 15, 47, 65
and state
in Christian nations 155
in Israel 65, 75, 152, 167, 169–170, 171–172, 181–182, 184–185, 202, 234–235, 255, 258, 262, 273, 286–288, 291–292, 304–307, 310, 315, 317–318, 329, 345, 353
see also Jewish religion
religious authorities, in Jewish religion 9
religious education 345
religious elite, among Mizrakhim 68–69
religious fundamentalism 4 n. 1
religious law
different from Diaspora in Land of Israel 189–190
governing marriage and divorce in Israel 145, 171–172, 181, 202–203, 234–235, 252, 262, 282, 304–306, 310–311, 315, 330, 342
religious political parties, in Israel 69
religious studies, importance in Jewish religion 9
'resident alien' (ger toshav) 134, 203, 214, 360
'resident Jews' 43, 259–260, 316
see also 'Hebrews'
Rifkind, Simon H. 293
Ritterband, P. 90 n. 8
Roman Empire, spread of Judaism in 139
Romans, objecting to conversion to Judaism 135–136
Rosenzweig, Franz 18, 155, 166
Russian immigrants
in Israel 70–72, 79, 106
national-territorialist attitude towards Jewish identity 109
Russian language, use by Jews from former Soviet Union 71 n. 4
Ruth
conversion of 125, 126, 159
example of 39, 155, 209, 233

Sabbath, celebration of 161
sabras *see* native born Israelis

sacrificial offering
  abolishment of human sacrifice by
    Jews   160
  as part of conversion   137, 139,
    140, 141, 213
Sadducees, dispute with Pharisees
  139
  the Sages, writings of   209, 211,
    212, 214, 224, 228, 231, 233,
    238, 250, 275, 276, 310, 325,
    338, 339, 340, 342, 348, 350
"Sages of Israel"
  debate with David Ben-Gurion   xix,
    xxv–xxvi, 7, 32–36, 117
  on definitions of Jewish identity   36,
    40–41, 43, 52, 104–106
  in Diaspora   36, 43–45, 50–51, 104
  free thinkers   33, 35, 51
  Israeli   36, 45–46, 47–50
  Modern Orthodox   33–35, 37,
    40–41, 43
  Non-Orthodox observant   33–35,
    41, 47–52
  and Orthodox rules regarding
    Jewishness   105
  place of residence   34–35, 36
  secular   43–44
  traditional   33, 35
  ultra-Orthodox   33–34, 37–40, 52
Samaria and Judea, as part of the
  Land of Israel   63–64
Samaritans   129 n. 65, 130–131,
  211–212
  dispute with exiles returning from
    Babylon   131
Sarne, Yekhezkiel   39, 294–295
Schechter, Joseph   49–50, 296–297
Schekner, J.   83 n. 2
Scherer, Emmanuel   93
Schindler, Rabbi Alexander   85
Schmueli, A.   9
Schneerson, Rabbo Menachem Mendel
  37–38, 298–299
Scholem, Gershom   xi, xiii, xvi
Science of Judaism   21
secular Jewish society
  in Diaspora   241, 348
  relations with ultra-Orthodox
    communities in Israel   61–63
secular "Sages of Israel"   43–44
Sefer Mitzvot Hagadol (ben Jacob)
  188–189
self-declared Jewish identity   32, 45,
  173, 182, 217, 218, 226, 250–251,

263, 264, 269–270, 279, 326, 331,
  337, 339, 350, 352, 357–358
'self-made' proselytes   211, 279, 350
Sephardic Jews   70
settlements, promotion of   64
Shafir, G.   77
Shalom, Sh. (Shalom Joseph Shapira)
  49, 300–302
Shapira, Yonatan   75–76
Sharot, S.   9
Shas party   79, 106, 363
  establishment of   69–70
Shor, Joshua Heshel   21
Shulkhan Arukh (Caro)   43, 151, 188,
  201, 205–206, 207–208, 214, 363
Silberg, Moshe   48, 303–307
Silberstein, L.J.   78
Simon, Akiva Ernst   50, 308–315
Simon, Leon (Arye)   51, 316–320
sincere proselytes   133, 157, 159, 162,
  190, 203, 227, 266
Smith, A.   5
Smolenskin, Peretz   22
social boundaries
  between Jews and non-Jews in
    United States   83–84, 107
  of Judaism   xx, 118, 314
social disadvantage, connected with
  cultural singularity   68, 72
socialism, Jewish   25
Socialist movement, Jewish
  participation in   25 n. 3
Society for Culture and Science for
  the Jews   21
Soloveitchik, Rabbi Joseph Dov   38,
  321–322
space of identities framework   99, 100,
  110
spiritual nationality   334–335, 344
state
  and religion
    in Christian nations   155
    in Israel   65, 75, 152, 167,
      169–170, 171–172, 181–182,
      184–185, 202, 234–235, 255,
      258, 262, 273, 286–288,
      291–292, 304–307, 310, 315,
      317–318, 329, 345, 353
Stein, Edith, example of   167
Steinberg, Meir Halevy   37, 220–222
structuralist school, on constitutive
  elements of identities   xxiv
superior caste   41
Swift, Morris   37, 220–222

Talmud 138, 142, 251, 342, 359, 363
  on conversion of minors 214
  on intermarriage and their offspring 205, 206, 232, 243–244, 281
  on proselytes 140, 141, 200–201, 203, 210, 212, 214–215, 279
Tami, establishment of 69
temple, introduction of term for house of worship 17
territorial conception of conversion 125–127
territorialization of Judaism 23
territory, seen as basis for Israeli nation 73–75, 79
tertio-Isaiah, prophesies of 128
Toaff, Rabbi Alfredo Shabtai 38, 323–326
Toaff, Rabbi Elio Raffaele 38, 327–328
Torah 363
  commandments of 161, 238, 335
  forbidding marriage with Canaanites, Ammonites, Moabites, Edomites, Egyptians and former inhabitants of the Land of Israel 131–132, 225, 244
  importance of 270–271, 297, 339–340
  laws of 164, 178, 190, 192–193, 224, 226, 243, 268, 294–295, 306, 339, 357
  on status of mixed parentage children 207, 278–279, 298
  see also God and Torah of Israel
Torat Kohanim 206
Tosafists 188, 191–192
Touraine, A. 80
tradition, invented 4
traditional, "Sages of Israel" 33, 35
traditional Judaism
  and Jewish state 14, 343–344
  response to modernism 13–30, 50, 100

ultra-Orthodox Judaism 15, 33, 98, 102
  acceptance of State of Israel 103
  caste syndrome attitude towards Jewish identity 103, 107, 108, 109
  in Israel 61–63, 98, 110
  opposition to secular Zionism 86–87
  in United States 86–87, 96–97, 98
  views on conversion to Judaism 36, 39, 41
ultra-Orthodox "Sages of Israel" 33–34
  caste syndrome attitude 37
  on definition of Jewish identity 36, 37–40, 52
United States
  anti-Semitism in 91
  assimilation of Jews in 91–92
  attitude of American Jews towards Israel 86–87, 91, 92–94, 95, 107–108
  congregation emphasized by Judaism in 89–90
  Conservative Judaism in 87–88
  cultural ethnicity of Jews in 94–98, 107
  educational achievements of Jews in 82–83
  ethno-cultural syndrome attitude by Jews in 94–98, 107–108
  Humanistic Judaism in 89
  intermarriages between Jews and non-Jews 84–85, 86
  Jewish community 82–98
  Jewish culture in 82, 90
  Jewish studies in 91–92
  mixed marriages in 84–85, 86
  modern Orthodox Judaism in 87
  practising Judaism in 90–91
  proselytizing practised by Jews among Christians 85–86
  Reconstructionists 88
  Reform Judaism in 17–19, 87, 88, 202, 313, 349
  ultra-Orthodox Judaism in 86–87, 96–97, 98
  Zionism in 94–95
universalism versus particularism dilemma in Judaism xxii, 162, 266
Urbach, A.A. 13
Urbach, Ephraim A. 48, 329–332

Vienna, assimilation of Jews in 91

Waxman, ? 93–94
Weinberg, Rabbi Yekhiel 38–39, 333–346
Weingrod, A. 68 n. 3

Wessely, Naphtali Herz   16
Wittgenstein, L.   xxiii, xxv, 6
    on collective identity   3
    notion of 'family resemblance'
        100, 111
Wolfson, Tsevi (Harry A.)   42,
    347–350
women
    conversion in Biblical times   127
    foreign, expulsion in times of Ezra
        131, 132, 164, 185–186, 206,
        232, 270
    performing ritual duties in Judaism
        87
Words of Peace and Truth (Wessely)
    16

Yemenite Jews   67, 68, 232
Yiddish
    being replaced by Hebrew   23, 62
    language of choice for the Bund
        29
    place in caste syndrome attitude
        towards Jewish identity   53
    as seen by Orthodox Movement
        29
    use of
        by American Jews   96
        by Ashkenazim   102
        by Bund   102

Yossef, Ovadia   70
the 'Youngsters'   63–64

Zaccai, Rabbi Jonathan ben   141
Zechariah   227
Zeitlin, Aaron   50–51, 351–354
Zevin, Rabbi Shlomo   39–40,
    355–358
Zhirkova, Elisheva   354
Zhitlowsky, Chaim   26
Zion
    current return to   282
    first return to   281
Zionism   22–26, 27–28, 29–30, 100,
    101, 102, 114, 258
    critics of   xxii, 76–77, 78
    currant   78
    equation with racism in UN
        resolution (1975)   94 n. 11
    negative views on Diaspora Jewry
        52, 59, 74
    as a new form of Jewish identity
        58
    Nietzchean influence   59
    opposed by ultra-Orthodox
        86–87
    traditionalist   67
    in United States   94–95
    versus pro-Israeli attitude   94
    see also post-Zionism

DATE DUE